Evaluation Models

Evaluation in Education and Human Services

Editors:

George F. Madaus, Boston College, Chestnut
   Hill, Massachusetts, U.S.A.
Daniel L. Stufflebeam, Western Michigan
   University, Kalamazoo, Michigan, U.S.A.

Previously published books in the series:

Evaluation Models
Viewpoints on Educational and
Human Services Evaluation

George F. Madaus
Michael S. Scriven
Daniel L. Stufflebeam

Kluwer-Nijhoff Publishing
Boston   The Hague   Dordrecht   Lancaster

Distributors for North America:

Kluwer Academic Publishers
101 Philip Drive
Assinippi Park
Norwell, MA 02061

Distributors outside North America:

Kluwer Academic Publishers Group
Distribution Centre
P.O. Box 322
3300AH Dordrecht,
THE NETHERLANDS

Library of Congress Cataloging in Publication Data

Main entry under title:

Evaluation models.

(Evaluation in education and human services)
includes index.
1. Educational surveys — Addresses, essays, lectures.
2. School management and organization — Evaluation —
Addresses, essays, lectures. 3. Curriculum evaluation —
Addresses, essays, lectures. I. Madaus, George F.
II. Scriven, Michael. III. Stufflebeam, Daniel L. IV. Series.
LB2823.E87   1983   379.1'54   82-22562
ISBN 0-89838-132-0 Professional edition
ISBN 0-89838-132-0 Text edition

Thirteenth Printing, 2000

Printed in the United States of America

Contents

v

List of Figures and Tables

List of Figures

List of Tables

Preface

Attempting formally to evaluate something involves the evaluator coming to grips with a number of abstract concepts such as value, merit, worth, growth, criteria, standards, objectives, needs, norms, client, audience, validity, reliability, objectivity, practical significance, accountability, improvement, process, product, formative, summative, costs, impact, information, credibility, and — of course — with the term *evaluation* itself. To communicate with colleagues and clients, evaluators need to clarify what they mean when they use such terms to denote important concepts central to their work. Moreover, evaluators need to integrate these concepts and their meanings into a coherent framework that guides all aspects of their work. If evaluation is to lay claim to the mantle of a profession, then these conceptualizations of evaluation must lead to the conduct of defensible evaluations.

The conceptualization of evaluation can never be a one-time activity nor can any conceptualization be static. Conceptualizations that guide evaluation work must keep pace with the growth of theory and practice in the field. Further, the design and conduct of any particular study involves a good deal of localized conceptualization. In any specific situation, the evaluator needs to define and clarify for others the following: the audiences and information requirements, the particular object to be evaluated, the purposes of the study, the inquiry approach to be employed, the concerns and issues to be examined, the variables to be assessed, the bases for interpreting findings, the communication mode to be used, the anticipated uses of the findings, and the standards to be invoked in assessing the quality of the work.

It is a small wonder, then, that attempts to conceptualize evaluation have been among the most influential works in the fast-growing literature of evaluation. The contents of this anthology attest to the fact that there has been a rich array of theoretical perspectives on evaluation. Given the complexity of evaluation work, the wide range of evaluative situations, the political contexts within which studies occur, the service orientation of evaluations, and the varied backgrounds and beliefs of those who write about evaluation, it is easy to understand why the various generalized conceptualizations of evaluation found in the literature differ in many important respects. The ways that evaluation is conceptualized differ over the role of objectives in the process, the desirability of presenting convergent or divergent findings, the use or absence of experimental controls, and the place of hard or soft data in arriving at conclusions. It is also understandable that given evaluators sometimes follow one general approach in one kind of evaluation assignment and a quite different approach in another setting. Since the contexts in which evaluations take place are so variable, it is fortunate that evaluators can look to the literature for optional ways to conceptualize the evaluation process in order to find one which best suits a particular context.

Amidst this diversity of conceptual approaches to evaluation, however, a consensus has begun to emerge regarding the principles that should undergird all evaluations. This consensus is embodied in the two major sets of standards for evaluations that have been issued recently by the Joint Committee on Standards for Educational Evaluation and by the Evaluation Research Society. The appearance of these standards is one sign — but a sure one — that evaluation has begun to mature as a profession.

This book is an up-to-date reflection of the conceptual development of evaluation, particularly program evaluation, and is divided into three major sections. The first includes a historical perspective on the growth of evaluation theory and practice and two comparative analyses of the various alternative perspectives on evaluation. The second part contains articles that represent the current major schools of thought about evaluation, written by leading authors in the field of evaluation, including, articles by Tyler, Scriven, Stake, Eisner, Floden, Airasian, Guba and Lincoln, Stufflebeam, Cronbach, Steinmetz (on Provus's work), Weiss and Rein, Madaus, and Koppelman. These articles cover objectives-oriented evaluation, responsive evaluation, consumer-oriented evaluation, decision and improvement-oriented evaluation, naturalistic evaluation, discrepancy evaluation, adversarial evaluation, connoisseur evaluation, accreditation, accountability, and social experimentation. This section concludes with a forecast on the future of evaluation by Nick Smith. The final section describes and discusses the recently released *Standards for Evaluations of Educational Programs, Projects, and Materials* and summarizes the 95 theses recently issued by Cronbach and Associates in calling for a reformation of program evaluation.

In one sense, the core of this book presents a set of alternative evaluation models. These are not models in the sense of mathematical models used to test given theories, but they are models in the sense that each one characterizes its author's view of the main concepts involved in evaluation work and provides guidelines for using these concepts to arrive at defensible descriptions, judgments, and recommendations. We are aware that some writers in the field have urged against according alternative perspectives on evaluation the status of models; but we think the alternative suggestion that these alternatives be called something else, such as persuasions or beliefs, would do little more than puzzle the readers. We are comfortable in presenting the alternative conceptualizations of evaluation that appear in the second part of the book, not as models *of* evaluation as it does occur, but as models *for* conducting studies according to the beliefs about evaluation that are held by the various authors. In this sense, they are idealized or "model" views of how to sort out and address the problems encountered in conducting evaluations.

We owe an enormous debt to the authors of the articles that appear in this book. We would like also to thank the various journals that gave us permission to reprint key pieces. We especially wish to thank Ralph Tyler and Peter Airasian for writing articles specifically for this book, as well as Egon Guba and Yvonna Lincoln, who adapted their article to fit within our space limitations. We also are grateful to Phil Jones, our publisher, who consistently supported our developmental effort. Thanks is extended also to Carol Marie Spoelman, Caroline Pike, and Mary Campbell for their competent clerical assistance. Special thanks to Rita Comtois for her administrative assistance throughout the project. Bernie Richey's editorial help throughout is appreciated.

We believe this book should be of interest and assistance to the full range of persons who are part of any evaluation effort, including, especially, the clients who commission evaluation studies and use their results, evaluators, and administrators and staff in the programs that are evaluated. We believe the book should be useful as a text for courses in program evaluation and for workshops as well. Further, it should prove to be an invaluable reference book for those who participate in any aspect of formal evaluation work. We hope that this book will assist significantly those involved in program evaluation to increase their awareness of the complexity of evaluation; to increase their appreciation of alternative points of view; to improve their ability to use theoretical suggestions that appear in the literature; to increase their testing and critical appraisal of the various approaches; and, ultimately, to improve the quality and utility of their evaluations.

I AN OVERVIEW OF MODELS AND CONCEPTUALIZATIONS

1 PROGRAM EVALUATION:
A Historical Overview
George F. Madaus, Daniel Stufflebeam, and Michael S. Scriven

Program evaluation is often mistakenly, viewed as a recent phenomenon. People date its beginning from the late 1960s with the infusion by the federal government of large sums of money into a wide range of human service programs, including education. However, program evaluation has an interesting history that predates by at least 150 years the explosion of evaluation during the era of President Johnson's Great Society and the emergence of evaluation as a maturing profession since the sixties. A definitive history of program evaluation has yet to be written and in the space available to us we can do little more than offer a modest outline, broad brush strokes of the landscape that constitutes that history. It is important that people interested in the conceptualization of evaluation are aware of the field's roots and origins. Such an awareness of the history of program evaluation should lead to a better understanding of how and why this maturing field has developed as it did. As Boulding (1980) has observed, one of the factors that distinguishes a mature and secure profession from one that is immature and insecure is that only the former systematically records and analyzes its history. Therefore since program evaluation continues to mature as a profession, its origins and roots need to be documented.

Where to begin? For convenience we shall describe six periods in the life of program evaluation. The first is the period prior to 1900, which we call the *Age of Reform;* the second, from 1900 until 1930, we call the *Age of Efficiency and*

Testing; the third, from 1930 to 1945, may be called the *Tylerian Age;* the fourth, from 1946 to about 1957, we call the *Age of Innocence;* the fifth, from 1958 to 1972, is the *Age of Expansion* and finally the sixth, from 1973 to the present, the *Age of Professionalization.*

The Age of Reform 1800–1900

This period in the history of program evaluation encompasses the nineteenth century. It was the Industrial Revolution with all of its attendant economic and technological changes, which transformed the very structure of society. It was a period of major social changes, of cautious revisionism and reform (Pinker, 1971). It was a time of drastic change in mental health and outlook, in social life and social conscience, and in the structures of social agencies. It was when the laissez-faire philosophy of Bentham and the humanitarian philosophy of the philanthropists was heard (Thompson, 1950). It was a period marked by continued but often drawn out attempts to reform educational and social programs and agencies in both Great Britain and the United States.

In Great Britain throughout the nineteenth century there were continuing attempts to reform education, the poor laws, hospitals, orphanages, and public health. Evaluations of these social agencies and functions were informal and impressionistic in nature. Often they took the form of government-appointed commissions set up to investigate aspects of the area under consideration. For example, the Royal Commission of Inquiry into Primary Education in Ireland under the Earl of Powis, after receiving testimony and examining evidence, concluded that "the progress of the children in the national schools of Ireland is very much less than it ought to be."[1] As a remedy, the Powis Commission then recommended the adoption of a scheme known as "payment by results" already being used in England, whereby teachers' salaries would be dependent in part on the results of annual examinations in reading, spelling, writing, and arithmetic (Kellaghan & Madaus, 1982). Another example of this approach to evaluation was the 1882 Royal Commission on Small Pox and Fever Hospitals which recommended after study that infectious-disease hospitals ought to be open and free to all citizens (Pinker, 1971).

Royal commissions are still used today in Great Britain to evaluate areas of concern. A rough counterpart in the United States to these commissions are presidential commissions (for example, the President's Commission on School Finance), White House panels (e.g., the White House Panel on Non Public Education), and congressional hearings. Throughout their history royal commissions, presidential commissions and congressional hearings have served as a means of evaluating human services programs of various kinds through the examination of evidence either gathered by the Commission or presented to it in testimony by concerned parties. However, this approach to evaluation was some-times merely emblematic or symbolic in nature. N.J. Crisp (1982) captures the pseudo nature of such evaluations in a work of fiction when one of his characters discusses a royal commission this way: ''Appoint it, feel that you've accomplished something, and forget about it, in the hope that by the time it's reported, the problem will have disappeared or been overtaken by events.''[2]

In Great Britain during this period when reform programs were put in place, it was not unusual to demand yearly evaluations through a system of annual reports submitted by an inspectorate. For example, in education there were schools inspectors that visited each school annually and submitted reports on their condi-tion and on pupil attainments (Kellaghan & Madaus, 1982). Similarly the Poor Law commissioners had a small, paid inspectorate to oversee compliance with the Poor Law Amendment Act of 1834 (Pinker, 1971). The system of maintaining an external inspectorate to examine and evaluate the work of the schools exists today in Great Britain and Ireland. In the United States, external inspectors are employed by some state and federal agencies. For example, the Occupational Safety and Health Administation (OSHA) employs inspectors to monitor health hazards in the workplace. Interestingly, the system of external inspectors as a model for evalua-tion has received scant attention in the evaluation literature. The educational evaluation field could benefit from a closer look at the system of formal inspectorates.

Two other developments in Great Britain during this period are worthy of note in the history of evaluation. First, during the middle of the nineteenth century a number of associations dedicated to social inquiry came into existence. These societies conducted and publicized findings on a number of social problems which were very influential in stimulating discussion (for example, Chadwick's Report on the Sanitary Condition of the Laboring Population of Great Britain in 1842 [Pinker, 1971]). Second, often in response to these private reports, bureaucracies that were established to manage social programs sometimes set up committees of enquiry. These were official, government-sponsored investigations of various social programs, such as provincial workhouses (Pinker, 1971). Both these examples are important in that they constitute the beginnings of an empirical approach to the evaluation of programs.

In the United States perhaps the earliest formal attempt to evaluate the perform-ance of schools took place in Boston in 1845. This event is important in the history of evaluation because it began a long tradition of using pupil test scores as a principal source of data to evaluate the effectiveness of a school or instructional program. Then, at the urging of Samuel Gridley Howe, written essay examina-tions were introduced into the Boston grammar schools by Horace Mann and the Board of Education. Ostensibly the essay exam, modeled after those used in Europe at the time, was introduced to replace the *viva voce* or oral examinations. The latter mode of examination had become administratively awkward with increased numbers of pupils and was also seen as unfair because it could not be standardized for all pupils. The interesting point in terms of program evaluation was the hidden policy agenda behind the move to written examinations; namely, it was the gathering of data for inter-school comparisons that could be used in decisions concerning the annual appointment of headmasters. Howe and Mann attempted to establish differential school effects and used these data to eliminate headmasters who opposed them on the abolition of corporal punishment. This is an interesting early example of politicization of evaluation data.

Between 1887 and 1898, Joseph Rice conducted what is generally recognized as the first formal educational-program evaluation in America. He carried out a comparative study on the value of drill in spelling instruction across a number of school districts. Rice (1897), like Mann and Howe before him, used test scores as his criteria measures in his evaluation of spelling instruction. He found no significant learning gains between systems which spent up to 200 minutes a week studying spelling and those which spent as little as ten minutes per week. Rice's results led educators to re-examine and eventually revise their approach to the teaching of spelling. More important from the point of view of this history of program evaluation is his argument that educators had to become experimentalists and quantitative thinkers and his use of comparative research design to study student achievement (Rice, 1914). Rice was a harbinger of the experimental design approach to evaluation first advanced by Lindquist (1953) and extended and championed by Campbell (Campbell & Stanley, 1963; Campbell, 1969) and others in the 1960s and 1970s.

Before leaving this very brief treatment of what has been characterized as the age of reform, another development should be mentioned. The foundation of the accreditation or professional-judgment approach to evaluation can be traced directly to the establishment of the North Central Association of Colleges and Secondary Schools in the late 1800s. The accreditation movement did not, however, gain great stature until the 1930s when six additional regional accrediting associations were established across the nation. Since then the accrediting movement has expanded tremendously and gained great strength and credibility as a major means of evaluating the adequacy of educational institutions. (Cf. chapter 15 by Floden for a treatment of the accreditation approach to evaluation.)

The Age of Efficiency and Testing 1900–1930

During the early part of the twentieth century the idea of scientific management became a powerful force in administrative theory in educational as well as in industrial circles (Biddle & Ellena, 1964; Callahan, 1962; Cremin, 1962). The emphasis of this movement was on systemization; standardization; and, most importantly, efficiency. Typifying this emphasis on efficiency were the titles of the fourteenth and fifteenth yearbooks of the National Society for the Study of Education (NSSE), which were, respectively, *Methods for Measuring Teachers' Efficiency* and the *Standards and Tests for the Measurement of the Efficiency of Schools and School Systems*.

Surveys done in a number of large school systems during this period focused on school and/or teacher efficiency and used various criteria (for example, expenditures, pupil dropout rate, promotion rates, etc.). By 1915, thirty to forty large school systems had completed or were working on comprehensive surveys on all phases of educational life (Kendall, 1915; Smith & Judd, 1914). A number of these surveys employed the newly developed "objective" tests in arithmetic, spelling, handwriting, and English composition to determine the quality of teaching. These tests were often developed in large districts by a bureau or department set up specifically to improve the efficiency of the district. For example, the Department of Educational Investigation and Measurement in the Boston public schools developed a number of tests that today would be described as objective referenced (Ballou, 1916). Eventually tests like those in Boston took on a norm-referenced character as the percentage of students passing became a standard by which teachers could judge whether their classes were above or below the general standard for the city (Ballou, 1916). In addition to these locally developed tests there were a number of tests developed by researchers like Courtis, Ayers, Thorndike, and others, which were geared to measuring a very precise set of instructional objectives. These tests by famous researchers of the day had normative data that enabled one system to compare itself with another (Tyack & Hansot, 1982).

Many of these early twentieth-century surveys were classic examples of muckraking, "often initiated by a few local people who invited outside experts to expose defects and propose remedies."[3] Another problem associated with these early surveys — a problem not unknown to evaluators today — was that the "objective" results obtained were often used as propaganda "to build dikes of data against rising tides of public criticism."[4] However, researchers at the time did recognize that such surveys could and should avoid muckraking and public relations use and should indeed be constructive, be done in cooperation with local advisors, and be designed to produce public support for unrecognized but needed change (Tyack & Hansot, 1982).

With the growth of standardized achievement tests after World War I, school districts used these tests to make inferences about program effectiveness. For example, May (1971) in an unpublished paper on the history of standardized testing in Philadelphia from 1916 to 1938 found that commercially available achievement tests, along with tests built by research bureaus of large school districts, were used to diagnose specific system weaknesses and to evaluate the curriculum and overall system performance, in addition to being used to make decisions about individuals. Throughout its history, the field of evaluation has been closely linked to the field of testing. Test data have often been the principal data source in evaluations; this use of tests has been a mixed blessing as we shall see presently.

During the late 1920s and 1930s, university institutes specializing in field studies were formed and conducted surveys for local districts. The most famous of these institutes was the one headed by George Strayer at Teachers College (Tyack & Hansot, 1982). These institutes could be considered the precursors of the university centers dedicated to evaluation that grew up in the 1960s and 1970s.

It is important to point out that studies of efficiency and testing were for the most part initiated by, and confined to, local school districts. In contrast to the national curriculum development projects of the late 1950s and early 1960s, curriculum development before the 1930s was largely in the hands of a teacher or committee of teachers. It was natural, therefore, that evaluations of that period were addressed to localized questions. This focus or emphasis on local evaluation questions continued into the 1960s despite the fact that the audience for the evaluations was statewide or nationwide; this resulted in many useless educational evaluations being carried out during the 1960s. It was only in the 1970s that educators and evaluators recognized and began to deal with this problem of generalizability.

The Tylerian Age 1930–1945

Ralph W. Tyler has had enormous influence on education in general and educational evaluation and testing in particular. He is often referred to, quite properly we feel, as the father of educational evaluation. Tyler began by conceptualizing a broad and innovative view of both curriculum and evaluation. This view saw curriculum as a set of broadly planned school-experiences designed and implemented to help students achieve specified behavioral outcomes. Tyler coined the term "educational evaluation," which meant assessing the extent that valued objectives had been achieved as part of an instructional program. During the early and mid-1930s, he applied his conceptualization of evaluation to helping instructors at Ohio State improve their courses and the tests that they used in their courses.

During the depths of the Great Depression, schools, as well as other public institutions, had stagnated from a lack of resources and, perhaps just as importantly, from a lack of optimism. Just as Roosevelt tried through his New Deal programs to lead the economy out of the abyss, so too John Dewey and others tried to renew education. The renewal in education came to be known as the Progressive Education Movement, and it reflected the philosophy of pragmatism and employed tools from behavioristic psychology.

Tyler became directly involved in the Progressive Education Movement when he was called upon to direct the research component of the now-famous Eight-

Year Study (Smith & Tyler, 1942). The Eight-Year Study (1932–1940), funded by the Carnegie Corporation, was the first and last large study of the differential effectiveness of various types of schooling until well after World War II. The study came about when questions were asked in the early 1930s about the efficacy of the traditional high school experience relative to the progressive secondary school experience. As a result of these questions, leading colleges began to refuse progressive-school graduates admittance because they lacked credits in certain specific subjects. To settle the debate, an experiment was proposed in 1932 in which over 300 colleges agreed to waive their traditional entrance requirements for graduates from about 30 progressive secondary schools. The high school and college performance of students from these secondary schools would be compared to the high school and college performance of students from a group of traditional secondary schools.

The Eight-Year Study introduced educators throughout America to a new and broader view of educational evaluation than that which had been in vogue during the age of efficiency and testing. Evaluation was conceptualized by Tyler as a comparison of intended outcomes with actual outcomes. His view of evaluation was seen by advocates as having a clear-cut advantage over previous approaches. Since a Tylerian evaluation involves internal comparisons of outcomes with objectives, it need not provide for costly and disruptive comparisons between experimental and control groups, as were required in the comparative experimental approach that Rice had used. Since the approach calls for the measurement of behaviorally defined objectives, it concentrates on learning *outcomes* instead of organizational and teaching *inputs*, thereby avoiding the subjectivity of the professional judgment or accreditation approach; and, since its measures reflect defined objectives, there was no need to be heavily concerned with the reliability of differences between the scores of individual students. Further, the measures typically cover a much wider range of outcome variables than those associated with standardized norm-referenced tests.

Clearly by the middle of the 1940s Tyler had, through his work and writing, laid the foundation for his enormous influence on the educational scene in general and on testing and evaluation in particular during the next 25 years. (A more detailed treatment by Tyler of his rationale for program evaluation can be found in chapter 4.)

The Age of Innocence 1946–1957

We have labeled the period 1946–1957 as the *Age of Innocence,* although we might just as well have called it the *Age of Ignorance.* It was a time of poverty and despair in the inner cities and in rural areas, but almost no one except the victims seemed to notice. It was a period of extreme racial prejudice and segregation, but most white people seemed oblivious to the disease. It was when exorbitant consumption and widespread waste of natural resources were practiced without any apparent concern that one day these resources would be depleted. It was a period of vast development of industry and military capabilities with little provision for safeguards against damage to the environment and to future generations.

More to the point of this review, there was expansion of educational offerings, personnel, and facilities. New buildings were erected. New kinds of educational institutions, such as experimental colleges and community colleges, emerged. Small school districts consolidated with others in order to be able to provide the wide range of educational services that were common in the larger school systems, including: mental and physical health services, guidance, food services, music instruction, expanded sports programs, business and technical education, and community education. Enrollments in teacher-education programs ballooned, and, in general, college enrollments increased dramatically. Throughout American society, the late 1940s and 1950s were a time to forget the war, to leave the depression behind, to build and expand capabilities, to acquire resources, and to engineer and enjoy a "good life."

This general scene in society and education was reflected in educational evaluation. While there was great expansion of education, optimism, plenty of tax money, and little worry over husbanding resources, there was no particular interest on the part of society in holding educators accountable. There was little call for educators to demonstrate the efficiency and effectiveness of any developmental efforts. Educators did talk and write about evaluation, and they did collect considerable amounts of data (usually to justify the need for expansion or for broad, new programs). However, there is little evidence that these data were used to judge and improve the quality of programs or even that they could have been useful for such a purpose. During this period there was considerable development of some of the technical aspects of evaluation; this was consistent with the then-prevalent expansion of all sorts of technologies. This was especially true of the testing approach to evaluation, but was also true of the comparative experimental and "congruence between objecties and outcomes" approaches. Chief among these developments was the growth in standardized testing. Many new nationally standardized tests were published during this period. Schools purchased these tests by the thousands and also subscribed heavily to machine scoring and analysis services that the new technology made available. The testing movement received another boost in 1947 when E.F. Lindquist, Ralph Tyler, and others helped establish the Educational Testing Service.

By the 1950s, the practice of standardized testing had expanded tremendously, and the professional organizations concerned with testing initiated a series of steps designed to regulate the test-related activities of their members. In 1954, a committee of the American Psychological Association prepared *Technical*

Recommendations for Psychological Tests and Diagnostic Techniques (APA, 1954). In 1955, committees of the American Educational Research Association and the National Council on Measurements Used in Education prepared *Technical Recommendations for Achievement Tests* (AERA and NCMUE, 1955). These two reports provided the basis for the 1966 edition of the joint AERA/APA/NCME *Standards for Educational and Psychological Tests and Manuals* (APA, 1966) and the 1974 revision entitled, *Standards for Educational and Psychological Tests* (APA, 1974). The latter report recognized the need for separate standards dealing with program evaluation. (At this writing a joint committee is at work revising the 1974 Standards.)

This rapid expansion of testing was not the only technical development related to program evaluation during this period. Lindquist (1953) extended and delineated the statistical principles of experimental design. Years later, many evaluators and educators found that the problems of trying to meet simultaneously all of the required assumptions of experimental design (for example, constant treatment, uncontaminated treatment, randomly assigned subjects, stable study samples, and unitary success criteria) in the school setting were insurmountable.

During the 1950s and early 1960s there was also considerable technical development related to the Tylerian view of evaluation. Since implementing the Tyler approach in an evaluation required that objectives be stated explicitly, there was a need to help educators and other professionals to do a better job articulating their objectives. Techniques to help program staffs make their objectives explicit, along with taxonomies of possible educational objectives (Bloom et al., 1956; Krathwohl, 1964), were developed to fill this need. The Tyler rationale was also used extensively during this period to train teachers in test development.

During this period evaluations were, as before, primarily within the purview of local agencies. Federal and state agencies had not yet become deeply involved in the evaluation of programs. Funds for evaluation that were done came from either local coffers, foundations, voluntary associations such as the community chest, or professional organizations. This lack of dependence on taxpayer money for evaluation would end with the dawn of the next period in the history of evaluation.

The Age of Expansion 1958–1972

The age of innocence in evaluation came to an abrupt end with the call in the late 1950s and early 1960s for evaluations of large-scale curriculum development projects funded by federal monies. This marked the end of an era in evaluation and the beginning of profound changes that would see evaluation expand as an industry and into a profession dependent on taxpayer monies for support.

As a result of the Russian launch of Sputnik I in 1957, the federal government enacted the National Defense Education Act of 1958. Among other things, this act provided for new educational programs in mathematics, science, and foreign language; and expanded counseling and guidance services and testing programs in school districts. A number of new national curriculum development projects, especially in the areas of science and mathematics, were established. Eventually funds were made available to evaluate these curriculum development efforts.

All four of the approaches to evaluation discussed so far were represented in the evaluations done during this period. First, the Tyler approach was used to help define objectives for the new curricula and to assess the degree to which the objectives were later realized. Second, new nationally standardized tests were created to better reflect the objectives and content of the new curricula. Third, the professional-judgment approach was used to rate proposals and to check periodically on the efforts of contractors. Finally, many evaluators evaluated curriculum development efforts through the use of field experiments.

In the early 1960s it became apparent to some leaders in educational evaluation that their work and their results were neither particularly helpful to curriculum developers nor responsive to the questions being raised by those who wanted to know about the programs' effectiveness. The best and the brightest of the educational evaluation community were involved in these efforts to evaluate these new curricula; they were adequately financed, and they carefully applied the technology that had been developed during the past decade or more. Despite all this, they began to realize that their efforts were not succeeding.

This negative assessment was reflected best in a landmark article by Cronbach (1963; cf. chapter 6). In looking at the evaluation efforts of the recent past, he sharply criticized the guiding conceptualizations of evaluations for their lack of relevance and utility, and advised evaluators to turn away from their penchant for post hoc evaluations based on comparisons of the norm-referenced test scores of experimental and control groups. Instead, Cronbach counseled evaluators to reconceptualize evaluation — not in terms of a horse race between competing programs but as a process of gathering and reporting information that could help guide curriculum development. Cronbach was the first person to argue that analysis and reporting of test item scores would be likely to prove more useful to teachers than the reporting of average total scores. When first published, Cronbach's counsel and recommendations went largely unnoticed, except by a small circle of evaluation specialists. Nonetheless, the article was seminal, containing hypotheses about the conceptualization and conduct of evaluations that were to be tested and found valid within a few years.

In 1965, guided by the vision of Senator Hubert Humphrey, the charismatic leadership of President John Kennedy, and the great political skill of President Lyndon Johnson, the War on Poverty was launched. These programs poured billions of dollars into reforms aimed at equalizing and upgrading opportunities for all citizens across a broad array of health, social, and educational services. The expanding economy enabled the federal government to finance these programs, and there was widespread national support for developing what President Johnson termed the Great Society.

Accompanying this massive effort to help the needy came concern in some quarters that the money invested in these programs might be wasted if appropriate accountability requirements were not imposed. In response to this concern, Senator Robert Kennedy and some of his colleagues in the Congress amended the Elementary and Secondary Education Act of 1964 (ESEA) to include specific evaluation requirements. As a result, Title I of that Act, which was aimed at providing compensatory education to disadvantaged children, specifically required each school district receiving funds under its terms to evaluate annually — using appropriate standardized test data — the extent to which its Title I projects had achieved their objectives. This requirement, with its specific references to standardized-test data and an assessment of congruence between outcomes and objectives, reflects the state-of-the-art in program evaluation at that time. More importantly, the requirement forced educators to shift their concern for educational evaluation from the realm of theory and supposition into the realm of practice and implementation.

When school districts began to respond to the evaluation requirement of Title I, they quickly found that the existing tools and strategies employed by their evaluators were largely inappropriate to the task. Available standardized tests had been designed to rank order students of average ability; they were of little use in diagnosing needs and assessing any achievement gains of disadvantaged children whose educational development lagged far behind that of their middle-class peers. Further, these tests were found to be relatively insensitive to differences between schools and/or programs, mainly because of their psychometric properties and content coverage. Instead of measuring outcomes directly related to the school or to a particular program, these tests were at best indirect measures of learning, measuring much the same traits as general ability tests (Madaus, Airasian & Kellaghan, 1980).

There was another problem with using standardized tests: such an approach to evaluation conflicted with the precepts of the Tylerian approach. Because Tyler recognized and encouraged differences in objectives from locale to locale it became difficult to adapt this model to nationwide standardized-testing programs. In order to be commercially viable, these standardized-testing programs had to overlook to some extent objectives stressed by particular locales in favor of objectives stressed by the majority of districts. Further, there was a dearth of information about the needs and achievement levels of disadvantaged children that could guide teachers in developing meaningful behavioral objectives for this population of learners.

The failure of attempts to isolate the effects of Title I projects through the use of experimental/control group designs was due primarily to an inability to meet the assumptions required of such designs. Further, project-site visitation by experts

— while extensively employed by governmental sponsors — was not acceptable as a primary evaluation strategy because this approach was seen as lacking the objectivity and rigor stipulated in the ESEA legislation. When the finding of "no results" was reported, as was generally the case, there were no data on the degree to which the "treatment" had in fact been implemented; the evaluator had overlooked the messy "black box" that constituted the "treatment." Further, we encased the word treatment in quotes advisedly since the actual nature of the treatment rendered to subjects was generally unknown. The technical description was nothing more than a vague description of the project. For example, the term Title I itself was often used to describe an amorphous general treatment. In any event, the emphasis on test scores diverted attention from consideration of the treatment or of treatment implementation.

As a result of the growing disquiet with evaluation efforts and with the consistent negative findings, the professional honorary fraternity Phi Delta Kappa set up a National Study Committee on Evaluation (P.D.K., 1971). After surveying the scene, this committee concluded that educational evaluation was "seized with a great illness"; and called for the development of new theories and methods of evaluation as well as for new training programs for evaluators. At about this same time many new conceptualizations of evaluations began to emerge. Provus (1969 & 1971), Hammond (1967), Eisner (1967), and Metfessel & Michael (1967) proposed reformation of the Tyler model. Glaser (1963), Tyler (1967), and Popham (1971) pointed to criterion-referenced testing as an alternative to norm-referenced testing. Cook (1966) called for the use of the systems-analysis approach to evaluate programs. Scriven (1967), Stufflebeam (1967 & 1971, with others), and Stake (1967) introduced new models of evaluation that departed radically from prior approaches. These conceptualizations recognized the need to evaluate goals, look at inputs, examine implementation and delivery of services, as well as measure intended and unintended outcomes of the program. They also emphasized the need to make judgments about the merit or worth of the object being evaluated. (Overviews of these developments can be found in chapters 2 and 3.) The late 1960s and early 1970s were vibrant with descriptions, discussions, and debates concerning how evaluation should be conceived; however, this period in the history of program evaluation ended on a down note. A number of important evaluations resulted in negative findings. First, Coleman's famous study, *Equality of Educational Opportunity* (1966, with others), received considerable notice. Particular attention went to his famous conclusion that "schools bring little influence to bear on a child's achievement that is independent of his background and general social context."[5] Title I evaluations (Picariello, 1968; Glass et al., 1970; U.S. Office of Education, 1970) argued against the efficacy of those programs. The Westinghouse/Ohio University Head Start investigation (Cicirelli et al., 1969) turned up discouraging results. Likewise, the results of the evaluation of *Sesame Street* (Ball & Bogatz, 1970; Bogatz & Ball, 1971) — when critically analyzed (Cook) — were discouraging. These disheartening findings raised serious questions about evaluation in general and certain methodologies in particular. For many supporters of these programs, this set the stage for our next period which we call the Age of Professionalization.

The Age of Professionalization 1973–Present

Beginning about 1973 the field of evaluation began to crystallize and emerge as a distinct profession related to, but quite distinct from, its forebears of research and testing. While the field of evaluation has advanced considerably as a profession, it is instructive to consider this development in the context of the field in the previous period.

At that time, evaluators faced an identity crisis. They were not sure whether they should try to be researchers, testers, administrators, teachers, or philosophers. It was unclear what special qualifications, if any, they should possess. There was no professional organization dedicated to evaluation as a field, nor were there specialized journals through which evaluators could exchange information about their work. There was essentially no literature about program evaluation except unpublished papers that circulated through an underground network of practitioners. There was a paucity of pre-service and in-service training opportunities in evaluation. Articulated standards of good practice were confined to educational and psychological tests. The field of evaluation was amorphous and fragmented — many evaluations were carried out by untrained personnel; others by research methodologists who tried unsuccessfully to fit their methods to program evaluations (Guba, 1966). Evaluation studies were fraught with confusion, anxiety, and animosity. Evaluation as a field had little stature and no political clout.

Against this backdrop, the progress made by educational evaluators to professionalize their field during the 1970s is quite remarkable indeed. A number of journals, including *Educational Evaluation and Policy Analysis, Studies in Evaluation, CEDR Quarterly, Evaluation Review, New Directions for Program Evaluation, Evaluation and Program Planning,* and *Evaluation News* were begun; and these journals have proved to be excellent vehicles for recording and disseminating information about the various facets of program evaluation. Unlike 15 years ago, there are now numerous books and monographs that deal exclusively with evaluation. In fact, the prolem today is not trying to find literature in evaluation but to keep up with it. The May 12th Group,[6] Division H of the AERA, the Evaluation Network, and the Evaluation Research Society have afforded excellent opportunities for professional exchange among persons concerned with the evaluation of education and other human service programs.

Many universities have begun to offer at least one course in evaluation methodology (as distinct from research methodology); a few universities — such as the University of Illinois, Stanford University, Boston College, UCLA, the University of Minnesota, and Western Michigan University — have developed graduate programs in evaluation. Nova University was perhaps the first to require an evaluation course in a doctoral program. For seven years the U.S. Office of Education has sponsored a national program of inservice training in evaluation for special educators (Brinkerhoff et al., in press), and several professional organizations have offered workshops and institutes on various evaluation topics. Centers have been established for research and development related to evaluation; these include the evaluation unit of the Northwest Regional Educational Laboratory, the Center for the Study of Evaluation at UCLA, The Stanford Evaluation Consortium, the Center for Instructional Research and Curriculum Evaluation at the University of Illinois, The Evaluation Center at Western Michigan University, and the Center for the Study of Testing, Evaluation and Educational Policy at Boston College. The Evaluation Institute of the University of San Francisco briefly expanded evaluation out into the product and personal areas. The state of Louisiana has established a policy and program for certifying evaluators (Peck, 1981), and Massachusetts is currently working on a similar certification program for evaluation. Recently Dick Johnson (1980) issued a first draft of a directory of evaluators and evaluation agencies.

Increasingly, the field has looked to meta evaluation (Scriven, 1975; Stufflebeam, 1978) as a means of assuring and checking the quality of evaluations. A joint committee (Joint Committee, 1981, a), appointed by 12 professional organizations, has issued a comprehensive set of standards for judging evaluations of educational programs, and materials (Joint Committee, 1981a), and has established a mechanism (Joint Committee, 1981b) by which to review and revise the *Standards* and assist the field to use them. (Cf. chapter 23 for an overview of these standards.) In addition, several other sets of standards with relevance for educational evaluation have been issued (cf. *Evaluation News,* May 1981).

During this period, evaluators increasingly realized that the techniques of evaluation must achieve results previously seen as peripheral to serious research; serve the information needs of the clients of evaluation; address the central value issues; deal with situational realities; meet the requirements of probity; and satisfy needs for veracity. While the field has yet to develop a fully functional methodology that meets all these requirements, there have been some promising developments, including: goal-free evaluation (Scriven, 1974; Evers, 1980); adversary-advocate teams (Stake & Gjerde, 1974; cf. chapters 11–13); advocate teams (Reinhard, 1972); meta analysis (Glass, 1976; Krol, 1978); responsive evaluation (Stake, 1975; cf. chapter 17); and naturalistic evaluation (Guba & Lincoln, 1981; cf. chapter 18). Under the leadership of Nick Smith (1981a; 1981b), a large number of writers have examined the applicability to evaluation of a wide range of investigatory techniques drawn from a variety of fields (cf. chapter 22). Eisner (1975) and his students have explored and developed techniques for applying the techniques used by critics in evaluating materials from the arts (cf. chapter 19). Webster (1975) and his colleagues have operationalized Stufflebeam's CIPP model within the context of a school district (cf. chapter 7). Stake (1978; cf. chapter 17), has adapted case study methods for use in evaluation. Roth (1977; 1978), Suarez (1980), Scriven & Roth (1978), Stufflebeam (1977) and others have begun to make both conceptual and operational sense of the crucial yet elusive concept of needs assessment. Personnel of the Toledo Public Schools, in collaboration with Bunda (1980) and Ridings (1980), have devised catalogs of evaluative criteria and associated instruments to help teachers and administrators tailor their data collection efforts to meet their information requirements. Finally, a great deal of work has been done to encourage the use of objective-referenced tests in evaluation studies. A particularly fruitful application of this latter technique is seen in curriculum-embedded evaluations, which provide teachers and students with an ongoing assessment of attainment in relation to the sequential objectives of a curriculum (Chase, 1980; Bloom, Madaus, & Hastings, 1981).

This substantial professional development in evaluation has produced mixed results. First, while there is undoubtedly more, and certainly better, communication in the field, there has also been an enormous amount of chatter (Cronbach, 1980). Second, while progress has been made in improving the training and certification of evaluators to ensure that institutions obtain services from qualified persons, some observers worry that this development may result in a narrow and exclusive club (Stake, 1981). Third, the cooperation among professional organizations concerned with educational evaluation, fostered by the Joint Committee on Standards for Educational Evaluation, is a promising but fragile arrangement for promoting the conduct and use of high-quality evaluation work. Finally, while the creation of new professional organizations has increased communication and reduced fragmentation in the evaluation field, there, unfortunately, remains a fairly sharp division between Division H of the AERA, the Evaluation Network, and the Evaluation Research Society of America.

Even though there has been increased communication between those advocating positivistic/quantitative approaches to evaluation and proponents of phenomenological/qualitative approaches, there is a present danger of a polarization developing between these camps. The roots of this polarization are not primarily methodological, but instead reflect ideological differences. Madaus & McDonagh (1982) describe the dangers of this polarization:

> In both cases, the evaluator, if not careful, could become a priest class which gives warning and advice, but does not take it, a class which preaches on the one hand in the name of science and on the other through charismatic personality.[7]

Finally, in spite of growing search for appropriate methods, increased communication and understanding among the leading methodologists, and the development of new techniques, the actual practice of evaluation has changed very little in the great majority of settings. Clearly, there is a need for expanded efforts to educate evaluators to the availability of new techniques, to try out and report the results of using the new techniques, and to develop additional techniques. In all of these efforts, the emphasis must be on making the methodology fit the needs of society, its institutions, and its citizens, rather than vice versa (Kaplan, 1964).

Conclusion

Evaluators need to be aware of both contemporary and historical aspects of their emerging profession — including its philosophical underpinnings and conceptual orientations. Without this background, evaluators are doomed to repeat past mistakes and, equally debilitating, will fail to sustain and build on past successes.

We have portrayed program evaluation as a dynamic, yet immature, profession. While the profession is still immature, there can be no doubt that it has become increasingly an identifiable component of the broader governmental and professional establishment of education, health, and welfare. The prediction commonly heard in the 1960s that formalized program evaluation was a fad and soon would disappear proved false, and there are strong indications that this field will continue to grow in importance, sophistication, and stature. The gains over the past 15 years are impressive, but there are many obvious deficiencies, and we still lack sufficient evidence about the impact of evaluations on education and human services. There is a need to improve research, training, and financial support for program evaluation. Leaders of the evaluation profession must ensure that efforts to improve their profession are geared to the service needs of their clients, not merely designed to serve their private or corporate needs. Ultimately the value of program evaluation must be judged in terms of its actual and potential contributions to improving learning, teaching and administration, health care and health, and in general the quality of life in our society. All of us in the program evaluation business would do well to remember and use this basic principle to guide and examine our work.

Notes

1.   Ireland. Royal Commission of Inquiry into Primary Education, 1870.
2.   N.J. Crisp, 1982, p. 148.
3.   D. Tyack and E. Hansot, 1982, p. 161.
4.   D. Tyack and E. Hansot, 1982, p. 155.
5.   J.S. Coleman, E.Q. Campbell, C.J. Hobson et al., 1966, p. 325.
6.   In the early 1970s a group of evaluators met on May 12th to discuss issues in evaluation. The group, with added members continues in existance and meets annually to discuss current issues and problems in the field.
7.   G.F. Madaus and J.T. McDonagh, 1982, p. 36.

References

American Educational Research Association and National Council on Measurements Used in Education. *Technical Recommendations for Achievement Tests*. Washington, D.C.: Author, 1955.

American Psychological Association. *Technical Recommendations for Psychological Tests and Diagnostic Techniques*. Washington, D.C.: Author, 1954.

American Psychological Association. *Standards for Educational and Psychological Tests and Manuals*. Washington, D.C.: Author, 1966.

American Psychological Association. *Standards for Educational and Psychological Tests*. Washington, D.C.: Author, 1974.

Ball, S., and Bogatz, G.A. *The First Year of Sesame Street: An Evaluation*. Princeton, New Jersey: Educational Testing Service, 1970.

Ballou, F.A. "Work of the Department of Educational Investigation and Measurement, Boston, Massachusetts." In: G.M. Whipple, (ed.), *Standards and Tests for the Measurement of the Efficiency of Schools and School Systems*. National Society for the Study of Education, Fifteenth Yearbook, Part I. Chicago: University of Chicago Press, 1916.

Biddle, B.J., and Ellena, W.J. (eds.) *Contemporary Research on Teacher Effectiveness*. New York: Holt, Rinehart & Winston, 1964.

Bloom, B.S.; Engelhart, M.D.; Furst, E.J.; Hill, W.H.; and Krathwohl, D.R. *Taxonomy of Educational Objectives Handbook I: The Cognitive Domain*. New York: David McKay Co., 1956.

Bloom, B.S.; Madaus, G.F.; and Hastings, J.T. *Evaluation to Improve Learning*. New York: McGraw-Hill Book Co., 1981.

Bogatz, G.A., and Ball, S. *The Second Year of Sesame Street: A Continuing Evaluation*. 2 vols. Princeton, New Jersey: Educational Testing Service, 1971.

Boulding, K.E. "Science, Our Common Heitage." *Science*, no. 4433, 207 (1980), 831–36.

Brinkerhoff, R. "Evaluation Technical Assistance: Reflections on a National Effort." *CEDR Journal*, forthcoming.

Bunda, M.A. *Catalog of Criteria for Evaluating Student Growth and Development*. Toledo: Toledo, Ohio Public Schools and the Western Michigan University Evaluation Center, 1980.

Callahan, R.E. *Education and the Cult of Efficiency*. Chicago: University of Chicago Press, 1962.

Campbell, D.T. "Reforms as Experiments." *American Psychologist*, no. 4, 24 (1969), 409–29.

Campbell, D.T., and Stanley, J.C. "Experimental and Quasi-Experimental Designs for Research on Teaching." In: N.L. Gage (ed.), *Handbook of Research on Teaching*, Chicago: Rand McNally, 1963.

Chase, F. *Educational Quandries and Opportunities*. Dallas, Texas: Urban Education Studies, 1980.

Cicirelli, V.G. et al. *The Impact of Head Start: An Evaluation of the Effects of Head Start on Children's Cognitive and Affective Development*. Study by Westinghouse Learning Corporation and Ohio University. Washington, D.C.: Office of Economic Opportunity, 1969.

Coleman, J.S.; Campbell, E.Q.; Hobson, C.J. et al. *Equality of Educational Opportunity*. Washington, D.C.: Office of Education, U.S. Department of Health, Education, and Welfare, 1966.

Cook, D.L. *Program Evaluation and Review Technique Applications in Education.* Washington, D.C.: Government Printing Office, 1966.

Cremin, L.A. *The Transformation of the School.* New York: Knopf, 1962.

Crisp, J.J. *The Brink.* New York: Viking Press, 1982.

Cronbach, L.J. "Course Improvement through Evaluation." *Teachers College Record,* 64 (1963): 672–83.

Cronbach, L.J. *Toward Reform of Program Evaluation.* San Francisco: Jossey-Bass Publishers, 1980.

Eisner, E.W. "Educational Objectives: Help or Hindrance?" *The School Review,* 75 (1967): 250–60.

Eisner, E.W. *The Perceptive Eye: Toward the Reformation of Educational Evaluation.* Stanford, California: Stanford Evaluation Consortium, December 1975.

Evaluation News. Sponsored by the Evaluation Network, Sage Publications, no. 2, 2 (1981).

Evers, J.W. "A Field Study of Goal-Based and Goal-Free Evaluation Techniques." Unpublished doctoral dissertation, Western Michigan University, 1980.

Glaser, R. "Instructional Technology and the Measurement of Learning Outcomes: Some Questions." *American Psychologist* 18 (1963): 519–21.

Glass, G.V. "Primary, Secondary, and Meta Analysis of Research." *Educational Reseacher,* no. 10, 5 (1976), 3–8.

Glass, G.V. et al. *Data Analysis of the 1968–69 Survey of Compensatory Education, Title I, Final Report on Grant No. OEG8–8–961860 4003–(058).* Washington, D.C.: Office of Education, 1970.

Guba, E.G. *A Study of Title III Activities: Report on Evaluation.* Indiana University, National Institute for the Study of Educational Change, October 1966.

Guba, E.G., and Lincoln, Y.S. *Effective Evaluation.* San Francisco: Jossey-Bass Publishers, 1981.

Hammond, R.L. "Evaluation at the Local Level." Address to the Miller Committee for the National Study of ESEA Title III, 1967.

Ireland. Royal Commission of Inquiry into Primary Education. *Report of the Commissioners.* (H.C. 1870, xxviii, part i).

Johnson, R. *Directory of Evaluators and Evaluation Agencies.* New York: Exxon Corporation 1980.

Joint Committee on Standards for Educational Evaluation. *Standards for Evaluations of Educational Programs, Projects, and Materials.* New York: McGraw-Hill Book Co., 1981*a.*

Joint Committee on Standards for Educational Evaluation. *Principles and By-Laws.* Western Michigan University Evaluation Center, 1981*b.*

Kaplan, A. *The Conduct of Inquiry.* San Francisco: Chandler, 1964.

Kellaghan, T. and Madaus, G.F. Trends in Educational Standards in Great Britain and Ireland. In G.R. Austin & H. Garber (eds.), *The Rise and Fall of National Test Scores.* New York: Academic Press, 1982.

Kendall, C.N. "Efficiency of School and School Systems." In *Proceedings and Addresses of the Fifty-third Annual Meeting of the National Education Association,* 389–95, 1915.

Krathwohl, D.R.; Bloom, B.S.; and Masia, B.B. *Taxonomy of Educational Objectives: the Classification of Educational Goals. Handbook II: Affective Domain.* New York: David McKay Co., 1964.

Krol, R.A. "A Meta Analysis of Comparative Research on the Effects of Desegregation on Academic Achievement." Unpublished doctoral dissertation, Western Michigan University, 1978.

Lindquist, E.F. *Design and Analysis of Experiments in Psychology and Education*. Boston: Houghton-Mifflin, 1953.

Madaus, G.F.; Airasian, P.W.; and Kellaghan, T. *School Effectiveness*. New York: McGraw-Hill Book Co., 1980.

Madaus, G.F., and McDonagh, J.T. "As I Roved Out: Folksong Collecting as a Metaphor for Evaluation." In N.L. Smith (ed.), *Communicating in Evaluation: Alternative Forms of Representation*. Beverly Hills, California: Sage Publications, 1982.

May, P. "Standardized Testing in Philadelphia, 1916–1938." Unpublished manuscript, 1971.

Metfessel, N.S. and Michael W.B. "A Paradigm Involving Multiple Criterion Measures for the Evaluation of the Effectiveness of School Programs." *Educational and Psychological Measurement* 27 (1967): 931–43.

National Society for the Study of Education. *Methods for Measuring Teachers' Efficiency*. Fourteenth Yearbook, Part II. Chicago: University of Chicago Press, 1916.

Peck, H. "Report on the Certification of Evaluators in Louisiana." Paper presented at the meeting of the Southern Educational Research Association, Lexington, Kentucky, Fall 1981.

Phi Delta Kappa Commission on Evaluation. *Educational Evaluation and Decision Making*. Itasca, Illinois: Peacock Publishers, 1971.

Picariello, H. *Evaluation of Title I*. Washington, D.C.: American Institute for the Advancement of Science, 1968.

Pinker, R. *Social Theory and Social Policy*. London: Heinemann Educational Books, 1971.

Popham, W.J. *Criterion-referenced Measurement*. Englewood Cliffs, New Jersey: Educational Technology Publications, 1971.

Provus, M. *Discrepancy Evaluation Model, 1969*. Pittsburgh, Pennsylvania: Pittsburgh Public Schools, 1969.

Provus, M. *Discrepancy Evaluation*. Berkeley, California: McCutcheon Publishing Co., 1971.

Reinhard, D. "Methodology Development for Input Evaluation Using Advocate and Design Teams." Unpublished doctoral dissertation, Ohio State University, 1972.

Rice, J.M. "The Futility of the Spelling Grind." *The Forum* 23 (1897): 163–72.

Rice, J.M. *Scientific Management in Education*. New York: Hinds, Noble & Eldredge, 1914.

Ridings, J. *Catalog of Criteria for Evaluating Administrative Concerns in School Districts*. Toledo: Toledo, Ohio Public Schools and the Western Michigan University Evaluation Center, 1980.

Roth, J. "Needs and the Needs Assessment Process." *Evaluation News* 5 (1977): 15–17.

Roth, J.E. "Theory and Practice of Needs Assessment With Special Application to Institutions of Higher Learning." Unpublished doctoral dissertation, University of California, Berkeley, 1978.

Scriven, M.S. "The Methodology of Evaluation." In *Perspectives of Curriculum Evaluation*. AERA Monograph Series on Curriculum Evaluation, no. 1. Chicago: Rand McNally, 1967.

Scriven, M.S. "Pros and Cons about Goal-Free Evaluation." *Evaluation Comment* 3 (1974): 1–4.

Scriven, M.S. *Evaluation Bias and its Control.* Occasional Paper Series no. 4. Western Michigan University Evaluation Center, 1975.

Scriven, M. and Roth, J.E. "Needs Assessment." *Evaluation News* 2 (1977): 25–28.

Scriven, M. and Roth, J.E. "Needs Assessment: Concept and Practice." *New Directions for Program Evaluation* 1 (1978): 1–11.

Smith, E.R., and Tyler, R.W. *Appraising and Recording Student Progress.* New York: Harper, 1942.

Smith, H.L., and Judd, C.H. *Plans for Organizing School Surveys.* National Society for the Study of Education, Thirteenth Yearbook, Part II. Bloomington, Illinois: Public School Publishing Co., 1914.

Smith, N.L. *Metaphors for Evaluation: Sources of New Methods.* Beverly Hills, California: Sage Publications, 1981a.

Smith, N.L. *New Techniques for Evaluation.* Beverly Hills, California: Sage Publications, 1981b.

Stake, R.E. "The Countenance of Educational Evaluation." *Teachers College Record* 68 (1967): 523–40.

Stake, R.E. "Setting Standards for Educational Evaluators." *Evaluation News* no. 2, 2 (1981), 148–52.

Stake, R.E. "The Case-Study Method in Social Inquiry." *Educational Researcher* 7 (1978): 5–8.

Stake, R.E. "Setting Standards for Educational Evaluators." *Evaluator News* no. 2, 2 (1981), 148–52.

Stake, R.E., and Gjerde, C. *An Evaluation of T-City, the Twin City Institute for Talented Youth.* AERA Monograph Series in Curriculum Evaluation, no. 7. Chicago: Rand McNally, 1974.

Stufflebeam, D.L. "The Use and Abuse of Evaluation in Title III." *Theory into Practice* 6 (1967): 126–33.

Stufflebeam, D.L. *Needs Assessment in Evaluation.* Audio-tape of presentation at the American Educational Research Association Meeting, San Francisco, September 1977. Published by the American Educational Research Association.

Stufflebeam, D.L. "Meta Evaluation: An Overview." *Evaluation and the Health Professions,* no. 2, 1 (1978).

Stufflebeam, D.L. et al. *Educational Evaluation and Decision-Making.* Ithaca, Illinois: Peacock Publishers, 1971.

Suarez, T. "Needs Assessments for Technical Assistance: A Conceptual Overview and Comparison of Three Strategies." Unpublished doctoral dissertation. Western Michigan University, 1980.

Thompson, D. *England in the Nineteenth Century (1815–1914).* Baltimore: Penguin Books, Inc., 1950.

Tyack, D., and Hansot, E. *Managers of Virtue.* New York: Basic Books, Inc., 1982.

Tyler, R.W. "Changing Concepts of Educational Evaluation." In: R.E. Stake (ed.), *Perspectives of Curriculum Evaluation,* vol. 1, New York: Rand McNally, 1967.

U.S. Office of Education. *Education of the Disadvantaged: An Evaluation Report on Title I, Elementary and Secondary Education Act of 1965, Fiscal Year 1968.* Washington, D.C.: Author, 1970.

Webster, W.J. *The Organization and Functions of Research and Evaluation Units in a Large Urban School District.* Dallas Texas: Dallas Independent School District, 1975.

2 AN ANALYSIS OF ALTERNATIVE APPROACHES TO EVALUATION
Daniel L. Stufflebeam and William J. Webster

The field of educational evaluation has developed dramatically over the past ten years. Following a period of relative inactivity in the 1950s, educational evaluation efforts experienced a period of revitalization in the mid 1960s. This revitalization was influenced by articles by Cronbach (1963), Scriven (1967), Stake (1967), and Stufflebeam (1966). The field's development was further stimulated by the evaluation requirements of the Great Society programs that were launched in 1965; by the nationwide accountability movement that began in the early 1970s; and, most importantly, by the mounting responsibilities and resources that society assigned to educators.

Developments of particular interest are the diverse ways in which educational evaluation has been conceptualized. This paper is an attempt to characterize and assess the different theoretical approaches to evaluation.

The study of alternative approaches is important for both the operation and the scientific advancement of evaluation. Operationally, a critical review of alternatives can help evaluators to consider and assess optional frameworks which they

Stufflebeam, Daniel L. and Webster, William J. "An Analysis of Alternative Approaches to Evaluation." *Educational Evaluation and Policy Analysis*, no. 3, 2 (May-June 1980), 5–19. Copyright © 1980, American Educational Research Association, Washington, D.C. Reprinted with permission.

can use to plan and conduct their studies. Scientifically, such a review can help evaluation researchers to identify issues, assumptions, and hypotheses that should be assessed. However, a main value in studying alternative approaches is not to enshrine any of them; on the contrary, the purpose is to discover their strengths and weaknesses and to obtain direction for devising better approaches.

Thirteen types of studies that have been conducted in the name of educational evaluation are identified and assessed in this paper. These 13 types are each unique and comprise most efforts to evaluate education. Whereas some of these types are used legitimately to assess worth, others are used illegitimately to create a false impression of an object's worth.

In analyzing the 13 types of studies, prior assessments regarding the state of the art of educational evaluation were consulted. Stake's analysis of nine evaluation approaches provided a useful application of advance organizers (the types of variables used to determine information requirements) for ascertaining different types of evaluation studies.[1] Hastings' review of the growth of educational evaluation theory and practice helped to place the field in an historical perspective.[2] Finally, Guba's presentation and assessment of six major philosophies in educational evaluation was provocative.[3] Although we did not always agree with the conclusions put forward in each of these papers, all of the prior assessments helped sharpen the issues addressed.

Alternative Conceptualizations of Educational Evaluation

In developing a characterization and assessment of different evaluation approaches, careful consideration was given to different kinds of activities conducted in the name of educational evaluation. These activities were classified according to their degree of conformity to a particular definition of educational evaluation. According to that definition, an educational evaluation study is one that is designed and conducted to assist some audience to judge and improve the worth of some educational object. This definition should be widely acceptable because it agrees with definitions of evaluation that appear in most dictionaries. However, it will become apparent that many studies done in the name of educational evaluation either do not conform to this definition or directly oppose it.

The proposed definition of an evaluation study was used to classify studies into three main approaches. The first approach includes politically oriented evaluations, which promote a positive or negative view of an object, irrespective of its actual worth. The second approach includes evaluations that are oriented to answer specified questions whose answers may or may not assess an object's worth. The third approach involves studies that are designed primarily to assess and/or improve the worth of some object.

Of the 13 types of studies identified, two pertain to the political approach, five to the questions-oriented approach, and six to the values-oriented approach.

Each type is further analyzed in terms of seven descriptors: (1) advance organizers, that is, the main cues that evaluators use to set up a study; (2) the main purpose served; (3) the sources of questions that are addressed; (4) the questions that are characteristic of each study type; (5) the methods that typically are used; (6) the persons who pioneered in conceptualizing each study type; and (7) other persons who have extended development and use of each study type. Using these descriptors, comments on each of the 13 types of studies are presented.

Politically Oriented Studies (or Pseudo-Evaluations)

Politically Controlled Study

The first type of study is labeled the politically controlled study. Its advance organizers are implicit or explicit threats faced by the client for an evaluation. The client's purpose in commissioning a politically controlled study is to secure assistance in acquiring, maintaining, or increasing the client's sphere of influence, power, or money. The questions addressed are those of interest to the client and special groups that share the client's interest. The main questions of interest to the client are: What information would be advantageous in a potential conflict situation? and, What data might be used advantageously in a confrontation? Typical methods of conducting the politically controlled study include covert investigations, simulation studies, and private information files. Generally, the client wants information obtained to be as technically adequate as possible, but the client also wants guarantees that he or she can control the dissemination of the information. Because the information might be released selectively to create a distorted picture of an object's worth, this type of study must be labeled a pseudo-evaluation study.

It should be noted that persons have not been nominated to receive credit as pioneers or developers of the politically controlled study, although real cases do exist.

To avoid the inference that the politically controlled type of study is imaginary, consider the following example. A superintendent of one of the nation's largest school districts once confided that he possessed an extensive notebook of detailed information about each of the school buildings in his district. The information included student achievement, teacher qualifications, racial mix of teachers and students, average per-pupil expenditure, socioeconomic characteristics of the student body, average length of tenure in the system for teachers in the school, and so forth. The aforementioned data revealed a highly segregated district. When asked why all the entries in the notebook were in pencil, the superintendent replied it was absolutely essential that he be kept informed about the current situation in each school; but, he said it was also imperative that the community-at-large, the board, and special interest groups in the community, in particular, not have access to the information. For, any of these groups might use the information to harm the district and to threaten his tenure there. Hence, one special assistant kept the document up-to-date; only one copy existed, and the superintendent kept that locked in his desk. The point of this example is not to make a negative judgment about the superintendent's behavior in this case. The point is that the superintendent's ongoing covert investigation and selective release of information was decidedly not a case of true evaluation, for it did not include full and open disclosure. Instead, this instance may appropriately be termed a pseudo-evaluation.

Public Relations-inspired Studies

The public-relations type of study is a similar case of politically oriented or pseudo-evaluation. In the public-relations type of study, the advance organizer is the propogandist's information needs. The purpose of the study is to help the client or propogandist create a positive public image for a school district, program, or process. The questions that guide such a study are derived from the public-relations specialists' and administrators' conceptions of which questions would be most popular with their constituents. In general, the public-relations study seeks information that would be most helpful in securing public support.

Typical methods used in public-relations studies are surveys, experiments, and the use of "expert" consultants. A pervasive characteristic of the public-relations evaluator's use of dubious methods is a biased attempt to nurture a good picture of the object of the evaluation.

A recent contact with an urban school district illustrates the second type of study. A superintendent requested a community survey for his district. The superintendent said, straightforwardly, he wanted a survey that would yield a positive report on the performance of the school district. He said such a positive report was desperately needed at the time so that community confidence in the school district could be restored. The superintendent did not get the survey and positive report, and it soon became clear why he thought one was needed. Several weeks after making the request, he was summarily fired.

Before addressing the next group of study types, perhaps a few additional comments should be made concerning politically oriented studies. Perhaps it is confusing to understand why any time at all has been taken to discuss the first two study types, since they certainly are not recommended in efforts to evaluate education. These studies have been considered because they are a prominent part of the educational evaluation scene. Sometimes evaluators and their clients are co-conspirators in performing the first two types of studies. On other occasions, evaluators, believing they are doing an objective assessment, discover that their client had other intentions. When the time is right, the client is able to subvert the study in favor of producing the desired biased picture. It is imperative that evaluators be more alert than they often are to these kinds of potential conflicts; otherwise, they will be unwitting accomplices in efforts to mislead through evaluation.

Questions-oriented Studies

Questions-oriented studies are so labeled because they start with a particular question and then move to the methodology appropriate for answering that question. Only subsequently do they consider whether the questions and methodology are appropriate for developing and supporting value claims. These studies can be called quasi-evaluation studies, because sometimes they happen to provide evidence that can be used to assess the worth of an object; while, in other cases, their focus is too narrow or is only tangential to questions of worth. Quasi-evaluation studies have legitimate uses apart from their relationship to evaluation; hence, the main caution is that these types of studies not be equated with evaluation.

Objectives-based Studies

The objectives-based study is the first questions-oriented study to be considered. In this type of study, some statement of objectives provides the advance organizer. The objectives may be mandated by the client, formulated by the evaluator, or specified by the teachers. The usual purpose of an objectives-based study is to determine whether the objectives have been achieved. Program developers, sponsors, and managers are typical audiences for such a study. The clients of objectives-based studies usually want to know which students have achieved which educational objectives.

The methods used in objectives-based studies essentially involve the collection and analysis of performance data relative to specified objectives. Ralph Tyler is generally acknowledged to be the pioneer in the objectives-based type of study, although Percy Bridgman and E.L. Thorndike probably should be credited along with Tyler.[4] Many people have furthered the work of Tyler by developing variations of his objectives-based evaluation model. A few of them are Bloom et al. (1956), Hammond (1972), Metfessel and Michael (1967), Popham (1969), and Provus (1971). Undoubtedly, the objectives based type of study has been the most prevalent type used in the name of educational evaluation. It is one that has good common sense appeal; educators have had a great amount of experience with it; and it makes use of technologies of behavioral objectives and standardized testing. Common criticisms are that such studies lead to terminal information that is of little use in improving a program, and that this information often is far too narrow in scope to constitute a sound basis for judging the worth of a program.

Accountability Studies

The accountability study became prominent in the early 1970s. Its emergence seems to have been connected with widespread disenchantment with the persistent stream of evaluation reports that indicated that massive state and federal investments in programs to improve education were not showing significant results. One proposed solution posited that accountability systems could be initiated to ensure both that educators would carry out their responsibilities to improve education and that evaluators would do a thorough job of identifying the effects of improvement programs.

The advance organizer for the accountability study is the set of responsibilities that personnel in institutions have for implementing educational programs. The purpose of the study, as already noted, is to provide constituents with an accurate accounting of results and to ensure that the results are primarily positive.

The questions that are addressed in accountability studies come from the constituents of programs, such as taxpayers; parent groups; school boards; and local, state, and national funding agencies. The main question that the groups want answered concerns whether the involved personnel and organizations charged with responsibility for educating students and for improving education are achieving all they should be achieving, given the investments of resources to support their work. Methods used in accountability studies include mandated testing programs; performance contracting; and procedures for auditing the design, process, and results of evaluation studies.

The person who is generally acknowledged as the pioneer in the area of educational accountability is Lessinger (1970). Some of the people who have extended Lessinger's work are Stenner and Webster, in their development of a handbook for conducting auditing activities,[5] and Kearney, in providing leadership to the State Department of Education in Michigan in developing the first statewide educational accountability system.

The main advantages of accountability studies are that they are popular among constituent groups and are aimed at improving the quality of education. A main disadvantage is that they produce a good deal of political unrest and acrimony among professional educators and between them and their constituents. Another disadvantage is that political forces tend to force the implementation of accountability efforts before the needed technology can be developed and field-tested.

Experimental Research Studies

The experimental research type of study is quite prominent in educational evaluation. It is labeled as a questions-oriented or quasi-evaluation strategy because it starts with questions and methodology that may or may not be related to assessing worth. The experimental research type of study calls to mind Kaplan's (1964) famous warning against the so-called "law of the instrument," whereby a given method is equated to a field of inquiry. In such a case, the field of inquiry is restricted to the questions that are answerable by the given method. Fisher (1951) specifically warned against equating his experimental methods with science.

The advance organizers in experimental studies are problem statements, hypotheses, and investigatory questions. The usual purpose of the experimental research study is to determine causal relationships between specified independent and dependent variables, such as a given instructional method and student standardized-test performance. It is particularly noteworthy that the sources of questions, investigated in the experimental research study, are researchers and the developers of educational programs, and not usually the constituents, practitioners, or financial sponsors.

The frequent question in the experimental study is: What are the effects of a given intervention on specified outcome variables? Typical methods used are experimental and quasi-experimental designs. Pioneers in using experimentation to study education are: Campbell and Stanley (1963), Cronbach and Snow (1969), and Lindquist (1953). Other persons who have developed the methodology of experimentation substantially for use in education are Glass and Maguire (1968), Suchman (1967), and Wiley and Bock (1967).

The main advantage of experimental studies in evaluation work is that they provide strong methods for establishing relatively unequivocal causal relationships between treatment and student achievement variables. The problems, however, are that the strategy is usually not workable in field settings and provides a much narrower range of information than is needed to evaluate educational programs. In addition, experimental studies tend to provide terminal information that is not useful for guiding the developmental process.

Testing Programs

Since the 1930s, American education has been inundated with standardized-testing programs. Probably every school district in the United States has some type of standardized testing program, and, formerly, many educators have tended to equate the results of a standardized-testing program with the information needed to evaluate the quality of a school district, a school, a program, and, in some cases, even a teacher.

Advance organizers for the testing study include areas of the school curriculum, tests that are available from publishing companies, and specified norm groups. The main purpose of testing programs is to compare the test performance of individual students and groups of students to that of selected norm groups.

The sources of questions that are addressed by the testing programs are usually test publishers and test selection committees; the typical question addressed by tests concerns whether the test performance of individual students is at or above the average performance of local, state, and national norm groups. The main process involved in using testing programs is to select, administer, score, and report standardized-test results.

One of the major pioneers in this area was Lindquist (1951), who was instrumental in developing the Iowa Testing Program, the American College Testing Program, the National Merit Scholarship Testing Program, and the General Educational Development Testing Program, as well as the Measurement Research Center at the University of Iowa. Many people have contributed substantially to the development of educational testing in America, including Ebel (1965), Flanagan (1939), Lord and Novick (1968), and Thorndike (1971).

The main advantages of standardized-testing programs are that they are efficient in producing valid and reliable information on student performance in many areas of the school curriculum and that they are a familiar strategy at every level of the school program in virtually all districts in the United States. The main limitations are: they provide data only about student performance, they reinforce students' multiple-choice test-taking behavior rather than their writing and speaking behavior, and, in many cases, they are perhaps a better indicator of the socioeconomic levels of the students in a given school or school district than they are of the quality of teaching and learning in that district. It has also been argued effectively by Stake (1971) that standardized tests are poor approximations of what teachers actually teach.

Management Information Systems

The management information system is the final type of question-oriented study. It is like the politically controlled studies, except that it supplies managers with the information they need to conduct their programs, as opposed to supplying them with the information they need to win a political advantage. The management information type of study is also like the decision-oriented study, which will be discussed later, except that the decision-oriented study provides information needed both to develop and defend the worth of a program, which goes beyond providing information that managers need to implement their management responsibilities.

The advance organizers in most management information systems include program objectives, specified activities, and projected program milestones or events. The purpose of a management information system, as already implied, is to continuously supply the information managers need to plan, direct, and control their programs.

The source of questions addressed is the management personnel. The main question they typically want answered is: Are program activities being implemented according to schedule, according to budget, and with the expected results? Methods commonly used in management information systems are system analysis, Program Evaluation and Review Technique (PERT), Critical Path Method, Program Planning and Budgeting System (PPBS), Management by Objectives, computer-based information systems, and cost analysis.

Cook (1966) introduced the use of PERT in education, and Kaufman (1969) has written widely about the use of management information systems in education.

A major advantage of the use of management information systems is in giving managers information they can use to plan, monitor, and control complex operations. A major difficulty with the application of this industry-oriented type of system to education is that the products of education are not amenable to a narrow, precise definition as is the case with a profit-and-loss statement of a corporation. Also, the information gathered in management information systems typically lacks the scope required to assess the worth of a program.

Values-oriented Studies

Accreditation/Certification Studies

Most educational institutions have periodically been the subjects of an accreditation study, and most professional educators, at one time or another, have had to meet certification requirements for a given educational position. Such studies of institutions and personnel are in the realm of true evaluation efforts, since institutions and personnel are studied to prove whether they are fit to serve designated functions in society.

The advance organizers used in the accreditation/certification study usually are guidelines that have been adopted by some accrediting or certifying body. As previously suggested, the purpose of the study is to determine whether institutions, programs, or personnel should be approved to perform specified functions.

The source of questions for accreditation or certification studies is the accreditating or certifying agency. Basically, the question they address is: Are institutions, programs, and personnel meeting minimum standards, and how can their performance be improved?

Typical methods used in the accreditation/certification study are self-study and self-reporting by the individual or institution. In the case of institutions, panels of experts are assigned to visit the institution, verify a self-report, and gather additional information. The basis for the self-studies and the visits by expert panels are usually guidelines that have been specified by the accrediting agency.

Accreditation of education was pioneered by the College Entrance Examination Board around 1901. Since then, the accreditation function has been implemented and expanded, especially by the Cooperative study of Seconday School Standards, dating from around 1933. Subsequently, the accreditation approach has been developed, expanded, and administered by the North Central Association of Secondary Schools and Colleges, along with their associated regional accrediting agencies across the United States, and by many other accrediting and certifying bodies.

The main advantage of the accreditation or certification study is that it aids lay persons in making informed judgments about the quality of educational institutions and the qualifications of educational personnel. The main difficulties are that the guidelines of accrediting and certifying bodies typically emphasize the intrinsic and not the outcome criteria of education. Also, the self-study and visitation processes used in accreditation offer many opportunities for corruption and inept performance.

Policy Studies

The policy study is the second type of true evaluation. It is recognized as a true evaluation approach because it sets out to identify and assess, for society or some segment of society, the merits of competing policies.

The advance organizer for the policy study is a given policy issue, for example: What is the best way to meet federal guidelines for equal education opportunity? The purpose of the policy study is usually to identify and assess the potential costs and benefits of competing policies for a given institution or for society.

Legislators, policy boards, and special interest groups often posit the questions that are addressed by policy studies. A main question they pose is: Which of two or more competing policies will maximize the achievement cost?

Methods used in policy studies include the Delphi Technique (described by Anderson, Ball, Murphy, and Associates, 1973), experimental and quasi-experimental design, (as in New Jersey's negative income tax experiment[6]), scenarios, forecasting, and judicial proceedings.

Joseph Rice (discussed in Anderson et al., 1973) can be mentioned as the pioneer in this area, as he conducted massive studies around 1900 to help education decide on the merits of continued contentration on spelling. Other persons who have contributed substantially to the methodology for conducting policy studies in education are Coleman, Campbell, Hobson, McPartland, Mood, Weinfeld, and York, (1966); Jencks, Smith, Adand, Bane, Cohen, Gintis, Heynes, and Michelson (1972); Clark (1965); Owens[7]; and Wolf (1973).

The main advantage of policy studies is that they are essential in guiding institutions and society. The main problems are that policy studies, over and again, are corrupted or subverted by the political environment in which they must be conducted and reported.

Decision-oriented Studies

The decision-oriented study emphasizes that evaluation should be used proactively to help improve a program as well as retroactively to judge its worth. As mentioned previously, the decision-oriented study should be distinguished from management information systems and from politically controlled studies because of the emphasis in decision-oriented studies on questions of worth.

· Decision situations provide the advance organizer for decision-oriented studies. Basically, the purpose of the studies is to provide a knowledge and value base for making and defending decisions.

The source of questions addressed by the decision-oriented studies is involved decisionmakers, which include administrators, parents, students, teachers, school boards, taxpayers, and all others who make decisions about funding, conducting, and using the results of education. The main questions addressed are: How should a given enterprise be planned? How should a given plan be carried out? How should a program be revised? Answers to these questions are based on the underlying standard of good education, which is that educational enterprises should foster human growth and development at a reasonable cost.

Many methods may be used in a decision-oriented study. These include surveys, needs assessments, case studies, advocate teams, observations, and quasi-experimental and experimental designs.

Cronbach (1963) first introduced educators to the idea that evaluation should be reoriented from its objectives-based history to a concern for helping educators make better decisions about how to educate. Later, Stufflebeam (1966, 1967) introduced a conceptualization of evaluation that was based on the idea that evaluation should help educators make and defend decisions that are in the best interest of meeting students' needs. Many other persons have since contributed to the development of a decision-oriented concept of evaluation. Included among them are Alkin (1969), Reinhard (1972), Taylor (1974), Ashburn,[8] Guba,[9] Merriman,[10] Ott,[11] Walker,[12] and Webster.[13]

A main advantage of the decision-oriented strategy is that it encourages educators to use evaluation continuously and systematically in their efforts to plan and implement programs that meet educational needs. It also presents a rationale for helping educators to be accountable for decisions they have made in the course of implementing a program.

A main limitation is that the collaboration required between an evaluator and decision-maker introduces opportunities for biasing the evaluation results. External meta evaluation has been introduced to offset such opportunities for bias.

Consumer-oriented Studies

In the consumer-oriented approach, the evaluator is the "enlightened surrogate consumer." Advance organizers are societal values and needs. The purpose of a consumer study is to judge the relative merits of alternative educational goods and services and, thereby, to help taxpayers and practitioners to make wise choices in their purchase of educational goods and services.

Questions for the consumer-oriented study are derived from society, from constituents of educational institutions, and especially from the evaluator's frame-of-reference. The general question addressed is: Which of several alternative consumable education objects is the best buy, given their costs, the needs of the consumer group, and the values of society at large? Methods include checklists, needs assessments, goal-free evaluation, experimental and quasi-experimental designs, modus operandi analysis, and cost analysis (Scriven 1974). Also, a popular method is for an external, independent consumer advocate to conduct and report findings on studies of publicly supported educational programs.

Scriven (1967) pioneered the consumer-oriented approach in education, and there are strong parallels between his work[and the concurrent work of Ralph Nader in the general field of consumerism. Glass has been an avid supporter and developer of Scriven's work.[14]

One of the main advantages of this approach is that it is a hard-hitting, independent assessment intended to protect educators and the consumers of education from shoddy educational products and services. The approach has high credibility with consumer groups.

The main disadvantage of this approach is that it can be so independent from practitioners that it may not assist them to do a better job of serving consumers. Also, the consumer-oriented study requires a highly credible and competent expert plus sufficient resources to allow the expert to conduct a thorough study. Often this approach is too costly to be carried out well and produces faulty, unrealistic data.

Client-centered Studies

In direct contrast to the consumer-oriented study is the client-centered study. The client-centered study takes the local autonomy view and helps people who are involved in a program to evaluate it and use the evaluation to improve it.

The advance organizers are concerns and issues in the program itself. The purpose of the study is to help people in a local setting understand the operations of their program, the ways the operations are valued by the people affected by them, and the ways they are valued by people who are expert in the program area.

Community and practitioner groups in the local environment plus external educational experts are the sources of questions that are addressed by the client-centered study. In general, the groups usually want to know about the history and status of a program and the ways in which it is judged by involved persons and experts in the program area.

Typical methods used in the client-centered study are the case study, adversary reports, sociodrama, and what Stake (1970) has called "responsive evaluation."

Stake (1967) is the pioneer of the client-centered type of study, and his approach has been developed by McDonald (1975) in England, Rippey (1973), and, most recently, Guba (1978).

The main strength of this approach is that it is an action-research approach, in which people implementing programs are helped to conduct their own evaluation. Its main weakness is its lack of external credibility and its susceptibility to bias on the part of people in the local setting, since they, in effect, have great control over the evaluation study.

Connoisseur-based Studies

The connoisseur-based study is the most recent entry among the 13 study types. This study assumes that certain experts in a given field are capable of indepth analysis and evaluation that could not be done in other ways. Just as a national survey of wine drinkers would undoubtedly produce information concerning overall wine preferences among the group, it would not provide the detailed judgments of the qualities of different wines that might be derived from a single connoisseur who has devoted a professional lifetime to the study and grading of wines.

The advance organizer for the connoisseur-based study is the evaluator's special expertise and sensitivities. The purpose of the study is to describe critically, appraise, and illuminate the particular merits of a given object.

The source of questions addressed by the connoisseur-based evaluation is the expert evaluators; that is, the critics and authorities who have undertaken the evaluation. The major question they can be expected to ask is: What merits and demerits distinguish the particular object from others of the same general kind?

The methodology of connoisseurship includes the critics' systematic use of their perceptual sensitivities, past expeiences, and refined insights. The evaluator's judgment is then conveyed to help the audience appreciate and understand all of the nuances of the object under study.

Eisner has pioneered this strategy in education.[15] Guba (1978) and Sanders and Hershiser[16] have further explored and developed its use in educational evaluation.

The main advantage of the connoisseur-based study is that it exploits the particular expertise and finely developed insights of persons who have devoted much time and effort to the study of a precise area. They can provide an array of detailed information that the audience can then use to form a more insightful analysis than otherwise might be possible. The disadvantage of this approach is that it is dependent on the expertise and qualifications of the particular expert doing the evaluation, leaving much room for subjectivity, bias, and corruption.

Conclusion

This completes our review of the 13 types of studies used to evaluate education. As stated at the beginning of this article, a critical analysis of these study types has important implications for both the practitioner of evaluation and the theoretician who is concerned with devising better concepts and methods.

A main point for the practitioner is that evaluators may encounter considerable difficulties if their perceptions of the study being undertaken differ from those of their clients and audiences. Typically, clients want a politically advantageous study performed, while the evaluators want to conduct questions-oriented studies, since these allow the evaluator to exploit the methodology in which they were trained. Moreover, the audiences usually want values-oriented studies that will help them determine the relative merits of competing educational goods and services. If evaluators are ignorant of the likely conflict in purpose, the evaluation is probably doomed to failure from the start. The moral is: at the onset of the study, evaluators must be keenly sensitive to their own agendas for an evaluation study as well as those that are held by client and audience. Further, the evaluator should advise involved parties of possible conflicts in the purposes for doing the study and should negotiate a common understanding at the start. Presented alternatives could be legitimately either a quasi-evaluation study directed at assessing particular questions or a true evaluation-type study directed at searching for all evidence that could help the client and audience assess the worth of the object. It is not believed, however, that politically inspired and controlled studies serve appropriate purposes in the evaluation of education. Granted, they may be necessary in administration and public relations, but they should not be confused with, or substituted for, evaluation. Finally, it is imperative to remember that no *one* type of study consistently is the best in evaluating education.

A main point to be gleaned from the review of these 13 types of studies, for the benefit of the theoretician, is that they have both strengths and weaknesses. In general, the weaknesses of the politically oriented studies are that they are prone to manipulation by unscrupulous persons and may help such people mislead an audience into developing a particular opinion of a program's worth that is un-founded and perhaps untrue. The main problem with the questions-oriented studies is that they often address questions that are more narrow in scope than the questions needing to be addressed in a true assessment of worth. However, it is also noteworthy that these types of studies are frequently superior to true evalua-tion studies in the efficiency of methodology and technical adequacy of informa-tion employed. Finally, the values-oriented studies undertake an overly ambitious task for it is virtually impossible to assess the true worth of any object. Such an achievement would require omniscience, infallibility, and a singularly unquestioned value base. Nevertheless, the continuing attempt to consider questions of worth certainly is essential for the advancement of education.

In conclusion, there is clearly a need for continuing efforts to develop and implement better approaches to evaluation. Theoreticians should diagnose strengths and weaknesses of existing approaches, and they should do so in more depth than we have been able to demonstrate here. They should use these diagnoses to evolve better, more defensible approaches; they should work with practitioners to operationalize and test the new approaches; and, of course, both groups should collaborate in developing still better approaches. Such an ongoing process of critical review and revision is essential if the field of educational evaluation is not to stagnate, but instead is to provide vital support for advancing education.

A summary of our analysis appears in tables 2–1, 2–2, and 2–3.

TABLE 2–1. An Analysis of Political-Orientation Study Types (Pseudo-Evaluation)

Approaches	*Political Orientation (Pseudo-Evaluation)*	
Definitions	*Studies that promote a positive or negative view of an object irrespective of its worth*	
Study Types	*Politically Controlled Studies*	*Public Relations Inspired Studies*
Advance Organizers	Implicit or explicit threats	Propogandist's information needs
Purpose	To acquire, maintain, or increase a sphere of influence, power, or money	To create a positive public image for an object
Source of Questions	Special interest groups	Public relations specialists and administrators
Main Questions	What information would be best to report or withhold in a projected confrontation?	What information would be most helpful in securing public support?
Typical Methods	Covert investigations and simulation studies	Biased use of surveys, experiments, and "expert" consultants

TABLE 2-2. An Analysis of Questions-Orientation Study Types (Quasi-Evaluation)

Approaches	(Quasi-Evaluation)				
Definitions	Studies that address specified questions whose answers may or may not assess an object's worth				
Study Types	Objectives-based Studies	Accountability Studies	Experimental Research Studies	Testing Programs	Management Information Systems
Advance Organizers	Objectives	Personnel/institutional responsibilities	Problem statements, hypotheses, and questions	Areas of the curriculum, published tests, and specified norm groups	Program objectives, activities, and events
Purpose	To relate outcomes to objectives	To provide constituents with an accurate accounting of results	To determine the causal relationship between specified independent and dependent variables	To compare the test performance of individual students and groups of students to select norms	To supply continuously the information needed to fund, direct, and control programs
Source of Questions	Program developers and managers	Constituents	Researchers and developers	Test publishers and test selection committees	Management personnel
Main Questions	Which students achieved which objectives	Are those persons and organizations charged with responsibility achieving all they should achieve?	What are the effects of a given intervention on specified outcome variables?	Is the test performance of individual students at or above the average performance of the norm group?	Are program activities being implemented on schedule, at a reasonable cost, and with expected results?
Typical Methods	Analysis of performance data relative to specified objectives	Auditing procedures and mandated testing programs	Experimental and quasi-experimental design	Selecting, administering, scoring, and reporting standardized tests	System analysis PERT, CPM, PPBS, computer-based information systems, and cost analysis
Pioneers	Tyler	Lessinger	Lindquist, Campbell and Stanley, and Cronbach	Lindquist	Cook, Kerr
Developers	Bloom, Hammond, Metfessel and Michael, Popham and Provus	Stenner and Webster, Kearney	Suchman, Wiley, Glass	Flanagan, Lord and Novick, Hyronymous, Thorndike, and many	Kaufman

TABLE 2-3. An Analysis of Values-Orientation Study Types (True-Evaluation)

	Values-Orientation (True Evaluation)					
Approaches	*Studies that are designed primarily to assess some object's worth*					
Definitions						
Study Types	*Accreditation/ Certification Studies*	*Policy Studies*	*Decision-oriented Studies*	*Consumer-oriented Studies*	*Client-centered Studies*	*Connoisseur-based Studies*
Advance Organizers	Accreditation certification guidelines	Policy issues	Decision situations	Societal values and needs	Localized concerns and issues	Evaluators' expertise and sensitivities
Purpose	To determine whether institutions, programs and personnel should be approved to perform specified functions	To identify and assess the potential costs and benefits of competing policies for a given institution or society	To provide a knowledge and value base for making and defending decisions	To judge the relative merits of alternative educational goods and services	To foster understanding of activities and how they are valued in a given setting and from a variety of perspectives	To critically describe, appraise and illuminate an object
Source of Questions	Accrediting/ certifying agencies	Legislators, policy boards and special interest groups	Decision makers (administrators, parents, students, teachers) their constituents, and evaluators	Society at large, consumers, and the evaluator	Community and practitioner groups in local environments and educational experts	Critics and authorities
Main Questions	Are institutions, programs and personnel meeting minimum standards; and how can they be improved?	Which of two or more competing policies will maximize the achievement of valued outcomes at a reasonable cost?	How should a given enterprise be planned, executed, and recycled in order to foster human growth and development at a reasonable cost?	Which of several alternative consumable objects is the best buy, given their costs, the needs of the consumers, and the values of society at large?	What is the history and status of a program and how is it judged by those who are involved with it and those who have expertise in program areas?	What merits and demerits distinguish an object from others of the same general kind?

TABLE 2–3. continued.

Typical Methods	Self-study and visits by expert panels to assess performance in relation to specified guidelines	Delphi, experimental and quasi-experimental design, fore-scenarios, casting, and judicial proceedings	Surveys, needs assessments, case studies, advocate teams, observation, and quasi-experimental and experimental design	Checklists, needs assessment, goal-free evaluation, experimental and quasi-experimental designs, modus operandi analysis, and cost analysis	Case study, adversary reports, sociodrama, responsive evaluation	Systematic use of refined perceptual sensitivities and various ways of conveying meaning and feelings
Pioneers	College Entrance Examination Board (1901)	Rice	Cronbach, Stufflebeam	Scriven	Stake	Eisner
Developers	Cooperative study of secondary school standards (1933)	Coleman, Jenks, Clarke, Owens, Wolf	Alkin, Ashburn, Brickell, Estes, Guba, Merriman, Ott, Reinhard	Glass	McDonald, Rippey, and Guba	Guba, Sanders

Notes

1. Stake, R.E. *Nine approaches to educational evaluation.* Unpublished chart. Urbana, Illinois: Center for Instructional Research and Curriculum Evaluation, 1974.

2. Hastings, T. *A portrayal of the changing evaluation scene.* Keynote speech at the annual meeting of the Evaluation Network, St. Louis, Missouri, 1976.

3. Guba, E.G. *Alternative perspectives on educational evaluation.* Keynote speech at the annual meeting of the Evaluation Network, St. Louis, Missouri, 1976.

4. Presentation by Robert W. Travers in a seminar at the Western Michigan University Evaluation Center, Kalamazoo, Michigan, October 24, 1977.

5. Stenner, A.J. and Webster, W.J. (eds.) *Technical Auditing Procedures. Educational Product Audit Handbook,* 38–103. Arlington, Virginia: Institute for the Development of Educational Auditing, 1971.

6. Kershaw, D.N. The New Jersey negative income tax experiment: A summary of the design, operations and results of the first large-scale social science experiment. *Dartmouth/OECD Seminar on Social Research and Public Policies.* 1974.

7. Owens, T. *Application of adversary proceedings to educational evaluation and decision making.* Paper presented at the annual meeting of the American Educational Research Association, New York, 1971.

8. Ashburn, A.G. *Directing education research training toward needs of large school districts.* (mimeo) Texas A & M University, Office of Educational Administration, Prairie View, Texas: 1972.

9. Guba, E.G. *A study of Title III activities: Report on Evaluation.* (mimeo) Bloomington, Indiana: National Institute for the Study of Educational Change, Indiana University, 1966.

10. Merriman, H.O. *Evaluation of planned educational change at the local education agency level.* (mimeo) Columbus, Ohio: Ohio State University Evaluation Center, 1968.

11. Ott, J.M. *A decision process and classification system for use in planning educational change.* (mimeo) Columbus, Ohio: Ohio State University Evaluation Center, 1967.

12. Walker, J. *Influence of alternative structural, organizational, and managerial options on the role of evaluation.* Paper presented at the annual meeting of the American Educational Research Association, Chicago, 1974.

13. Webster, W.J. *The organization and functions of research and evaluation in large urban school districts.* Paper presented at the annual meeting of the American Educational Research Association, Washington, D.C., March, 1975.

14. Glass, G.V. *Design of evaluation studies.* Paper presented at the Council for Exceptional Children Special Conference on Early Childhood Education, New Orleans, Louisiana, 1969.

15. Eisner, E.W. *The perceptive eye: Toward the reformation of educational evaluation.* Paper presented at the annual meeting of the American Educational Research Association, Washington, D.C., March, 1975.

16. Sanders, J.R. and Hershiser, M.A. *A proposal to study the attributes of a classroom that determine its pervasive quality.* Kalamazoo, Michigan: Western Michigan University Evaluation Center, 1976.

References

Alkin, M.C. Evaluation theory development. *Evaluation Comment.* 1969, 2. 2–7.

Anderson, Scarvia B.; Ball, Samuel; Murphy, Richard T.; and Associates. *Encyclopedia of educational evaluation.* San Francisco, California: Jossey-Bass, 1973, 142.

Bloom, B.S.; Englehart, M.D.; Furst, E.J.; Hill, W.H.; and Krathwohl, D.R. *Taxonomy of educational objectives: Handbook I: Cognitive domain.* New York: David McKay, 1956.

Campbell, D.T., and Stanley, J.C. Experimental and quasi-experimental designs for research on teaching. In N.L. Gage (ed.), *Handbook of research on training.* Chicago: Rand McNally, 1963.

Clark, K. *Dark ghetto.* New York: Harper & Row, 1965.

Coleman, J.S.; Campbell, E.Q.; Hobson, C.J.; McPartland, J.; Mood, A.M.; Weinfeld, F.D.; and York, R.L. *Equality of educational opportunity.* Washington, D.C.: U.S. Department of Health, Education, and Welfare, Office of Education, 1966.

Cook, D.L. Program evaluation and review techniques, applications in education. *U.S. Office of Education Cooperative Monograph, 17,* (OE-12024), 1966.

Cronbach, L.J. Course improvement through evaluation. *Teachers College Record.* 1963, 64, 672–83.

Cronbach, L.J., and Snow, R.E. *Individual differences in learning ability as a function of instructional variables.* Stanford, California: Stanford University Press, 1969.

Ebel, R.L. *Measuring educational achievement.* Englewood Cliffs, New Jersey: Prentice-Hall, 1965.

Fisher, R.A. *The Design of experiments.* (6th ed.) New York: Hafner, 1951.

Flanagan, J.C. General considerations in the selection of test items and a short method of estimating the product-moment coefficient from data at the tails of the distribution. *Journal of Educational Psychology,* 1939, 30, 674–80.

Glass, G.V., and Maquire, T.O. *Analysis of time-series quasi-experiments.* (U.S. Office of Education Report No. 6–8329.) Boulder, Colorado: Laboratory of Educational Reseach, University of Colorado, 1968.

Guba, E.G. Toward a methodology of naturalistic inquiry in educational evaluation. *CSE Monograph Series in Evaluation,* Los Angeles, California: Center for the Study of Evaluation, 1978.

Hammond, R.L. *Evaluation at the local level.* (Mimeograph) Tucson, Arizona: EPIC Evaluation Center, 1972.

Jencks, C.; Smith, M.; Adand, H.; Bane, M.J.; Cohen, D.; Gintis, H.; Heynes, B.; and Michelson, S. *Inequality: A reassessment of the effect of family and schooling in America.* New York: Basic Books, 1972.

Kaplan, A. *The conduct of inquiry.* San Francisco, California: Chandler, 1964.

Kaufman, R.A. Toward educational system planning: Alice in Educationland. *Audiovisual Instructor,* 1969, 14, (May), 47–48.

Lessinger, L.M. *Every kid a winner: Accountability in education.* New York: Simon and Schuster, 1970.

Lindquist, E.F. (ed.). *Educational measurement.* Washington, D.C.: American Council on Education, 1951.

Lindquist, E.F. *Design and analysis of experiments in psychology and education.* Boston: Houghton-Mifflin, 1953.

Lord, F.M., and Novick, M.R. *Statistical theories of mental test scores.* Reading, Massachusetts: Addison-Wesley, 1968.

McDonald, B. Evaluation and the control of education. In D. Tawney (ed.), *Evaluation: The state of the art.* London: Schools Council, 1975.

Metfessel, N.S., and Michael, W.B. A paradigm involving multiple criterion measures for the evaluation of the effectiveness of school programs. *Educational and Psychological Measurement,* 1967, 27, 931–43.

Popham, W.J. Objectives and instruction. In: R. Stake (ed.), *Instructional objectives. AERA Monograph Series on Curriculum Evaluation,* (Vol. 3). Chicago: Rand McNally, 1969. 1969.

Provus, M.N. *Discrepancy evaluation.* Berkeley, California: McCutcheon, 1971.

Reinhard, D.L. *Methodology development for input evaluations using advocate and design teams.* Ph.D. dissertation, Ohio State University, 1972.

Rippey, R.M. (ed.). *Studies in transactional evaluation.* Berkeley, California: McCutcheon, 1973.

Scriven, M.S. The methodology of evaluation. In: R.E. Stake (ed.), *Curriculum evaluation. AERA Monograph Series on Curriculum Evaluation* (Vol. 1) Chicago: Rand McNally, 1967. 1967.

Scriven, M. Evaluation perspectives and procedures. In: W. James Popham (ed.), *Evaluation in Education: Current Applications.* Berkeley, California: McCutcheon, 1974.

Stake, R.E. The countenance of educational evaluation. *Teachers College Record.* 1967, 68, 523–40.

Stake, R.E. Objectives, priorities, and other judgment data. *Review of Educational Research,* 1970, 40, 181–212.

Stake, R.E. *Measuring what learners learn.* (mimeograph) Urbana, Illinois: Center for Instructional Research and Curriculum Evaluation, 1971.

Stufflebeam, D.L. A depth study of the evaluation requirement. *Theory into Practice,* 1966, 5, (June), 121–34.

Stufflebeam, D.L. The use of and abuse of evaluation in Title III. *Theory into Practice,* 1967, 6, (June), 126–33.

Suchman, E.A. *Evaluative research.* New York: Russell Sage Foundation, 1967.

Taylor, J.P. *An administrator's perspective of evaluation.* Kalamazoo, Michigan: Western Michigan University, 1974, (Occasional Paper #2).

Thorndike, R.L. *Educational measurement* (2nd ed.) Washington, D.C.: American Council on Education, 1971.

Wiley, D.E., and Bock, R.D. Quasi-experimentation in educational settings: Comment. *The School Review,* Winter, 1967, 353–66.

Wolf, R.L. How teachers feel toward evaluation. In: E.R. House (ed.), *School evaluation: The politics and process.* Berkeley, California: McCutcheon, 1973.

3 ASSUMPTIONS UNDERLYING EVALUATION MODELS
Ernest R. House[1]

The Major Models

One way of understanding evaluation is to compare the numerous evaluation models with one another. There are many possibilities for comparison, but perhaps the most significant comparisons are those among the underlying theoretical assumptions on which the models are based. In this way, one might see how logically similar the models are to one another and determine what logical possibilities do and do not exist.

The basic theme is that all the evaluation models are based on variations in the assumptions of liberal ideology, or if one prefers, the conceptions of liberal democracy. The models differ from one another as the basic assumptions vary. Assumptions I take here in the commonsense meaning of "things taken for granted" or "things taken to be true."

Table 3–1 presents a taxonomy of some evaluation models. In selecting the models I have made use of the classifications of several writers, especially Stake (1976), Popham (1975), and Worthen and Sanders (1973). There seems to be

House, Ernest R. "Assumptions Underlying Evaluation Models." *Educational Researcher* (March 1978), 4–12. Copyright © 1978, American Educational Research Association, Washington, D.C. Reprinted with permission.

agreement on what are the major models. I believe that most of the other models are similar to these, although certainly some approaches have been overlooked.
    A very brief sketch of each evaluation model is in order.

Systems Analysis.   In this approach one assumes a few quantitative output measures, usually test scores, and tries to relate differences in programs to variations in test scores. The data are often survey data and the outcome measures are related to the programs via correlational analyses. Recently, experimental design has been more heavily employed. One of the main antecedents for this approach was systems analysis as developed in the Department of Defense under Secretary McNamara. It has served as the major evaluation perspective in the Department of Health, Education, and Welfare since about 1965 (McLaughlin, 1975; House, 1977).

Behavioral Objectives.   The objectives of a program are spelled out in terms of specific student performances that can be reduced to specific student behaviors. These behaviors are measured by tests, either norm-referenced or criterion-referenced. Ralph Tyler was the originator of this approach.

Decision Making.   The evaluation is structured by the decisions to be made. The evaluator is to supply information on these particular decisions. Stufflebeam is the major figure here. The methodology tends to be questionnaire and interview surveys. The decisionmakers are administrators and managers, although the category has broadened somewhat recently.

Goal Free.   Scriven has been primarily concerned with reducing the effects of bias in evaluation. This model reduces the bias of searching only for the program developers' prespecified intents by not informing the evaluator of them. Hence, the evaluator must search for all outcomes. The consumer is the primary audience and Consumer's Union procedures are analogs to this approach.

Art Criticism.   Evolving from the traditions of art and literary criticism is the model of an educational critic, one who is attuned by experience and training to judge the important facets of educational programs. Eisner is the leading figure.

Accreditation.   For more than 50 years, schools have united cooperatively to evaluate each other. This is ordinarily done by a team of outside professionals visiting on-site. The local people have previously collected information and studied their program according to a set of external standards. The reviewers commend or disapprove of the local programs.

Adversary.   Quasi-legal procedures have been used by several people to present the pros and cons of a program. The adversary system ensures the presentation of both sides. These evaluations often take the form of trial-by-jury.

Transaction. This approach concentrates on the educational processes themselves: the classroom, the school, the program. It uses various informal methods of investigation and has been drawn increasingly to the case study as the major methodology. Stake is the leading figure.

In the first column of the taxonomy in table 3–1, the common names of the models are listed. In the top row are the critical dimensions of comparison: the audiences to whom the evaluation is addressed, what the model assumes consensus on, the methodology of data collection, the ultimate outcome expected, and the typical question that the approach tries to address. At one level of abstraction, these are the assumptions underlying the models.

In the taxonomy, the models are related to one another in a systematic way. Generally the more one progresses down the column of major audiences, the more democratic or less elitist the audience becomes. The more one moves down the consensus column, the less consensus is assumed on goals and other elements. The more one moves down the methodology column, the more subjective and less objective the research methodology becomes. The more one moves down the outcomes column, the less the overall concern becomes social efficiency and the more it becomes personal understanding. These are oversimplifications since the actual ordering is more complex.

The major elements in understanding the models are their ethics, their epistemology, and their political ramifications. The current models all derive from the philosophy of liberalism, with deviations from the mainstream being responsible for differences in approaches. The ethics, epistemology, and politics are not entirely separable from one another.

Liberalism itself grew out of an attempt to rationalize and justify a market society (MacPherson, 1966) that was organized on the principle of freedom of choice. Choice remains a key idea in the evaluation models, although whose choice, what choices, and the grounds upon which choices are made are matters of difference. Consumer's choice is the ultimate idea but the concept of the consumer differs.

A second key idea of liberalism is that of an individualist psychology. Each individual mind is presumed to exist prior to society. The individual is not conceived initially as a part of a greater collectivity, although he may submit to one later as in a social contract situation. Liberalism is profoundly methodologically individualist in its intellectual constructions.

Another key idea is the empiricist orientation. Often liberalism is radically empiricist. For example, John Stuart Mill, the apostle of liberalism, believed that even mathematics was inductively based. All the evaluation models here have such an empiricist flavor.

TABLE 3–1. A Taxonomy of Major Evaluation Models

Model	Proponents	Major Audiences	Assumes Consensus on	Methodology	Outcome	Typical Questions
Systems Analysis	Rivlin	Economists, managers	Goals; known cause & effect; quantified variables.	PPBS; linear programming; planned variation; cost benefit analysis.	Efficiency	Are the expected effects achieved? Can the effects be achieved more economically? What are the most *efficient* programs?
Behavioral Objectives	Tyler, Popham	Managers, psychologists	Prespecified objectives; quantified outcome variables	Behavioral Objectives; achievement tests	Productivity; accountability	Are the students achieving the objectives? Is the teacher producing?
Decision Making	Stufflebeam, Alkin	Decision-makers, esp. administrators	General goals; criteria	Surveys, questionnaires, interviews; natural variation	Effectiveness; quality control.	Is the program effective? What parts are effective?
Goal Free	Scriven	Consumers	Consequences; criteria	Bias control; logical analysis; modus operandi	Consumer choice; social utility.	What are *all* the effects?
Art Criticism	Eisner, Kelly	Connoisseurs, Consumers	Critics, standards,	Critical review	Improved Standards	Would a critic approve this program?
Accreditation	North Central Association	Teachers, public	Criteria, panel, procedures	Review by panel; self-study	Professional acceptance	How would professionals rate this program?
Adversary	Owens, Levine, Wolf	Jury	Procedures and judges	Quasi-legal procedures	Resolution	What are the arguments for and against the program?
Transaction	Stake, Smith, MacDonald, Parlett-Hamilton	Client, Practitioners	Negotiations; activities	Case studies, interviews, observations	Understanding; diversity	What does the program look like to different people?

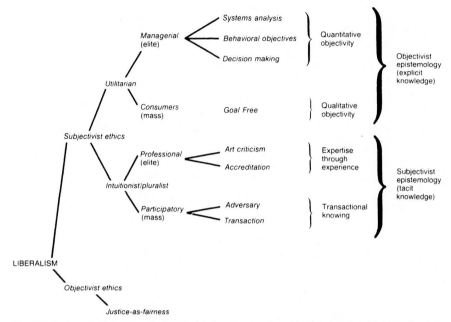

Figure 3–1.   A Scheme Relating Major Evaluation Models to the Philosophy of Liberalism.

The evaluation models also assume a free marketplace of ideas in which consumers will "buy" the best ideas. They assume that competition of ideas strengthens the truth. Ultimately they assume that knowledge will make people happy or better in some way. So the evaluation models partake of the ideas of a competitive, individualist, market society. But the most fundamental idea is freedom of choice, for without choice, of what use is evaluation? Figure 3–1 presents the evaluation models as they are related to liberalism.

Subjectivist Ethics

All the major evaluation models are subjectivist in ethics, although there is no necessity for this. One type of ethical subjectivism sees the end of ethical conduct as the realization of some type of subjective experience. This describes the top four models, which I have labeled utilitarian. Properly speaking, utilitarianism refers to the idea of maximizing happiness in society. Any activity that maximizes happiness is the "right" thing to do (House, 1976). Usually surrogate measures, like gross national product in economics or mean test scores in education, are used as the indicators for happiness.

Besides the systems analysis, behavioral objective, and decision making models, Scriven's goal-free model is also included in this classification. All these models try to arrive at a single judgment of overall social utility. The simplest approach is the homogenous scaling of the systems analysis approach, which tries to reduce all variables into a quantitative model like a regression analysis. Only one or a few outcome variables are employed.

The most complex model is that of Scriven, in which many outcome variables are considered, including secondary and tertiary effects. All these various scales must be weighted and combined somehow into an overall summative judgment. The analogy is to a Consumer's Union report in which many different criteria are summed up in an overall ranking of better and best. As in Consumer's Union, the final scaling will be ordinal rather than interval. It is utilitarian in the sense that there is *one* final scaling of merit, leading to best consumer choice and eventually to social utility.

The other four major evaluation models I have labeled intuitionist/pluralist. The ethical principles are not single in number nor explicitly defined as in utilitarian ethics. There are several principles derived from intuition and experience, but no set rules for weighting them. This captures another meaning of ethical subjectivism — that the ultimate criteria of what is good and right are individual feelings or apprehensions.

In the art criticism model, the critic has arrived at his invariably plural principles by long training and experience. His taste has been refined so that he is an expert judge. Much of his expertise lies in how well he can intuitively balance the principles of judgment. In the accreditation model, the principles may be spelled out in books like *Evaluative Criteria* (1969), but their origin and application remain very much a matter of professional intuitive judgment based on long experience.

In the adversary model, as in a quasi-trial, the jury is free to employ multiple criteria in an intuitive fashion. The adversaries are free to introduce anything in evidence that can be construed as relevant. Finally, in the transaction model, pluralistic criteria are introduced by soliciting the judgments of various people involved in the program. The data are weighted intuitively by the evaluator and by the audience of the evaluation.

Generally speaking, the utilitarian models tend to take explicitly defined techniques as the basis of ethics and knowledge, whereas the intuitionists/ pluralists take intuitive tacit knowledge derived from professional experience and participation as the basis.

Although all the major models are based on subjectivist ethics, there is no reason why this must be so. It would be possible to have an objectivist ethic within the liberal philosophy. For example, in his *Theory of Justice* (1971), John Rawls attempted to base his social ethics on two principles of justice. These principles were not justified on the presumption that they maximized some subjective feeling like happiness, nor on the fact that people intuitively held these principles. Rather, the principles were justified on the basis that rational analysis, namely the theory of minimizing losses, would lead *any* rational person to the same principles. They were objectivistic in the sense that they were based on inspectable public logic. Rawls' theory would still fit within the liberal tradition of free choice and methodological individualism.

The utilitarian group is differentiated internally by orientation to different audiences. The systems analysis, behavioral objectives, and decision making models are strongly oriented to supplying information to managers. The goal-free model is aimed more at consumers. This elite/mass differentiation is carried through among the intuitionists/pluralists as well. The art criticism and accreditation models rely on professional experts for judgments about the program being evaluated, while the adversary and transaction models require participation by both the practitioners and the public.

The Liberal Objectivist Epistemology

In their orientation toward management, the managerial models look for ways in which management can monitor and improve the programs. Accountability, efficiency, and quality control are major management concerns. Evaluation has something of a watchdog function. The managerial school also tends to be based on a common epistemology, which I will label ''objectivism.'' Evaluation information is considered to be ''scientifically objective.'' This objectivity is achieved by using ''objective'' instruments like tests or questionnaires. Presumably, results produced with these instruments are reproducible. The data are analyzed by quantitative techniques which are also ''objective'' in the sense that they can be verified by logical inspection regardless of who uses the techniques.

In its extreme form, objectivism in epistemology entirely excludes the non-quantitative. If it exists, it can be measured, the thought goes. Reduction into numbers sometimes becomes equated with objectivity. The origins of much of this extreme empiricism and objectivism can be found in the earlier epistemology of the liberal philosophy.

The origins of liberalism as a philosophy can be traced back, in part, to the first great British empiricist, Thomas Hobbes. An admirer of Galileo's mechanical view of the universe, Hobbes developed a mechanistic philosophy of mind based on the idea that sensations were produced in the mind by the motions of external bodies. Words have meaning only when associated with these sensations, and truth consists of the right ordering of names with sensations. Clear definitions are critical. Reasoning is equivalent to calculation and will be correct if the signs are attached to consistent images. Cause-and-effect is a direct reflection of the world. Thus, the way to truth is through clear definition and scientific method.

This epistemology was reformulated in turn by Locke, Berkeley, and Hume.

Two hundred years later came the last of the great British empiricists, John Stuart Mill, for whom the mind was a bundle of impressions. Psychological laws of association were the foundation of a science of society. Everything came from and had to be tested by experience, to the extent that even deductive logic, e.g., mathematics, had an inductive basis. Mill saw no fundamental difference between logical truths and factual truths. All knowledge, he felt, had to be grounded in and tested by experience. Knowledge was the pooled sum of individual observations.

This extreme methodological individualism ran deep in Mill's philosophy. To him, society was a collection of individual persons bound by common interests. His radical empiricism led him to formulate rules for the conduct of inductive inquiry in *A System of Logic* (Mill, 1893). Since the mind consisted of sensations, feelings, and their associations, the categories of the real world seemed to Mill to be easily accessible. But could these categories be relied upon? If they were ephemeral, one could not know anything. To overcome this problem, Mill *assumed* the world consisted of constant uniformities among classes of sensations.

Experimentation was essential for the scientific testing of theories. Valid causal connections could be established only through the meticulous sorting and independent variation of antecedent conditions and consequences. These were often concealed from causal observation. "Unwashed" appearances were deceptive; only techniques of inductive logic could clean them. It was here that techniques like the method of agreement, method of difference, or method of concomitant variation could be useful. The canons of induction were to provide a method for sifting evidence of correlations upon which scientific laws were based.

The scientific laws were what one was after. Science should be concerned with causal uniformities that held for all members of a given class. The assumption of the uniformity of nature was the key on which Mill's whole system of logic depended. In Mill's language:

> We must first observe that there is a principle in the very statement of what Induction is; an assumption with regard to the course of nature and the order of the universe; namely, that there are such things in nature as parallel cases; that what happens once will, under a sufficient degree of similarity of circumstances, happen again, and not only again, but as often as the same circumstances recur. . . . And if we consult the actual course of nature we find that the assumption is warranted. The universe, so far as known to us, is so constituted that whatever is true in any one case is true in all cases of a certain description; the only difficulty is, to find what description. (Mill, 1893)

Hamilton (1976) has identified some of Mill's key epistemological axioms:

There is a uniformity of nature in time and space. This lends a procedural certainty to inductive logic.

Concepts can be defined by direct reference to empirical categories, and laws of nature can be derived inductively using the proper procedures.

Large samples can suppress idiosyncracies in the data and reveal "general causes."

The social and natural sciences have the same aim of discovering general laws for purposes of prediction and explanation.

The social and natural sciences are methodologically similar; social science is just more complex.

This extreme empiricism relied on the belief that categories were rather easily obtainable, much like categories in the physical sciences. Using the proper techniques, one could define variables and establish relationships between them. Since nature was uniform, one could induce laws in social science just as in natural science. Furthermore, this could be done with survey methodology. The extreme emphasis on empiricism to the exclusion of theory has been inherited by evaluation from liberal epistemology: One can find relationships in nature without theoretical constructs.

Hamilton (1977) traces the introduction of some of these ideas into evaluation. A contemporary of Mill, Francis Galton, invented correlational techniques to relate Mill's easily discoverable categories to one another. Galton also provided an important basis for psychometrics in his work on individual differences. Cattell, greatly influenced by Galton, introduced mental testing into the United States.

The use of tests in education for sorting purposes was promoted by E.L. Thorndike. Thorndike also had a strong influence on the scientific management movement in education. The scientific management movement introduced efficiency engineering into the schools. Tests, rating scales, and quantitative techniques stimulated by Thorndike's work were used as devices for achieving efficiency in the schools (Callahan, 1962).

In its emphasis on task analysis, prespecification, and many other features, scientific management bears a strong resemblance to the systems analysis and behavioral objectives models of evaluation (House, 1978). In fact, one of the leading advocates of scientific management in education was Franklin Bobbitt. Later, Bobbitt and Charters adopted a task analysis skill job specification approach to curriculum development. One of Charters' graduate students was Ralph Tyler, who later originated the behavioral objectives model of evaluation. The managerial orientation to evaluation has long historical roots.

With or without the historical connections, the similarity of the managerial evaluation models to Mill's epistemology is strong. Perhaps the leading proponent of the systems analysis model has been Alice M. Rivlin. She was in the group that introduced cost benefit analysis to education and other social programs in the Department of Health, Education, and Welfare in the 1960s. Most of the large

federal evaluation efforts were based on the systems analysis logic (McLaughlin, 1975).
The key ideas in Rivlin's (1971) approach were these (House, 1978):

Key decisions will be made at higher governmental levels.

The end of evaluation is efficiency in the production of social services.

The only true knowledge is a production function specifying stable relationships between educational inputs and outputs.

The only way to such knowledge is through experimental methods and statistical techniques.

It is impossible to agree on goals and on a few output measures.

There is a direct parallel between production in social services and in manufacturing. The same techniques of analysis will apply.

Like Mill, Rivlin assumed the physical science paradigm would be appropriate. She saw social services and manufacturing as yielding to the same techniques of inquiry. The result would be generalizations (in this case production functions) that would hold in various circumstances, if one could only find what those circumstances were. Such a mechanistic conception goes back to Hobbes, and the uniformity of nature assumptions were straight out of J.S. Mill. Results would be consistent everywhere. Rivlin also believed, as did Mill, that large samples were necessary to rid oneself of idiosyncracies.

Mill felt that the chief moral problem was enlightenment, and that men were misled by their institutions. Rivlin believed that the major problem was ignorance in not knowing how to produce social services more effectively. Both believed in the use of experts to unravel these problems. Both also believed in using a few measures as surrogates of happiness. These are needed for calculations in order to enable the utilitarian ethics to work.

There is one place where the classic liberal J.S. Mill and a modern liberal diverge however. To Mill, liberty was necessary for enlightenment to occur. Mill was one of the great defenders of laissez-faire. The government should stay out of men's affairs. For Rivlin, a welfare-state liberal, the government would be deciding and acting. In order to find out what works, the government would need more control to conduct experiments. Mill was not for large-scale social planning, with the exception of special areas like education, where he allowed for planning and even coercion. Rivlin is the epitome of large-scale planning, as discussed later.

The objectivism of the managerial evaluation models, which tends to equate objectivity with quantification, relies on intersubjective agreement as the exclusive indicator of objectivity. Scriven (1972) calls this the quantitative sense of objectivity. One person's perception of something is regarded as being subjective

— the disposition of one individual. Being objective is what a *number* of observers experience. Common experiencing makes the observation public through inter-subjective agreement.

Objectivity has come to be equated with externalizing all references so that multiple witnessing can be achieved, since by the doctrine of intersubjectivism what cannot be experienced directly by others cannot be taken seriously. Hence, objectivity is often equated with being able to specify and explicate completely all data collection procedures. Complete externalization permits replication, the hallmark of reliability.

In describing systems analysis procedures, the Department of Defense puts it this way: "Perhaps the most important of these is the scientific method. This means that the data used in the analysis must be capable of verification, either by observation or by deduction from plausible premises, and that the procedures employed in the analysis must conform to accepted rules of logic. Systems analysis is characterized, in the second place, by the use of quantifiable data and mathematical techniques. . . . Explicitness is the final common denominator of systems analysis. The assumptions and criteria employed in an analysis are specified, and incommensurables and areas of uncertainty are carefully delineated." (Snyder, 1967).

"Reliable instruments" receive top priority following this reasoning. In fact, the higher the observer agreement (the reliability coefficient), the better the instrument or procedure appears to be. Unfortunately, reliability is no guarantee of validity, and the intersubjective fallacy can lead to the use of "instruments" on which one achieves high observer agreement as opposed to procedures which may have much greater validity. Instruments with high reliability are hallmarks of this epistemological objectivism. Validity often suffers accordingly.

There is a sense in which the intersubjective verification principle is carried through in the definition of goals as well as in the measurement of effects. It is assumed in the managerial models of evaluation that one can reach a consensus on the goals of a particular project. This assumption is critical in the systems analysis and behavioral objectives models, for the consensus defines what the evaluation will look for. In addition, the systems analysis model also assumes agreement on cause-and-effect relationships. Mill assumed cause-and-effect to be obvious and discernible in nature.

Hence, in objectivism the notion of objectivity becomes equated with proce-dures for determining intersubjectivity. This occurs in both the ethics and episte-mology. In fact, utilitarianism requires that there be a single standard of social utility against which to compare things.

Although I have placed Scriven's goal-free evaluation in the utilitarian group, it is somewhat more complex. Scriven employs the *qualitative* notion, in which objectivity is equated with being free from bias or distortion. Scriven's overriding concern is with the control of bias. He may employ experimental design like the managerial group, but he has evolved an arsenal of organizational and social devices for controlling biases in the broadcast sense (Scriven, 1975; 1976).

In Scriven's framework, it is possible for a single observer, unaided by any psychometric instrumentation, to be more objective than a battalion of observers loaded with reliable instruments — if the single observer is looking for the right thing and is sufficiently protected from numerous biases. Scriven does not equate objectivity with intersubjective agreement. Neither does he assume consensus on goals and objectives, as dramatically indicated by the goal-free approach. Goal-free evaluation probably does assume agreement on the consequences of the program. (Again the choice at issue is consumer's choice rather than that of the manager.) Scriven combines multiple criteria of consequences with ordinal scaling and relentlessly comparative approach.

The Subjectivist Epistemology

Utilitarian evaluation, then, is based on a subjectivist ethic, such as maximizing a state of mind like satisfaction, but employs an objectivistic epistemology in doing so. Once one has determined what is to be maximized, the methodology can then be employed objectivistically to allocate resources to satisfy various desires.

The intuitionist/pluralist evaluation models employ a subjectivist ethic of a different sort. Generally speaking, their research methodology also tends to be subjectivist. Procedures for an educational critic or an accreditation team to conduct their investigation are general rather than specific. Explicitness of detail and externalization of procedures so that others might observe the same thing are not the common denominators. Reproducibility is not the major criterion.

Likewise, in the adversary and transaction approaches how the jury will come to a decision or how a case study worker chooses certain material over other material is not made totally specific. There is a good deal of subjectivity in how the key actors conduct their investigations.

Whereas the objectivists rely on explicitness of detail in defining techniques which others can use, the intuitionists rely on training and experience to insure that truth is served. At the extreme in these models, both validity and utility are defined subjectively. Validity is conceived as being relative to the conditions of the human mind either because of universal limitations on the way people think or because of personal limitations. (In the objectivists' framework, validity often is conceived as predicting one observable category from another.)

Subjective validity means that truth is relative to human nature and perhaps even to particular humans. What is valid for one person may not be valid for another. Likewise, the subjective utility of something is based on personal judgment and personal desires. Each person is the best judge of events for himself.

Actually, the subjectivist epistemology is not quite as anarchic as it appears. Whereas the objectivist position is based on externalization and total specification of techniques, the subjectivist position is based on the tradition of the "closed case." Through training, experience, and socialization, the evaluator incorporates precedents into his judgments. The law is the most obvious example of a set of cases that guide judgment.

The subjectivists are less interested in arriving at a proposition that is true (in the generalizable sense) than in relating the evaluation to the particular experience of the audience. They attempt to obtain valid insights within the frame of reference of the group for whom they are working. It is assumed that there is a gap between language and experience. Tacit rather than explicit knowledge is what the evaluator seeks. The evaluation is intentionally context-bound and findings are interpreted in context. Since the audience may well have a firmer grasp of the context, based on greater experience, the audience's interpretation of an event may be superior to that of the evaluator. The subjectivist evaluator is more concerned in his work with specific causal statements (internal validity) than with general causal statements (external validity) (Ennis, 1973). Specific causal statements obtain for a particular time and place. Generalizations may be left to the audience.

The subjectivist methodology tends to be naturalistic. It aims at naturalistic generalization (based on the experience of the audience); is directed more at non-technical audiences like teachers or the general public; uses ordinary language and everyday categories of events; and is based more on informal than formal logic (House, 1977). Informal interviews and observations, often written up as case studies, are the favorite data collection devices.

The evaluator tries to collect multiple perspectives, although the perspectives may not agree with one another. Historical and longitudinal investigations also are critical. The historical mode of investigation is more appropriate than the natural science mode. Emphasis is on the qualitative rather than the quantitative.

In the subjectivist methodology, utility is in terms of the observer's interests. Theory and practice are blended together. Improving the understanding of particular individuals is the goal. In the objectivist approach, there is a rigid separation of observer and facts. Highly abstract theory is separated from application. Prediction is the goal.

The technique of the closed case and use of the precedent gives stability to the judgments derived from the subjectivistic epistemology. In fact, tradition is so strong in these evaluation models that this is a criticism of them. This is because the subjectivistic models rely heavily on practitioner judgment, which is in turn based on the experience of the classroom. The subjectivist models treat education and teaching as a craft rather than as a set of explicit, externalized techniques.

The transaction model of evaluation focuses on events occurring in and around the actual program in context. It is based on perception and knowing as a transactional process. In one version of transactional psychology, human perception is dependent on three features (Ittelson & Cantril, 1954). First, the facts of perception are always presented through concrete individuals dealing with concrete situations. Hence, one can study perceptions only by studying particular transactions in which the perceptions can be observed. All parts of the situation enter into the transaction as "active participants," and do not appear as separate already-existing entities.

Secondly, perceiving is always done by each person from his own unique position, experiences, and needs, including the scientist-observer. He affects and is affected by the situation; thus he is part of the transaction.

Third, each person creates his own psychological environment by attributing aspects of his experience to the environment. He believes the environment exists independently of his experience. In other words, he externalizes his experience. Consequently, the world as it is experienced is the *product* of perception, not the cause of it.

These presuppositions about perception are strikingly different from those of J.S. Mill and Hobbes. In the mechanistic Hobbesian view, the environment acts on the organism to produce perception. In the transactional view, the organism also works on the environment in an active manner so that perception is a product of the two. Categories are not easily discernible from the environment because they are inextricably entwined with one's own perceptions.

In the Hobbesian-Millean point of view, the world is taken as given. The mechanistic uniformity of nature assures that. Perceptions can be isolated and studied. One can communicate to another scientist statements that are reducible to what the other scientist will experience if he does certain things — the operational viewpoint. In the transactional point of view, reliability is not so easily obtained. What one observes is a function of the unique position and experience of each observer and even of the observer's purposes. Perceptions can only be studies in concrete real-life situations.

Not all the proponents of the transaction models of evaluation would subscribe to all these presuppositions. But this description captures the transactional viewpoint as a dialectical interaction of people and their environment that results in perceptions. Individual perceptions are a focus of study, and active participation is essential to knowing.

Political Assumptions of the Models — The Utilitarians

Liberalism is not only an ethical and epistemological theory; it is a profoundly political theory, too. As indicated earlier, although Rivlin and the modern liberals accept J.S. Mill's utilitarian ethics and extreme empiricism, they differ dramatically from Mill over the role of government in making decisions and taking action .

Rivlin's welfare liberalism holds that the government must make the major decisions, whereas Mill was the champion of laissez-faire, of keeping the government as far removed from decisions as possible. In this regard, the intuitionists are closer to classic liberalism than are the utilitarians.

For Mill, enlightenment was necessary for happiness and liberty. Freedom from government interference was necessary for enlightenment. For Rivlin, enlightenment will occur through government-sponsored research, and on the basis of this knowledge, the government will then take steps to alleviate the problems. In both cases, knowledge will make men happy.

For Mill there were two distinct spheres of activities — the internal and the external. The internal included the individual's own mind, body, and private actions. In the internal sphere the government had absolutely no right to interfere, no matter what. The individual could amuse or abuse himself as he saw fit in matters that concerned only himself (Wolff, 1968). The scope of government was limited only to that which concerned others — the external sphere.

Even in the external sphere in Mill's framework, societal interference was justified only on the basis of the principle of utility. That is, governmental interference was justified only when it would promote the greatest happiness of the greatest number of people by maximizing satisfactions.

> . . . actions are right in proportion as they tend to promote happiness; wrong as they tend to produce the reverse of happiness. By happiness is intended pleasure and the absence of pain; by unhappiness, pain and the privation of pleasure. (Mill, 1861)

Mill's arguments were strictly utilitarian, i.e., based on an estimate of future consequences of various alternatives. If the empirical estimates of consequences change, so could the conclusions. The modern welfare-state liberals have changed the empirical estimates and hence the conclusions. According to the modern liberals, the principle of utility requires that the government take strong action. The calculation of the utility principle leads to welfare-state liberalism eventually (Wolff, 1968).

For Mill, every person was the best judge of his own interest. (It should be noted that Mill was writing at a time when the masses had no vote. His theories applied only to the more "enlightened" citizenry.) For modern liberals like Rivlin (1971), the government is often considered the best judge. In Mill's framework, complete freedom of speech led to a competition of ideas, which stengthened truth. In a free market of ideas, the consumers would buy the best without government interference. For the modern liberal, the government must provide indices of effectiveness on which judgments are based and often must make the choice in the public interest. The classic and modern liberals agree on liberal political principles but disagree as to whether government interference will help or harm.

Mill felt that government interference would result in impeding individual development; in centralization and abuse of power; in inefficiency; in government doing indifferently and poorly what interested private parties could do better; and in suppression of individual initiative which would lay the groundwork for despotism. However, even Mill felt that if the buyer were not the best judge of a commodity, then the competition of the market did not exist. In cultural and educational affairs Mill did not think that the uncultured were the best judges. Therefore, the state might legitimately interfere, a position close to that of modern liberals.

But, generally, the calculation of the utility principle leads to strong government interference rather than away from it. It is not surprising then that all the utilitarian models of evaluation — systems analysis, behavioral objectives, decision making, and goal free — are based on strong government action, usually even government mandates. Most of these models also take as their major audiences the managers and administrators of government programs. The one exception is goal-free evaluation, which takes the consumer as the major audience.

Political Assumptions of the Intuitionists/Pluralists

How is one to conduct an evaluation if there is no single principle like the principle of utility to use as the criterion? There are two types of answers found among the intuitionist/pluralist models. One is professional authority, as in the educational critic and accreditation models, and the other is a combination of scientific authority and participation in the evaluation by those involved in the program. The accreditation model began as a voluntary association to ward off government interference.

The participatory models are attempts to establish more direct participation of the people who are most closely involved in the program. The adversary model does this by involving people in a decision-making operation like a mock trial. The transaction models involve people through negotiation, interviewing, and responding to drafts of the evaluation, although it is still the evaluator who writes the report. If people are to participate as major audiences, the evaluation must be immediate and comprehensible. The participatory school is aimed at establishing a more direct democracy among program participants rather than in relegating decision making to the government, as in utilitarian evaluation. Pluralistic principles are derived by the participation of diverse individuals and groups.

There are two distinct approaches to political pluralism. One is derived directly from the classic liberal philosophy of J.S. Mill, without his epistemology or utilitarian ethics. Classic liberalism sees society as an association of self-determining individuals who cooperate with others for self-interested ends. Following from Mill, it is essential that they have a direct hand in governing themselves, since they know themselves and their interests best. This version of pluralism accepts individual idiosyncracies and interpersonal conflicts as inevitable (Wolff, 1968).

The sanctity of the individual against the intrusion of society is paramount, and the inner sphere of the private man must be held inviolate. There can be no interference with his thoughts and practices. Individuality and diversity are encouraged rather than suppressed. Society is conceived as a marketplace in which each individual pursues his own private goals. Each man is free to pursue his own goals compatible with others pursuing theirs. In the public sphere, society has a right to impose some rules of equity. Otherwise, the market will automatically work things out.

The ideal society envisioned is that of a large, diverse city, like London or New York. Classic liberalism sees man as a rational calculator of pain and pleasure. Rationality is calculating prudence. Each individual views others as instruments in the pursuit of his private ends. Others are means to some end, not ends in themselves. This is sometimes called the instrumental theory of pluralism (Wolff, 1968).

Justice is the protection of the inner sphere of the person and a more-or-less equal opportunity for all to pursue their private goals. In more sophisticated versions, the pleasure maximizing is softened somewhat and the pursuit of higher goals is emphasized. Nonetheless, society is still viewed as a collection of independent "centers of consciousness," each pursuing its own private goals and confronting others as alien objects (Wolff, 1968).

Associated with this version of pluralism is the "referee" theory of government. The government will establish ground rules for individual and group competition but will not interfere in any other way. Action is to be *direct* action by the individuals and groups concerned and not action by the government. Each person must be free to engage directly in the decision processes, and this role cannot be delegated or usurped by government or anyone else. This version of direct democracy grows out of classic liberalism in which *each individual's* choice is maximized.

The evaluation model that most closely corresponds to this version of liberal pluralism is MacDonald's democratic evaluation (1974). MacDonald sees the evaluator as a "broker in exchanges of information between groups," representing a range of interests, presenting information accessible to non-specialists, giving informants confidentiality and control over the data, having no concept of information misuse, negotiating with sponsors and participants, and making no recommendations. The evaluator feeds information to audiences and lets the market work things out. Each person makes use of the information as he sees fit with the evaluator removed from interpretation. The evaluator operates on a set of procedural regulations, which control information flow.

MacDonald has also been most adamant about protecting the sanctity of the "inner sphere," giving informants veto power over what goes into the report. This is captured by his phrase, "People own the facts of their lives." Interference by the evaluator in either the private sphere or public sphere is rejected, except to facilitate information flow that will increase knowledge and, presumably, happiness by allowing individuals to pursue their goals better.

A somewhat different version of pluralism prevails in the United States. Based on the idea that every person achieves his identity from primary groups, it does not see man as a totally detached individual, as does classic liberalism. Since ethnic, religious, economic, and cultural groups determine what a person is, his interests must be expressed through the larger groups to which he belongs,. This version, called democratic pluralism or conservative liberalism, recognizes tolerance for established, diverse groups but not for idiosyncratic individuals. It is considered good for an individual to conform to some groups, but good for the groups to differ.

In this vision of pluralism as the conflict of permanent interest groups, community is a much stronger value than in classical liberalism. Pluralism is based on group rather than individual diversity. The ideal society is more like a small town than a large city. Tolerance and mutual acceptance are exercised among groups.

Associated with this vision of pluralism is the vector-sum or balance-of-power theory of government. The purpose is to get the government to act in a certain direction. The individual must work through his groups in order to do this since only they have the influence to guide the ship-of-state. As in classical liberalism, the individual must have immediacy, effectiveness, involvement, and participation in his group. The government (and evaluator) act as middlemen, absorbing directions and responding to shifts in pressure. In both types of pluralism, the capacity to see competing claims as legitimate is essential to make the system work.

Stake's "responsive" evaluation comes closest to the democratic pluralism version. The evaluator must remain responsive to any legitimate interests and pressures around the program; but he is not obliged to represent any point of view, nor is he obliged to represent points of view in the evaluation unless an interest group involved in the program is actively promoting that point of view. Active involvement is a criterion for representing a group's viewpoint in the evaluation.

Issues are defined by legitimate groups, and only a few issues are to be explored. Methods of investigation are to be chosen to fit the issues. Problems are best solved directly by local people close at hand (Stake, 1975). This is in contrast to utilitarian evaluation, in which the government evaluates, defines the problem, and takes action. The pluralistic evaluations tend to maximize local and individual choice rather than social utility. Both forms of pluralism are based on the concept of a free market of ideas. Justice tends to be identified with the free play of opposing individuals and groups, as the working out of a free market requires.

Although these evaluation models differ in the ways suggested, what they share are some of the basic tenets of the liberal ideology. This includes the principle of freedom of choice. Although who shall make the choice is at issue, choice is maximized. They are based on a strongly individualist psychology and their intellectual constructions reflect that. They are also thoroughly empiricist in orientation.

All the evaluation models also presume a free market of ideas from which, ideally, consumers will select the best. Through a competition of ideas, truth will be strengthened and education improved. Finally, the models all assume that increased knowledge will make people happy, better, or satisfied in some way.

This paper has been a description of the major evaluation models and an exploration of their premises. It is part of a longer work, which attempts to present a comprehensive analysis of evaluation. Each model has strengths and weaknesses, both in theory and in practice. A critique of the models is a necessary step to further understanding.

Note

1.   I wish to express my thanks for helpful comments to Robert Ennis, David Hamilton, and Bruce Stewart.

References

Callahan, R.E. *Education and the cult of efficiency*. Chicago, Illinois: University of Chicago Press, 1962.

Ennis, R. On causality. *Educational Researcher,* 1973, 2, 6.

Hamilton, D. *A science of the singular?* University of Illinois, 1976, mimeo.

Hamilton, D. Making sense of curriculum evaluation. In Lee Shulman (ed.), *Review of research in education,* Itasca, Illinois: F.E. Peacock, 1977.

House, E.R. Justice in evaluation. In Gene V. Glass (ed.), *Evaluation studies review annual,* Vol. 1, Beverly Hills, California: Sage Publishing Company, 1976.

House, E.R. *The logic of evaluative argument*. Center for the Study of Evaluation, UCLA, Monograph 7, 1977.

House, E.R. Evaluation as scientific management in U.S. school reform. *Comparative and International Education Review,* October 1978.

Ittelson, W.H. and Cantril, H. *Perception: A transactional approach*. New York: Doubleday Papers in Psychology, 1954.

Macdonald, B. *Evaluation and the control of education*. Norwich, England: Center for Applied Research in Education, 1974.

MacPherson, C.B. *The real world of democracy*. Oxford, England: Oxford University Press, 1966.

McLaughlin, M.W. *Evaluation and reform*. Cambridge, Massachusetts: Ballinger Publishing, 1975.

Mill, J.S. *A system of logic*. (8th ed.) New York: Harper Publishing, 1893.

Mill, J.S. *Utilitarianism*. Indianapolis, Illinois: Bobbs-Merrill Co., 1861. National Study of Secondary School Evaluation. *Evaluative criteria*. (4th ed.) Washington, D.C., 1969.

Popham, W.J. *Educational evaluation*. Englewood Cliffs, New Jersey: Prentice Hall, 1975.

Rawls, J. *A theory of justice*. Cambridge, Massachusetts: Belknap Press, 1971.

Rivlin, A.M. *Systematic thinking for social action*. Washington, D.C.: The Brookings Institution, 1971.

Scriven, M. *Objectivity and subjectivity in educational research. Philosophical Redirections in Educational Research*, National Society for the Study of Education, 1972.

Scriven, M. *Evaluation bias and its control*. Occasional Paper 4. Kalamazoo: The Evaluation Center, Western Michigan University, 1975.

Scriven, M. *Bias contol systems in evaluation*. Paper presented at the Annual Meeting of the American Educational Research Association, 1976.

Snyder, W. *Case studies in military systems analysis*. Washington, D.C.: Industrial College of the Armed Forces, 1967.

Stake, R.E. *Some alternative presumptions*. Urbana, Illinois: Center for Instructional Research and Curriculum Evaluation, October 1975, mimeo.

Stake R.E. *Evaluating educational programmes*. Organization for Economic Co-Operational Development, 1976.

Wolff, R.P. *The poverty of liberalism*. Boston, Massachusetts: Beacon Press, 1968.

Worthen, B.R. and Sanders, J.R. *Educational evaluation: Theory and practice*. Worthington, Ohio: Charles A. Jones, 1973.

II MODELS AND CONCEPTUALIZATIONS

4 A RATIONALE FOR PROGRAM EVALUATION
Ralph W. Tyler

There are two closely related rationales, each of which is often referred to as the *Tyler Rationale*. One was developed specifically for evaluation activities and was first published in 1934 under the title *Constructing Achievement Tests*.[1] The other evolved from my work as director of evaluation for the Eight-Year Study. It was a general rationale for curriculum development and was first published in 1945 as a mimeographed syllabus for my course at the University of Chicago, entitled *Basic Principles of Curriculum and Instruction*. This was later picked up by the University of Chicago Press and published as a book in 1949.[2] Each of these statements was formulated as an outgrowth of particular circumstances and is intended to furnish a defensible and orderly procedure to deal with such situations.

The Background of Constructing Achievement Tests

I was brought to the Ohio State University in 1929 by W.W. Charters, director of the university's Bureau of Educational Research, to head the Division of Accomplishment Testing. He believed that one of the major missions of the bureau was to provide assistance to the university in seeking to improve the instruction of undergraduates. At that time, the university administrator and many members of the Ohio legislature expressed great concern over the fact that a large percentage of

67

the students did not continue their university education beyond the freshman year. The faculties were urged to improve their teaching, particularly in first- and second-year classes where the failures and drop-outs were highly concentrated. Charters believed that teaching and learning in the university could be markedly improved with the aid of relevant research and the use of tests and measurements. He asked me to focus my initial efforts on research in the undergraduate courses. I began in the biology courses with the cooperation of the instructors.

The instructors told me of their difficulties in trying to help their students to understand biological phenomena so that they could explain the phenomena in terms of basic concepts and principles, and solve some common biological problems by drawing upon observations, making inferences from data, and applying relevant principles. Most of the students would perform well on written tests, but in class and laboratory few of them could explain newly observed phenomena or solve problems not taken up in class. I found that the instructors were using tests that demanded only that students recall specific information. None of the test exercises required the more complex behaviors that the courses were planned to help students learn. This was typical of the tests commonly in use at that time. The most widely used tests in high school and college appraised only recall of information on specific skills in mathematics and reading.

Using tests of this sort, the instructors were unable to assess objectively the progress of their students in learning what the courses were designed to help them learn. Furthermore, the use of tests of recall gave the students the wrong notion of what they were expected to learn. They were being rewarded by their good test performance on memorizing specific information and were given no opportunity in the examinations to demonstrate the behaviors that the instructors believed to be most important. As we discussed this observation, it seemed clear that new tests should be constructed, tests that would appraise the degree to which students were achieving the objectives of the courses.

At that time, the accepted methodology for constructing objective achievement tests was to sample the content of the textbooks and other instructional materials used by teachers, and to write questions requiring the students to reproduce this content. In my own earlier experience in constructing tests, I usually had in mind what I thought the student should be able to do with each category of content, and I believed that most skillful test-item writers had some notion of what the educational objectives should be, but these unexamined ideas were too idiosyncratic to substitute for an explicit statement by those responsible for the curriculum and instructional program. Hence, the first step in constructing tests useful in guiding instruction in these biology courses was to identify the educational objectives of these courses.

As I worked with the instructors, asking them what they expected students to be learning in and from their courses, I found that the first answers were usually very general and often vague. For example, "I am trying to teach them to think," "I am teaching the scientific method," "I want them to develop skill in the laboratory." Since the fundamental purpose of education is to help students acquire new ways of thinking, feeling, and acting, objectives should be defined clearly enough to indicate what the educational program is intended to help students develop — what kinds of behavior; what ways of thinking, feeling, or acting; and with what content.

As instructors recognized the need for clear definition they were able to set aside several afternoons during which we worked out definitions of the objectives they had in mind, expressing them in terms of *behavior* and *content*. For example, the definition they developed for understanding biological phenomena was: to explain common biological phenomena in terms of relevant concepts and principles. Then, they listed some 23 concepts and 93 principles that were dealt with in the course and that could be used to explain most of the common biological phenomena encountered in that geographic region. The objective, making inferences from experimental data, was defined as making logical inferences from data presented in dealing with common biological phenomena and presented in current publications in biology. The objective, skill in the use of laboratory instruments, was defined as using the compound microscope properly and making sections of common plant and animal tissues that can be mounted on slides. These are illustrations of the result of their efforts to clarify their educational goals. Other objectives that they defined were: application of biological principles, interest in biology, and recall of important facts and definitions.

As these objectives were defined, it became evident that the exercises to be constructed to test for them would require much more than multiple-choice test items and that, for some, no paper-and-pencil test would likely be valid. We thought that skillfully constructed multiple-choice tests would serve for appraising the students' recall of information and definitions, and some modifications of such paper-and-pencil tests could be used to assess the students' understanding of biological phenomena, their ability to draw inferences from experimental data, and their ability to apply principles in explaining biological phenomena. However, we saw no valid substitute for a direct test of performance in using laboratory instruments. Furthermore, an appraisal of students' interest in biology would require the development of a new test procedure.

This experience with the biology courses was repeated in work with instructors of courses in chemistry, mathematics, philosophy, accounting, history, and home economics in the period from 1930–34. It led to my writing the article, "A Generalized Technique for Constructing Achievement Tests," which appeared in the volume, *Constructing Achievement Tests,* referred to in the first paragraph of this paper.

As we developed tests for the objectives of the biology course, we used them to gain greater understanding of what the students were learning and where they seemed to have difficulty. For example, we found that the students were able to draw appropriate inferences from the data that the instructors were interpreting in class and laboratory, but few were able to interpret data that they had not seen before. This finding led naturally to modifying the course procedure so that students could have practice in reading and interpreting experimental data that had not previously been discussed in class. The instructors and I worked closely together in developing tests, studying and discussing the results, and trying to improve the courses where the test results suggested inadequacies. The changes in the courses were tested continuously in order to find out what changes seemed to remedy the faults identified earlier. Program evaluation proved to be a very useful means in assisting course improvements.

Generalizing from these Experiences

Although this rationale for achievement testing was conceived and developed to serve the particular purpose of furnishing assistance to instructors in under-graduate courses in the Ohio State University, I perceived it as having general usefulness and wrote the article mentioned above, "A Generalized Technique for Constructing Achievement Tests." This procedure involves the following steps:

1. *Identifying the objectives of the educational program.*

2. *Defining each objective in terms of behavior and content.* The definition should not be so specific that it is in conflict with the basic aim of all educational activities, which is to help students generalize, that is, to be guided by principles, modes of approaching situations, cognitive maps, and the like, rather than by rigid rules and habits. The objective should be clearly defined at the level of generality intended by those planning and conducting the course.

3. *Identifying situations where objectives are utilized.* The logic of this step should be obvious. If one has learned something, one has internalized it and can be expected to utilize it wherever it is appropriate. Hence, if we wish to find out whether a student has learned something, we should look at those situations where the learner can use what he has learned. A test, therefore, should sample these situations.

4. *Devising ways to present situations.* For the students to demonstrate what they have learned, the appropriate situations need to be presented in a way that

will evoke the reactions that the normal situations would evoke; or, alternatively, practical ways should be devised to observe the students' reactions in the situations that they normally encounter where the attainment of the objectives can be shown. It is often difficult to devise artificial situations in which the simulations seem so real as to assure the students' motivation to respond. This is the reason for using the term *evoke* rather than the more passive phrase, *requiring a response*.

5. *Devising ways to obtain a record.* In most written tests the students make the record by writing their response or by checking one or more of the responses presented to them. The popularity of the multiple-response test is due to the case of recording the responses as well as the apparent simplicity of appraising them. When the skill or ability is accurately indicated by a product the students make, such as a composition, a dress, or a work of art, the product itself becomes the record that can be preserved for careful appraisal. Observation checklists, anecdotal records, and photographs can furnish records of reactions that do not furnish their own record.

6. *Deciding on the terms to use in appraisal.* The tradition of scoring or grading tests in terms of the number of correct responses has often prevailed when the sum of correct responses does not furnish a useful or a reasonably accurate appraisal of the students' attainment of the objectives. An important consideration is to use terms or units that properly reflect the desirable characteristics of the students' reactions in contrast to the undesirable or less desirable. For example, in appraising the reactions of students in attacking a problem of resource allocations, the number of relevant major factors they consider can be the units of desirable characteristics, while the failure to work on their interrelation can be a descriptive term of an undesirable reaction. In some cases, as in diagnosis, the terms used may need to indicate syndromes or types of difficulties the learner is encountering. In appraising products like compositions, two appraisal schemes can be used — one indicating the level of quality of the total product and the other furnishing a report on the number of different desirable or undesirable features, like compound sentences and misspelled words.

7. *Devising means to get a representative sample.* We all know that human behavior may vary under different conditions, even when these conditions are clearly defined. One may read newspaper articles easily and find it hard to read the directions for assembling an appliance. One can use a large vocabulary in speaking of art and still be limited in the words used to discuss social issues. For a test to furnish reliable information about what students have

learned, it must be based on a representative and reliable sample of the situations in which this learning can be exhibited. To obtain a representative sample of something, it is necessary to define the universe of this *something* and then to draw random or stratified samples from this universe. For example, to obtain a representative sample of the reading situations for a sixth-grade test in comprehension, it is necessary to define the universe of things the sixth-grader reads, such as kinds of textbooks, stories, newspapers, directions, etc. It is from this universe that samples can be drawn for testing. A sample is likely to be representative if it is drawn from the universe by a random procedure or by being divided into strata, each randomly sampled and then put together with the samples from the other strata by the appropriate weights. The adequacy of the sample — that is, its required size — depends upon both the precision demanded for the purposes that the test is to serve and the variability of the students' reactions to the different situations. The more variable the student reactions are, the larger the sample required for the desired reliability.

The Background for the Curriculum Rationale

In 1934, I was asked to serve as director of evaluation for the Eight-Year Study. This study grew out of pressures for change in the high school curriculum, which came from several sources. The high schools of 1930 were still very much like those of 1920, particularly in terms of curriculum content and learning activities. High school staffs felt that they were prevented from making improvements because of the rigidity of college entrance requirements and of state accreditation regulations. Pressures for change were mounting, coming in part from the students themselves. Many of the young people entering high school came from elementary schools that had given them greater freedom and more opportunities for self-direction in learning than they were permitted as high school students. Moreover, with the onset of the Great Depression in 1929, new demands for change came with such force that they could no longer be denied. Many young people, unable to find work, enrolled in high school. Most of these new students did not plan to go to college, and most of them found little meaning and interest in their high school tasks. But still they went to school; there was no other place for them to go.

The high school curriculum of 1930 was not designed for these young people. Most teachers and principals recognized this fact, and many favored a move to reconstruct the high school curriculum and the instructional program both to meet the needs of these Depression youth and to respond to the pressures to give greater opportunities for self-direction in learning. At the same time, however, they did not want to jeopardize the chance of college admission for students who wished to go there, or to lose their state accreditation. This was the dilemma.

The Progressive Education Association took the lead in attacking the problem. Its officers appointed the Commission on the Relation of School and College and charged it with the task of devising a way out of the impasse. The commission served as a forum for the presentation of conflicting points-of-view. Finally, a sufficient degree of consensus was reached to enable the commission to recommend a pilot program. A small number of secondary schools — ultimately 30 schools and school systems — were to be selected by the commission and, for eight years, were to be permitted to develop educational programs that each school believed to be appropriate for its students, without regard to the current college entrance requirements or state accreditation regulations. The schools would be responsible for collecting and reporting information about what students were learning — information that would help the colleges in selecting candidates for admission. The commission would make sure that a comprehensive evaluation of the pilot program would be made and the findings reported.

The schools of the Eight-Year Study began their pilot efforts in September 1933. It soon became apparent that they needed assistance, both in curriculum development, and evaluation. The Progressive Education Association established the Commission on the Secondary School Curriculum, which sponsored a series of studies of adolescents. The adolescent studies, under Caroline Zachry's direction, were to provide helpful information about the interests, needs, activities, and learning characteristics of youth. Under the leadership of Harold Alberty, subject-matter committees were formed to draw upon these studies and others, and to publish volumes that would furnish statements, overall objectives, relevant subject-matter, and possible learning activities for these subjects.

To meet the need for assistance in evaluation, the Steering Committee asked me to serve as director of evaluation and to assemble a staff to develop the procedures and the instruments. The curriculum associates and the evaluation staff worked closely with the schools throughout the pilot period. Learning how to develop and operate a new curriculum and instructional program designed to be serviceable to high school students proved to be a highly significant experience.

Most of the schools began their curriculum development efforts with one or two ideas about what needed to be done, but they soon discovered that the problems were more complex than they had earlier conceived. Those who had become very conscious of the large gap between the needs and interests of students and the content of the curriculum soon found that there was also a serious problem of relating the curriculum to the opportunities and demands of the changing situations that students were encountering in life outside the school. Others who began with their focus on developing a curriculum relevant to the social changes so evident in the 1930s were soon faced with the fact that the students' motivation to learn was closely related to their perception of the value of what was being taught in terms of meeting their needs and interests. Further, all the schools were reminded of the fact that much of the current content was considered obsolete by many scholars in the several subject-matter fields. It soon became apparent that the development of the curriculum and instructional program and the plan of evaluation required more time than was available on weekends, when the working committees met during the first year-and-a-half of the program. It was then that we devised the summer workshops, in which representative teachers from all of the schools worked together with the Study staffs and subject-matter consultants for six weeks each summer to develop what was needed.

In 1936, the Curriculum Staff pointed out that the Evaluation Staff had an excellent rationale to guide its work, but there was no such rationale to guide the curriculum efforts. With the encouragement of my associate, Hilda Taba, we developed the rationale that is presented in the syllabus entitled, *Basic Principles of Curriculum and Instruction.* It, like the rationale for testing, evolved from the particular situations of the Eight-Year Study and was designed as a general procedure to guide the development activities in our summer workshops. However, as I participated later in other situations, particularly, in the Cooperative Study in General Education sponsored by the American Council in Education, I found the rationale applicable to those different contexts. This recognition led to my use of it in my courses in curriculum development.

The rationale is simply an orderly way of planning. It identifies four basic questions that should be answered in developing curriculum and plan of instruction. These questions are.

1. *What education objectives are the students to be helped to attain?* That is, what are they to be helped to learn? What ways of thinking, feeling, and acting are they to be helped to develop in this educational program?

2. *What learning experiences can be provided that will enable the students to attain the objectives?* That is, how will the students be helped to learn what is proposed?

3. *How will the learning experiences be organized to maximize their cumulative effect?* That is, what sequence of learning and what plan of integration of learning experiences will be worked out to enable students to internalize what they are learning and apply it in appropriate situations that they encounter?

4. *How will the effectiveness of the program be evaluated?* That is, what procedure will be followed to provide a continuing check on the extent to which the desired learning is taking place?

The efforts to answer these questions are not to be treated in a one-way, linear fashion. As committees worked on learning experiences, developing resources, and trying them out, they often obtained information or thought of new points that caused them to re-examine the objectives and to check on the organization of experiences, as well as to see that the evaluation procedure was appropriate for the learning activities proposed. Similarly, working out a plan for the sequence and integration of learning experiences often gave rise to re-examination of the treatment of the other three questions. Always, of course, evidence obtained from evaluation led to further consideration of objectives, learning experiences, and organization. The basic questions in the rationale were viewed as parts of a cyclical procedure rather than a linear one.

In connection with each question, the rationale suggests the kinds of empirical data that can inform the judgments that are made and the kinds of criteria to guide the judgments. Thus, in selecting educational objectives data regarding the demands and opportunities in contemporary society, information about the needs, interests, activities, habits, knowledge, and skills of the students, and the potential contributions of relevant subject-matters can inform the committees in a more comprehensive way than most curriculum groups have considered. Furthermore, the explicit formulation of the accepted philosophy of education and the state-of-the-art in the psychology of learning can provide criteria that are more thoughtfully considered than the intuitive judgments that committees often make.

In developing learning experiences, teachers were helped by recognizing the conditions commonly identified in conscious, complex, human learning. At the time the rationale was formulated, I found little empirical research on the effects of various ways of organizing learning experiences. Hence, the rationale suggests criteria for planning and evaluating the organization. The rationale's treatment of evaluation is largely a modification of the generalized procedure for achieving test construction.

Previous Practice and Theory of Evaluation

Prior to my use of the term *evaluation* in 1930, the common terms for appraisal of learning were *examining* and *testing*. Assessment of educational achievement has been practiced for several thousand years. The prevailing name for this activity changes from time to time — examining; quizzing; testing; measuring; evaluating; appraising; and, currently, assessing — but the primary function of ascertaining the educational attainment of students has remained constant. The scientific or systematic development of assessment has taken place largely in the twentieth century. During this relatively short period of time, some profound changes have taken place in both the purposes and expectations for testing.

The successful use of psychological and educational tests in World War I led to their wide adoption by schools and other civilian institutions. When America drafted two million men for military service in 1918, the problem of organizing and training this large number of persons who had had no previous military experience was overwhelming. Who were to be selected for officer training, and who for the variety of technical tasks — construction, battalions, signal corps, quartermaster corps, and the like? The psychological advisors developed the Army Alpha Test and other classification tests that provided the basis for selecting and classifying this large assortment of young men. After the war, groups tests, both of intelligence and achievement, were constructed and developed for school use, employing the same methodology that was formulated for the Army Alpha and other military classification tests.

This methodology is designed to arrange those who take the test on a continuum from those who make the highest score to those who make the lowest score. Such an arrangement permits one to identify the position of any individual in terms of his or her standing in the total group. By administering the tests to a representative sample of a defined population, like children in the third grade of U.S. schools, the continuum on which those best scores are arranged is the distribution of the scores of all American third graders. This makes it possible to overcome the limitations in comparisons within an individual classroom, school, city, or state by referring to a national norm. The original purpose was to sort students or to grade them from excellent to poor. Test items were selected that differentiated among students, and items that all or almost all students answered correctly and that few, if any, answered correctly were dropped after tryout. Hence, the resulting test was not a representative sample of what students were expected to learn.

As I began to work with the instructors at the Ohio State University, it was clear that they needed tests that would inform them about what students were learning and where they were having difficulty. Sorting students was not the purpose; instead, their concern was to improve the curriculum and the instructional program. I realized that test theory developed for purposes of sorting and based on measures of individual differences would not produce the kinds of evaluation instruments needed. Hence, I developed a procedure based on theories of instruction and learning.

Similarly, in formulating a rationale for curriculum development, I was guided by the theories of Dewey and Whitehead regarding educational aims and theories of instruction and learning. The prevailing curriculum development procedure was to identify significant content and to design ways of presenting the content. This left in limbo the question of learning objectives, that is, what the student is expected to do with the content. Furthermore, the then-usual procedure for preparing lesson plans was based on a very primitive view of student learning systems, that is, the several conditions necessary or helpful in assuring that the desired learning takes place.

Major Applications

At the time the rationales were developed, they were used first in the undergraduate colleges of Ohio State University, then in the Eight-Year Study and in the college chemistry tests of the Cooperative Test Service.

In 1938, the evaluation rationale became the basis for the development of the University of Chicago comprehensive examinations and the instruments constructed by the 22 colleges in the Cooperative Study in General Education. In 1943, I was made director of the Examinations Staff of the U.S. Armed Forces Institute, and the evaluation rationale guided the construction of the hundreds of tests and examinations developed for the Armed Forces.

The curriculum development rationale has been utilized most extensively in the construction and revision of curricula for some of the professions, for example, medicine, nursing, social work, engineering, and agriculture. I do not know how extensively it has been used in elementary and secondary schools.

Changes in Conceptualization

As the rationales began to be utilized in new situations, I made several changes in my own conceptions. Others who have used the rationales have probably made modifications that they found helpful. As evaluation became a term widely used in educational discourse, its meaning was greatly broadened. It is not often used to refer to any and all of the efforts to compare the reality of an educational situation with the conception that has guided the planning and execution. Thus, there is evaluation of a proposed educational program made by comparing the conception of the program with whatever relevant information or generalizations are appropriate to judge the soundness and practicability of the plan. The testing out of curriculum units and their modification in the light of the test results was a larger part of the evaluation in the Ohio State University course and in the Eight-Year Study, but it is now often given a special label of formative evaluation. Then, there is the evaluation of implementation, which was a significant activity in the evaluation of the New York City Activity Schools in the 1940s and was dramatically presented in Goodlad and Klein's "Behind the Classroom Doors." There is evaluation in the continuous monitoring of programs to identify significant changes, either improvements or deterioration. There is evaluation of the unintended outcomes of a program, as well as the effort to identify the extent to which the intended results are being achieved; and, finally, there is "follow-up" evaluation to ascertain the long-term effects as learners live and work in different environments, some of which are supportive and some otherwise.

In the use of evaluation as a means of both understanding an educational program and improving it, I have come to realize the importance of identifying and appraising factors in the environment that have a significant influence on learning in addition to the planned curriculum and the activities of the teacher. The need to evaluate, measure, or describe such matters as the classroom ethic, the learner's expectations, the teacher's concern for the students, and the standards the teacher believes the students can reach are illustrations of some of those environmental factors. In brief, my conception of evaluation has greatly expanded since 1929.

As we learn more about the ways in which persons acquire new kinds of behavior and develop this knowledge, these skills, and the attitudes and interests in various situations and changing environments, I believe our conceptions of the purposes, the procedures, and the appropriate instruments of evaluation will continue to expand as well as to be more sharply focused.

Notes

1. Ralph W. Tyler, *Constructing Achievement Tests,* Bureau of Educational Research, Columbus, Ohio: Ohio State University Bureau of Educational Research, 1934.
2. Ralph W. Tyler, *Basic Principles of Curriculum and Instruction,* Chicago: University of Chicago Press, 1949.

5 THE DISCREPANCY EVALUATION MODEL

Andrés Steinmetz

The word *evaluation* is used loosely to encompass many different activities and purposes. When educators evaluate a reading program, they may be referring to deciding which of several reading programs their school district should adopt; when evaluating a school-bell schedule, they may mean finding out how popular the schedule is among students and faculty and what the advantages and disadvantages of several other bell schedules may be; when evaluating students, they may mean administering achievement or psychological tests; and so on.

Also, the more educators stress the need for evaluation and the more it is associated with accountability and funding decisions, the more the term appears in their vocabulary. People become willing to call a lot of things evaluation when they need to show that they have done something called evaluation.

While a wide variety of activities is encompassed by the term, there is an apprehensiveness associated with it that seems to remain invariant. Evaluation suggests making judgments of worth, and these judgments are generally accompanied by strong emotional reactions. The term raises apprehension that judgments will be made which will affect the social and/or professional status of people, their career plans, their self esteem, the scope of their authority, and so on.

What all this amounts to is that when one is called upon to do evaluation, it is usually hard to escape first doing battle with a lot of expectations people have about what is going to happen. To work effectively, a practitioner is forced to clarify his/her position relative to all these expectations. The Discrepancy Evaluation Model (DEM)[1] represents an assembly of ideas and procedures arising out of attempts to respond constructively to such expectations. It represents a scheme with which to respond to the challenges presented by the difficult task of evaluating educational programs.

I. Basic Tenets of the Model

The Concepts of Standards, Performance, and Discrepancy

In order to evaluate something, we inevitably make comparisons. More specifically, we say that to evaluate a given object (whether a person, a motorcycle, or a program) it must be compared to a standard. By a standard we mean a list, description, or representation of the qualities or characteristics the object should possess. In other words, a description of how something *should be* is called the Standard (S).

Once we are clear about how things should be, we can proceed to find out whether they *actually are* that way. When we are engaged in finding out the actual characteristics of the object to be evaluated, we are taking Performance measures (P). Thus, evaluation is a matter of comparing S against P.

There is another term involved in the comparison between S and P. We say that the comparison yields Discrepancy (D) information, and thus we can speak of evaluation as being a matter of making judgments about the worth or adequacy of an object based upon D information between S and P.

The concepts of S, P, and D surface quite naturally whenever, under the name of evaluation, one wants to judge the adequacy or worth of something. Suppose, for example, that you want to purchase a motorcycle but are uncertain whether the specific one you are considering is in good mechanical condition, and you, therefore, arrange to have a mechanic examine it. We can use the concepts of S, P, and D to describe what the mechanic will do pursuant to your request to find out whether the motorcycle is in good mechanical condition. Essentially, the mechanic will take certain P measures and compare these to an S. The D information generated in making the comparison will somehow aggregate into a judgment about whether the motorcycle is or is not in good mechanical condition.

The mechanic has some ideas about how the motorcycle *should be* functioning when it functions adequately and he/she will proceed to test these out. For example, he/she may refer to the motorcycle specifications manual to find out what compression the pistons should generate, and that information will become part of the S. Then, as a P measure, he/she can find out whether the pistons do in fact generate the compression specified. He/She may also listen to the way the motorcycle is idling (P) and compare that to his/her experience in order to decide whether the engine sounds the way *it should* sound (S). Or, he/she may refer to both his/her experience and the specifications manual (S) in order to generate D information about the actual condition (P) of the brakes. As another P information-collecting strategy, the mechanic is also likely to drive the motorcycle and compare how it feels and sounds with how he/she thinks the motorcycle *should* feel and sound.

Thus, to find out whether the motorcycle is in good mechanical condition, the mechanic will do certain things, like measure compression, test the brakes, examine the spark plugs, etc., all of which represent gathering P information. Of course, the mechanic will probably restrict himself/herself to collecting P measures on a limited number of dimensions according to time available; the price he/she has agreed on with you; his/her experience about what is important to look at; and, also, the availability of an S governing what he/she is looking at. Note also that S will vary in specificity and will be a mixture of the mechanic's experience and the operating and engineering specifications of the motorcycle. The D information he/she generates by comparing S and P will become a basis for the conclusions he/she submits to you. In his/her conclusions, he/she is likely to pass a judgment by saying that the motorcycle is or is not in good condition. He/she will probably substantiate his/her conclusion by referring to some of his/her findings. He/She might add things like, ''the piston rings are worn,'' or ''it needs a new clutch'' and thus roll into one phrase a P statement, an S, D information between the two, and a conclusion indicating what to do about it. Furthermore, knowing that you are trying to decide whether or not to buy the motorcycle, he/she is likely to make a recommendation such as, ''it's OK for the price,'' or ''I wouldn't buy it.''

In similar fashion, the S, P and D concepts can be shown to underlie the making of any judgment of adequacy or worth. More than that, they seem to underlie any cybernetic process and much of human behavior. Under the DEM, however, the important thing is how these concepts are applied. To discuss how they are applied, I would first like to make some summary observations about the work of the mechanic in the example considered above. Then, I will consider the role of a DEM evaluator by elaborating a bit further on the same motorcycle example. At that point, we will be in a position to understand the application of the DEM and can go on to apply it to something a bit more complex than a motorcycle — an educational program.

Summary Observations

1. The person you consulted to determine whether the motorcycle is in good mechanical condition is considered by you to be an expert in motorcycle mechanics.
2. Both the S and the specific characteristics of the motorcycle to be examined (the specific P information to be gathered) were selected and determined by the mechanic. In particular, the sources of the S were the mechanic's experience and knowledge, and the manufacturer's specifications.
3. Much of the S was left implicit. You might ask to have the S applied, verbalized or explained to you, but the custom governing the exchange between you, the client, and the mechanic (as expert and as evaluator) tends to keep that sort of conversation to a minimum and on a relatively superficial level. And, whatever conversations might be held about S are usually jargon-loaded and assume knowledge over the very conditions or phenomena which, as client, you don't have, and which led to your turning to someone else in the first place. Thus, the specific S brought to bear on certain performance information may remain unknown to you and, to some extent because they are not articulated by him/her, less than consciously known to the mechanic. For example, in examining the condition of the spark plugs the mechanic may notice that they are a brand which he/she considers inferior to another brand. That, in itself, may tend to make him/her more willing to consider their life exhausted than he/she might otherwise be. And the influence of that bias in his/her judgment is something the mechanic may not be ready to acknowledge.
4. You are not likely to see the specific performance information obtained. The mechanic is likely to report to you an overall judgment about the mechanical condition of the motorcycle, elaborate a bit on some of his/her findings, and respond to some questions you might have. He/She is unlikely, however, to itemize P and D information for you or to be explicit about how he/she aggregated the D information to arrive at his/her judgment. He/She may also recommend to you a course of action — repair, price negotiation, etc.

The Role of the Evaluator

We have seen how what the mechanic was asked to do can be discussed in terms of S, P and D. Thus, we can say that the mechanic was evaluating the mechanical adequacy of the motorcycle. But we would not say that he/she was applying the DEM, even though we can describe what he/she did in terms of S, P and D, because the critical thing about the DEM is the *manner* in which these concepts are applied. The crucial thing rests in the role relationship that is assumed by the evaluator vis-a-vis the client. In particular, the DEM evaluator would neither set S

nor judge the comparisons made between S and P, though he/she would normally collect P. Instead, he/she would assist the client to do these things for himself/herself.

Let's suppose, to explore this role relationship, that you come to me, a DEM evaluator and neither a motorcycle expert nor mechanic, and ask me to help you with your larger problem — namely, to evaluate a specific motorcycle with the aim of deciding whether or not to purchase it. As a DEM evaluator, the first thing I would be concerned about is the existence of an S. I would want to know from you what you are looking for in a motorcycle, what characteristics or qualities you feel that motorcycle *should* possess. If my turning to you for an S seems a little odd at this point, it may be because we have some different ideas about and expectations from an evaluation. Remember that this role characteristic of the evaluator is chosen in order to permit constructive response to technical, political, organizational, and emotional problems encountered in the applied situation.

As a DEM evaluator, I would be seeking a model representing the kind of motorcycle you are looking for, which can then be used as the S against which to compare any particular motorcycle. This stands in contrast to summary observations (1) and (2) above, which noted how the mechanic (as evaluator) was considered an expert authority and the source of the S governing mechanical functioning. I might begin by helping you make a list of the characteristics or qualities you value or find desirable, as shown in table 5–1.

While this first attempt at an S gives an idea of the kinds of characteristics you feel the desired motorcycle *should* possess, I would still need further guidance from you before I could collect P information that would be useful to you. I would ask you to formulate some questions — evaluation questions — which you would want answered relative to each characteristic making up the S. These would be questions which ask directly whether the quality, condition, or characteristic desired and specified by the S obtains in reality. Let's take cost and power, for example. In the case of cost, an evaluation question might be: What does this specific motorcycle cost? In getting ready to answer this question, I would make a little work plan, something like that shown in table 5–2, which I would review with you.

Table 5–1. First Attempt at a Standard

Characteristics the motor cycle should possess:

— *Cost:* should not cost over $800
— *Power:* should be able to cruise at 60 mph
— *Stability:* should be large and heavy enough to stay on the road
— *Noise:* should be quiet
— *Appearance:* should have the classic "World War I look"
— *Mechanical Condition:* should be in good condition and not presently need repairs

Table 5-2. Elements of an Evaluation Workplan

Evaluation Question	Standard	Source of Information	Instrument	Data Collector	Date Info is Needed
1. How much does this motorcycle cost	The motocycle should not cost more than $800	Seller of motorcycle	Interview	Evaluator	Next Friday
2. Does this motorcycle cruise at 60 mph?	Should be able to cruise at 60 mph				

Table 5-3. Elements of an Evaluation Workplan

Evaluation Question	Standard	Source of Information	Instrument	Data Collection	Date Info Needed
1. How much does this motorcycle cost?	The motorcycle should not cost more than $800	Seller of Motorcycle	Interview	Evaluator	Next Friday
2. Does this motorcycle cruise at 60 mph?	It should maintain 60 mph with 2 passengers on a straightaway all day.	Engineering specifications	Review of engineering specs	Evaluator	Next Friday
	It should maintain 60 mph with 2 adults up the mile-long hill on Rt. 629	Motorcycle	Road test	Evaluator	Next Friday

It would be clear that when I get the answer to question one in dollars, it will be easy for you to determine whether or not the S is met, since you have said it should not cost over $800. Let's consider power, however. As shown in table 5–2, an evaluation question here might be: Does this motorcycle cruise at 60 mph? In thinking through the elements of the evaluation work plan here, however, I would be faced right away with a basic problem, and I would turn to you for clarification of the following points: I can answer the question in many different ways and still meet your Standard. For example, I could ride down a long incline and maintain 60 mph, or drive a straightaway with no passengers or wind and maintain 60 mph for one-half hour, or I could find that the engineering specifications say the motorcycle will cruise at 65 with one passenger, or so on. So, I would think through these difficulties with you and urge you to set an S that restricted more severely the number of different conditions and answers that would satisfy it. We might thus end up with a more specific S as shown in table 5–3.

Let's now turn to another aspect of the S mentioned in table 5–1, i.e., stability. We can see right away that the same problem with the S reappears here. You claim a relationship between size, weight, and stability, but if we don't know what it is, then simply finding out the size and weight of a given motorcycle will not let you know whether your S for stability will have been met. Again, I would urge you to decide what you will consider adequate stability and to agree with me on an appropriate way of taking performance measures. If you could reach no conclusion on your own, I would help you think through a number of different options. You could consult motorcycle engineers for constellations of variables and conditions that might define stability; you could launch a research project yourself aimed at defining stability and the factors involved, etc. You could also decide to remove the whole matter of stability from your S. While I would facilitate an S-setting process and seek to confront you with decisions you would need to make in order to have an S available, I would not get involved in the work or decisions involved in creating the S itself. Thus, for example, I would not carry out the research project that would build the S — unless I completely changed my contract with you, and it was made clear I would no longer be an evaluator. To me, evaluation would presume the existence of the S and would entail merely looking at a specific object or event to see whether pertinent characteristics or conditions are present.

Under most circumstances, I would not even collect any data unless the pertinent S was explicitly stated. Otherwise, you, as client, would be left open to the possibility that I, and not you, would make the ultimate judgment of adequacy in the evaluation. Suppose you decide that the research questions concerning stability are too time-consuming and expensive given that you want to reach a decision within a brief time period. Thus, you are in the position of remaining interested in a certain quality (stability) yet find yourself without an S for it. This certainly is a common enough situation in most daily affairs, and there is a popular method for dealing with it: leave the S unexplicated and decide on the adequacy of the *P* information as you collect it. Applying this method to our example, one could drive the motorcycle and draw some conclusion about how "stable" one feels — which involves conjuring up an *S* based on the immediate experience. One would be contrasting the immediate experience to an ideal implicit model of stability. One could also make a comparative judgment by riding a number of motorcycles and comparing the feelings of stability involved. Either way, one collects some psycho-motor knowledge about the stability one desires, formulates an *S,* and generates *D* information while test driving. However, if this latter route were chosen in order to obtain *P* measures on stability, then *you,* as client, would have to do the test driving. You are the one, after all, who is primarily interested in knowing whether a specific motorcycle meets your *S.* If the *S* is left unobservable and if I, as evaluator, do the test driving, the matter of stability would end up being judged against *my* (implicit) *S* and not yours.

Review

While the work of both the mechanic and the DEM evaluator can be described in terms of the *S, P* and *D* concepts and thus be called evaluation, there are important differences in the way each discharged his/her role. These differences can be summarized in terms of the relationship of the mechanic and the evaluator of *S* involved. The mechanic was the source of *S,* selected *S,* defined the *P* measures to be made, the procedures involved, and also collected the *P* information. He/She then compared *S* and *P* in each case and formed an overall judgment concerning the mechanical adequacy of the motorcycle based on the *D* information generated. He/She was also not particularly concerned with making *S* explicit nor with presenting *P* in any great detail. At least, he/she did so only as it seemed necessary to make his/her conclusions plausible and convincing to the client, or in answer to specific questions.

In contrast, the DEM evaluator approached the problem by helping the client articulate the dimensions involved in *S* by making it clear that the responsibility for deciding what *S should be* rests with the client. The evaluator also made it clear that the client had to specify the kind of evidence that would be an acceptable index of the *S* as well as what would be considered criterion performance. Moreover, the significance attached to all discrepancies found and, thus, the overall judgment of adequacy, was also left to the client. The DEM evaluator was thus the facilitator of a process. The actual evaluator, in the sense of making the judgment of worth, was the client.

To ensure that the client would be in the position of making the judgment of worth, both the *S* and *P* information to be collected had to reach a certain level of specificity independent of the personality of the DEM evaluator. This is one thing that makes the role of the evaluator tricky. While the DEM evaluator would generally consider it part of his/her responsibility to collect P information, he/she would not do so in cases where it would evidently compromise the client's ability to compare S and P and thus give D significance. The example involving stability was a case in point. We saw that by leaving S embedded in personal experience, the very definition and collection of P tacitly set S. Therefore, in that instance, the client was asked to collect P himself/herself.

There are two aspects of the posture of the DEM evaluator that require further comment. They have to do with the interest of distinguishing clearly between the acts of setting S and determining whether S has been met. First, as already noted, setting S is the responsibility of the client, but facilitating the process is the responsibility of the evaluator. If the client is unable to formulate a pertinent S, then he/she can undertake whatever activity necessary to create it, which may involve consulting experts or launching research projects. He/She may also engage an expert to do the "evaluation" for him/her. This was the situation in the example above, where a mechanic was engaged to judge the mechanical condition of the motorcycle because the client did not feel he/she had the expertise to do it himself/herself. Yet, because of the way in which this "evaluation" was performed, or, more exactly, because of the client's relation to it, we would not consider it a DEM evaluation. The major reason for this is that the client is not expressly setting S, and this would be considered pre-empting his/her decison making role and responsibility. It may be objected that the client is still free to accept or reject whatever the expert ends up recommending. That is, of course, true, but the point is not so much that the client end up making the final decisions as it is that he/she expand his/her awareness of the raw ingredients that go into making the decision. Choosing to accept or reject a formed judgment is different from being a party to the making of that judgment.

The second matter is a variation of the difficulty often encountered in specifying S. One can say that leaving the definition of something like stability to an unexplicated feeling derived from test driving is not objective, is not scientific, or does not provide the evaluator with an operational or observable definition. And not being objective or scientific in this sense is generally shunned. I prefer, however, not to talk about the issue in this way. I think it is better to discuss the issue in terms of roles and responsibilities. The client is the one who has to live with the choice made. He/She is the one who has to take responsibility for the evaluation and the decisions resulting from it. The specific data or performance information one responds to in comparing P and S is certainly a matter of one's belief structure and one's preferred way of relating to the world. If nothing other than empirical or scientific data will do, then certainly one could proceed to construct an empirical definition of "stability." But I don't think that is automatically the best or most appropriate way to proceed. A client may find his/her own personal judgment based on *feel* or unexplicated criteria satisfactory, and if *he/she* does, I will too. That doesn't mean that I would not try to explore with the client other alternatives or the consequences of doing things in different ways. It also doesn't mean that I would accept any evaluation contract whatsoever. It means that the credibility of evidence is a function of one's beliefs and that quantitative objective data is not necessarily the thing to strive for.

An interesting corollary here is that, in the case of program evaluation, absolutely any program objective is an adequate objective as far as the DEM evaluator is concerned. There is no need to insist on behavioral or other kinds of objectives. The role description already provided emphasizes freedom to set S as seems desirable and pertinent to the client, who carries the responsibility for the program. Rules for expressing criterion performance, in particular, are not necessarily deduced from a certain methodological orientation or logical framework. Acceptable S and P are seen, rather, as a function of the set of agreements and beliefs that make up the world of the client.

These role characteristics may be unwieldly when a layperson wants to evaluate a motorcycle, but they are essential to the comprehensive and useful evaluation of something like an educational or social service program. This is because programs represent organized human activity and, as such, always represent normative states of affairs. For here, $S's$ ultimately are issues in social and moral philosophy, and, immediately, ideological and political matters. The position taken here is that S not be left to experts dissociated from the responsibilities of program operation and management. For program staff to choose and commit themselves to the S pertinent to their clients' contexts and personalities is fully as important as having an S that is rooted in abstract empirical generalizations (i.e., expert knowledge).

Finally, it should be evident that setting the role of the evaluator in this way formalizes the common human evaluative activity that is associated with any deliberate act. When applied to a program, DEM evaluation refers to making explicit the procedures and norms governing the *SPD* cycles that make up planning, implementation, and review activities. Thus, DEM program evaluation is aimed at program improvement. With the client in control of S and guiding the collection of P, D information can be used to keep action flexible, responsive, and informed. Since D is the result of comparing S and P, we can reduce D by changing S or changing P. Changing S involves program redesign, perhaps changing basic objectives or activities. To change only P in a program requires that management exert greater control over operations.

II. The Application of the DEM to an Educational Program

Review of the Model

We have said that evaluation always consists of comparing *Performance (P)* with a *Standard (S)*. This comparison yields *Discrepancy (D)* information, which can be used as a basis for making a judgment of value or worth about the object being evaluated.

To evaluate something, we must have a pertinent S available. Obtaining such an S is usually not easy and, in most circumstances, has to be created — a job done by the client, assisted by the evaluator, to clarify and make conscious the S that should govern the activity or object being evaluated. Usually the extent to which S can be made explicit and observable is a matter of degree — important dimensions of it remaining implicit.

The evaluator collects data for which an explicit S is available; but, in order to do so, the evaluator and client must first agree on both the specific P information to be collected and the source of that information. This may involve the client and evaluator working together to continually clarify S.

Basic Steps in the Application of the DEM to a Program

The first thing to do is to understand that the purpose of the evaluation is to improve the program by making SPD cycles explicit and public insofar as is possible. This includes agreeing to the role distinctions between client and evaluator discussed above, and clearing the way for the first task, which is to create S.

Creating S is action-oriented planning. The client must turn both to existing knowledge and to his/her own experiences, values, and purposes in order to construct S. He/She must seek to involve others on his/her staff, those affected by the program, or those for whom the program is designed, in order to end up with an adequate and realistic S. Creating S is thus very much an exercise in applied goal- and value-clarification and may be thought of as creating a concrete model of a program.

A useful way to proceed in order to create S is to do a component analysis: to break the program into its major activities, functions, or components. Each component, in turn, can then be broken into its subcomponents and so on, until a level of detail is reached suitable to the needs of program management. For example, suppose the program we are concerned about is a teacher in-service program. We can represent it as shown in figure 5–1. However, upon thinking through the basic organization, we might decide that the program really consists of three major components: selection, curriculum development, and instruction. These can then be represented as subcomponents of the teacher in-service program as shown in figure 5–2.

Each time we break a component into subcomponents, we reach a new level of detail. Thus, we call figure 5–1 level I analysis and figure 5–2 level II analysis. Figure 5–3 shows a level III analysis for the selection component. While selection alone has been chosen for the sake of brevity, the other components would be similarly broken down when constructing a program design.

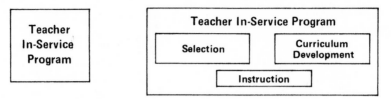

Figure 5–1.   Level I Analysis.   Figure 5–2.   Level II Component Analysis.

In order to write a practical description of each component and subcomponent, we do an input-process-output analysis for each. This means that we assume program activity is not random, that it is goal-directed and that each activity has one or more objectives. These objectives, which may be conditions, behaviors, tangible products, or any purpose an activity is trying to realize, are *outputs*. The things we do to bring about the outputs are *processes*. Processes indicate what will be done, who will do it, how, when, and where. They describe how resources will be combined or transformed to produce outputs. The resources themselves, the personnel, facilities, materials, prerequisites, etc., that are needed to support the processes, are *inputs*.

Let's assign the entire program the numeral 1.0. We could then call the selection component 1.1, curriculum development 1.2, and instruction 1.3. Similarly, staff selection can be 1.1.1. and participant selection, 1.1.2. (This numbering system offers a convenient way to refer to components and follows the usual outlining form.) An abbreviated input-process-output description for each might look as shown in table 5–4.

In the same way, a program design or S would be developed for each of the other subcomponents, breaking these down further into their components (thus going to level IV detail), if that is useful. Notice that the output of 1.1.1, two teacher trainers, is referenced: "to 1.1.2, 1.2, and 1.3." This indicates that the output of 1.1.1 is used as input to 1.1.2, 1.2, and 1.3. In other words, the teacher trainers will be inputs to the participant selection, curriculum development, and in-service instruction activities. The input-process-output description for 1.1.2 shows this relationship between 1.1.1 and 1.1.2 with the entry "teacher trainers (from 1.1.1)" in the input column. We would thus expect to find the contribution of the teacher trainers mentioned in the description of the process for 1.1.2, participant selection. The design also shows that the ten teachers from each school are inputs to component 1.3, in-service instruction (that makes sense, of course, since they will be the beneficiaries of the program).

These input-to-output relationships are shown in the network in figure 5–4, which is the same as figure 5–3, except that the component numbers and some arrows between components have been added. An arrow between components means that one component produces at least one output that is an input to the other

Table 5-4. Input-Process-Output Description for Two Components

INPUT	PROCESS	OUTPUT
— Program director — 3 principals — 3 building coordinators — teacher needs assessment data — $30,000 personnel budget — Personnel Office procedures	1.1.1 STAFF SELECTION. The program director meets with the principals and building coordinators of each of the 3 schools in order to: — write job descriptions for 2 full-time teacher trainers based on needs assessment data; — coordinate with the school district personnel office and their recruitment procedures; — plan the applicant screening and selection procedures; — carry out the selection procedure.	— 2 teacher trainers (to 1.1.2, 1.2, 1.3).
— Program director — teacher trainers (from 1.1.1) — teacher needs assessment data — 3 building coordinators	1.1.2 PARTICIPANT SELECTION. (Describes how the participants for the in-service program will be selected.)	— 10 teachers from each school (to 1.3).

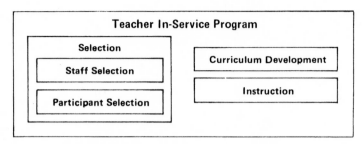

Figure 5–3.   Level III Component Analysis of the Teacher In-Service Program.

component. Thus, the fact that teacher trainers selected in 1.1.1 are an input to 1.1.2, as already noted, is shown with an arrow connecting 1.1.1 and 1.1.2. The other (input-output) relationships among components are also shown with arrows. This additional information to the component analysis of figure 5–3 leads us to call figure 5–4 a network.

This kind of component and relationship analysis eventually produces a detailed program design. It will consist of input-process-output narratives for each component, along with a network showing all components (and subcomponents) and the major relationships among them. This design then acts as $S;$ specifying what *should* be, the intent of the program. As we will see in a moment, P data can then be collected on any aspect of the program to determine whether what should be occurring or resulting (S) is *actually* taking place (P).

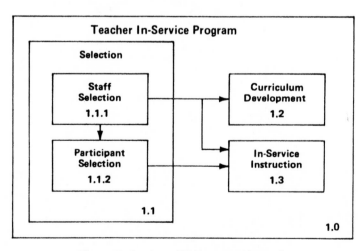

Figure 5–4.   Level III Program Network.

It should be evident that this planning procedure stands to surface differences in values, approaches, procedures, philosophical orientations, etc. Properly facilitated by the DEM evaluator, planning promotes resolution or negotiation of these differences and agreement on the *S* that will govern formal evaluation. As these plans are implemented and periodically reviewed in light of *P* information, they may be changed or amended; that is, the *S* may change as conditions change and as continuous assessment of results occurs. Thus, programmatic decisions and actions utilize feedback. The evaluator's job includes gathering that feedback and putting it at the disposal of the evaluator's client(s).

The input-process-output description suggests different kinds of information that may be deliberately or formally gathered in order to assist feedback-guided action. These are summarized in table 5–5.

Design evaluation in table 5–5 refers to judging the adequacy of program intentions. The object being evaluated here is the program plan. Any program is bound to have a basis in social and moral philosophy, as well as empirical research, and the critique of these bases may be referred to as the problem of construct validity. But the program plans may also be examined for their comprehensiveness, appropriateness to the situation, relationship to known interests and needs, and so on. An analysis may also be made to see whether resources, such as the kinds and qualifications of personnel and materials, seem adequate to support the activities that the program intends to undertake. Similarly, one may critique the logical relationship between program objectives and the activities designed to bring them about. Design evaluation, then, refers to the construct and logical or operational validity of a set of intentions. The standards involved in this sort of evaluation are often not entirely explicit in advance and are made explicit incrementally. The method used is that of logical argument and the evaluation itself is readily understood in terms of the *S, P, D* concepts.

Program plans may themselves serve as *S* for other evaluation undertaken during the life cycle of the program. Program plans specify and direct program implementation and, as such, may serve as *S* to input, process, and outcome evaluation. For example, any program utilizes certain kinds and amounts of resources over time. Program plans that specify the number and kind of resources to different activities and purposes can act as an *S* governing the installation of the program. Thus, *P* information may be gathered concerning the extent to which the resources planned for are indeed available and are in fact deployed as required (input evaluation). A program whose design has been judged adequate may nevertheless falter if it does not have the proper resources available when they are needed. Input evaluation is aimed at helping management make sure these resources are available when necessary.

Process evaluation involves determining whether planned activities are carried out in the manner called for by the program plans and whether they are of the

Table 5-5. Kinds of Evaluation Useful to Program Improvement

MANAGEMENT ACTION	KINDS OF EVALUATION	STANDARDS RELATIVE TO:
Program Planning	Design Evaluation	— design adequacy; construct validity, comprehensiveness, internal or logical consistency, relationship to need, appropriateness.
Program Implementation	Input Evaluation	— availability of resources; extent to which prerequisites and preconditions are met, extent to which program resources (moneys, people, materials, etc.) are available and deployed as planned.
	Process Evaluation	— extent to which activities are carried out as planned; existence or frequency, intensity, manner, and other qualities and characteristics of the activities.
	Outcome Evaluation	— interim outcomes; outcomes which are prerequisite to other outcomes; terminal outcomes.

quality expected. Again, the S here is the program plan, which specifies and describes the program processes to be set into motion. Because of the complex interaction between S and action (which was known first?), thorough process evaluation overlaps with action research.

Outcome evaluation refers to determining the extent to which planned outcomes are achieved. It is useful to distinguish at least two classes of outcomes. Enabling or interim outcomes refer to milestones or sub-objectives essential to the execution of the program from month to month. In contrast, terminal objectives refer to the major purposes or aims of the program.

It should be clear that properly specifying inputs, processes, and outputs for each component and subcomponent and specifying the relationships among all subcomponents, amounts to making available the S essential for input, process, and outcome evaluation. This makes it possible to conduct evaluation on a continuous basis throughout the life of the project, because P data can be gathered relative to a larger class of program characteristics than just terminal objectives. Finally, the D information produced in the course of evaluation may be used to support two broad categories of management action. It may be used, on the one hand, to exert greater control over program operations in order to insure that P meets S. On the other hand, management may decide that the S originally set is inappropriate or unrealistic and may thus change the S involved.

Now it is, of course, impossible to formally collect empirical information on *all* inputs, processes, and outputs. Thus, program management is faced with setting some priorities. Management must identify the P information that would be most useful to it, given its limited resources and its internal and external needs. There will be P information useful primarily to program management in the day-to-day operation of the program, and there will be information that has to be provided to individuals and other organizations in the environment that serves to justify the program. Thus, management must set priorities around its needs for proper internal management and its need to remain accountable to the external environment. The decisions involved are made by management, not the DEM evaluator, although the latter again facilitates the deliberations involved. Having a complete program design available literally points out trouble spots and helps in making the trade-offs involved.

The collection of P information is guided by what the DEM evaluator calls "evaluation questions." Such questions ask whether what *should be* actually *is;* whether inputs are available *as specified;* whether processes are carried out *as planned;* and whether outcomes are being achieved *as intended.*[2] In other words, evaluation questions direct attention to the P information needed in order to determine whether the applicable S has been met. Examples might be: Are there ten participants from each school, and do they meet selection criteria? (outcome evaluation; the S required that there be ten from each school meeting certain criteria); Is the needs assessment data available? (input evaluation; the S required

Table 5–6. Summary of Data Collection Plan

(a) Evaluation Questions	(b) Design Referent	(c) Standard	(d) Data Collection Strategy	(e) Instrument	(f) Date Information Needed
(The specific question about the program and its operation that management wants answered. These questions give feedback important to determining whether standards should be changed or whether greater control over performance should be exerted. The standards applicable to each evaluation question must be known.)	(Names the component, its number, and whether the evaluation question is dealing with an input, process, or output. This refers you to the design where the standards governing the evaluation question are described.)	(Summarizes the standards pertinent to the evaluation question. This information is extracted from the program design.)	(Lists sources of information and techniques for obtaining the information Represents the thinking that must lead to the ''instrument'' in the next column and to table 5–7.)	(A general term standing for the method or procedure to be used in gathering data; i.e., test, questionnaire, interview, observation, etc.)	(Dates are crucial particularly when information is supposed to support program planning and operation.)

Table 5-7. Summary of Data Collection Plan (continued)

(a) Instrument	(b) Evaluation Question Addressed	(c) Instrument Administration Schedule	(d) Data Collector	(e) Respondents	(f) Sample	(g) Data Analysis Procedure & Analyst	(h) Audience	(i) Report Preparation and Date
(From column (e) in table 5-6.)	(Shows the number of each evaluation question for which the instruments gather data. Often any one instrument is designed to answer more than one question.)	(Shows data collection dates and times.)	(Shows who is responsible for administering the instrument or collecting the data.)	(Shows the direct source of data: people, files, etc.)	(Usually limited resources demand that the respondents be sampled.)	(Who will analyze data and how the analysis will be done must be thought through in advance.)	(All persons or places expecting the information gathered are listed.)	(Names the persons with primary report preparation responsibility and the date by which reports must be ready.)

that needs assessment data be available to the people planning the selection of staff); or, Is the personnel committee meeting as planned? (process evaluation; the *S* specifies who should meet to design and carry out the staff selection). There might also be evaluation questions about the operation of the other components, similarly aimed at ensuring effective program operation. And, no doubt, there would be evaluation questions aimed at determining whether the terminal outcomes have been realized.

It is important to notice the very narrow definition given to evaluation questions. Evaluation questions assume the existence of an *S*. This is because evaluation is defined as the comparison between what *is* and what *might be* and is impossible unless the *S* is specified. The DEM evaluator will not let himself/herself get involved in collecting *P* information to answer questions for which no *S* exists. But, as already discussed, he/she will work with the client to articulate the *S* and to define the action that needs to be taken in order to make a pertinent *S* available.

The connection between the program design, the *intent* or expectations of the program, in short, the program *S,* and the program as it *actually is,* is provided by the evaluation questions. Dozens of these questions may be asked and many can be answered through informal interviews, meetings, or planning sessions. Some will be pursued more formally, depending upon the interests and needs of management and the problems and cost involved in collecting the information. The major steps essential to the collection of *P* information are summarized in tables 5–6 and 5–7. Thus, a DEM evaluation will consist of an *S* (a detailed program design showing a network and input-process-output descriptions for all components and subcomponents) and a data collection plan filled out for each evaluation question asked. In this way, an internal feedback cycle can be set up so that the program is managed as much as possible on the basis of *D* information generated by comparing *S* and *P;* that is, on the basis of systematic evaluation.

III. Conclusion

The Discrepancy Evaluation Model offers a pragmatic, systematic approach to a wide variety of evaluation needs. From the daily activities of an individual teacher to educational program evaluation, the DEM can be utilized to structure the gathering of information essential for well-informed decision making. A major feature of the DEM is its emphasis on self-evaluation and systematic program improvement.

Notes

1.   The DEM was first put forth by Malcolm Provus; see *Discrepancy Evaluation,* McCutchan, 1971. It was further developed at the Evaluation Research Center in 1971–1975 by a team of people,

including the author, led by Malcolm Provus. Different versions of the DEM have arisen. The views presented here are those of the author.

2. This does not necessarily mean that the DEM evaluator will not be open to unexpected events. How to handle this problem is negotiated between client and evaluator; the important thing, again, is for the evaluator to stay away from setting S and deciding on his/her own what information to collect.

6 COURSE IMPROVEMENT THROUGH EVALUATION
Lee J. Cronbach

The national interest in improving education has generated several highly important projects attempting to improve curricula, particularly at the secondary-school
level. In conferences of directors of course content improvement programs sponsored by the National Science Foundation, questions about evaluation are frequently raised.[1] Those who inquire about evaluation have various motives, ranging
from sheer scientific curiosity about classroom events to a desire to assure a
sponsor that money has been well spent. While the curriculum developers sin-
cerely wish to use the skills of evaluation specialists, I am not certain that they have
a clear picture of what evaluation can do and should try to do. And, on the other
hand, I am becoming convinced that some techniques and habits of thought of the
evaluation specialist are ill-suited to current curriculum studies. To serve these
studies, what philosophy and methods of evaluation are required? And, particularly, how must we depart from the familiar doctrines and rituals of the testing game?

Decisions Served by Evaluation

To draw attention to its full range of functions, we may define evaluation broadly
as the *collection and use of information to make decisions about an educational*

From *Teachers College Record,* 64 (1963), 672–83. Copyright 1963, Teachers College, Columbia
University, New York. Reprinted with permission of the author and publisher using an edited version
found in R.W. Heath, *New Curricula,* Harper & Row, 1964, at Professor Cronbach's request.

program. This program may be a set of instructional materials distributed nationally, the instructional activities of a single school, or the educational experiences of a single pupil. Many types of decision are to be made, and many varieties of information are useful. It becomes immediately apparent that evaluation is a diversified activity and that no one set of principles will suffice for all situations. But measurement specialists have so concentrated upon one process — the preparation of pencil-and-paper achievement tests for assigning scores to individual pupils — that the principles pertinent to that process have somehow become enshrined as *the* principles of evaluation. "Tests," we are told, "should fit the content of the curriculum." Also, "only those evaluation procedures should be used that yield reliable scores." These and other hallowed principles are not entirely appropriate to evaluation for course improvement. Before proceeding to support this contention, I wish to distinguish among purposes of evaluation and relate them to historical developments in testing and curriculum making.

We may separate three types of decisions for which evaluation is used:

1. Course improvement: deciding what instructional materials and methods are satisfactory and where change is needed.
2. Decisions about individuals: identifying the needs of the pupil for the sake of planning his instruction, judging pupil merit for purposes of selection and grouping, acquainting the pupil with his own progress and deficiencies.
3. Administrative regulation: judging how good the school system is, how good individual teachers are, etc.

Course improvement is set apart by its broad temporal and geographical reference; it involves the modification of recurrently used materials and methods. Developing a standard exercise to overcome a misunderstanding would be course improvement, but deciding whether a certain pupil should work through that exercise would be an individual decision. Administrative regulation likewise is local in effect, whereas an improvement in a course is likely to be pertinent wherever the course is offered.

It was for the sake of course improvement that systematic evaluation was first introduced. When that famous muckraker Joseph Rice gave the same spelling test in a number of American schools and so gave the first impetus to the educational testing movement, he was interested in evaluating a curriculum. Crusading against the extended spelling drills that then loomed large in the school schedule — "the spelling grind" — Rice collected evidence of their worthlessness so as to provoke curriculum revision. As the testing movement developed, however, it took on a different function.

The greatest expansion of systematic achievement testing occurred in the 1920s. At that time, the content of any course was taken pretty much as established and beyond criticism, save for small shifts of topical emphasis. At the administrator's direction, standard tests covering this curriculum were given to assess the efficiency of the teacher or the school system. Such administrative testing fell into disfavor when used injudiciously and heavy-handedly in the 1920s and 1930s. Administrators and accrediting agencies fell back upon descriptive features of the school program in judging adequacy. Instead of collecting direct evidence of educational impact, they judged schools in terms of size of budget, student-staff ratio, square feet of laboratory space, and the number of advanced credits accumulated by the teacher. This tide, it appears, is about to turn. On many university campuses, administrators wanting to know more about their product are installing "operations research offices." Testing directed toward quality control seems likely to increase in the lower schools as well, as is most forcefully indicated by the statewide testing just ordered by the California legislature.

After 1930 or thereabouts, tests were given almost exclusively for judgments about individuals: to select students for advanced training, to assign marks within a class, and to diagnose individual competences and deficiencies. For any such decisions, one wants precise and valid comparisons of one individual with other individuals or with a standard. Much of test theory and test technology has been concerned with making measurements precise. Important though precision is for most decisions about individuals, I shall argue that in evaluating courses we need not struggle to obtain precise scores for individuals.

While measurers have been well content with the devices used to make scores precise, they have been less complacent about validity. Prior to 1935, the pupil was examined mostly on factual knowledge and mastery of fundamental skills. Tyler's research and writings of that period developed awareness that higher mental processes are not evoked by simple factual tests and that instruction that promotes factual knowledge may not promote — indeed, may interfere with — other more important educational outcomes. Tyler, Lindquist, and their students demonstrated that tests can be designed to measure general educational outcomes, such as ability to comprehend scientific method. Whereas a student can prepare for a factual test only through a course of study that includes the facts tested, many different courses of study may promote the same *general* understandings and attitudes. In evaluating today's new curricula, it will clearly be important to appraise the student's general educational growth, which curriculum developers say is more important than mastery of the specific lessons presented. Note, for example, that the Biological Sciences Curriculum Study offers three courses with substantially different "subject matter" as alternative routes to much the same educational ends.

Although some instruments capable of measuring general outcomes were prepared during the 1930s, they were never very widely employed. The prevailing philosophy of the curriculum, particularly among progressives, called for developing a program to fit local requirements, capitalizing on the capacities and experiences of local pupils. The faith of the 1920s in a "standard" curriculum was replaced by a faith that the best learning experience would result from teacher-pupil planning in each classroom. Since each teacher or each class could choose different content and even different objectives, this philosophy left little place for standard testing.

Many evaluation specialists came to see test development as a strategy for training the teacher in service, so that the process of test making came to be valued more than the test — or the test data — that resulted. The following remarks by Bloom (1961) are representative of a whole school of thought:[2]

> The criterion for determining the quality of a school and its educational functions would be the extent to which it achieves the objectives it has set for itself. . . . (Our experiences suggest that unless the school has translated the objectives into specific and operational definitions, little is likely to be done about the objectives. They remain pious hopes and platitudes.) . . . Participation of the teaching staff in selecting as well as constructing evaluation instruments has resulted in improved instruments on one hand, and, on the other hand, it has resulted in clarifying the objectives of instruction and in making them real and meaningful to teachers. . . . When teachers have actively participated in defining objectives and in selecting or constructing evaluation instruments, they return to the learning problems with great vigor and remarkable creativity. . . . Teachers who have become committed to a set of educational objectives which they thoroughly understand respond by developing a variety of learning experiences which are as diverse and as complex as the situation requires.

Thus "evaluation" becomes a local, and beneficial, teacher-training activity. The benefit is attributed to thinking about the data to collect. Little is said about the actual use of test results; one has the impression that when test-making ends, the test itself is forgotten. Certainly there is little enthusiasm for refining tests so that they can be used in other schools, for to do so would be to rob those teachers of the benefits of working out their own objectives and instruments.

Bloom and Tyler describe both curriculum making and evaluation as integral parts of classroom instruction, which is necessarily decentralized. This outlook is far from that of course improvement. The current national curriculum studies assume that curriculum making can be centralized. They prepare materials to be used in much the same way by teachers everywhere. It is assumed that having experts draft materials and revising these after tryout produces better instructional activities than the local teacher would be likely to devise. In this context, it seems wholly appropriate to have most tests prepared by a central staff and to have results returned to that staff to guide further course improvement.

When evaluation is carried out in the service of course improvement, the chief aim is to ascertain what effects the course has — that is, what changes it produces in pupils. This is not to inquire merely whether the course is effective or ineffective. Outcomes of instruction are multidimensional, and a satisfactory investigation will map out the effects of the course along these dimensions separately. To agglomerate many types of post-course performance into a single score is a mistake, since failure to achieve one objective is masked by success in another direction. Moreover, since a composite score embodies (and usually conceals) judgments about the importance of the various outcomes, only a report that treats the outcomes separately can be useful to educators who have different value hierarchies.

The greatest service evaluation can perform is to identify aspects of the course where revision is desirable. Those responsible for developing a course would like to present evidence that their course is effective. They are intrigued by the idea of having an ''independent testing agency'' render a judgment on their product, but to call in the evaluator only upon the completion of course development, to confirm what has been done, is to offer him a menial role and make meager use of his services. To be influential in course improvement, evidence must become available midway in curriculum development, not in the home stretch when the developer is naturally reluctant to tear open a supposedly finished body of materials and techniques. Evaluation, used to improve the course while it is still fluid, contributes more to improvement of education than evaluation used to appraise a product already placed on the market.

Insofar as possible, evaluation should be used to understand how the course produces its effects and what parameters influence its effectiveness. It is important to learn, for example, that the outcome of programed instruction depends very much upon the attitude of the teacher; indeed, this may be more important than to learn that on the average such instruction produces slightly better or worse results than conventional instruction.

Hopefully, evaluation studies will go beyond reporting on this or that course and help us to understand educational learning. Such insight will in the end contribute to the development of all courses rather than just of the course under test. In certain of the new curricula, there are data to suggest that aptitude measures correlate much less with end-of-course achievement than they do with achievement on early units (Ferris, 1962). This finding is not well-confirmed, but is highly significant if true. If it is true for the new curricula and only for them it has one implication; if the same effect appears in traditional courses, it means something else. Either way, it provides food-for-thought for teachers, counselors, and theorists. Evaluation studies should generate knowledge about the nature of the abilities that constitute educational goals. Twenty years after the Eight-Year Study of the Progressive Education Association, its testing techniques are in good repute, but we still know very little about what these instruments measure. Consider ''Applications of Principles in Science.'' Is this in any sense a unitary ability? Or has the able student only mastered certain principles one-by-one? Is the ability demonstrated on a test of this sort more prognostic of any later achievement than is factual knowledge? Such questions ought to receive substantial attention, though to the makers of any one course they are of only peripheral interest.

The aim of comparing one course with another should not dominate plans for evaluation. To be sure, decisionmakers have to choose between courses, and any evaluation report will be interpreted in part comparatively. But formally designed experiments pitting one course against another are rarely definitive enough to justify their cost. Differences between average test scores resulting from different courses are usually small, relative to the wide differences among and within classes taking the same course. At best, an experiment never does more than compare the present version of one course with the present version of another. A major effort to bring the losing contender nearer to perfection would be very likely to reverse the verdict of the experiment.

Any failure to equate the classes taking the competing courses will jeopardize the interpretation of an experiment, and such failures are almost inevitable. In testing a drug, we know that valid results cannot be obtained without a double-blind control, in which the doses for half the subjects are inert placebos; the placebo and the drug look alike, so that neither doctor nor patient knows who is receiving medication. Without this control, the results are useless even when the state of the patient is checked by completely objective indices. In an educational experiment, it is difficult to keep pupils unaware that they are an experimental group, and it is quite impossible to neutralize the biases of the teacher as those of the doctor are neutralized in the double-blind design. It is thus never certain whether any observed advantage is attributable to the educational innovation, as such, or to the greater energy that teachers and students put forth when a method is fresh and experimental. Some have contended that any course, even the most excellent, loses much of its potency as soon as success enthrones it as the traditional method.[3]

Since group comparisons give equivocal results, I believe that a formal study should be designed primarily to determine the post-course performance of a well-described group, with respect to many important objectives and side effects. Ours is a problem like that of the engineer examining a new automobile. He can set himself the task of defining its performance characteristics and its dependability. It would be merely distracting to put his question in the form: ''Is this car better or worse than the competing brand?'' Moreover, in an experiment where the treatments compared differ in a dozen respects, no understanding is gained from the fact that the experiment shows a numerical advantage in favor of the new course. No one knows which of the ingredients is responsible for the advantage. More analytic experiments are much more useful than field trials applying markedly dissimilar treatments to different groups. Small-scale, well-controlled studies can profitably be used to compare alternative versions of the same course; in such a study the differences between treatments are few enough and well-enough defined that the results have explanatory value.

The three purposes — course improvement, decisions about individuals, and administrative regulation — call for measurement procedures having somewhat different qualities. When a test will be used to make an administrative judgment on the individual teacher, it is necessary to measure thoroughly and with conspicuous fairness; such testing, if it is to cover more than one outcome, becomes extremely time-consuming. In judging a course, however, one can make satisfactory interpretations from data collected on a sampling basis, with no pretense of measuring thoroughly the accomplishments of any one class. A similar point is to be made about testing for decisions about individuals. A test of individuals must be conspicuously fair and extensive enough to provide a dependable score for each person. But if the performance will not influence the fate of the individual, we can ask him to perform tasks for which the course has not directly prepared him, and we can use techniques that would be prohibitively expensive if applied in a manner thorough enough to measure each person reliably.

Methods of Evaluation

Range of Methods

Evaluation is too often visualized as the administration of a formal test, an hour or so in duration, at the close of a course. But there are many other methods for examining pupil performance, and pupil attainment is not the only basis for appraising a course.

It is quite appropriate to ask scholars whether the statements made in the course are consistent with the best contemporary knowledge. This is a sound, even a necessary, procedure. One might go on to evaluate the pedagogy of the new course by soliciting opinions, but here there is considerable hazard. If the opinions are based on some preconception about teaching method, the findings will be controversial and very probably misleading. There are no theories of pedagogy so well established that one can say, without tryout, what will prove educative.

One can accept the need for a pragmatic test of the curriculum and still employ opinions as a source of evidence. During the tryout stages of curriculum making, one relies heavily on the teachers' reports of pupil accomplishment — "Here they had trouble"; "This they found dull"; "Here they needed only half as many exercises as were provided"; etc. This is behavior observation, even though unsystematic, and it is of great value. The reason for shifting to systematic observation is that this is more impartial, more public, and sometimes more penetrating. While I bow to the historian or mathematician as a judge of the technical soundness of course content, I do not agree that the experienced history or mathematics teacher who tries out a course gives the best possible judgment on its effectiveness. Scholars have too often deluded themselves about their effectiveness as teachers — in particular, they have too often accepted parroting of words as evidence of insight — for their unaided judgment to be trusted. Systematic observation is costly and introduces some delay between the moment of teaching and the feedback of results. Hence, systematic observation will never be the curriculum developer's sole source of evidence. Systematic data collection becomes profitable in the intermediate stages of curriculum development, after the more obvious bugs in early drafts have been dealt with.

The approaches to evaluation include process studies, proficiency measures, attitude measures, and follow-up studies. A process study is concerned with events taking place in the classroom, proficiency and attitude measures with changes observed in pupils, and follow-up studies with the later careers of those who participated in the course.

The follow-up study comes closest to observing ultimate educational contributions, but the completion of such a study is so far removed in time from the initial instruction that it is of minor value in improving the course or explaining its effects. The follow-up study differs strikingly from the other types of evaluation study in one respect. I have already expressed the view that evaluation should be primarily concerned with the effects of the course under study rather than with comparisons of courses. That is to say, I would emphasize departures of attained results from the ideal, differences in apparent effectiveness of different parts of the course, and differences from item to item. All these suggest places where the course could be strengthened; but this view cannot be applied to the follow-up study, which appraises effects of the course as a whole and which has very little meaning unless outcomes can be compared with some sort of base rate. Suppose we find that 65 percent of the boys graduating from an experimental curriculum enroll in scientific and technical majors in college. We cannot judge whether this is a high or low figure save by comparing it with the rate among boys who have not had this course. In a follow-up study, it is necessary to obtain data on a control group equated at least crudely to the experimental cases on the obvious demographic variables.

Despite the fact that such groups are hard to equate and that follow-up data do not tell much about how to improve the course, such studies should have a place in research on the new curricula, whose national samples provide unusual opportunity for follow-up that can shed light on important questions. One obvious type of follow-up study traces the student's success in a college course founded upon the high school course. One may examine the student's grades or ask him what topics in the college course he found himself poorly prepared for. It is hoped that some of the new science and mathematics courses will arouse greater interest than usual among girls; whether this hope is well-founded can be checked by finding out what majors and what electives these ex-students pursue in college. Career choices likewise merit attention. Some proponents of the new curricula would like to see a greater flow of talent into basic science as distinct from technology, while others would regard this as potentially disastrous; but no one would regard facts about this flow as lacking significance.

Attitudes are prominent among the outcomes that course developers are concerned with. Attitudes are meanings or beliefs, not mere expressions of approval or disapproval. One's attitude toward science includes ideas about the matters on which a scientist can be an authority — about the benefits to be obtained from moon shots and studies of monkey mothers, and about depletion of natural resources. Equally important is the match between self-concept and concept of the field: what roles does science offer a person like me? Would I want to marry a scientist? and so on. Each learning activity also contributes to attitudes that reach far beyond any one subject, such as the pupil's sense of his own competence and desire to learn.

Attitudes can be measured in many ways; the choices revealed in follow-up studies, for example, are pertinent evidence. But measurement usually takes the form of direct or indirect questioning. Interviews, questionnaires, and the like are quite valuable when not trusted blindly. Certainly, we should take seriously any *un*desirable opinion expressed by a substantial proportion of graduates of a course (e.g., the belief that the scientist speaks with peculiar authority on political and ethical questions, or the belief that mathematics is a finished subject rather than a field for current investigation).

Attitude questionnaires have been much criticized because they are subject to distortion, especially where the student hopes to gain by being less than frank. Particularly if the questions are asked in a context far removed from the experimental course, the returns are likely to be trustworthy. Thus, a general questionnaire administered through homerooms (or required English courses) may include questions about liking for various subjects and activities; these same questions administered by the mathematics teacher would give much less trustworthy data on attitudes toward mathematics. While students may give reports more favorable than their true beliefs, this distortion is not likely to be greater one year than another or greater among students who take an experimental course than among those who do not. In group averages, many distortions balance out. But questionnaires insufficiently valid for individual testing can be used in evaluating curricula, both because the student has little motive to distort and because the evaluator is comparing averages rather than individuals.

For measuring proficiency, techniques are likewise varied. Standardized tests are useful, but for course evaluation it makes sense to assign *different* questions to different students. Giving each student in a population of 500 the same test of 50 questions will provide far less information to the course developer than drawing for each student 50 questions from a pool of, say, 700. The latter plan determines the mean success of about 75 representative students on every one of the 700 items; the former reports on only 50 items (See Lord, 1962). Essay tests and open-ended questions, generally too expensive to use for routine evaluation, can profitably be employed to appraise certain abilities. One can go further and observe individuals or groups as they attack a research problem in the laboratory or work through some other complex problem. Since it is necessary to test only a representative sample of pupils, costs are not as serious a consideration as in routine testing. Additional aspects of proficiency testing will be considered below.

Process measures have especial value in showing how a course can be improved, because they examine what happens during instruction. In the development of programed instructional materials, for example, records are collected showing how many pupils miss each item presented; any piling up of errors implies a need for better explanation or a more gradual approach to a difficult topic. Immediately after showing a teaching film, one can interview students, perhaps asking them to describe a still photograph taken from the film. Misleading presentations, ideas given insufficient emphasis, and matters left unclear will be identified by such methods. Similar interviews can disclose what pupils take away from a laboratory activity or a discussion. A process study might turn attention to what the teacher does in the classroom. In those curricula that allow choice of topics, for example, it is worthwhile to find out which topics are chosen and how much time is allotted to each. A log of class activities (preferably recorded by a pupil rather than the teacher) will show which of the techniques suggested in a summer institute are actually adopted, and which form part of the new course only in the developer's fantasies.

Measurement of Proficiency

I have indicated that I consider item data to be more important than test scores. The total score may give confidence in a curriculum or give rise to discouragement, but it tells very little about how to produce further improvement. And, as Ferris (1962) has noted, such scores are quite likely to be mis- or overinterpreted. The score on a single item or on a problem that demands several responses in succession is more likely than the test score to suggest how to alter the presentation. When we accept item scores as useful, we need no longer think of evaluation as a one-shot, end-of-year operation. Proficiency can be measured at any moment, with particular interest attaching to those items most related to the recent lessons. Other items calling for general abilities can profitably be administered repeatedly during the course (perhaps to different random samples of pupils) so that we can begin to learn when and from what experiences change in these abilities comes.

In course evaluation, we need not be much concerned about making measuring instruments fit the curriculum. However startling this declaration may seem and however contrary to the principles of evaluation for other purposes, this must be our position if we want to know what changes a course produces in the pupil. An ideal evaluation would include measures of all the types of proficiency that might reasonably be desired in the area in question, not just the selected outcomes to which this curriculum directs substantial attention. If you wish only to know how well a curriculum is achieving *its* objectives, you fit the test to the curriculum; but if you wish to know how well the curriculum is serving the national interest, you measure all outcomes that might be worth striving for. One of the new mathematics courses might disavow any attempt to teach numerical trigonometry and, indeed, might discard nearly all computational work. It is still perfectly reasonable to ask how well graduates of the course can compute and can solve right triangles. Even if the course developers went so far as to contend that computational skill is no proper objective of secondary instruction, they will encounter educators and laymen who do not share their view. If it can be shown that students who come through the new course are fairly proficient in computation despite the lack of direct teaching, the doubters will be reassured. If not, the evidence makes clear how much is being sacrificed. Similarly, when the biologists offer alternative courses emphasizing microbiology and ecology, it is fair to ask how well the graduate of one course can understand issues treated in the other. Ideal evaluation in mathematics will collect evidence on all the abilities toward which a mathematics course might reasonably aim, likewise in biology, English, or any other subject.

Ferris states that the ACS Chemistry Test, however well constructed, is inadequate for evaluating the new CBA and CHEM programs, because it does not cover their objectives. One can agree with this without regarding the ACS test as inappropriate to use with these courses. It is important that this test not stand alone, as the sole evaluation device. It will tell us something worth knowing, namely, just how much "conventional" knowledge the new curriculum does or does not provide. The curriculum developers deliberately planned to sacrifice some of the conventional attainments and have nothing to fear from this measurment, if it is competently interpreted (particularly if data are examined item-by-item).

The demand that tests be closely matched to the aims of a course reflects awareness that examinations of the usual sort "determine what is taught." If questions are known in advance, students give more attention to learning their answers than to learning other aspects of the course. This is not necessarily detrimental. Wherever it is critically important to master certain content, the knowledge that it will be tested produces a desirable concentration of effort. On the other hand, learning the answer to a set question is by no means the same as acquiring understanding of whatever topic that question represents. There is, therefore, a possible advantage in using "secure" tests for course evaluation. Security is achieved only at a price: one must prepare new tests each year and cannot make before-and-after comparisons with the same items. One would hope that the use of different items with different students and the fact that there is less incentive to coach when no judgment is to be passed on the pupils and the teachers would make security a less critical problem.

The distinction between factual tests and tests of higher mental processes, as elaborated for example in the *Taxonomy of Educational Objectives,* is of some value in planning tests, although classifying items as measures of knowledge, application, original problem solving, etc., is difficult and often impossible. Whether a given response represents rote recall of reasoning depends upon how the pupil has been taught, not solely upon the question asked. One might, for example, describe a biological environment and ask for predictions regarding the effect of a certain intervention. Students who had never dealt with ecological data would succeed or fail according to their general ability to reason about complex events; those who had studied ecological biology would be more likely to succeed, reasoning from specific principles; and those who had lived in such an ecology or read about it might answer successfully on the basis of memory. We rarely, therefore, will want to test whether a student *knows* or *does not know* certain material. Knowledge is a matter of degree. Two persons may be acquainted with the same facts or principles, but one will be more expert in his understanding, better able to cope with inconsistent data, irrelevant sources of confusion, and apparent exceptions to the principle. To measure intellectual competence is to measure depth, connectedness, and applicability of knowledge.

Too often, test questions are course-specific, stated in such a way that only the person who has been specifically taught to understand what is being asked for can answer the question. Such questions can usually be identified by their use of conventions. Some conventions are commonplace, and we can assume that all the pupils we test will know them. But a biology test that describes a metabolic process with the aid of the symbol presents difficulties for students who can think through the scientific question about equilibrium but are unfamiliar with the symbol. A trigonometry problem that requires use of a trigonometric table is unreasonable, unless we want to test familiarity with the conventional names of functions. The same problem in numerical trigonometry can be cast in a form clear to the average pupil *entering* high school; if necessary, the tables of functions can be presented along with a comprehensible explanation. So stated, the problem becomes course-independent. It is fair to ask whether graduates of the experimental course can solve such problems, not previously encountered, whereas it is pointless to ask whether they can answer questions whose language is strange to them. To be sure, knowledge of a certain terminology is a significant objective of instruction; but, for course evaluation, testing of terminology should very likely be separated from testing of other understandings. To appraise understanding of processes and relations, the fair question is one comprehensible to a pupil who has not taken the course. This is not to say that he should know the answer or the procedure to follow in attaining the answer, but he should understand what he is being asked. Such course-independent questions can be used as standard instruments to investigate any instructional program.

Pupils who have not studied a topic usually will be less facile than those who have studied it. Graduates of my hypothetical mathematics course will take longer to solve trigonometry problems than will those who have studied trigonometry.

But speed and power should not be confused; in intellectual studies, power is almost always of greatest importance. If the course equips the pupil to deal correctly, even though haltingly, with a topic not studied, we can expect him to develop facility later when that topic comes before him frequently.

The chief objective in many of the new curricula seems to be to develop aptitude for mastering new materials in the field. A biology course cannot cover all valuable biological content, but it may reasonably aspire to equip the pupil to understand descriptions of unfamiliar organisms, to comprehend a new theory and the reasoning behind it, and to plan an experiment to test a new hypothesis. This is transfer of learning. It has been insufficiently recognized that there are two types of transfer. The two types shade into one another, being arranged on a continuum of immediacy of effect; we can label the more immediate pole *applicational transfer,* and speak of slower-acting effects as *gains in aptitude* (Ferguson, 1954).

Nearly all educational research on transfer has tested immediate performance on a partly new task. We teach pupils to solve equations in x and include in the test equations stated in a or z. We teach the principles of ecological balance by referring to forests and, as a transfer test, ask what effect pollution will have on the population of a lake. We describe an experiment not presented in the text and ask the student to discuss possible interpretations and needed controls. Any of these tests can be administered in a short time. But the more significant type of transfer may be the increased ability to learn in a particular field. There is very likely a considerable difference between the ability to draw conclusions from a neatly finished experiment and the ability to tease insight out of the disordered and inconsistent observations that come with continuous laboratory work on a problem. The student who masters a good biology course may become better able to comprehend certain types of theory and data, so that he gains more from a subsequent year of study in ethnology; we do not measure this gain by testing his understanding of short passages in ethnology. There has rarely been an appraisal of ability to work through a problem situation or a complex body of knowledge over a period of days or months. Despite the practical difficulties that attend an attempt to measure the effect of a course on a person's subsequent learning, such *learning to learn* is so important that a serious effort should be made to detect such effects and to understand how they may be fostered.

The technique of programed instruction may be adopted to appraise learning ability. One might, for example, test the student's rate of mastery of a self-contained, programed unit on heat or some other topic not studied. If the program is truly self-contained, every student can master it, but the one with greater scientific comprehension hopefully will make fewer errors and progress faster. The program might be prepared in several logically complete versions, ranging from one with very small steps to one with minimal internal redundancy, on the hypothesis that the better-educated student could cope with the less redundant program. Moreover, he might prefer its greater elegance.

Conclusion

Old habits of thought and long-established techniques are poor guides to the evaluation required for course improvement. Traditionally, educational measurement has been chiefly concerned with producing fair and precise scores for comparing individuals; educational experimentation has been concerned with comparing score averages of competing courses; but course evaluation calls for description of outcomes. This description should be made on the broadest possible scale, even at the sacrifice of superficial fairness and precision.

Course evaluation should ascertain what changes a course produces and should identify aspects of the course that need revision. The outcomes observed should include general outcomes ranging far beyond the content of the curriculum itself: attitudes, careers choices, general understandings and intellectual powers, and aptitude for further learning in the field. Analysis of performance on single items or types of problems is more informative than analysis of composite scores. It is not necessary or desirable to give the same test to all pupils; rather, as many questions as possible should be given, each to a different moderate-sized sample of pupils. Costly techniques, such as interviews and essay tests, can be applied profitably to samples of pupils, whereas testing everyone would be out of the question.

Asking the right questions about educational outcomes can do much to improve educational effectiveness. Even if the right data are collected, evaluation will have contributed too little if it only places a seal of approval on certain courses and casts others into disfavor. Evaluation is a fundamental part of curriculum development, not an appendage. Its job is to collect facts the course developer can and will use to do a better job and facts from which a deeper understanding of the educational process will emerge.

Notes

1.   My comments on these questions and on certain more significant questions that *should* have been raised, have been greatly clarified by the reactions of several of these directors and colleagues in evaluation to a draft of this paper. J. Thomas Hastings and Robert Heath have been especially helpful. What I voice, however, are my personal views, deliberately more provocative than *authoritative*.

2.   Elsewhere, Bloom's paper discusses evaluation for the new curricula. Attention may also be drawn to Tyler's highly pertinent paper (1951).

3.   The interested reader can find further striking parallels between curriculum studies and drug research (see Modell, 1963).

References

Bloom, B.S. (ed.) *Taxonomy of educational objectives,* New York: Longmans, Green, 1956.

Bloom, B.S. Quality control in education. *Tomorrow's teaching.* Oklahoma City: Frontiers of Science Foundation, 1961. Pp. 54–61.

Ferguson, G.A. On learning and human ability, *Canadian J. Psychol.,* 1954, 8, 95–112.

Ferris, F.L., Jr. Testing in the new curriculums: Numerology, tyranny, or common sense? *School rev.,* 1962, 70, 112–131.

Lord, F.M. Estimating norms by item-sampling. *Educ. psychol. Measmt.,* 1962, 22, 259–268.

Tyler, R.W. The functions of measurement in improving instruction. In E.F. Lindquist (ed.), *Educational measurement.* Washington, D.C.: Amer. Council Educ., 1951, Pp. 47–67.

7 THE CIPP MODEL FOR PROGRAM EVALUATION
Daniel L. Stufflebeam

*The most important purpose of program
evaluation is not to prove but to improve*

This chapter is a review and update of the so-called CIPP Model[1] for evaluation. That model (Stufflebeam, 1966) was developed in the late 1960s as one alternative to the views about evaluations that were most prevalent at that time — those oriented to objectives, testing, and experimental design. It emerged with other new conceptualizations, especially those developed by Scriven (1966) and Stake (1967). (For a discussion of these historical developments, see Chapter 1 of this book.) The CIPP approach was applied in many institutions; for example, the Southwest Regional Educational Laboratory in Austin, Texas; the National Center for Vocational and Technical Education; the U.S. Office of Education; and the school districts in Columbus, Toledo, and Cincinnati, Ohio; Dallas, Forth Worth, Houston, and Austin, Texas; and Saginaw, Detroit, and Lansing, Michigan. It was the subject of research and development by Adams (1971), Findlay (1979), Nevo (1974), Reinhard (1972), Root (1971), Webster (1975), and others. It was the central topic of the International Conference on the Evaluation of Physical Education held in Jyvaskyla, Finland in 1976 and was used as the advance organizer to group the evaluations that were presented and discussed during that week-long conference. It was also the central topic of the Eleventh National Phi Delta Kappa Symposium on Educational Research, and, throughout the 1970s it was referenced in many conferences and publications. It was most fully explicated in the Phi Delta Kappa book, *Educational Evaluation and Decision Making* (Stufflebeam et al., 1971) and most fully implemented in the Dallas Independent School District. Its conceptual and operational forms have evolved in response to critiques, applications, research, and parallel developments; and it continues to be referenced and applied in education and other fields.

The CIPP approach is based on the view that the most important purpose of evaluation is not to prove but to improve. It is a move against the view that evaluations should be "witch hunts" or only instruments of accountability. Instead it sees evaluation as a tool by which to help make programs work better for the people they are intended to serve. This position is consistent with those recently presented by Patton (1978) and Cronbach and Associates (1980). However, the orientation of this chapter is not intended to discount the likelihood that some programs are unworthy of efforts to improve them and thus should be terminated. By promoting the demise of unneeded or hopelessly flawed programs, evaluations also serve an improvement function by helping to free resources for allocation to more worthy efforts. Fundamentally, the use of the CIPP Model is intended to promote growth and to help the responsible leadership and staff of an institution systematically to obtain and use feedback so as to excel in meeting important needs, or, at least, to do the best they can with the available resources.

The purpose of this chapter is to present an up-to-date interpretation of the CIPP Model. Especially, it is intended to convey background information and a general guide to anyone who is interested in applying the approach. I will begin by setting the CIPP approach in its historical context to show how and why it was developed and how it came to have its current form. I will analyze how it is similar to and different from other major conceptualizations and how they have influenced its evaluation. I will underscore its main orientation towards fostering improvement and will characterize its potential role in assisting institutions to improve their services. I will provide an up-to-date overview of its main concepts. Finally, I will describe a structure for designing evaluation studies.

Development of the CIPP Model

CIPP was conceptualized as a result of attempts to evaluate projects that had been funded through the Elementary and Secondary Education Act of 1965 (ESEA). This act provided billions of dollars to school districts throughout the United States for the purpose of improving the education of disadvantaged students and, more generally, for upgrading the total system of elementary and secondary education. The act also required educators to evaluate their funded projects. This requirement created a crisis, since educators were not prepared to design and conduct evaluation studies. They lacked evaluation training and experience, and they soon found that the available evaluation approaches were no match for the evaluation needs of the ESEA (see Guba, 1969). As a consequence, several agencies attempted to develop new and better ways of evaluating education and to provide training in the use of these approaches. The Ohio State University Evaluation Center was one such agency. It was through the work of that center in the late 1960s that the original version of the CIPP model was developed.

The Evaluation Center had been created in 1965 for the purpose of assisting educational agencies to improve their evaluation programs. The center was to do this by providing evaluation service to school districts and other educational agencies, by studying these service experiences, by conceptualizing improved ways of doing evaluation, by devising tools and strategies to carry out new ideas about evaluation, and by training educators to use the new tools and strategies.

As one means of pursuing these goals, the center contracted with the Columbus, Ohio Public Schools to evaluate their Elementary and Secondary Education Act projects. These three-year projects included a pre-kindergarten project, mathematics and reading improvement projects, an after-school study center, a health services project, and several others; the projects were supported by a $6.6 million federal grant. The Columbus district subcontracted about eight percent of this amount to the Evaluation Center to sponsor their work in evaluating the eight projects and in helping the district to develop its own evaluation system.

The center staff set about their evaluation task in a traditional way. They sought to determine whether the eight projects were achieving their objectives. According to this approach, we were to identify the behavioral objectives for each project, select or develop appropriate instruments for measuring student performance, administer these instruments after instruction, and then compare student performance with project objectives. Many of you will recognize this as the Tylerian Evaluation Rationale (Tyler, 1942), which has been a mainstay of American educational evaluation theory for over 30 years.

We soon found that this approach was not adequate for evaluating the Columbus projects. The assumption that educators knew or could easily determine what student behaviors should result from the projects was far from realistic. The original objectives contained in the funding proposal were general and did not reflect data about the functioning of the students to be served. In fact, the objectives usually had been written by consultants and administrators who had little or no direct experience with these students. What's more, the project staff could not agree, even after the project had started, on what specific objectives should be adopted. In retrospect, they and we wasted valuable time in trying to do so, since the needs of the students were highly variable and had not been the subject of serious study, and since no common set of objectives could have been responsive to their varied developmental levels and needs. A related technical problem was the fact that existing tests were not geared to the language patterns and functional levels of disadvantaged students, and developing such tests in time to use them in evaluating the ESEA projects presented great problems of feasibility. Also, and more seriously, our employment of the Tylerian approach promised to yield reports only at the end of each project year, which was far from the most useful evaluative feedback that might have been provided.

This became apparent to me when I visited project staff members and observed their project activities. While I expected to find the projects being implemented across schools and classrooms with some degree of consistency, I found nothing of the sort. Instead there was widespread confusion on the part of the teachers concerning what they were supposed to be doing. Most of them had not had an opportunity to read the proposal that they were supposed to be implementing. Many of those who had seen the proposal were in disagreement with it or confused by it. Not surprisingly, the activities within a given project were not consistent across classrooms, and these activities bore little resemblance to those that had been described in the funding proposal. As I considered this situation, the outcome data that my staff and I were planning to collect seemed of low importance.

I decided that educators needed a broader definition of evaluation than one constrained to determine whether objectives had been achieved. The needed definition should lead to evaluations that would aid in managing and improving programs. It seemed to me that the best hope of doing this would be to supply the school administrators, project directors, and school staff with information they could use to decide on and bring about needed changes in the projects. As an alternative to the Tylerian definition, I proposed that evaluation be redefined as a process of providing useful information for decision making (Stufflebeam, 1969). To my surprise, this proposal soon received widespread support, especially from the U.S. Office of Education, several large school districts, research and development agencies, and many educational administrators.

Since I wanted to gear evaluation to serve the information requirements of decisionmakers, it seemed appropriate to identify the main types of decisions that typically confronted them; then to derive appropriate evaluation strategies. Based on the experience with the Columbus ESEA projects, decisions of immediate concern seemed to be those associated with implementing the project designs, e.g., how to bring teachers "up to speed" in carrying out the projects, how to allocate resources, how to assign and remodel facilities, how to obtain and sustain community support, how to schedule the needed transportation of students, how to adapt instructional materials, and how to foster communication among those participating in the projects. To service these and other *implementation* decisions, I directed my staff and other staff members to start interacting with the observing the activities of project staff on a continuous basis and to report *process* results at least once each two weeks to project staff so that operational problems could be detected or highlighted and solved. The other main type of decision, especially in view of the government's annual funding cycle, quite apparently included decisions related to continuing or terminating a project, increasing or decreasing funding, merging the project with another one, institutionalizing the project, etc. I called these *recycling* decisions and suggested that they should be supported by information about what a project had *produced*. Accordingly, my staff and I continued our efforts with project staff to clarify what evidence of project outcomes would be appropriate, and we developed and administered quite a few tailor-made performance tests and rating scales. To summarize, at this point, this reconceptualization of evaluation included *process evaluation* to guide *implementation* and *product evaluation* to serve *recycling decisions*. Process evaluation was a relatively new entry in the lore of educational evaluation; product evaluation, of course, was akin to what Tyler had meant by evaluation per se.

Shortly after developing this scheme, I was invited to describe it in an Ohio State faculty-student colloquium. One key reaction was that the proposed conceptualization was a decided improvement over classical ideas about educational evaluation, since it evidenced a concern for process as well as product. However, three philosophers in the group charged that the approach ignored the fundamental concern for assessing goals.

They were correct. The selection of goals places constraints on what is hoped for and attempted in a project, and thus is a key decision. I had neither included the choice of goals as a decision to be served by evaluation nor proposed any evaluation strategies that would assist evaluators in choosing or assessing goals. Also, I knew that the choice of goals to guide the Columbus projects had been based more on a review of literature concerning disadvantaged children and educational innovations in general than on a systematic study of the needs of the students in Columbus. I suspected that the goals of the eight ESEA projects were only generally reflective of the needs of the students in Columbus, and there was no evidence to the contrary. To address this deficiency, I proposed that evaluators assess and report on student needs and system problems as a means of aiding educators to choose sound goals. The language that was added to the emerging CIPP framework advised educators to conduct *context evaluation* as a means of servicing *planning decisions*. However, this insight came too late for us to be able to conduct and report a context evaluation as a basis for selecting and shaping project goals. In retrospect, however, we probably should have performed one anyway to provide a sounder base than the armchair objectives for interpreting project outcomes. Later, the Columbus evaluators developed a school profile system, which assessed student and school characteristics and achievement results; the annual school profile reports provided information for periodic context evaluations across the district and for each school. That is, they provided information for locating both school-level and district-wide deficiencies that needed to be corrected.

There was an obvious gap in this scheme, since it did not consider decisions that are required in specifying what *means* are required to achieve a given set of goals, or a set of assessed needs. These decisions are illustrated by the procedures, schedules, staffing plans, and budgets that appear in proposals that are sent to school boards and funding agencies, and, in general, by the choice of one plan over other possibilities. I called these decisions *structuring decisions* and proposed that they be serviced by *input evaluation,* which are studies that identify and assess the relative merits of alternative project designs.

At this point, the basic framework of the CIPP Framework was complete (context evaluation to inform planning decisions, input evaluation to serve structuring decisions, process evaluation to guide implementing decisions, and product evaluation to serve recycling decisions.) Howard Merriman, who was a student in the Evaluation Center at the time and who later became the director of the Columbus schools' new department of evaluation (which our project developed), observed that the first letters of the labels for the four evaluation concepts would provide a convenient acronym to help people remember them, and the label CIPP was thus affixed to the scheme.

CIPP Compared to Other Evaluation Proposals

While my colleagues and I were developing the CIPP framework, Bob Stake was developing the *Countenance of Evaluation* approach, which he has since incorporated in his *Responsive Approach.* We exchanged drafts of our working papers in 1966, and I was interested to see whether or not we had been independently developing similar or different approaches.

The consistency between the CIPP and Countenance frameworks was considerable, but there were also some notable differences. Both approaches called for assessment of outcomes, but Stake emphasized the need to search for side effects as well as intended effects, which was an excellent recommendation that I have incorporated in my views of product evaluation. His provision for observing and analyzing "transactions within a project" was similar to process evaluation. While Stake provided no analogue for input evaluation, it and context evaluation could be assumed to be covered in his provision for identifying and assessing "antecedent conditions" (those that existed before the project started and before the evaluator entered the scene.) Clearly, the use of either approach called for a more comprehensive assessment of a project than was embodied in the outcomes-oriented Tylerian rationale. One difference concerned how the two approaches dealt with the so-called "point of entry" problem. By relegating concerns for assessing needs and project plans to the category of antecedents, Stake seemed to assume that the evaluator would enter during the implementation stage, when it would be most appropriate to look at ongoing transactions. CIPP provided for entry either before or during a project and allowed for the possibility of conducting a single type of evaluation only (context, input, process, or product) or some combination, depending on the needs of the audiences. Neither approach gave much credence to entering after a project to perform a post mortem (or motivate a celebration), since both emphasized the improvement function of an evaluation. While both approaches were geared to helping particular audiences use evaluation to carry out their assignments, the Stake approach was geared most directly to serving the involved project staff and teachers, whereas the CIPP approach was oriented more to the needs of those charged with planning and administering the projects. Another difference concerned the bases used by the two approaches to form conclusions about the success of projects. In the Stake approach, such conclusions were to be derived by collecting and analyzing judgments from all persons and groups with an interest in the project; whereas the CIPP approach looked more to whether assessed needs had been met. Both approaches evidenced a tension — and I believe a healthy one — between obtaining a comprehensive view of a project while tailoring the evaluation to address the most important information needs of the relevant audiences.

Michael Scriven's *Formative-Summative* approach offered a fairly sharp contrast to both the Countenance and CIPP approaches (for an updated version of his approach see pages 229 to 260.) He defined evaluation as the systematic and objective determination of the worth or merit of an object, and said this definition could best be implemented by engaging an independent evaluator to render a judgment of an object based on the accumulated evidence about how it compared with similar objects in meeting the needs of consumers. He called this approach summative evaluation and said it was fundamentally more important than formative evaluation, in which an evaluator collects and reports data and judgments to assist the development of an object. Based on this rationale, Scriven (1970) charged that the CIPP approach was flawed because it almost totally ignored the fundamental role of summative evaluation, due to its preoccupation with fostering improvement.

At a meeting of the May 12th Group of Evaluation,[2] Michael Scriven and I debated the relative merits of an improvement orientation versus a summative-judgment orientation. Later, the American Educational Research Association (AERA) put this debate on the road, so to speak, as we were commissioned to co-direct and team-teach four traveling training institutes. Subsequently, NIE commissioned us to chair teams that designed competing plans for the evaluation of regional educational laboratories and research and development centers. Through these contacts, I became convinced that our different views of evaluation were more apparent than real and that they mainly reflected different perspectives and experiences. In my work with the Columbus schools, an orientation towards a final, externally-based judgment of worth would have been stifling and nonresponsive to the staff's need for guidance toward ''shaking down'' and improving their ESEA projects. Likewise, given that Scriven had been extensively involved in advising groups concerned with evaluating competing national curriculum packages, it is easy to see why he was placing emphasis on comparative summative evaluations. His main audience included the potential purchasers of these packages and they obviously were interested not in data by which to improve the packages, but in recommendations about which of the alternatives would serve them best. Finally, the compatibility of our views was confirmed when our two teams' designs for the NIE evaluation work turned out to be highly similar, even though they had been independently developed (Reinhard, 1972).

Nevertheless, these experiences pointed up the need to clarify and extend the CIPP model to ensure that it would serve needs for summative as well as formative evaluation. Accordingly, I issued an article on the applicability of the CIPP approach to accountability (Stufflebeam, 1971). In this article, I characterized evaluation for decision making as formative or proactive in nature and evaluation for accountability mainly as summative or retroactive. In the main, this article was written to explain a version of the chart presented in table 7–1. This chart shows that context, input, process, and product evaluations may be used both to guide decision making, the formative role, and to supply information for accountability, the summative role. Based on this scheme, the evaluators would design and conduct evaluation so as to assist a staff to plan and implement their program. Regardless of how narrow or broad the information requirements of the developers, they would also keep in mind and try to address the full range of information needs of external audiences that someday would want to form conclusions about the worth and merit of the educational effort. Moreover, they would maintain a record of the information collected and evidence of the extent that the developers used it to guide their work. While such information would not answer all the questions of an external summative evaluator, it would certainly help in answering some of them. Especially, a full implementation of the CIPP approach would yield information to use in addressing the following questions:

1. What needs were addressed, how pervasive and important were they, and to what extent were the project's objectives reflective of assessed needs (addressed by context information)?
2. What procedural and budgeting plan was adopted to address the needs, what alternatives were considered, why was it chosen over them, and to what extent was it a reasonable, potentially successful, and cost effective response to the assessed needs (addressed by input information)?
3. To what extent was the project plan implemented, and how and for what reasons did it have to be modified (addressed by process information).
4. What results — positive and negative as well as intended and unintended — were observed, how did the various stakeholders judge the worth and merit of the outcomes, and to what extent were the needs of the target population met (product information)?

CIPP as a Strategy for Improving Systems

Compared to the Stake and Scriven orientations, CIPP evaluation is geared more to a system view of education. It is concentrated not so much on guiding the conduct

Table 7–1. The Relevance of Four Evaluation Types to Decision Making and Accountability

	Evaluation Types			
	Context	*Input*	*Process*	*Product*
Decisionmaking (formative orientation)	Guidance for choice of objectives and assignment of priorities	Guidance for choice of program strategy Input for specification of procedural design	Guidance for implementation	Guidance for termination, continuation, modification, or installation
Accountability (summative orientation)	Record of objectives and bases for their choice along with a record of needs, opportunities, and problems	Record of chosen strategy and design and reasons for their choice over other alternatives	Record of the actual process	Record of attainments and recycling decisions

of an individual study but on providing ongoing evaluation services to the decisionmakers in an institution. This orientation towards helping to maintain and improve the quality of institutional operations is illustrated in the flow model that appears in figure 7–1.

Starting in the upper left-hand corner, figure 7–1 indicates that the operations of a school, or some other institution, include various and perhaps uncoordinated evaluation efforts; but that, periodically, the institution needs to undergo a special context evaluation. Such an evaluation would examine the needs of the institution's clients; expose opportunities such as funding programs, advanced educational technologies, or industries with a willingness and capacity to aid the institution; collect and examine perceptions about problems in the institution that warrant change; and assess the efficacy of institutional goals and priorities. Such a context evaluation might be motivated from inside the institution as a regular "state of the institution" assessment or as a response to indications from some sector of dissatisfaction about the institution's performance. A context evaluation might also be motivated from outside the institution, as when an accrediting agency requires a self-study or a funding agency requires a "needs assessment" as a basis for justifying a funding request. Such studies may be targeted on specified areas of concern or focused more generally on a wide range of institutional functions. In general, such studies aid in system renewal and promotion of better

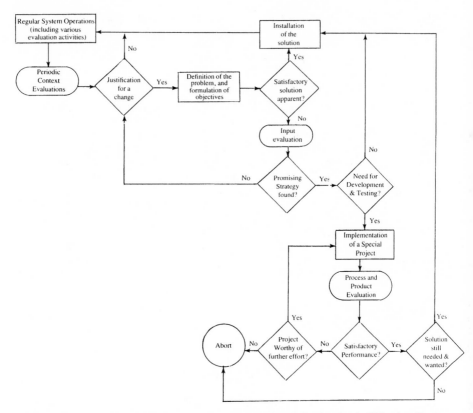

Figure 7–1.   A Flowchart Depicting the Role of CIPP Evaluation in Effecting System Improvement.

and more efficient service, in diagnosis of particular problems and targeting of improvement efforts, and in communication about the institution's strengths and weaknesses with its constituency.

The results of the context evaluation, ideally, would lead to a decision about whether to introduce some kind of a change in the system. If decided in the negative, then the institution's staff would continue with their program operations as usual. However, if a decision to change the institution in some way were made, then the program staff would clarify the problem(s) to be solved and formulate their objectives. Next, they would consider whether some appropriate solution strategy is apparent and readily adaptable to their situation. It so, they would install it and redirect their attentions to using it and evaluating it in the ongoing program of the institution.

If no satisfactory solution were apparent, then the staff, according to the flow model, would conduct an input evaluation. Such an evaluation would search the relevant literature, query personnel in other institutions that may have dealt successfully with a similar problem, draw on the ingenuity and creativity of the institution's staff and constituent groups, and possibly involve outside experts. Subsequently, one or more teams would be assigned to write up one or more proposed solution strategies. The resulting proposal(s) would then be assessed against such criteria as responsiveness to the defined needs, problems, and objectives; theoretical soundness; and feasibility.

The results of the input evaluation would be used to decide whether a sufficiently promising solution strategy had been found to warrant going ahead with its further development. If not, the staff would reconsider whether the desired change is sufficiently important to warrant further search, and, if so, would recycle through the search for a solution strategy. If a promising strategy had been found, then the staff would decide whether or not the strategy could justifiably be installed without further testing. If much were known about the strategy and there was little concern about being able to install it, the staff would be likely to turn their attention directly to incorporating the change into their regular ongoing activities.

However, if they decided to test it further, they would direct their attention to a field test of the strategy, and they would subject it to process and product evaluation over whatever time period would be required to shakedown and debug the procedure and reach the desired level of performance and readiness for installation. At some point, however, if the project has not performed satisfactorily or is viewed as too costly, the leadership of the institution might conclude that no further effort is warranted and, in accordance with this conclusion, decide to abort the effort. Such decisions frequently have been made at the conclusions of federally supported projects, when the grantee had to decide whether or not to allocate local funds for the institutionalization of a project. As shown in the bottom right hand corner of figure 7–1, even if a project had succeeded the institution's leadership might determine that conditions in the institution had changed sufficiently that the previously desired change was no longer needed, and, accordingly, they would terminate the effort. Under the assumption that the project was a success and the solution it afforded was still needed and wanted, the institution would install the proven project and return to regular operations, including regularized evaluation of the ongoing program.

The preceding analysis of evaluation in the context of an institution's change process points up a number of important features of a systems approach to evaluation.

1. Evaluation is an integral part of an institution's regular program and not merely a specialized activity involved in innovative projects, and the implementation of CIPP or any other specialized approach is only a part of the total mosaic of informal and formal evaluation that goes on in the institution.
2. Evaluations have a vital role in stimulating and planning changes.

3. The employment of each type of evaluation in the CIPP model is indicated only if information beyond what already exists is needed, not by the inherent value in doing each kind of evaluation. In other words, context, input, process, and product evaluations are only a part of a larger milieu of evaluation that goes on in any institution, and the most important function of those commissioned studies is in serving the institution's marginal needs for evaluative information.

4. The development of new programs should include the provision for their ongoing employment and use of evaluation once they have been installed, through something akin to curriculum-embedded evaluation (wherein evaluation is built in to the implementation of a curriculum and, as a matter of course, yields feedback of use in diagnosing, prescribing, and checking progress).

5. Evaluation information not only provides guidance for institutional problem solving, but, if recorded and made available for public review, it also provides a basis for judging whether decisions either to abort or institutionalize a special project were made on defensible grounds.

6. While the CIPP Model makes no special provision for formulating and testing hypotheses, it does, through its provision for context, input, and process information, provide a rich array of background data against which to interpret and understand outcomes.

An Overview of the CIPP Categories

In addition to viewing the CIPP approach in an institutional or system context, it is instructive to examine each type of study more closely. The matrix in table 7–2 is presented as a convenient overview of the essential meanings of context, input, process, and product evaluation. These four types of studies are defined in relation to their objectives, methods, and uses.

Context Evaluation

The primary orientation of a context evaluation is to identify the strengths and weaknesses of some object, such as an institution, a program, a target population, or a person, and to provide direction for improvement. The main objectives of this type of study are to assess the object's overall status, to identify its deficiencies, to inventory the strengths at hand that could be used to remedy the deficiencies, and to diagnose problems whose solution would improve the object's well-being. A context evaluation also is aimed at examining whether existing goals and priorities are attuned to the needs of whoever is being served. Whatever the focal object, the results of a context evaluation should provide a sound basis for adjusting its existing goals and priorities and targeting needed changes.

Table 7-2. Four Types of Evaluation

	Context Evaluation	Input Evaluation	Process Evaluation	Product Evaluation
Objective	To define the institutional context, to identify the target population & assess their needs, to identify opportunities for addressing the needs, to diagnose *problems* underlying the *needs*, & to judge whether proposed objectives are sufficiently responsive to the assessed needs.	To identify & assess *system capabilities*, alternative program *strategies*, procedural *designs* for implementing the strategies, budgets, & schedules.	To identify or predict, in process, *defects* in the procedural design or its implementation, to provide information for the pre-programed decisions, and to record & judge procedural events & activities.	To collect descriptions & judgments of outcomes & to relate them to objectives & to context, input, & process information; & to interpret their worth & merit.
Method	By using such methods as system analysis, survey, document review, hearings, interviews, diagnostic tests, & the Delphi technique.	By inventorying & analyzing available human & material resources, solution strategies, & procedural designs for relevance, feasibility & economy; and by using such methods as literature search, visits to exemplary programs, advocate teams, & pilot trials.	By monitoring the activity's potential procedural barriers & remaining alert to unanticipated ones, by obtaining specified information for programed decisions, by describing the actual process, & by continually interacting with & observing the activities of project staff.	By defining operationally & measuring outcome criteria, by collecting judgments of outcomes from stakeholders, & by performing both qualitative & quantitative analyses.
Relation to Decision-making in the Change Process	For deciding upon the *setting* to be served, the *goals* associated with meeting needs or using opportunities, & the *objectives* associated with solving problems, i.e., for *planning* needed changes; and for providing a basis for judging outcomes.	For selecting *sources of support*, solution *strategies*, & procedural *designs*, i.e., for *structuring* change activities; and to provide a basis for judging implementation.	For *implementing and refining the program design and procedure*, i.e., for effecting *process control*; & to provide a log of the actual process for later use in interpreting outcomes.	For deciding to *continue, terminate, modify, or refocus a* change activity, & present a clear record of effects (intended & unintended, positive & negative).

The methodology of a context evaluation may involve a variety of measurements of the object of interest and various types of analysis. A usual starting point is to interview the clients for the study in order to obtain their perceptions of strengths, weaknesses, and problems. Hearings and further interviews may be conducted to generate additional hypotheses about what changes are needed. These hypotheses may be used to construct a survey instrument, and it may be administered both to a carefully defined sample of stakeholders and made available more generally to anyone who wishes to provide input, with the analyses of the two sets of responses kept separate. Existing records should also be examined to identify performance patterns and background information; special diagnostic tests might be administered; an expert review panel might be engaged to visit and closely observe a program; a consensus-building technique, such as Delphi, might be used to secure agreements about priority needs; and a workshop might be conducted to help the clients to study and apply the findings.

A context evaluation may have a number of constructive uses. It may provide a means by which a school district communicates with its public to gain a shared conception of the district's strengths and weaknesses, needs and opportunities, and priority problems. It may be used to convince a funding agency that a proposed project is directed at an area of urgent need or to convince an electorate of the need to pass a tax issue. It might be used to formulate objectives for staff development and/or curriculum revision. It could be used to select particular schools for priority assistance. Of course, it would often be used to help students and their parents to focus their attention on developmental areas where more progress is needed. Also, it could be used to help decide how to cut programs, hopefully to help the institution get stronger while getting smaller. These are but a few examples of how a context evaluation could assist individuals and groups to set priorities for improvement efforts. Another use comes later, when there is a need to assess what has been accomplished through an improvement project. One basis for judging outcomes is by assessing whether they are adequately responsive to the needs that were identified through the context evaluation. Finally, context evaluation records are an excellent means by which to defend the efficacy of one's goals and priorities.

Input Evaluation

The main orientation of an input evaluation is to help prescribe a program by which to bring about needed changes. This type of study should identify and rate relevant approaches (including any that are already in operation) and assist in explicating and "shaking down" the one that is chosen for installation or continuation. It should also search the client's environment for barriers, constraints, and potentially available resources that need to be taken into account in the process of activating the program. The overall intent of an input evaluation is to help the clients consider alternatives in the context of their needs and environmental circumstances and to evolve a plan that will work for them; another important function is to help clients avoid the wasteful practice of pursuing proposed innovations that predictably would fail or at least waste resources.

The methods involved may be described in a series of stages, although there is no set sequence of steps for conducting an input evaluation. One might begin by reviewing (via literature search and visits to exemplary programs) the state of practice with respect to meeting the specified needs. This information could be used to judge whether potentially acceptable solution strategies exist. In turn, any promising approaches could be rated for potential effectiveness and feasibility; then the client could be advised about whether to seek a novel solution. If so, the client and evaluators might next structure a request for proposal, obtain competing proposals, and rate them for potential effectiveness and feasibility. Subsequently, the evaluators might analyze the potentially acceptable proposals and suggest how their best features could be combined. In addition, a site visit might be conducted to obtain a realistic appraisal of resources and barriers that, in some way, need to be dealt with in the process of installing the solution.

The *advocacy team technique* is a relatively new procedure for conducting input evaluation that deserves special mention. This technique is especially applicable in situations where appropriate effective means to meet specified needs are not available. Two or more teams of experts are convened; they are given the objectives for which a program is needed, provided specifications for designing a program proposal, and oriented to the criteria by which the competing response will be judged. The advocacy team reports are rated by a panel of experts and/or pilot-tested in accordance with the pre-established criteria. Subsequent steps involve members of the user system in operationalizing the winning strategy or combining and operationalizing the best features of the *two* or more competing strategies. Advantages of the advocacy team technique are that it provides:

1. An explicit procedure for generating and assessing competing program strategies;
2. An explicit accountability record of why a particular solution strategy was selected;
3. A forum that exploits bias and competition in a constructive search for alternatives; and
4. A means of involving personnel from the adopting system, either as advocacy team members or as members of the team that performs the convergence and operationalization activities following the ranking of the competing strategies.

Additional information, including a technical manual and the results of five field tests of the technique, is available in a doctoral dissertation by Diane Reinhard (1972).

Input evaluations have a number of applications. A chief application is in preparing a proposal for submission to a funding agency or an institution's policy board. Another is to assess one's existing program — whether or not it seems to be working — against what is being done elsewhere and proposed in the literature.

Input evaluation has also been used in the Dallas Independent School District as a device for screening out locally generated proposals for innovation whose projected costs could be shown to exceed the projected benefits. Another use is to provide a structure and forum by which historically antagonistic groups can reach agreement on some course of action. In addition, the records from an input evaluation study help those in authority to be accountable for their choice of one course of action above other possibilities.

Process Evaluation

In essence, a process evaluation is an ongoing check on the implementation of a plan. One objective is to provide feedback to managers and staff about the extent to which the program activities are on schedule, are being carried out as planned, and are using the available resources in an efficient manner. Another objective is to provide guidance for modifying or explicating the plan as needed, since not all aspects of a plan can be determined in advance and since some of the initial decisions may later prove to be flawed. Still another objective is to assess periodically the extent to which program participants accept and are able to carry out their roles. Finally, a process evaluation should provide an extensive record of the program that was actually implemented and how it compared to what was intended, and a full account of the various costs incurred in carrying it out and how observers and participants judged the quality of the effort overall.

The lynch-pin of a sound process evaluation is the process evaluator. More often than not, a program staff's failure to obtain guidance for implementation and to document their activities is due to a failure to assign anyone to do this work. Erroneously, it is too often assumed that the managers and staff can and will do an adequate job of process evaluation as a normal part of their assignments. While some review and documentation can be done through routine activities, such as staff meetings, these are not a sufficient means of meeting the requirements of a sound process evaluation. In my experience, these requirements can be met well only by assigning one or more persons to provide ongoing review, feedback, and documentation.

There is much work for a process evaluator to do in a program. The following scenerio is provided as an illustration of what might be done. Initially, the process evaluator could review the program plan and any prior evaluation on which it is based to identify important aspects of the program that should be monitored. Some examples that might be identified are staff development sessions, development and implementation of materials centers, counseling of students, liaison with parents, tutoring services, staff planning sessions, skill grouping of students, classroom instruction, field trips, homework assignments, and use of diagnostic tests. As another means of identifying what should be looked at, the evaluator might form an advisory group, broadly representative of program participants, and periodically ask them to identify concerns and questions that should be addressed. Other questions of relevance will occur to the evaluator as he observes program activities.

With questions and concerns such as those mentioned above in mind, the process evaluator could develop a general schedule of data collection activities and begin carrying them out. Initially, these activities probably should be as unobtrusive as possible in order not to threaten program staff or get in their way. Subsequently, as rapport is developed, the process evaluator can use a more structured approach. At the outset, the process evaluator might try to get an overview of how the program is operating by visiting and observing centers of activity, reviewing program documents, attending staff meetings, and interviewing key participants. He then could prepare a brief report that summarizes his data collection plan, reviews what he has learned, and points up what he sees as key issues. He could then present this report at a staff meeting and invite the staff director to lead a discussion of it and to use it for program revision as he and his staff see fit. Later in the meeting, he could review with the staff his plans for further data collection and a subsequent report. He could ask for their reactions about what feedback would be most useful at a subsequent meeting, and solicit their suggestions about how best to obtain certain items of information, e.g., observations, staff-kept diaries, interviews, or questionnaires. On the basis of feedback from the staff, the evaluator would schedule future feedback sessions, modify the data collection plan as appropriate, and proceed accordingly. He should continually demonstrate that the main purpose of process evaluation is to assist the staff in carrying out their program, through a kind of quality assurance process. Throughout this interactive process, the evaluator periodically should prepare and file reports on his perception of the extent that the program plan has been implemented. He should describe main deviations from the plan and should make special note of variation within the program concerning how different persons and subgroups are carrying out the plan. He should also characterize the ongoing planning activity and trace the evolution of the basic plan on which the program is based.

The main use of process evaluation is to obtain feedback that can aid staff to carry out a program as it was planned, or, if the plan is found to be seriously flawed, to modify it as needed. Some managers see regularly scheduled process evaluation feedback sessions as a means of keeping staff on their toes and abreast of their responsibilities. Process evaluation records are also useful for accountability, since funding agencies, policy boards, and constituents typically want to know whether grantees did what they had proposed. Process evaluations can also help external audiences learn what was done in the program in case they want to conduct a similar one. Further, a process evaluation is a vital source of information for interpreting product evaluation results; since, in considering why program outcomes turned out as they did, one would want to know what was actually done in carrying out the program; in this respect, process evaluation, in addition to promoting improvement and supporting accountability, also fosters understanding of phenomena under study.

Product Evaluation

The purpose of a product evaluation is to measure, interpret, and judge the attainments of a program. Feedback about what is being achieved is important both during a program cycle and at its conclusion. Also, product evaluation often should be extended to assess long-term effects. The main objective of a product evaluation is to ascertain the extent to which the program has met the needs of the group it is intended to serve. In addition, a product evaluation should look broadly at the effects of the program, including intended and unintended effects and positive and negative outcomes. A product evaluation should gather and analyze judgments of the program's success from a broad range of people associated with the program. Sometimes it should compare the outcomes of the program under study with those of alternative programs. Frequently the client wants to know how the attainments compare to previously stated objectives and the extent the outcomes are worth more than the cost of attaining them. Also, it is usually quite important to offer interpretations of the extent that failure to achieve objectives or meet needs was correlated with a failure to implement the program plan. Finally, a product evaluation usually should view outcomes from several vantage points: in the aggregate, by subgroupings of program recipients who might be differentiated by needs and services received, and sometimes by individuals. An outcome associated with an individual may be classified as a success or failure depending on whether it has satisfied a diagnosed need of the individual; such product evaluation at the level of individuals also allows aggregation across individuals to get an overall index of the extent to which the program has succeeded in meeting the collective and differential needs of individuals.

There is no set algorithm for conducting a product evaluation, but there are many applicable methods. The following scenerio is intended to illustrate the range of techniques that might be employed. In general, a combination of techniques should be used to obtain a comprehensive view of effects and to provide crosschecks on the various findings.

The product evaluators might begin by assessing performance in relation to previously diagnosed needs. Such assessments might be made based on test performance compared to a profile of previously assessed needs, pretest performance, selected norms, specified performance standards, or the performance of a comparison group. The tests used might be published objective tests, specially made criterion-referenced tests, or applied performance tests (see Sanders and Sachse 1977). Performance assessments might also be based on ratings of performance by observers, employers, and/or the program recipients themselves. And experts might assess work products and compare them to previously developed needs profiles for the program recipients who produced them.

In order to assess performance beyond that related to intended outcomes, evaluators need to make an extensive search for unanticipated outcomes, both positive and negative. They might conduct hearings or group interviews to generate hypotheses about the full range of outcomes and follow these up with clinical investigations intended to confirm or disconfirm the hypotheses. They might conduct case studies of the experiences of a carefully selected sample of participants in order to obtain an in-depth view of the effects of the program. They might survey, via telephone or mail, a sample of participants to obtain their judgments of the project and their views of both positive and negative findings. They might ask the participants to submit concrete examples, e.g., pieces they have written, of how the project has influenced their work. They might engage observers to view the performance of program and comparison groups in regular settings and to develop and validate tests that distinguish between their performance, thus giving a view of the unique contributions of the program, pro and con (see Brickell, 1976). They might search out and examine program outcomes in relation to a comprehensive checklist of outcomes that have been observed for similar programs. As a final example, they might conduct a jury trial by which to introduce and examine all available evidence that reflects on the success or failure of the programs (see Wolf, 1974).

Reporting of product evaluation findings may occur at different stages. Interim reports may be submitted during each program cycle to indicate the extent the targeted needs are being addressed and met. End-of-cycle reports may sum up the results achieved and interpret them in the light of the preassessed needs, costs incurred, and the extent the plan was carried out. Follow-up reports may also be submitted to indicate what if any long term impacts can be found. In such reports, the results might be analyzed in the aggregate, for subgroups, and for individuals.

The basic use of a product evaluation is to determine whether a given program is worth continuing, repeating, and/or extending into other settings. It also should provide direction for modifying the program so that it better serves the needs of all members of the target audience and so that it will become more cost effective. Product evaluations have psychological implications, since by showing signs of growth and/or superiority to competing efforts they reinforce the efforts of both staff and program recipients; likewise, they may dampen enthusiasm when the results are poor. Product evaluation information is an essential component of an accountability report; and, when there is evidence of significant achievement, it can aid in securing additional financial and political support from the community and funding agencies. When this information reveals no important gains that are warranted by the associated costs, product evaluation can help avoid continued wasteful investments in the program. Moreover, a record of the results obtained, especially in consideration of the program approach used and the costs involved, can assist other developers to decide on the wisdom of pursuing a similar course of action.

The preceding discussion indicates that context, input, process, and product evaluation serve unique functions, but that they are also synergistic. It further shows that a variety of methods are applicable to each type of evaluation, but it doesn't deal with the evaluator's practical problem in deciding which methods to employ in a particular study. This problem is treated in the next and final section of this article.

Designing Evaluations

To guide the implementation of an evaluation — whether context, input, process, or product evaluation (or some combination) — the evaluator obviously needs to design the work to be done. This involves preparing the preliminary plans and subsequently modifying and explicating them as the study procedes. These plans must deal with a wide range of choices pertaining to the conduct of the evaluation, e.g., the key audiences and questions; the object to be assessed; whether a context input, process, and/or product evaluation is indicated; the timing and location of the study; the extent and nature of controls to be imposed; the contrasts to be made; the sources of needed information; the methods, instruments, and schedule for data collection; the formats and procedures for labeling, storing, and retrieving information; the methods of analysis and interpretation; provisions for communicating findings; and criteria and arrangements for assessing the evaluation results. Decisions about such evaluation activities form the basis for contracting and financing the evaluation work, working out protocol with the involved institutions, staffing the study, and scheduling and guiding staff activities.

We might wish that evaluators could finalize design decisions at the outset and then follow them precisely. However, the dynamic and interactive qualities of many evaluations, plus their service orientation, make difficult, if not impossible, the accurate long-range projection of specific information needs. Consequently, technical plans for data collection and analysis, made prior to the start of a study, often are based on erroneous assumptions and later found to be inappropriate or incomplete. Rigid adherence to the original evaluation design — especially if it had been defined in specific terms — often would detract greatly from the utility of the study by directing it to the wrong questions, using erroneous assumptions to guide it, and/or convincing members of the audience that the evaluator has an ivory tower orientation.

Hence, evaluators are faced with a dilemma. On the one hand, they need to carefully plan their evaluation activities so they can carry them out efficiently and with an acceptable amount of rigor and convince their clients that they know what they are doing. One the other hand, they need to approach the design of evaluation studies flexibly and provide for periodically reviewing and otherwise modifying the design so that the evaluation remains responsive to the needs of the audiences. This dilemma is especially troublesome to evaluators, since clients often expect or demand up-front technical designs and later become disenchanted when rigid adherence to the original design yields much information that is no longer perceived as useful. The client often perceives that somehow the evaluator should have been smarter in projecting information needs and more skilled in planning the data collection activities.

To address this dilemma evaluators must view design as a process, not a product, and they need to get their clients to do likewise. Evaluation goals and procedures should be sketched in advance, but they should be periodically reviewed, revised, expanded, and operationalized. Fundamentally, this process should be guided by a defensible view of what constitutes sound evaluation, by a sensitivity to factors in the real world that often interfere with evaluation work, and by ongoing communication between the evaluators and their audiences about the pertinence and adequacy of the design.

At the outset of the process, I believe it is important to listen and probe. Who are the primary clients? What do they want from the evaluation? Why? What type(s) of evaluation (context, input, process, product) would be most responsive? How do the clients think the evaluation should be conducted? What timeline do they have in mind? Who do they see as the main audience? Who might get hurt as a consequence of the evaluation? Why? Whose cooperation will be essential? What information already exists? What's the relevant history? Realistically, what positive benefits from the evaluation could be expected? What deleterious effects are real possibilities? How could they be avoided? What qualifications are required to do the job? etc. Whenever there is a choice, an evaluator should pursue questions like these before agreeing that an evaluation should be done or that he's the right person to do it.

Assuming a positive decision to go ahead, the evaluator should sketch an overall plan. This plan should take into account what the evaluator has learned about the setting and particular needs for the evaluation, and it should conform to generally accepted standards of sound evaluation. In addition, it should speak, at least in a general way, to the full range of tasks to be done.

Table 7–3 provides a general outline of the points to be addressed in an evaluation design. These points are applicable when developing the initial design or later, when revising or explicating it. Of course, they serve only as general indications of the detailed information that eventually must be provided to flesh out and operationalize the design.

The formulation of the design requires that the client and evaluators collaborate, from the outset, when they must agree on a charge. The client needs to identify the object, e.g., the program to be evaluated, and the evaluator can help by guiding the client to define clear and realistic boundaries around what will be looked at. The client is a prime source for identifying the various groups with potential interest in the study, but the evaluator also needs to touch base with the potential audiences and think about the evaluation within the relevant social context in order to identify

Table 7–3.   Outline for Documenting Evaluation Designs

Review of the Charge

Definition of the object of the evaluation
Identification of the client and audiences
Purpose(s) of the evaluation
Type of evaluation (e.g., context, input, process, or product) to be employed
Principles of sound evaluation (i.e., standards) to be observed

---

Plan for Obtaining Information

The general strategy
Working assumptions to guide measurement, analysis, and interpretation
Collection of information (i.e., sampling, instrumentation, and data collection)
Organization of information (i.e., coding, filing, and retrieving)
Analysis of information (both qualitative and quantitative)
Interpretation of findings

Plan for Reporting the Results

Preparation of reports
Dissemination of reports
Provision for follow-up activities to promote impact of the evaluation

---

Plan for Administering the Study

Summarization of the evaluation schedule
Plan for meeting staff and resource requirements
Provision for meta evaluation
Provision for periodic updating of the evaluation design
Budget
Memorandum of agreement or contract

---

the full range of legitimate audiences. The client and other audiences need to identify the purpose of the study, i.e.,. indicate what information they need and how they plan to use it, and the evaluator needs to pursue clarifying questions in order to sort out different (perhaps conflicting) purposes and to get the client to assign priorities. The evaluator needs to indicate what general type(s) of study, e.g., context, input, process, and/or product, seems needed; and the client should confirm this general choice or help to modify it. In rounding out the charge, the evaluator needs to make clear that the evaluation will be conditioned to meet a certain set of standards (see the chapters on standards and theses for sound evaluation that appear in the final part of this book), and the client should be asked to help select and assign priorities to the applicable standards.

Basically, the plan for obtaining information should be worked out by the evaluator, but it should be subjected to careful review by the client and modified accordingly. The evaluator should provide an overview of the general strategy to be employed — survey, case study, site visitation, advocacy teams, goal-free search for effects, adversary hearings, or field experiment — and technical plans for collecting, organizing, and analyzing the needed information. While the client should at least react to the technical plans, they should exert a major influence in deciding how the findings will be interpreted, e.g., against objectives, against the results of prior needs assessments, based on the evaluator's professional judgment, or through some type of formal group process. The evaluator and client should anticipate that the plan for obtaining information will likely change and expand during the course of the evaluation, as new audiences are identified and information requirements change.

The part of the evaluation design devoted to reporting results should be geared to promote utilization. The client and audience should be involved in projecting the contents and timing of needed reports. They should also assist in planning how the results will be disseminated, i.e., formatted, displayed, delivered, reviewed, revised, and documented for later use. Moreover, the client and evaluator should seriously consider whether the evaluator might play an important role — beyond the delivery of the final report — in helping the client and audience to apply the findings to their work. Overall, the plan for reporting should be directed to promote impact through whatever means seem appropriate, e.g., oral reports and hearings, multiple reports targeted to specified audiences, press releases, socio-dramas to portray and explore the findings, and workshops aimed at applying the findings.

The final part of the design, the plan for administering the study, is oriented towards operationalizing the conceptual and technical plans. The evaluator needs to identify and schedule the evaluation tasks consistent with the client's needs and in consideration of the relevant practical constraints. Staff who will carry out the evaluation work and special resources, such as office space and data processing facilities, need to be identified; and the client needs to assure that the proposed personnel have the necessary level of credibility as viewed by the audiences. The evaluator and client need to agree on how the evaluation plans, processes, and reports will be assessed against the agreed-upon standards. They also should agree on a mechanism by which to periodically review, update, and document the evolving evaluation design; they need to lay out a realistic budget; and, in my view, they should summarize and formalize their general agreements about the form and function of the evaluation in a memorandum of agreement or a contract.

The foregoing discussion of table 7–3 has been necessarily general, but it indicates that designing an evaluation is a complex and ongoing task. It highlights the need for continued collaboration between evaluator and client and emphasizes the need to evolve the evaluation design consistent with client and audience needs. Nevertheless, it emphasizes the need to maintain professional integrity in the evaluation work. One of the most useful references for helping to flesh out an evaluation design and ensure that it adheres to widely shared principles of sound evaluation is the *Standards for Evaluations of Educational Programs, Projects, and Materials* (Joint Committee, 1981) (see chapter 23).

Conclusion

Michael Scriven once said that "evaluation is nervous making," and it is. I have often been reminded of the biblical warning to "Judge not, lest ye be judged."

But evaluation is also a necessary concomitant of improvement. We cannot make our programs better unless we know where they are weak and strong and unless we become aware of better means. We cannot be sure that our goals are worthy unless we can match them to the needs of the people they are intended to serve. We cannot plan effectively if we are unaware of options and their relative merits; and we cannot convince our constituents that we have done good work and deserve continued support unless we can show them evidence that we have done what we promised and produced beneficial results. For these and other reasons, public servants must subject their work to competent evaluation, which must help them sort out the good from the bad and point the way to needed improvements.

This paper has stressed the improvement function of evaluation. It has updated the CIPP model, shown how it was developed, contrasted it to other approaches, shown how it can be used to guide improvement efforts and serve accountability needs, and explained its main concepts. It has provided general guidelines for designing evaluation studies. Moreover, by referencing the *Standards for Evaluation of Educational Programs, Projects, and Materials,* it has placed the CIPP model within what appears to be an emerging consensus about what constitutes good and beneficial evaluation.

Notes

1.   CIPP is an acronym that includes the first letters of labels for four kinds of evaluation. The *C* stands for *context evaluation,* which is a kind of needs assessment. The *I* represents *input evaluation,* which is a means of identifying and assessing competing plans. The first *P* denotes *process evaluation,* which assesses and guides the implementation of plans. And the second *P* refers to *product evaluation,* which involves assessing outcomes.

2.   This is a small, informal group of about fifty specialists in educational evaluation. It was organized by Bob Stake and others in the late 1960s for the purpose of ongoing discussion of the problems in educational evaluation. It has continued to meet at least annually.

References

Adams, James A. "A Study of the Status, Scope, and Nature of Educational Evaluation in Michigan's Public K–12 School Districts." Unpublished doctoral dissertation, Ohio State University, 1971.

Brickell, Henry M. *Needed: Instruments as Good as Our Eyes*. Occasional Paper Series, no. 7. Kalamazoo, Michigan: Western Michigan University Evaluation Center, July 1976.

Cronbach, Lee J. and Associates. *Toward Reform of Program Evaluation*. San Francisco: Jossey-Bass Publishers, 1980.

Findlay, Donald. "Working Paper for Planning an Evaluation System." Unpublished, The Center for Vocational and Technical Education, Ohio State University, 1979.

Guba, Egon G. "The Failure of Educational Evaluation" *Educational Technology*, 9 (1969) 29–38.

Nevo, David. "Evaluation Priorities of Students, Teachers, and Principals." Unpublished doctoral dissertation, Ohio State University, 1974.

Patton, Michael Quinn. *Utilization-Focused Evaluation*. Beverly Hills: Sage Publications, 1978.

Reinhard, Diane L. "Methodology Development for Input Evaluation Using Advocate and Design Teams." Unpublished doctoral dissertation, Ohio State University, 1972.

Root, Darrell. "The Evaluation Training Needs of Superintendents of Schools." Doctoral dissertation, Ohio State University, 1971.

Sanders, James R. and Sachse, T.P. "Applied Performance Testing in the Classroom." *Journal of Research and Development in Education,* 10 (Spring 1977) 92–104.

Scriven, Michael. "The Methodology of Evaluation." no. 110, Layfayette, Indiana: the Social Science Education Consortium, Purdue University, 1966.

Scriven, Michael. "Critique of the PDK Book, *Educational Evaluation and Decision Making.*" Presentation at the annual meeting of the American Educational Research Association, New York City, 1970.

Stake, Robert. "The Countenance of Educational Evaluation." *Teachers College Record,* no. 7, 68 (April 1967).

Stufflebeam, Daniel L. "Evaluation as Enlightenment for Decision Making." In Walcott, A. Beaty (ed.) *Improving Educational Assessment and an Inventory of Measures of Affective Behavior*. Washington, D.C.: Assoc. for Supervision and Curriculum Development, 1969.

Stuffiebeam, Daniel L. "The Relevance of the CIPP Evaluation Model for Educational Accountability." *Journal of Research and Development in Education,* (Fall 1971).

Tyler, R.W. "General Statement on Evaluation." *Journal of Educational Research,* 35 (1942), 492–501.

Webster, W.J. "The Organization and Functions of Research and Evaluation in Large Urban School Districts." Paper presented at the annual meeting of the American Educational Research Association, Washington, D.C., March 1975.

Wolf, R.L. "The Application of Select Legal Concepts to Educational Evaluation." Unpublished doctoral dissertation, University of Illinois, 1974.

8 THE EVALUATION OF BROAD-AIM PROGRAMS:
Experimental Design, Its Difficulties, and an Alternative
Robert S. Weiss and Martin Rein

There is an approach to the evaluation of social action programs which seems so sensible that it has been accepted without question. The underlying assumption is that action programs are designed to achieve specific ends and that their success can be established by demonstrating cause-effect relationships between the programs and their aims. In consequence, the preferred research design is an experimental one in which aspects of the situation to be changed are measured before and after implementation of the action program. To support the argument that the program is responsible for the observed changes, the anticipated effects may be measured simultaneously in a control situation that does not receive the program (Campbell & Stanley, 1966). This plausible approach misleads when the action programs have broad aims and take unstandardized forms.

The term *broad-aim program* is intended to describe programs that hope to achieve nonspecific forms of change-for-the-better and which also, because of their ambition and magnitude, involve unstandardized, large-scale interventions and are evaluated in only a few sites. These characteristics have been shared by a

Weiss, Robert S. and Rein, Martin. "The Evaluation of Broad-Aim Programs: Experimental Design, Its Difficulties, and an Alternative." *Administrative Science Quarterly*, no. 1, 15 (March 1970), 97–109. Copyright 1970, Administrative Science Quarterly, Ithaca, NY. Reprinted by permission of publisher.

number of social action programs launched during the 1960s — the delinquency prevention and grey area programs, portions of the poverty program, and the model cities planning program. These programs attempted to produce increased community competence, increased participation of low-income citizens in community action, and more effective utilization of existing institutions. All these aims could be realized in many alternative ways, and none of these programs could be judged by whether one particular end was achieved.

In the evaluation of broad-aim programs, experimental design creates technical and administrative problems so severe as to make the evaluation of questionable value. A more historically oriented, more qualitative evaluation has greater value. The experimental model has been criticized by Stufflebeam (1968), Suchman (1968), and Schulberg and Baker (1968). However, only Schulberg and Baker have agreed with the position taken here that the experimental model is intrinsically unsuitable to the evaluation of broad-aim programs. Even among critics of experimental designs for program evaluation, this is a minority position.

A Case in Point

The difficulties encountered in evaluation by experimental design may be illustrated by a case study. The failures and frustrations encountered in this case, we will argue, derived from the inability of experimental design to respond to critical issues in the evaluation of broad-aim programs. Certainly they cannot be attributed to incompetence or indolence among the research staff; the project directors were well-trained, committed, and hard-working, and, in addition, in the first year of the study they incorporated in their planning the advice of several men who are greatly respected as experts in social research.

Let us call the program the Neighborhood Benefit Program. Its aim was to change existing community institutions — social agencies, schools, employment services — so that they might be more useful to citizens of the community and especially to underprivileged youth. It was a broad-aim program, as we use the term: general aims, unstandardized intervention, virtually unreplicated evaluation.

Criterion Development

An evaluation study was required by the federal agency that funded the program. The agency, acting on the advice of its scientific consultants, recommended that the evaluation study be as methodologically rigorous as possible. In addition, the agency made clear that the program should be construed as primarily a test of its form of intervention in functioning systems, rather than as a remedy specific to the ills of the city in which it was being introduced. This meant that the research group should emphasize generalizable assessments of the overall worth of the program, rather than assessments which would focus on benefits that might have been unique to the program's city. The agency made no mention of the possible use of research personnel to develop information that could help the program administration make policy decisions.

At the very beginning, program administrators hoped that the research group might contribute to policy formulation through the development of relevant information. The research group, though they wanted to oblige, could not give much of their energy to such matters. The sociologists who staffed the research group were sympathetic to the aim of rigorous research and felt that the study of day-to-day problems, though possibly a service to the program, was a distraction. Someone trained in an applied field — social work or planning — or someone trained in a field-work tradition in sociology or anthropology might not have agreed, but even if it had been possible to locate such research personnel, the federal directive made rigor mandatory.

One of the first concerns of the research group was the development of evaluation criteria, and one of their first difficulties was that institutional change, the primary aim of the project, would be difficult to assess. After consideration, the study of institutional change was rejected as unfeasible. There were so many institutions — schools, playgrounds, manpower agencies, other social agencies — that quantitative study of each would have required more staff time than was available. In addition, there was reason to believe that some of the institutions would resist study by a parallel, and possibly rival, agency. It was therefore decided that the object of study should be the impact of the program on youth in the area and that changes in their attitudes or behavior which suggested better adaptation to society would be taken as indicating program success.

The next problem was the necessity of deciding which individuals living within the area had in fact exposed to the Neighborhood Benefit Program. Exposure was not easy to judge. What about the students who had dutifully sat in a school auditorium while speakers talked about the job market? What about the youth who came to a playground once and left without doing more than lean against a swing? And what about those youths who showed up for nothing, but whose fathers had found jobs through the program? Clearly a distinction between possible exposure and active participation, however difficult each might be to specify, was likely to be useful. The research group developed forms to be filled out by playground supervisors and manpower specialists.

A related problem was that of evaluating the relative effects of the large number of activities sponsored by the program. If the same children were exposed to school enrichment and playground enrichment, how does one decide which results to associate with which activity? One proposal the research group made was that different change attempts should be introduced into different districts of the area — a change in the schools in one district, a change in playgrounds in another, and so on. The program administrators, concerned with cajoling, persuading, bribing, or intimidating other institutions into enlarging their programs, and absorbed by the task of making even limited headway against institutional inertia, found the idea charming and unrealistic. The research group was asked to evaluate the net impact on exposed youths, irrespective of what they participated in, or even whether they participated in anything.

The government agency sponsoring the program may have been pleased by the decision to evaluate net impact, since the official view was that the Neighborhood Benefit Program was a unitary program, though a multifaceted one. The research group, as is noted above, nevertheless arranged for participation records so that individuals who had been active in one or another activity could later be identified. They recognized that problems of self-selection, small numbers, and difficulties in defining participation would hamper utilization of this information, but it later turned out that there were other problems as well: the records were often poorly kept and this, plus variations in the ways names were recorded, made it difficult to match participation records with questionnaire forms.

Research Activities during the Program

The study design which finally emerged anticipated the collection of questionnaire data from 1500 young people in the area and from 500 young people in a similar area in a neighboring city. This represented a 25 percent sample of eligible youths in the two cities.

Fully 90 percent of the sampled youths were located and interviewed, a remarkable response rate considering that many of the young people were not in school and not regularly at home. A great deal of information about each respondent was collected through an extensive questionnaire, a personal interview, and information from his school. The code book contained several hundred items regarding the backgrounds, behaviors, beliefs, perceptions, attitudes, experiences, plans, and concerns of these youths.

Although the research design used the framework of a controlled experiment, data-gathering had more in common with survey research. Because there were many ways in which individual youths might display the effects of exposure, the study could not focus on specific changes which theory and hypothesis suggested might take place, as would be more usual in experiments, but instead was required to cast a wide net.

Development of the data-collection instruments and collection of base-line data absorbed the first year of the project. Since the collection of post-program data would use instruments already developed and the program would run three years, the research group had time for other work before starting to evaluate impact. During the interim, the research group analyzed the base-line data, examining the distributions of behaviors, beliefs, perceptions, and attitudes by age, sex, race, and school status. The findings were interesting, but had no greater relationship to the functioning of the Neighborhood Benefit Program than would have the findings from any other study of a low-income area.

The research group launched a few additional small studies. They hired two talented but untrained individuals to observe the street life of the area and to talk with neighborhood residents about their concerns; this field observation team produced a set of journalistic materials which suggested something of the neighborhood's style of life. The research group also compared young people who were believed by their neighbors to be the most troublesome in the area with young people who were believed to be highly promising. But the problem youths were just as difficult when filling out questionnaires as in their other contacts with authorities, and there was much doubt regarding the validity of their responses. This study, like the analysis of base-line data, addressed itself to issues unrelated to evaluation of the Neighborhood Benefit Program and was only marginally helpful in suggesting new program activities.

By the end of the second year, it had become clear to the administrators of the program that the evaluation project had little relationship to their immediate concerns. They did not know exactly what the research group was studying, but the questions seemed to be in the realm of basic research and to have little relation to the program. Some administrators found it difficult to accept that the program evaluation work of the research group could only be prepared after the program ended, and they thought the research should at least produce hints of what was wrong or right while there was still time to change.

There were other reasons for distrust of the research group among the program administrators. The research group seemed more defensive, more inclined toward mystification, and less convincing, as they repeatedly argued that analysis of base-line data was undertaken as a secondary project until the time came for collecting post-program data. Increasingly, the program administrators felt that the research group was deeply committed to analyzing the base-line data and hoped through it to make a significant contribution to their field and that their references to the comparison with post-program data were intended to fend off scrutiny of their operation. Program administrators began wondering whether there would be funds and staff for the pre-post comparison.

Moreover, the promise of evaluating program impact had attracted the administrators at the beginning of the program, when they had hopes of producing major changes in their community. After two years of frustrating experience of the difficulty in producing significant changes, they were less convinced that their successes would be adequately represented by changes in the neighborhood youth. They had initiated a few programs, had strengthened some others, and had perhaps initiated movement in some institutions; but they knew that what they had been able to do was outweighed by what they had not been able to do. Though some neighborhood residents, including some who were young, had been helped to use their leisure time profitably, or even to find a job, it was no longer possible to assume that the result had been change in the personalities or perceptions of the helped, let alone in those of other young people. The loss of optimism resulted in loss of faith in the promise of experimental evaluation. After two years of experience, the administrators would have preferred to be told which youths used their services rather than which youths showed greater attitudinal changes than their comparison group, and to be told what differences the services made in how youths looked for a job rather than their effect on feelings of citizenship. The administrators were more interested in whether they had been able to make a difference at all and if so, with whom, than in the possibly more lasting and far-reaching effects of their efforts on a total population.

A Consultant's Report

At this point it became clear that gathering the post-program data would require an extremely expensive locating process, that analyzing the data would also be extremely expensive, and that the two together would require more time and money than had been budgeted. The program administrators, uneasy about backing the research group's request for further funds, called in the first author of this paper as consultant. Chief among the issues to which the consultant attended was the likely value of findings. Would they be worth the cost?

Findings showing that youths in the program area dramatically differed from youths in the comparison city might demonstrate the desirability of the program and be worthwhile, whatever the cost. However, the differences would have to be large enough to rule out chance or minor differences between the communities as their explanation, and they would have to be so closely related to the activities of the program that they could not be ascribed to major but irrelevant differences between the communities. In addition, the differences would have to be socially significant if they were to justify the program's cost; differences only in attitudes toward the visiting nurse service would be insufficient. The program administrators believed that such differences were unlikely to be found — not because the program had failed, but because its successes had to do with improving job placement services, providing more play space, and providing child-care centers — and these interventions have little impact on the way individuals view themselves and their world.

What seemed likely was that the research would disclose small, statistically significant differences between youths in the two communities and that these differences could be explained by community differences other than the presence of the Neighborhood Benefit Program in one. A major political difference between the communities was demonstrated simply by the fact that one had acquired government funds for the Neighborhood Benefit Program and the other had not. The communities probably also differed in job markets, in school systems, in police attitudes, and in local leadership — to mention only a few possibilities.

Negative findings would not be conclusive evidence that the program had not worked. The program administrators had impressionistic evidence of success in promoting useful services and felt that the planned research was insufficiently sensitive to the ways in which new or improved services might contribute to the well-being of area residents' reports.

> Negative results might mean that the program did not change anything so far as adolescents were concerned. But negative results might also mean that changes took place that weren't measured: e.g., adolescents might have gone into different jobs as a result of the program, or different courses in school, or been launched on a career whose implications will display themselves only in the future. Negative results might also mean . . . the measuring instruments were not sensitive enough. . . . One would also get negative results if only a few activities had effects, and then only with those youths who participated at a high level; their responses would be overwhelmed by those of the youths who had not been affected. . . . Finally it might be noted . . . that the aims of the action programs have not been to change the values, attitudes, or behaviors of youths, but rather to change the situations they live in, to make life better for them, and we frankly do not know whether this results in personality change, but we might think it desirable nevertheless.

Positive findings, too, would be easy to discount. First there would be the possibility of important uncontrolled differences between the compared communities. Then, if this were dealt with by limiting analysis to the program community and comparing participants with nonparticipants, there would be difficulties having to do with self-selection. Those who had participated were a self-selected group and therefore differences between them and others might be expected irrespective of program effects. In any event, as has been noted, participation records had been so badly kept that this last analytic plan was not feasible.

Epilogue

The research group and the program administrators agreed to conduct a pilot evaluation study that might furnish enough information to make it possible to estimate the difficulties of the planned larger study and the usefulness of the data which would be gathered. However, a key member of the research group had earlier accepted another position and now left the project. The pilot study proved difficult to manage without him. The program administrators became increasingly unsympathetic and increasingly unwilling to sponsor the research group to their funding agency. The director of the research group left the project, with bad feelings all around.

Technical Difficulties with Experimental Designs

Similar accounts can be obtained from many evaluation projects. Here the evaluation team was responsible to the program administrators, and this produced tensions. Yet even when an external agency has been responsible, the experimental or near-experimental study of an unstandardized, virtually unreplicated action program has encountered problems of cost, administrative irrelevance, and difficulty of interpretation. Marris and Rein (1967) and Thernstrom (1969) have described situations where rigorous evaluation designs for broad-aim programs went astray, and Rossi (1966) has described the problems inherent in relationships between program administrators and personnel concerned with evaluation, even when research is administratively independent.

Not all of these difficulties stem from the commitment to experimental evaluation. Some have to do with discord between a research group's responsibilities for information regarding the effectiveness of a program and their professional preference for more basic studies. Some stem from over-optimistic judgments regarding the potential impact of a large-scale social program. But some of the difficulties do have their roots in the commitment to experimental evaluation, and we examine these more closely in what follows. We begin with difficulties inherent in the method and then turn to difficulties deriving from the relationship between research and administration which the method imposes.

It is difficult to select satisfactory criteria.   A narrow-aim program might be intended to increase an individual's language facility, to prepare him for a job, or to upgrade the quality of his housing. The criteria of success are evident in the statment of aims, or, said another way, the aims are nearly operational. Broad-aim programs frustrate a research person who feels he must know specifically what the program hopes to change in order that he may gather base-line data. There is temptation to force the program administrators to operationalize program aims as nonspecific as a more responsive institutional system, a richer cultural atmosphere, or increased opportunity for the poor. Freeman and Sherwood (1965, p. 17), for example, suggest that the evaluation research personnel "participate or even take a major responsibility for the development of the action framework."

The difficulty is not that the aims of the broad-aim program are unformulated — although there may be different interpretations and the interpretations may change over time — but rather that the aims may be specified in many ways. The administrators are apt not to know exactly how the desired change will manifest itself. Although they can be prevailed upon to list the changes they hope will result, they will nevertheless be opportunistic in their program management and will direct program resources to changes which appear within reach, whether or not these were included among their initial aims. The attempt to evaluate success in terms of narrowly defined criteria misrepresents the actual aims of broad-aim programs.

Is it not possible to develop operational measures of system change? The appraisals of knowledgeable observers might, for example, be one such measure. But while such measures are possible and experts' judgments have been used to appraise programs on a number of occasions, practical problems impede the use of such judgments in the evaluation of broad-aim programs and, to our knowledge, have not yet so been used. The task would be formidable: to judge whether the system has changed during the preceding two or three years.

One faulty response to the criterion problem in broad-aim programs was illustrated in the case study. Since change may evidence itself in many ways, each of these ways is a possible criterion; information regarding the multiple criteria is collected through a survey instrument administered before the introduction of the program and again after the completion of the program; and analysis takes the form of fishing for differences between the pre-program and post-program data (Selvin & Stuart, 1966). Of course, the larger the number of criteria included in the survey, the more likely that differences will be found. Whether particular significant differences result from the program or from chance can only be solved by good theory or by the utilization of data from other studies. In most situations of this sort neither seems easily available. Moreover, the variables which show differences are likely to be unduly identified as the successfully achieved goals of the program, although had the system been only a bit different it might well have taken a different path and other variables might have signaled the change.

Predetermined criteria, whether only a few or many are employed, present another problem: programs representing large inputs of resources are likely to produce unanticipated consequences whose importance may rival, if not outweigh, the intended ends. For example, a poverty program may fail to change the economic condition of the poor, yet alter the political climate. An evaluation study which ignores unanticipated consequences produces a limited assessment of the impact of a program.

The situation is essentially uncontrolled. Setting up comparison situations attempts to ensure that observed changes are not mistakenly credited to the action program when in fact exogenous factors are responsible. The idea is that every factor except the experimental intervention will also be present in the comparison situation, and, therefore, changes in the experimental situation which do not occur in the comparison situation can confidently be ascribed to the intervention. But this is a misapplication of the experimental method because it fails to recognize the numerous ways in which two communities differ — from the personalities of their mayors through the employment policies of their industries.

Of course, the situation is not totally controlled (and sometimes controlled very little) even in the best laboratory experiments, but since treatments are there randomly distributed among replications, uncontrolled factors within the replications should not produce statistically significant differences corresponding to treatments. There are many problems in the application of this idea to broad-aim programs. First, the numbers of replications are usually insufficient to provide statistically useful samples of the experimental and comparison situations. Second, the distribution of treatments to replications is never random; communities which apply for action program funds differ systematically from communities which do not apply, and the communities accepted for funding are almost always a rationally-selected subset of the applicants. Third, communities which are not chosen for a program nevertheless are likely to be affected by it, because a program's ideas diffuse throughout society.

The treatments are not standardized.   The form assumed by an action program differs from community to community, in response to the needs and tolerances of the communities. For example, in the model cities planning program, cities adopted different approaches to eliciting neighborhood participation, in part because of different degrees of organization of their neighborhoods. Because different communities experience different forms of the program, it is misleading to think that one is evaluating the program by evaluating a small number of specific realizations of the program. Some potential realizations of the program may not be feasible with any of the sample communities because, for example, of their political structures. Consequently, one important research function should be the description of the forms the program takes and of the forces shaping these forms. Experimental evaluation neglects such description entirely, being based on the assumption that what took place was what was supposed to take place.

The experimental design is limited in the information it can produce.   The possible results of an experiment can be listed in advance; the independent variable, singly or in combination, will or will not produce the hypothesized effects. The experimenter ordinarily hopes to find positive results, because these will corroborate an existing theory and suggest fruitful further developments. Negative results are not very helpful; they indicate that the theory or its operationalization is faulty, but they do not identify the flaw. The experimenter is apt to follow the trail of his positive results, discarding negative results as signs of blind alleys. He learns what was amiss in one trial of a hypothesis by developing new trials of the hypothesis.

An action program may be the only trial a social innovation will be given, and the great capacity of a community to resist change, even when the program is an ambitious one, makes negative results more likely than positive ones. Research cannot merely document that the program failed and go on to study a modification of the program; it must identify the causes of failure. In this way, the experience can become a basis for designing more effective programs.

Evaluations of broad-aim programs should identify the forces which shaped the program, the nature of the opposition encountered, the reasons for success or failure, and the program's unanticipated consequences. Then, in addition, the research might decide whether or not anticipated changes occurred. The issue in the evaluation of broad-aim programs is not "Does it work?" but "What happened?"

Administrative Difficulties with Experimental Designs

The issues raised above are technical ones concerning the appropriateness of experimental design to broad-aim programs. There are, in addition, administrative problems.

There may be conflict over program development. In the case reported above, the research group did not attempt to direct the program's development except for the suggestion that different sections of the community be exposed to different activities. But in other cases, evaluation groups have attempted to ensure that they remain stable while being evaluated, instead of constantly changing from one form to another. Any effective administrator, who is committed to his program's success, will insist on modifying the program as he learns more about his staff, his situation, and the difficulties faced by the program. If the research group objects to these changes or, finding itself helpless to prevent them, withdraws from association with the program administration, the breach betweeen administration and research widens.

The research group may be dependent on uncommitted record-keepers. If members of the target population can involve themselves in many different program activities, the research group may want to separate individuals having great involvement with particular activities from individuals having less involvement or having involvement with different activities. But to do this, the research will ordinarily be dependent on participation records kept by program personnel who are not committed to the research effort. The records are almost certain to be unreliable and, even if reliable, difficult to coordinate with other research information. In addition, reliance on operating personnel introduces an opportunity for their attitudes to bias the data.

Operationalizations may become primary goals. Once the research group and program administrators have agreed that particular operationalizations of the program aims indeed represent what the administrators hope to achieve, these operationalizations may take on an importance they would not otherwise have had. For example, if the administrators agree that their program could be evaluated in terms of the numbers of individuals helped to find full-time employment, employment may take on added importance in the minds of the administrators.

The research staff may not know what is going on. A commitment to an experimental model is apt to result in the paradoxical development of the research staff being relatively ignorant about what is happening in the field. Administrators, far from being able to call on the research group for consultation, are likely to discover that the group is totally absorbed in managing large quantities of data and has neither knowledge of the day-to-day operations nor desire to learn about them. Experimental research, though it competes in the present for money, of which it requires a great deal, provides no illumination until after the project's end.

A Role for Experimental Design

There is a role for experimental design in the evaluation of broad-aim programs. When one aim of a program, or a single objection to a program, is important enough to justify collecting data which will lead to a relatively unquestionable conclusion and when the program can be given the form of standardized replications within relatively controlled situations, experimental design is fully justified.

The exploratory program of negative taxation in New Jersey met all the criteria. Although negative taxation is intended to better the condition of the poor without special commitment to a particular form of betterment, one specific issue, the impact of negative taxation on incentive to work, has assumed special importance. Impact on incentive is, then, a single criterion variable of social importance. In addition, negative taxation is a perfectly standardizable treatment which can be repeated in enough cases to build an adequate sample of experiences. Of course, an evaluation of impact on incentive would not properly assess the overall worth of the negative income tax, since only one criterion would be examined (Watts, 1969).

In the taxation problem, experimental design provides a convincing test of the possible connection between the program and a consequence about which critics are concerned. Where convincing statements regarding relationships are needed and where the nature of the program permits, experimental design is clearly the methodology to be recommended.

An Alternative Methodology

An approach that is generally superior to experimental design for evaluating broad-aim programs is one that might be characterized as *process-oriented qualitative research, historical research,* or *case study* or comparative research. The first characterization emphasizes the type of data to be collected — although there is no need to exclude quantitative data. The second characterization emphasizes the method's concern with the development of events though time. The third emphasizes the use of a single case or small set of cases as a basis for generalization to a larger class. The aim of the approach is to develop a coherent and nearly complete description of the relevant community systems before the intervention, of the form taken by the intervention, and of the new systems which develop incorporating the intervention as a dynamic constituent.

Conceptual Frameworks

Research to tell the story of an intervention and to derive generalization from such a story must be structured by a conceptual framework. In experimental work, this conceptual framework is organized around the idea of determination, especially causal determination (Bunge, 1959). For historical descriptions, the potential frameworks include system theory, the drama-like unfolding of events, and the interaction of political forces. Such conceptual frameworks are not in the forefront of an historical study; rather, the conceptual frameworks guide attention to the events which should be recorded, to the questions which must be answered, and to the connections which should be demonstrated.

The three frameworks noted above are mutually complementary. The systems framework suggests what events or phenomena should be included within the inquiry and provides concepts for dealing with linkages among actors and institutions. The dramaturgic approach is useful for describing small-scale events and for relating individual actions to the outcomes of the events. The political framework, with its focus on coalitions and conflicts among interest groups, aids description of events which unfold over long periods of time and involve large numbers of individuals.

Systems. The general ideas of systems theory have been presented by Miller (1965a and 1965b) and in application to evaluation research by Schulberg and Baker (1968). Their usefulness in evaluation research extends from the initial conceptualization of the problem, which may be cast as change in concrete intermeshed systems, to the organization of observations and conclusions in a final report, to which systems theory can supply coherence.

In its concept of system boundaries, the systems outlook offers the research worker a guide to balancing his desire to learn about everything and his resource limitations. It suggests that the research worker focus his attention on the smallest set of interacting groups and individuals that will account for most of what happens and most of what determines what happens.

Systems should be identified in relation to issues, and different issues require different system definitions. The system studied when evaluating a model cities planning program would differ from the system studied in connection with a police department community relations program. Even in a study of the same program, different systems may become relevant to different issues.

System boundaries are easy to identify in studies of organizations, but are hard to identify in studies of communities. Indeed, openness is an important characteristic of most communities. Yet even in communities, key actors and institutions should be apparent. The systems perspective alerts the investigator to the need to identify the interrelations of actors and groups, and then to identify the program's impact on these interrelations, the events in which aspects of the program are reacted to, the new actors the program introduces, and the ways in which individuals and institutions move in and out of the network of interrelationships.

The systems framework also alerts the investigator to the likelihood that important forces having few interrelations with the system will appear. These new forces can be treated as exogenous sources of impact whose prior history and subsequent fate need not be understood further. For instance, in a model cities planning program, the deadline for submitting the plan was changed by the office to whom the plan was to be sent. This affected the planners and their interrelations, but it was not necessary in the study of the course of this program to ask why the deadline had been changed. Of course, before an unexpected event is categorized as exogenous, the investigator should consider whether events having to do with the program induced the intrusion. For example, when the staff of a radically-oriented community action program discovered, after a series of confrontations with local government officials, that the application procedure for new funds had been changed to their disadvantage, an investigator might have decided that the program was imbedded in a larger system than he had previously considered — a system activated by the controversy the program created.

Dramaturgic unfolding. In dramaturgic unfolding, the basic strategy is to construct a story about actors who engage in coalitions and conflicts and whose interactions form plots and subplots moving to a resolution. This framework is similar to the approach of "methodological individualism" (Watkins, 1953), which seeks to explain events by analyzing the actions of individuals within situations.

The dramaturgic framework is particularly useful for describing meetings, conferences, and other time-limited situations in which individuals interact to resolve an issue. One among a number of schemes for structuring observation suggests attention to the following issues:

1. identification of the issues which bring the individuals together,
2. identification of the actors and their commitments in relation to the issues,
3. description of the action which takes place, and
4. statement of the resolution (Kaplan, 1969; Burke, 1945).

Political forces. The interaction of political forces constitutes a complex conceptual framework; it is probably more useful when the task is to describe a connected series of events than when the task is to organize observation of a single event. Attention is directed to conflicts and coalitions, as in the dramaturgic framework, but the actors are perceived as representing interest groups, and their actions are interpreted as expressing a strategy. Of particular interest is how groups mobilize their resources in response to the program intervention, in what way they commit themselves to affect events, and with what success.

The systemic, dramaturgic, and political frameworks organize and discipline observation and reporting. Two alternative conceptual frameworks worth consideration are functional analysis, which examines the contributions of activities to the maintenance or goals of some system, and pattern analysis, which looks for expressions of a common theme in a variety of phenomena. These perspectives may be developed independently or other frameworks or may be assimilated into them.

Sample Selection

Because evaluation research on broad-aim programs quickly produces masses of data, the number of cases which can be usefully studied is limited. It seems intuitively that 15 or 20 instances should be sufficient to develop an understanding of program potentials; but, even if well chosen, a sample of 20 may provide inaccurate estimates of population characteristics. For case research, the sampling problem is to select one instance from which it will be possible to generalize to a significant proportion of the class of instances, if not the class as a whole. In comparative research — which aims at learning about different structures within a class — the sample should represent the important varieties within the class. If the problem is evaluation of a community action program, a sample including at least one instance of each important type of community would be adequate. Representative samples would be wasteful. Suppose that 50 percent of the cities in which a program is introduced are economically dependent on manufacturing and a much smaller number are economically dependent on extractive industry. It would nevertheless be better to represent manufacturing cities by three or four instances, and to represent extractive industry cities by the same number of instances than to have manufacturing cities make up 50 percent of the cases studied, and extractive industry cities make up a smaller proportion. The latter approach would very likely produce more data than necessary about the first type of city, less data than necessary about the second.

Data Gathering and Analysis

There are three sources of data for historical studies: interviews, observation of events, and documents. Interviews provide information regarding the aims of individuals and groups, their perceptions of the aims of others, and their perceptions of events, including events the investigator did not witness. Observation informs about the emergence of coalitions and conflicts, milestones, and the imagery of the intervention experience. Documents outline the sequence of events as well as fill in details. For example, a series of memoranda may define the negotiating positions of conflicting organizations and state understandings and misunderstandings. Interviews can then make clear the perceptions and aims which gave rise to the negotiating positions and the nature of the interchanges mentioned in the documents. Since there are no data-reduction techniques for qualitative data, only techniques for organizing the data, the individuals responsible for report writing have to be concerned that they are not overwhelmed by information (Glaser & Strauss, 1967).

Data analysis may be directed at any of three levels of generalization:

1. materials may be organized to describe what happened in concrete cases;
2. reports may describe in more general terms the types of systems and processes observed; and
3. a report may present a general model of the introduction of a change program of the sort studied in various types of communities.

Ethical Problems

In addition to many technical problems, this approach is likely to give rise to important ethical issues. Some of the ethical issues result from the value that data about process have to actors in the situation. The data often can affect the social standings and careers of individuals, as well as the success of the strategies of interest groups. It is fairly easy for an investigator not to divulge what he has learned to members of the community until an appropriate date for feedback, although he may feel himself in a moral dilemma should individuals who have been helpful to him seem unaware of some potentially dangerous aspect of their situation. However, it may be difficult for him to withhold important information from program administrators — especially if he is administratively responsible to them.

Investigators are committed to report, after the conclusion of their study, all data which bear on evaluation of the program. This commitment limits the situation in which they can promise confidentiality. Yet even if they have not made this promise, they often feel constrained to do no damage to those who have cooperated with them. At times it may appear that investigators are more protective of members of the community than those members are of themselves, but the investigator must remain aware of the potential effect of his appraisals on individuals and groups. If there is no way an investigator can describe what happened without making clear that one individual blocked action or another failed to carry through an agreement, then perhaps the best he can do is state the circumstances from all perspectives so that a reader can understand that the behaviors were plausible in the circumstances.

It is extremely difficult to avoid assigning positive and negative roles to individuals and groups, both in data gathering and in reporting. Bias need not be blatant — it can occur in the coloring of descriptions of positions or actors — and it can express either the investigator's sympathies or a competing position, when the investigator's caution against his own sympathies is exaggerated. One guard against bias is full and conscientious reporting of all viewpoints. Another is review of the report to actors in the situation. But in the latter case, to what extent should the investigator respect objections? The danger is that the investigator may unintentionally form alliances with one party or another through the way he checks his report.

There are different traditions within disciplines regarding publication which identifies individuals and institutions by name. Political scientists use real names; sociologists disguise both individuals and communities. For examples, compare Banfield (1964) and Thernstrom (1969) with Vidich and Bensman (1958). If there is a sponsoring agency which requires information regarding the viability of its program, there can be no disguises of critical information without compromising the initial commitment of the investigator.

The Role of Values

Evaluation appraises the extent to which a program realizes certain goals. When evaluation is based on an experimental design, the evaluation criteria are imbedded in the program at its inception. The value framework is that of the program's administrators, and there is no incentive to use alternative criteria.

In a qualitative study, it is possible to appraise both the extent to which the program realized its initial objectives and the extent to which the program realized other goals as well. The investigator can ask whether members of the population suffered losses — perhaps by attack on a coherent way of life — as well as gains. He need not restrict his attention to the target population, but can describe the consequences for individuals in other sectors of the community. The investigator can consider the program both from the perspectives of clients and from the perspectives of competing agencies or of local government. The investigator can evaluate the program from a radical perspective, and consider the extent to which the program has in marginal ways improved an inherently unsatisfactory system, and so reduced the likelihood of fundamental changes. Qualitative appraisal permits values to re-enter evaluation openly, and it permits the development of appraisals from different perspectives.

The advocated approach has the potential of freeing the investigator responsible for evaluation research from the constraint described by Merton and Lerner (1951, no. 306):

> The American social scientist now increasingly finds himself called upon to "solve" practical problems. But often the problem is stated for him by an executive whose acquaintance with the uses and limits of social science is not intimate. The scientist is called upon to contribute information useful to implement a given policy, but the policy itself is "given," not open to question. . . . So long as the social scientist continues to accept a role in which he does not question policies, state problems, and formulate alternatives, the more does he become routinized in the role of bureaucratic technician.

The qualitative approach to evaluation permits the social scientist to evaluate programs without having either to act solely as a technician or alternatively to give up his commitment to careful empirical work as a basis for his judgments.

References

Banfield, Edward. *Political Influence*. New York: Free Press, 1964.

Bunge, Mario. *Causality*. Cambridge: Harvard University Press, 1959.

Burke, Kenneth, *Grammar of Motives*. Englewood Cliffs, New Jersey: Prentice-Hall, 1945.

Campbell, Donald, and Julian Stanley. *Experimental and Quasi-Experimental Design for Research*. Chicago: Rand McNally, 1966.

Freeman, Howard, and Clarence C. Sherwood. "Research in Large-scale Intervention Programs." *Journal of Social Issues*, 21:11–28, 1965.

Glaser, Barney and Anselm Strauss. *Discovery of Grounded Theory*. Chicago: Aldine, 1967.

Kaplan, Marshall. *Instructions to research staff*. Working paper, Marshall Kaplan, Gans and Kahn, San Francisco, 1969.

Marris, Peter, and Martin Rein. *Dilemmas of Social Reform*. New York: Atherton, 1967.

Merton, Robert K., and Daniel Lerner. "Social Scientists and Research Policy." In: Daniel Lerner and Harold D. Lasswell (eds.), *The Policy Sciences*, 282–307. Stanford: Stanford University Press, 1951.

Miller, James G. "Living Systems: Basic Concepts." *Behavioral Science*, 10:193–237, 1965a.

Miller, James G. "Living Systems: Structure and Process." *Behavioral Science*, 10:337–379. 1965b.

Rossi, Peter. *Booby Traps and Pitfalls in the Evaluation of Social Action Programs*. Working paper, Department of Sociology, University of Chicago, 1966.

Schulberg, Herbert C., and Frank Baker. "Program Evaluation Models and the Implementation of Research Findings." *American Journal of Public Health*, 58:1248–55, 1968.

Selvin, Hanan C., and Alan Stuart. "Data Dredging Procedures in Survey Analyasis." *American Statistician*, 20:20–23, 1966.

Stufflebeam, Daniel L. *Evaluation as Enlightenment for Decision Making*. Working paper, Evaluation Center, Ohio State University, 1968.

Suchman, Edward. *Action for What? A Methodological Critique of Evaluation Studies.* Working paper, University of Pittsburgh, 1968.

Thernstrom, Stephan. *Poverty, Planning, and Politics in the New Boston.* New York: Basic Books, 1969.

Vidich, Arthur J., and Joseph Bensman. Small Town in Mass Society. Princeton: Princeton University Press, 1958.

Watkins, J.W.N. ''Ideal Types and Historical Explanation.'' In: Herbert Feigl and May Brodbeck (eds.), *Readings in the Philosophy of Science:* 723–43. New York: Appleton-Century-Crofts, 1953.

Watts, Harold. *Graduated Work Incentives: An Experiment in Negative Taxation.* Working paper, Institute for Research on Poverty, University of Wisconsin, 1969.

9 SOCIETAL EXPERIMENTATION[1]

Peter W. Airasian

Introduction

It is a special feature of modern societies that we identify, plan, and carry out programs designed to improve our social systems. It is also our experience that the programs do not always produce their intended improvements. Often, it is difficult to decipher whether programs have any impact at all, so complex is the ongoing social system into which programs are introduced and so inadequate are our methodologies for determining impact. To overcome these problems, to help obtain valid empirical evidence about the effectiveness of new social programs, a branch of methodology termed societal experimentation was suggested by Campbell (1969). Common pseudonyms for societal experimentation are evaluation research (Suchman, 1967), social experiments, experimental policy research, and field experiments.

This discussion will highlight the historical context which kindled interest in societal experimentation, define the rationale underlying societal experiments, and identify major obstacles to carrying out such experiments. It obviously is impossible to do full justice to these topics in a short paper. Nuances must be overlooked, history over-generalized, and practical strategies all but omitted. The purpose of this discussion is to provide a general, introductory overview of a recent and important addition to program evaluation theory and practice.

History

In the 1950s, Americans rediscovered the problems of poverty, racial injustice, and unequal opportunity. Characteristically, the response to these problems was swift and overly optimistic; by the mid-1960s, the federal government had undertaken an unprecedented range of social initiatives designed to put an end to racial discrimination, to poverty, and to school achievement differences between advantaged and disadvantaged groups (Moynihan, 1973). Variously called the New Frontier, the War on Poverty, and the Great Society — the label shifted with each incoming political administration — these efforts sought to make the problems of the poor America's number one priority and to bring substantial resources to bear on these problems. The programs quickly attained a momentum of their own, aided no doubt by almost universal public confidence that it was within the power of government to bring about quick, dramatic, and lasting social change.

But the premise underlying many of the reform programs of the 1960s was different from the premise which guided earlier social reform efforts (Rossi, 1972). Most federal intervention efforts before 1960 could be classified as maintenance or distributive programs (Tobin, 1966), programs intended to provide the goods or services denied individuals because of deficiencies in the wider economic, educational, and social systems. A presumption underlying these programs was that nothing was *wrong* with the individual citizen per se. He or she was out of work, dispossessed, or denied quality schooling because of systemic forces beyond his or her control. Reform efforts, therefore, were generally directed toward maintaining individuals during hard times, rather than endeavouring to make basic changes in the characteristics of the individuals themselves.

In the 1960s, societal reform, particularly in the realm of education and social work, took on a new orientation and the solution to the economic, social, and educational plight of the disadvantaged came to be viewed as requiring more direct attempts to change the personal qualities of individuals. Breaking the cycle of poverty involved more than treating its economic symptoms, it involved overcoming the cognitive, attitudinal, and experiential deficits which were seen to be at the root of these symptoms (Jencks et al., 1972). While the causes of the deficits generally were seen as residing outside the individual per se and, in fact, were the focus of a whole set of new maintenance programs (e.g., medicare, aid to dependent children, public housing, etc.), the deficits themselves were seen as personal.

While previous experience had made governmental agencies fairly proficient at carrying out distributive and maintenance-type programs, efforts to change individuals directly represented a move into relatively uncharted territory. Here the focus was to be less upon *access* to social and educational services than it was to be upon the *performance* of those who received the services. Moreover, those who were to be the recipients of the new programs and services were not a cross section of the American public, but rather individuals with so-called hard core learning and employment problems. As a society, we had had little experience with the structural, person-specific type of reform called for in the 1960s. Further, the optimism which characterized the period made it easy to gloss over the key issue of specifying the particular changes that needed to be brought about in the disadvantaged populace. Legislation tended to include only broadly stated goals such as "improve the quality of life in urban neighborhoods" or "improve the quality of education for poor children" (Rossi, 1972). It was never made clear how program personnel were to go about the task of changing people, nor did conventional wisdom suggest the variables that were most influential in effecting change. It was hard enough to change individuals, but it was doubly hard to change them in nebulously stated ways.

These issues would have receded into unimportance had the various ameliorative programs proved to be effective in overcoming the cognitive and motivational problems of the disadvantaged. Such was not the case however, and the late 1960s witnessed a host of studies which appeared to show that reform programs had had little discernible effect in changing the characteristics of their participants (Averch et al., 1972; Cicirelli et al., 1969; Coleman et al., 1966; Gilbert, Light, & Mosteller, 1975; Jencks, et al., 1972; McDill et al., 1969; Mullen et al., 1972). Fueled in part by media over-generalization of these findings and in part by underlying value conflicts regarding the ends of social reform, a vigorous debate over the validity of the research conclusions ensued, with the lines of disagreement encompassing both philosophical and methodological issues (Madaus, Airasian, & Kellaghan, 1980; Grant, 1973; Hodgson, 1973; Moynihan, 1968; Rossi & Williams, 1972). The idea of societal experimentation is one by-product of this debate.

By about 1970, a number of loosely related trends and events had combined to establish a receptive climate for the concept of societal experimentation. First, as noted, the disappointing impact of reform efforts had convinced many that the desire to "do something good" was, alone, insufficient to overcome the problems of the disadvantaged. Noble intentions had to be supplemented by thoughtful planning and a systematic examination of the effectiveness of programs. Second, by about 1970, a "guns or butter" debate was underway in Washington, with competition between the domestic commitments to the Great Society and the demands of an ever more expensive foreign war putting increasing pressure on the federal coffers. The onus fell upon domestic programs to justify their effectiveness in order to receive new or continued funding. Third, and somewhat more tenuously, the accountability movement, which had its origins in the Defense Department in the 1960s, began to be applied seriously to ameliorative social and educational programs. Accountability may be conceived of as a form of consumer protection, where the effectiveness of programs must be demonstrated to the ultimate supporters of these programs, the taxpayers. Simply put, the notion was that program effectiveness must be demonstrated in order to justify the dollars expended on the programs. These events, combined with methodological limitations in the studies performed to that time (e.g., Averch et al., 1972; Mosteller & Moynihan, 1972; Smith, 1972; Rotberg & Wolf, 1974) created an interest in more rational, quantitative strategies for determining the worth of social and educational reform programs.

Many individuals, frustrated by the evaluation research results obtained from non-experimental studies, viewed societal experiments as the appropriate avenue for obtaining valid, unequivocal data about the effectiveness of new social programs (Abt, 1976; Campbell, 1969, 1970, 1971; Campbell & Boruch, 1975; Gilbert & Mosteller, 1972; Kershaw, 1972; Mosteller & Moynihan, 1972; Riecken & Boruch, 1974; Rivlin, 1971; Stanley, 1972). On the basis of an experimental approach to social reform, new programs designed to cure specific social ills would be tried out on a limited scale, experimental evidence would be gathered to determine whether these programs were effective, and decisions to retain, modify, or discard the programs would be made in light of the empirical data. In many respects, the orderly, rational, quantitative features of such an approach were appealing, particularly to the many individuals who craved evaluations that provided clear answers about program effectiveness, instead of only more questions.

Societal Experimentation

Essentially, societal experimentation is an attempt to apply the method of experimental trials prevalent in laboratory settings to the evaluation of the effectiveness of social programs. In its simplest form, the experimental method may be characterized as a three-stage process. Initially, two groups of people (or classes, schools, factories, etc.) are drawn at *random* from a single, well-defined population. Then, one group is administered the *treatment* (program) of interest while the second group is not. Alternatively, if two different treatments or programs are of interest, one group is administered the first while the other group receives the second. Finally, measurements are made to determine how some relevant aspects of behavior following treatment differ from that of the non-treated or comparison group. It should be emphasized that the use of the word *experiment* or *experimental* in this context is *not* synonymous with the words *new* or *novel*, as in the common parlance, "my experimental (i.e., new) program." Rather, *experiment* or *experimental,* as used here, implies a set of data-gathering procedures involving randomization, control, treatment, and comparison.

Experiments are persuasive because they permit the investigator to establish cause and effect chains of logic among programs and their outcomes. Of principal concern in any piece of research are the answers to the questions. "How unambiguous are the data on which the conclusions are based?" and "How certain can we be that an observed difference — or lack of difference — between the treated and non-treated group is a true reflection of the effectiveness of the program per se and not of some extraneous variable?'' (Campbell & Stanley, 1966; Cook & Campbell, 1979). By selecting two groups at random from a single population, providing the groups different treatment, and measuring differences between the groups after completion of treatment, an investigator satisfies the conditions required to establish causal links between treatments and their outcomes (Airasian, 1974; Cook & Campbell, 1979). He or she is, in essence, able to state that observed differences at the end of the treatment period were *caused* by the programs themselves and not by extraneous factors unrelated to the programs.

It is important to recognize that societal experimentation differs from other approaches to evaluating social programs in three ways. First, societal experiments are predicated on the idea that new programs be implemented on a limited scale, so that effectiveness may be evaluated prior to the programs' being made universally available. To date, most reform programs succumbed to the political exigency that they be treated as though they were certain to be effective and be pushed into broad practice with no serious effort to determine the likelihood of their success. In the end, unrestricted adoption precludes the possibility of identifying suitable comparison groups to settle the question of program effectiveness, which inevitably arises after the fact.

Second, societal experimentation requires formal measurement of the effects of programs on their ultimate recipients. While this emphasis may appear commonsensical, many attempts to judge program effectiveness go no further than obtaining testimonial evidence about the effort, activities, and attitudes of the program staff. Such information is of interest, but it is not a substitute for evidence about the measurable effects of the program on its ultimate clientele.

Third, and perhaps most subtly, societal experimentation represents an attempt to apply a model of knowledge acquisition widely used in many academic disciplines to the formation of public policy knowledge. The experimental method, however, is not only a set of procedures for acquiring valid data about phenomena; it is also a particular approach to knowing, in the sense that knowing by induction is a different process than knowing by, say, deduction. Thus, when one accepts the laboratory model of experimentation to study programs in the social arena, one also is accepting a set of implicit concepts regarding the gradualness of knowledge acquisition, the stability of research settings, the essential timelessness of the research process, the need to test and constantly revise theoretical premises, and so forth. Too often, the tendency has been to view program evaluation in general and societal experimentation in particular solely as a set of procedures for data collection, ignoring the fact that they also are more general approaches to the process of knowing.

As its name implies, societal experimentation is carried out not in the rarified controlled atmosphere of the laboratory, but in the *real,* everyday social context in which the subjects of the investigation live and function. The conditions in which the experiment is carried out, then, should mirror the actual situation in which the program or treatment to be evaluated will be practiced (Airasian, Kellaghan & Madaus, 1971). The term *societal* is applied to this kind of study because it takes place in *real life* settings where the population for investigation is representative of a significant social group, and the benefits of the proposed program are expected to be widespread throughout a society. Experiments at the social level, however, obviously carry with them a series of constraints not usually encountered in laboratory experiments. Some of these constraints will now be considered.

Constraints on the Practice of Societal Experimentation

At a practical level, there are a number of constraints on the societal experimenter which, individually or in concert, hamper efforts to conduct truly experimental studies. Many of these constraints are encountered in other evaluation approaches. Empirical examination of program effectiveness is threatening to those involved in the conduct and administration of the program. Especially if there is a pre-existing commitment to the correctness and efficacy of the program — as there normally is on the part of those responsible for its day-to-day conduct — information about the true effectiveness of the program has immediate political implications. Many administrators wisely prefer to confine examination to those variables that they can control. Ambiguity, lack of suitable comparison groups, and lack of concrete evidence all serve to increase the administrator's control over the experiment. Societal experimentation is most often a political activity and is recognized as such by program staff and administrators. It is in their interest to maintain as much control over the evaluation parameters as possible — even to the extent of crippling the experimental framework (Airasian, 1974; Campbell, 1969; House, 1973; Zaltman & Duncan, 1977).

However, even with the best cooperation from program administrators and staff, there are additional problems that arise. For example, since the experimental approach requires the identification of a control group, the treatment must be withheld from a group of individuals whose need for the program is equivalent to that of its recipients.[2] Moreover, whether or not one is to receive the program is left to chance; that is, to random procedures. Although random selection is the fairest means to allocate a resource when the demand for that resource exceeds its supply, it is generally difficult to justify random allocation of a plentiful resource solely on the grounds of experimental expediency. The prevalent tendencies in program allocation have been either to provide the program to the most needy or to provide the program to all who wish it. While these strategies are laudable on ethical grounds, they subvert the possibility of conducting controlled experiments by removing the opportunity to identify appropriate control groups against which to compare the outcomes attained by the program recipients. The evaluator then must adopt quasi-experimental methods (Cook & Campbell, 1979). Withholding a program from those whom it might benefit is neither an ethically nor politically popular strategy.

In a sense, the public has been so bombarded by new programs and new approaches, each more elaborate and expensive than its predecessors, that false expectations and a desire to "keep up with the Joneses" have been created. Under such circumstances, new social programs are often perceived as being good simply beause they are new; for many, new is, by definition, better.[3] Given this attitude, it can be extremely difficult for the evaluator and the program administrator to withstand pressures for making a program available to all who wish it.

In addition to the problems associated with obtaining full cooperation and disclosure from program administrators, randomly determining who will receive a program, and withholding the program from some needy individuals, other practical problems can plague the societal experimenter. Among these are inability to control program implementation at local sites (Rivlin & Timpane, 1975; Williams, 1976), erosion of control groups (Cook & Campbell, 1979), and the corruptibility of outcome measures (Campbell, 1975). Because societal experimentation is carried out in the real world setting, it is subject to a variety of real world influences not present in the controlled laboratory setting. These influences may make it difficult to satisfy the conditions required for true experimentation and useful program evaluation.

While practical constraints may limit the opportunity to conduct societal experiments, there are more basic issues associated with the relevancy of societal experiments as a path to social action. First among these issues is a question of morality (American Psychological Association, 1973; Kelman, 1968; Russell Sage Foundation, 1970). Selecting and assigning groups of individuals to one treatment or another involves some degree of manipulation of the lives of human beings. Few moral questions arose as long as scientists confined their experiments to study of the physical world; but when researchers began to use feeling, animate subjects in their studies, it became appropriate to question whether the search for knowledge provided sufficient justification for the manipulation of experimental subjects. Of course, the urgency of the moral issue may vary with the manipulation proposed; some interventions are relatively innocuous while others may be quite strong and potentially harmful. Moreover, just as one may question the morality of manipulating human beings in societal experiments, one might question also the morality of expending huge amounts of public monies on untested programs of unproven worth or, for that matter, the morality of continually raising and then dashing the expectations of the disadvantaged by promising that social programs will deliver more than they ultimately do. The moral dilemmas posed by an experimental approach to social reform are real, but they are by no means simple or one-dimensional. (Airasian, Kellaghan & Madaus, 1971).

A second issue of concern has to do with the relevancy of the criteria on which social experimenters judge programs to be effective. The experimental approach is an excellent way to obtain quantitative evidence about the comparative benefits of a social program; experiments can tell us that recipients read better, are happier, or love school more than an equivalent group of non-recipients. But the goals of social programs are usually multi-layered and political support for a program may bear no direct relation to the outcomes social experimenters strive so hard to measure. For example, many of the compensatory education programs instituted in the United States during the 1960s and 1970s had as their ostensible goal to improve the basic cognitive skills of disadvantaged youngsters; but, at a different level, the compensatory programs represented a means for legislators to provide direct financial support to the schools in their constituencies. One commentor has suggested that compensatory program funding was the educational equivalent to federal rivers-and-harbors bills, which allocate monies to Congressmen's districts for the improvement of rivers and harbors regardless of whether the district is on the seacoast or landlocked in the middle of a desert (Cohen, 1970). Moynihan (1973) has noted that the existence of programs, independent of their effectiveness, has a strong political benefit. ''In their ritualistic aspects, the programs are of particular value. They give psychic satisfaction to the patrons of the poor, convince outsiders — especially the media — that 'something is being done,' and indicate to the urban poor that someone up there really cares'' (p. 153).

It may be that societal experiments will provide unambiguous answers to questions of program evaluation that are relatively unimportant from the perspective of political program support and continuation. A decade of research has failed to turn up evidence of significant or lasting effects from compensatory education programs, yet such programs continue to receive legislative support and funding. The initial concept of Project Head Start was that is was to be an experimental program reaching a limited number of disadvantaged children. However, the idea was simply too attractive, and Head Start became an ideal symbol for the new war on poverty. Head Start generated immediate national support, quickly expanded into a national program, and has maintained its immense popularity in the face of evaluation evidence suggesting its relative ineffectiveness in attaining its ostensible aims. It is difficult for quantitative evidence of program ineffectiveness to compete with the political benefits associated with federal support for local schools or with those omni-present photographs of smiling youngsters eagerly working at their local preschool centers.

Those who see experiments as a rational problem-solving strategy in the relatively hermetic atmosphere of the laboratory may find that a different conception of rationality prevails in the cruel, realistic world. Politicians and bureaucrats generally are not scientists and are unlikely to let empirical evaluation evidence, no matter how fastidiously gathered, be their sole decision making guide — except perhaps when it suits some prior purpose.

A further point on this cold, hard world theme concerns the inherent gradualness of the experimental process. Rarely do scientists, in a single experiment, obtain definitive answers to complex questions. Rather, the experimental process, as a way of accumulating knowledge, usually proceeds at a slower pace, through successive stages of trial and error; a fledgling theory leads to an experiment which produces findings which in turn lead to theory revision — and the process is repeated again and again. In the social sciences, we are at a disadvantage because we have such poor theories about social phenomena and processes; generally, it is not until we have completed a number of investigations that the real problems at issue become clear to us. Often we have little more than a vague conventional wisdom to guide our reform efforts. While conventional or common sense wisdom is important, it often turns out to be wrong — or at least simplistic — so that the process of identifying and validating strong and effective remedial treatment can involve a time-consuming series of successive approximations.

This strategy would be quite adequate were it not for the fact that the problems which galvanize a society's interest typically have a brief life; society has a short attention span. While problems do not disappear after their period in the limelight, they do recede in importance, to be replaced by ever more urgent problems which require immediate solution. In succeeding years — sometimes months — the focus of society's concern has turned from the problem of disadvantaged children to the problem of the aged, to the problem of the unemployed, to the energy crisis, and to the economy, with a few unmentioned stops in between. The importance of program evaluation in a particular problem areas waxes and wanes with the area's perceived importance. We are willing to tolerate uncertainties about the effectiveness of older reform programs while we divert attention and effort toward examination of our newest social problems and programs.

In theory, nothing seems more reasonable than trying out programs, rigorously evaluating their effectiveness, and applying this knowledge to policy decisions. However, the systemic stability implicit in the experimental approach may not hold in complex social settings. Social problems and the experimental process may have a timelessness about them, but the attention span of society does not. It may be frustrating for a societal experimenter to hear the constant lament that his or her experiments do not tell us what is effective, only what is not effective, but the experimenter may be even more frustrated when he or she works out a definitive answer to a problem and then finds that nobody is interested.

Conclusions

It is obvious that applying the experimental paradigm to the evaluation of real, ongoing social and educational programs is fraught with attitudinal, organizational, ethical and methodological problems. However, the installation and conduct of social experiments, while problematical, is possible; under the right set of circumstances, societal experiments have been conceived and carried out in the real world. These experiments have ranged from small-scale evaluations carried out in a single institution (Skipper & Leonard, 1968) to nationwide experiments involving tens of thousands of subjects (Kellaghan, Madaus, & Airasian, 1982). Catalogs of efforts to apply societal experimentation to program evaluation in a variety of disciplines are found in Boruch (1974) and Gilbert, Light, and Mosteller (1975).

On the whole, however, it is fair to say that societal experimentation, the application of true experimental methods to program evaluation, has been more talked about than practiced. Campbell's 1969 vision of the experimenting administrator has not come to pass, probably for all the reasons that Campbell and others (e.g., House, 1973) recognized and might have hoped would be overcome. Societal experimentation is not the panacea for hard-headed, data-based program evaluation that many thought it would be only a few years ago.

The legacy of societal experimentation to program evaluation — if it is appropriate to talk in terms of a legacy for a movement barely 15 years old — has been a burgeoning field of methodology which seeks to identify methods for obtaining valid evaluation data in real world settings that do not manifest all the parameters necessary for the conduct of a true societal experiment. Societal experimentation represents the ultimate ideal of empirically based program evaluation approaches. It is, as suggested previously, an ideal which is rarely realized in its fullest form. Quasi-experimental strategies represent attempts to accommodate the real world exigencies that preclude true experiments. Through the development and refinement of quasi-experimental methods, (Airasian, 1974; Bennett & Lumsdaine, 1975; Campbell, 1969, 1970, 1971, 1975; Campbell & Erlebacher, 1970; Caro, 1971; Cook & Campbell, 1979; Glass, Wilson, & Gottman, 1974; Riecken & Boruch, 1974), comparative, data-based program evaluation has been enhanced enormously. Moreover, the very process of identifying real world impediments to true experiments — regardless of whether methodologists have been able to overcome these impediments — has contributed a great deal to understanding the sociology of program implementation, conduct, and evaluation.

Notes

1.   Revised version of a symposium address presented at the Annual Conference of the British Psychological Association, University of Exeter, Exeter, England, April, 1977. Financial support for this address was provided by the Carnegie Corporation, the Russell Sage Foundation, the National Institute of Education, the Spencer Foundation, and the Department of Education of the Irish Government. The views expressed are solely those of the author.

2.   Actually, the problem is more complicated than the mere providing or withholding a particular treatment from sample groups. The intrinsic desirability of various social and educational treatments is often perceived to be quite different. Consequently, as much controversy may arise as a result of providing groups with treatments perceived to be of different worth as may arise as a result of completely withholding a treatment.

3. In the past two or three years, public expectations in America have diminished and, in some areas, education for example, retrenchment and focus on the basic skills have eroded the attitude that new is necessarily better.

References

Abt, Clark C. (ed.). *The Evaluation of Social Programs*. Beverly Hills, California: Sage Publications, 1976.

Airasian, P.W. "Designing Summative Evaluation Studies at the Local Level." In: W.J. Popham (ed.), *Evaluation in Education*. Berkeley, California: McCutchan Publishing Co., 1974, 145–200.

Airasian, P.W., Kellaghan, T., and Madaus, G.F. *Societal Experimentation*. Position paper prepared for a conference on "The Consequences of Educational Testing: A Societal Experiment," funded by the Russell Sage Foundation, Dublin, Ireland, October, 1971.

American Psychological Association, *Ethical Principles in the Conduct of Research with Human Participants*, 1973.

Averch, H.A. et al. *How Effective is Schooling?* Santa Monica, California: Rand Corporation, 1972. Prepared for President's Commission on School Finance.

Bennett, C.A. and Lumsdaine, A.A. *Evaluation and Experiment*, New York: Academic Press, Inc., 1975.

Boruch, R.F. "Bibliography: Illustrated Randomized Field Experiments for Program Planning and Evaluation." *Evaluation*, no. 1, 2 (1974), 83–87.

Campbell, D.T. "Reforms as Experiments." *American Psychologist*, no. 4, 24 (1969), 404–29.

Campbell, D.T. "Considering the Case Against Experimental Evaluations of Social Innovations." *Administrative Science Quarterly*, no. 1, 15 (1970), 110–13.

Campbell, D.T. *Methods for an Experimenting Society*. Paper presented to the Eastern Psychological Association, April 17, 1971, and to the American Psychological Association, Sunday, September 5, Washington, D.C.

Campbell, D.T. "Assessing the Impact of Planned Social Change." In: Lyons, G.M. (ed.), *Social Research and Public Policies*, Hanover, New Hampshire: The Public Affairs Center, Dartmouth College, 1975, 3–45.

Campbell, D.T. and Boruch, R.F. "Making the Case for Randomized Assignment to Treatments by Considering the Alternatives: Six Ways in Which Quasi-Experimental Evaluations in Compensatory Education Tend to Underestimate Effects." In: Bennett, C.A., and Lumsdaine, A.A. (eds.), *Evaluation and Experiment*, New York: Academic Press, Inc., 1975, pp. 195–296.

Campbell, D.T. and Erlebacher, A.E. "How Regression Artifacts in Quasi-Experimental Evaluations Can Mistakenly Make Compensatory Education Look Harmful." In Hellmuth, J. (ed.), *Disadvantaged Child*, vol. 3, *Compensatory Education: A National Debate*. New York: Brunner/Mazel, 1970.

Campbell, D.T. and Stanley, J.C. *Experimental and Quasi-Experimental Designs for Research*. Chicago: Rand McNally, 1966.

Caro, F.G. (ed.) *Readings in Evaluation Research*. New York: Russell Sage Foundation, 1971.

Cirirelli, V.G. et al. *The Impact of Head Start: An Evaluation of the Effects of Head Start on Children's Cognitive and Affective Development*. A report presented to the Office of Economic Opportunity pursuant to Contract B89–4536, June 1969. Westinghouse Learning Corporation, Ohio University. (Distributed by Clearinghouse for Federal Scientific and Technical Information, U.S. Department of Commerce, National Bureau of Standards, Institute for Applied Technology, PV 184 328).

Cohen, D.K. "Politics and Research: Evaluation of Social Action Programs in Education." *Review of Educational Research*, no. 2, 40 (1970), 213–38.

Coleman, J.S. et al. *Equality of Educational Opportunity*. U.S. Department of Health, Education and Welfare, U.S. Office of Education, Washington, D.C., 1966.

Cook, T.D. and Campbell, D.T. *Quasi-Experimentation: Design and Analysis Issues for Field Settings*. Chicago: Rand McNally, 1979.

Gilbert, J.P., and Mosteller, F. "The Urgent Need for Experimentation." In: Mosteller, F. and Moynihan, D.P. (eds.) *On Equality of Educational Opportunity*. New York: Random House, 1972, 371–83.

Gilbert, J.P., Light, R.T., and Mosteller, F. "Assessing Social Innovations: An Empirical Base for Policy." In: Bennett, C.A. and Lumsdaine, A.A. (eds.), *Evaluation and Experiment*, New York: Academic Press, Inc., 1975, 39–194.

Glass, G.V., Wilson, V.L. and Gottman, J.M. *Design and Analysis of Time Series Experiments*, Boulder, Colorado: University of Colorado Press, 1974.

Grant, G. "Shaping Social Policy: The Politics of the Coleman Report," *Teachers College Record*, no. 1, 75 (1973), 17–54.

Hodgson, G. "Do Schools Make a Difference?" *Atlantic Monthly*, (March 1973), 35–46.

House, E.R. (ed.) *School Evaluation, the Politics and Process*. Berkeley, California: McCutchan Publishing Co., 1973.

Jencks, C. et al. *Inequality: A Reassessment of the Effect of Family and Schooling in America*. New York: Basic Books, 1972.

Kellaghan, T., Madaus, G.F. and Airasian, P.W. *The Effects of Standardized Testing*. Boston, Massachusetts: Kluwer–Nijhoff, 1982.

Kelman, H.C. *On Human Values and Social Research*. San Francisco, California: Jossey-Bass Inc., 1968.

Kershaw, D.N. Issues in Income Maintenance Experiments. In: Rossi, P. and Williams, W. (eds.), *Evaluating Social Action Programs: Theory, Practice and Politics*. New York: Seminar Press, 1972, 221–245.

Madaus, G.F., Airasian, P.W., Kellaghan, T. *School Effectiveness: A Reassessment of the Evidence*. New York: McGraw-Hill, 1980.

McDill, E.L., McDill, M.S., and Sprehe, J.T. *Strategies for Success in Compensatory Education*. Baltimore, Maryland: Johns Hopkins Press, 1969.

Mosteller, F. and Moynihan, D.P. (eds.), *On Equality of Educational Opportunity*. New York: Random House, 1972.

Moynihan, D.P. "Sources of Resistance to the Coleman Report." *Harvard Educational Review*, no. 1, 38 (1968), 23–25.

Moynihan, D.P. *The Politics of a Guaranteed Income. The Nixon Administration and the Family Assistance Plan*. New York: Random House, 1973.

Mullen, E.J. et al. *Evaluation of Social Intervention*. San Francisco, California: Jossey-Bass, Inc., 1972.

Riecken, H.W. and Boruch, R.F. *Social Experimentation*. New York: Academic Press, 1974.

Rivlin, A.M. *Systematic Thinking for Social Action*. Washington, D.C.: The Brookings Institution, 1971.

Rivlin, A.M. and Timpane, P.M. (eds.) *Planned Variation in Education*. Washington, D.C.: The Brookings Institution, 1975.

Rossi, P.C. "Testing for Success and Failure in Social Action." In: Rossi, P.C. and Williams, W. (eds.), *Evaluating Social Action Programs: Theory, Practice and Politics*. New York: Seminar Press, 1972, 11–49.

Rossi, P.C. and Williams, W. (eds.). *Evaluating Social Action Programs: Theory, Practice and Politics*. New York: Seminar Press, 1972.

Rotberg, I.C. and Wolf, A. *Compensatory Education: Some Research Issues*. Policy Studies Program, Division of Research, National Institute of Education, Washington, D.C., 1974.

Russell Sage Foundation, *Guidelines for Collection, Maintenance and Dissemination of Pupil Records*, 1970.

Skipper, J.S. and Leonard, R.C. "Children, Stress, and Hospitalization: A Field Experiment." *Journal of Health and Social Behavior*, 9 (1968), 275–87.

Smith, M.S. "Equality of Educational Opportunity: The Basic Findings Re-considered." In: Mosteller, F. and Moynihan, D.P. (eds.), *On Equality of Educational Opportunity*. New York: Random House, 1972, 230–342.

Stanley, J.C. "Controlled Field Experiments as a Model for Evaluation." In: Rossi, P. and Williams, W. (eds.) *Evaluating Social Action Programs: Theory, Practice and Politics*. New York: Seminar Press, 1972, 67–71.

Suchman, E.A. *Evaluation Research*. New York: Russell Sage Foundation, 1967.

Tobin, J. "The Case for an Income Guarantee." *Public Interest*, (Summer 1966), 31–41.

Williams, W. "Implementation Problems in Federally Funded Programs." In: Williams, W. and Elmore, R.F. (eds.), *Social Program Implementation*. New York: Academic Press, 1976, 15–40.

Zaltman, G. and Duncan, R. *Strategies for Planned Change*. New York: Wiley Interscience, 1977.

10 RATIONALITY TO RITUAL:
The Multiple Roles Of Evaluation in Governmental Processes
Robert E. Floden and Stephen S. Weiner

There is a growing disillusion with social science evaluation and the role it has played in the conduct of massive social programs (Speizman, 1974; Horowitz & Katz, 1975; Orlans, 1971; Williams & Evans, 1969; Cohen, 1975). In retrospect, it appears that the social science evaluations of the past decade were undertaken with impossibly high ambitions and relied upon restrictive assumptions concerning the functions that evaluation serves in governmental processes.

The dominant model has taken evaluation to be an activity which functions to alter and enlighten the pursuit of programmatic goals. Such a view is too narrow and may actually be misleading. Other functions of evaluation can be identified, including conflict resolution and complacency reduction. Recognition of these functions leads to a desire for differently structured evaluations; but such evaluations cannot be conducted without changes in the pattern of evaluation funding and in the composition of the evaluation community. This recognition also suggests that the evaluator may have more options than he realized.

Floden, Robert E. and Weiner, Stephen S. "Rationality to Ritual: The Multiple Roles of Evaluation in Governmental Processes." *Policy Sciences,* 9 (1978), 9–18. Copyright 1978, Elsevier Scientific Publishing Company, Amsterdam. Reprinted by permission of authors and publisher.

The Stanford Evaluation Consortium is supported by a grant from the Russell Sage Foundation.

The Decisionistic Model

Conventional wisdom concerning the relationship between evaluation and governmental processes emphasizes the impact of evaluation upon discrete decisions made by public managers. The language of various proponents of evaluation varies, but three fundamental assumptions regarding goals, information, and utilization appear and reappear (Stufflebeam et al., 1971; Popham, 1975; Provus, 1971; Alkin, 1969; Stake, 1967):

1. *Goals.* Social programs are enacted with stable, consensual, publicly proclaimed goals. Politicians initiate programs with these goals in mind; the programs function to achieve these goals.
2. *Information.* Evaluations serve to collect information on the way in which programs function and on the effectiveness of programs in meeting proclaimed goals. This information will reveal any discrepancies between program performance and goals.
3. *Utilization.* Decision makers and program managers will utilize evaluative information to make discrete, identifiable decisions intended to improve programs. Decision makers and managers are constantly in search of ways to improve program performance.

Because the dominant theme of these premises is that evaluation aids in making discrete decisions, these three premises will be called the *decisionistic model* of the function of evaluation.[1]

The decisionistic model depicts governmental and social systems, under the influence of evaluation, as highly adaptive. Information about government performance, measured against widely shared goals for public policy, is quickly fed back into the policy-making process where course corrections are made.

The decisionistic model is a familiar one in the literature of evaluation. Although it is cast here in simplistic terms, this description captures many of the basic ideas that motivated both program-planning-budgeting systems (PPBS) and the drive for rational decision making in government (Hitch, 1970; Schultze, 1968; Rivlin, 1971; Riecken & Boruch, 1975).

Many nationwide evaluations designed to fit this model have been conducted. For example, in the field of education, we now have documentation on evaluations of Title I of the Elementary and Secondary Education Act (McLaughlin, 1975), Follow Through (Elmore, 1972, 1975), Head Start (Williams & Evans, 1969), Head Start Planned Variation (Rivlin & Timpane 1975), and performance contracting (Gramlich & Koshel, 1975). The effects of these evaluations are not those predicted by the decisionistic model. As Cohen and Garet say:

> In general, efforts to improve decision making by producing better knowledge appear to have had disappointing results. Program evaluations are widely reported to have little

effect on school decisions; there is similar evidence from other areas of social policy. The recent national experiments in preschool and early childhood education (Headstart Planned Variation and Project Follow Through) do not seem to have affected federal decisions about priorities within such compensatory programs. There is little evidence to indicate that government planning offices have succeeded in linking social research and decision making.[2]

Part of the apparent failure of evaluations to influence decisions is probably due to the inconsistent quality of the evaluations conducted. But consideration of the premises of the decisionistic model suggests that even "good" evaluations may fail to aid decisionmakers.

The Goals Premise

It is naive to assume that governmental decisions are made primarily in accordance with universally accepted goals (Orlans, 1971). The goals of public policy often involve private, conflicting objectives in addition to public, consensual ends. Politicians and bureaucrats experience immense difficulty in defining the public interest. Further, they are concerned about the interests of the particular groups with whom they identify and from whom they derive political support.

Evaluators usually report to a heterogeneous, rather than homogeneous, audience. The evaluator who chooses to measure the performance of social programs against public rhetoric offers little to decisionmakers with private or narrowly political aims. For example, the report on whether student achievement improves in schools that use paraprofessionals is likely to say little to administrators who value the program because it provides local employment and increased political support.

The diversity of ends served by public policy should not be viewed as a pathology, however. Few goals have majority support. Hence, public programs can only be established by appealing to the partly divergent goals of a number of groups. The goals written into legislation will be sufficiently vague to allow various constituencies to read in their own goals. As David Truman said, "Ambiguity and verbal compromise may be the very heart of a successful political formula."[3]

The Information Premise

It is naive to assume that the information collected in an evaluation will always reveal discrepancies between program performance and goals. Evaluations have faced numerous difficulties in obtaining believable results. (For examples of these difficulties, see Campbell & Erlebacher, 1970; Gilbert, Light, & Mosteller, 1976.)

Outcomes of the programs are obscured by the complexity of the social context in which they take place; furthermore, the public goals often change during the course of the evaluation.

Since social programs can seldom be isolated from the rest of society, the outcomes measured are affected by many factors not intentionally included in the program. Since the effects of factors such as the strength of the national economy and the whims of local governments may have large, unknown impacts on the outcome measures, the evaluation may be unable to isolate and assess the effects specific to the program. In many cases, this problem is compounded by the inability of the evaluator to randomly assign subjects to program and control groups. In this case, the program effects are also confounded with pre-existing group differences.

Prospects for discovery of discrepancies in the short run are further compromised by the growing realization that it is time consuming to carefully design and execute evaluations that can detect accurately the small effects of many new social programs. A decade may be required for the testing, design, and implementation of programs on an experimental basis (Rivlin & Timpane, 1975). In this time, quite different program goals may have evolved, but the carefully designed evaluation may only be able to detect discrepancies between program effects and the previous, now obsolete, goals.

While it is optimistic to assume that an evaluation will collect useful information, the decisionistic model is restrictive in its assumption that evaluations function *only* to collect information. Evaluators usually collect information on the activities and effectiveness of programs, but this is not all they do. Evaluations are often large-scale programs in their own right, affecting the lives of people in the program and providing support for those in the evaluation industry. Considering evaluations only as sources of information may lead to a failure to recognize substantial effects of evaluation efforts.

The Utilization Premise

Are organizations constantly in search of ways to improve their performance? Organizational theorists say not (March & Simon, 1958; Cyert & March, 1963; Steinbruner, 1974). Rather than continually seeking optimal performance, organizations search for new ideas and practices only when current performance falls below satisfactory levels. For governmental organizations, satisfaction ordinarily disappears only when external pressure causes substantial discomfort within the organization. An agency is content to maintain business as usual unless public pressure focuses on problems in its domain. At such a time, the organization is likely to search for ways to improve its programs or at least alter public perceptions of its programs. The organization will usually start by using strategies which have previously helped to reduce public pressure. Some of these strategies use information regarding program performance and effectiveness.

The public, however, is extremely fickle in its concerns. Each social problem rises into public view, captures center stage for a time, and fades away to be replaced by the next fashionable issue (Downs, 1971). Each problem area, such as health or education, experiences alternating periods of public concern and public neglect. For example, the urban riots of 1967 sparked a public determination to "do something." When the costs of ameliorating the conditions of black ghettos were realized and initial steps did not deliver rapid social improvement, the public became bored with media coverage of street mobs; issues of urban decay fell into neglect.

Once public excitement passes, the stimulus to improve services fades as well. Evaluations commissioned in the first blush of program operation are of little interest when completed, if the public has turned to other issues. Although evaluations are not predestined to irrelevance, utilization depends on the chance conjunction of available results, public concern, and bureaucratic receptivity. In the majority of cases, this conjunction does not occur, and the evaluative evidence is filed, not used.

The utilization premise can fail in another way. The time required for evaluative evidence to influence decisionmakers in considerably longer than the decisionistic model implies (Cohen & Garet, 1975). While the decisionistic view assumes that evaluations will provide information for a particular decision in the short run, the decisions that are actually affected may come much later. A decision making structure consists of roles and relationships, sets of beliefs and values, commitments already accepted, and courses of action already in progress. Plans can rarely be altered until current commitments have been met. Only when plans are open to influence can the evaluator's report have impact. Further, the ultimate impact of evaluations often depends on altered belief structures; such alterations may come only after a series of studies has confirmed initial findings.

Belief in the efficacy of compensatory education was not substantially shaken by the first adverse evaluation; a multitude of evaluations, conducted over the period of several years, did erode such beliefs. The possibility that evaluative results can alter policy in the short run is seriously diminished by the inertia of the decision making structure.[4]

Limitations of the Decisionistic Model and Some Alternatives

The foregoing recitation is not intended to bolster an assertion that evaluations never fit into a decisionistic framework. It is plausible to assume that evaluators are sometimes called upon in situations where program goals are consensual, consistent, and operational; where evaluative results can be reported while managerial interest is still high; where the program directors are free to consider a wide range of alternatives; where new alternatives can be implemented within standard operating procedures and where the utilization of evaluation does not require a reversal of deeply rooted attitudes. But no one should be surprised when some or all of these conditions are absent. When such conditions do not hold, the evaluation will fail to perform the function outlined by the decisionistic model.

But we need not conclude that such evaluations serve no useful social function. Evaluations may influence governmental processes in ways not envisioned in the decisionistic model. Evaluations have at least two additional functions. These functions may be served whether or not the decisionistic model is applicable.

Evaluation as Conflict Resolution

Evaluation can be viewed as a means for managing conflict so as to promote gradual social change. Evaluation is a signal that the program under study is subject to further negotiation and compromise. When groups with opposing views on a program agree to a test of its worth, they commit themselves to some compromise related to evaluation results. Social experimentation and evaluation resemble political debates. Candidates with strongly differing opinions will refuse to discuss issues with each other, each hoping for total victory. When they agree to debate, they acknowledge the worth of at least some part of their opponents' position and acknowledge their willingness to compromise. Likewise, a shift in the debate from program strategies to evaluation strategies indicates that both sides of the debate have tacitly agreed to investigate at least one new program.

In a similar vein, evaluations in the form of social experiments often act to produce social change. Differing parties may agree to a social experiment, each side feeling confident that the results of the experiment will help consolidate their position. But part of the experiment, however, is the creation of a pilot program; such pilot programs seldom disappear at the end of the experiment. Thus the conduct of a social experiment often leads to some form of social change, regardless of the outcome of the experiment (Floden, 1974).

Evaluation as Complacency Reduction

The very act of participating in an evaluation may spur the consideration of new practices by practitioners — managers, teachers, probation officers, social workers. Participation in evaluative efforts can prompt both the clarification of standard operating procedures and their revision.

Such complacency reduction serves at least two purposes. First, while working with the evaluator to determine how to measure program success, program participants clarify program goals. Second, participation in evaluation can lead to the rejection of previous goals and to the stimulation of alternatives. In the complacency reduction model, evaluation serves as a prod to program participants; it leads them to be clear about what they are trying to accomplish and to consider alternatives to the complacently accepted verbal goals.

The complacency reduction model resembles organization theory models of participatory decision making. These models make two distinct claims for gains from employee participation. The strong claim is that decisions made with greater employee participation are likely to be better decisions. The weaker claim is that the quality of life in the organization is improved, i.e., everyone is happier with the decision made (March & Simon, 1958).

The advantages of complacency reduction suggested above fall under the strong claim, e.g., complacency reduction leads to greater clarity and more alternatives, which in turn leads to a better program. The weaker claim suggests the additional benefit of an increased satisfaction with the administration and evaluation of the program.

The Eight-Year Study sponsored by the Progressive Education Association in the 1930s provides a classic example of complacency reduction (Smith & Tyler, 1942). In this instance, the evaluation effort had as its purpose the direct involvement of teachers in the formulation of program goals, the collection of data concerning performance, and the consideration of alternatives. The final project report only presented the various instruments and exercises (developed jointly with teachers) and eschewed the presentation or analysis of data. The impact of the evaluation was achieved not through conclusions or advice to management but through the involvement of program participants in asking questions about their own activities.[5]

Some Implications

Evaluations may serve to shape managerial decisions, to resolve conflict among policy elites, and to reduce complacency among program participants. Any particular evaluation is likely to function, to some extent, in each role. An adequate assessment of the impact of evaluation upon governmental processes must take notice of all these functions.

The decisionistic model has so dominated theoretical discussion of evaluation that other perspectives have been neglected or ignored. The model has had a deep imprint on recommendations designed to enhance the positive contribution of evaluation in the development of social programs. Thus, for example, advocacy of social experimentation clearly presumes the decisionistic model. Yet, the roles of evaluations in resolving conflict and reducing complacency are also important. The extent to which public officials understand and value these other evaluative functions is unclear. The rhetoric of the process through which evaluations are commissioned is dominated by the decisionistic model. "Requests for Proposals," the prime bureaucratic device for procuring evaluations, speak only of the gathering and analysis of data and the marshaling of evidence in the form of written reports. Put simply, the dominant pattern of thought that lies behind the commissioning process has been limited by the decisionistic model.

The skills that can be easily summoned from the professional evaluation community are biased when compared to the diverse functions served by evaluative effort. Experts in testing, econometrics, opinion surveys, quantitative analysis, and the techniques of proposal writing and report preparation are in ample supply. Those with interpersonal skills, with skills in drawing out assumptions and hidden goals, and with training in arbitration and mediation are less in evidence in the institutions that conduct evaluations. Evaluators are drawn almost exclusively from the fields of psychology and economics; fields such as political science, history, and anthropology are underrepresented. The skills of the evaluation industry will continue to be restricted to the narrow and traditional domains of experimental design and regression analysis until government officials are prepared to expand the skills summoned in the commissioning process.

The process of change cannot take place from the bottom up. Local administrators of publicly funded programs find it difficult to justify hiring evaluators with non-standard skills. Middle management in a controversial social intervention will find it difficult to facilitate conflict resolution. Similarly, such administrators are often in an awkward position to stimulate complacency reduction. This suggests that performance of the non-decisionistic functions of evaluation can be improved only through encouragement at higher levels of government.

The recognition of these additional functions also has implications for the evaluator. Although he may assign different priorities to the fulfillment of the various functions, the evaluator can make a contribution in more than one way. If he is unable to contribute information to any discrete decision, he may change his emphasis to complacency reduction or the mediation of conflicts. The evaluator tied to the decisionistic model may experience only frustration, while the evaluator with a wider perspective may find satisfaction with the results of his work.

Policy-makers and professional evaluators may be uncomfortable with a depiction of evaluation as an exercise in arbitration or complacency reduction. Their discomfort is evidence of the influence of scientism in thought about the relation of social science to government. The evaluation of governmental processes may profit from analogies with the scientific laboratory, but the laboratory is no more an apt metaphor than the psychiatrist's couch or the bargaining table. Our vision of evaluation and our repertoire of evaluative behavior must attend to each.

Two paths diverge from the current state of affairs. Down one path lies an increasing acceptance of evaluation as a vehicle for questioning existing institutions and practices. The work of Ralph Nader and his colleagues is the exemplar in this respect. Down the other path lies an increasing willingness of evaluators to join in efforts to bring conflicting policy elites into at least temporary agreements concerning the next programmatic steps to be attempted.

We urge a schizophrenic stance of fostering both. Governmental processes need to be subjected to more intensive questioning; mechanisms are also needed to contain the resulting conflicts.

Evaluation as Ritual: A Speculation

This discussion has not exhausted the possible functions of evaluation, but has merely drawn attention to previously suggested functions. We wish to suggest yet another function of evaluation, albeit a speculative one.

Evaluation may be seen as a ritual whose function is to calm the anxieties of the citizenry and to perpetuate an image of governmental rationality, efficacy, and accountability. The very act of requiring and commissioning evaluations may create the impression that government is seriously committed to the pursuit of publicly espoused goals, such as increasing student achievement or reducing malnutrition. Evaluations lend credence to this image even when programs are created primarily to appease interest groups.

The picture of a committed government serves two functions. First, it improves the image of public officials. In both democratic and authoritarian systems, political leaders must appear to be confident, efficacious, and "in control" if they hope to produce any changes (Arnold, 1935; Ellul, 1965). The government needs public cooperation to conduct any large-scale program. This cooperation is most likely to be forthcoming when the government maintains the impression that it can cope with problematic situations. When this appearance cannot be maintained, cooperation may disappear, and no government solution to the problem will be possible. Thus, government effectiveness is improved by the conduct of evaluations, whether or not the results are actually used.

The impression of government rationality also promotes a feeling of security in the citizenry. Societal problems are often magnified by the media to the point where a crisis seems imminent. The threat of crisis leads to a widespread sense of helplessness and hopelessness. Evaluations serve to combat this feeling by fostering the belief that the government is acting on everyone's behalf to find solutions to pressing problems. The publicity given to these efforts reduces the level of public anxiety, whether or not evaluations produce useful information.

Evaluations may also serve as a focal point for the reduction of complex social problems to a choice between relatively well-defined alternatives. This reduction of apparent complexity acts both to make the problems seem manageable and to give citizens the sense that they have a firm understanding of the issues involved (Ellul, 1965).

Ironically, the ritual functions of evaluation are best fostered by not acknowledging their existence. These functions depend on the creation of a particular impression; such an impression may be destroyed by announcing the intent. Just as one defeats the intent of a propaganda broadcast by announcing, "We will now attempt to portray Russia as a world menace," one destroys the impression of government competence by commissioning an evaluation for that express purpose. Nonetheless, evaluations may serve this function; in cases where this function is particularly desired (albeit not acknowledged), its action may be promoted by increasing the publicity given to the existence of the evaluation.

Note that the ritual function is not conspiracy of the governing to deceive the governed. It is a ritual in which individuals at all levels of governance participate in some way in order to bolster a common faith.

Cries of the failure of evaluation have assumed only one narrow model of the function of evaluation. This model represents only a part of the whole picture. Evaluation serves functions of complacency reduction and conflict management; it may serve other functions as well.

Notes

1. This name was suggested by Martin Rein.
2. Cohen and Garet, 1975, p. 19.
3. Truman, 1951, p. 393.
4. The likelihood of delay in acceptance is not symmetrical with respect to evaluative results. That is, it may require longer for negative results concerning program impact to "sink in" than is required for the acceptance of positive results. Given the rarity of "positive evaluations," however, there remains a high probability of the need for cumulative results.
5. A recent study of evaluative impact in California's educational system noted a similar effect of on-site visits by evaluation teams from the State Department of Education (Berke et al., 1976).

References

Alkin, Marvin C. "Evaluation Theory Development." *Evaluation Comment* 2 (1969), 2–7.
Arnold, Thurman W. *The Symbols of Government*. New Haven: Yale University Press, 1935.
Berke, Iris, Elaine French, Susan Heck, Michael Kirst and Stephen Weiner. *The Impact of State Mandated Evaluation Procedures Upon the Educational Programs of Local School Districts in California*. Report submitted to the California State Board of Education, Stanford University, 1976.
Campbell, D.T., and A. Erlebacher. "How Regression Artifacts in Quasi-Experimental Evaluations Can Mistakenly Make Compensatory Education Look Harmful." In: J. Helmuth (ed.), *Compensatory Education: A National Debate. Vol. III: The Disadvantaged Child*. New York: Brunner/Mazel, 1970, 185–210.
Cohen, David. "The Value of Social Experiments." In: Alice M. Rivlin and P. Michael Timpane (eds.), *Planned Variation in Education: Should We Give Up or Try Harder?* Washington, D.C.: The Brookings Institution, 1975, 147–76.

Cohen, David and M. Garet. "Reforming Educational Policy with Applied Social Research." *Harvard Educational Review* 45 (1975), 17–43.

Cyert, Richard M. and James G. March. *A Behavioral Theory of the Firm.* Englewood Cliffs: Prentice-Hall, 1963.

Downs, Anthony. "The Issue-attention Cycle and Improving Our Environment." Unpublished. Chicago: Real Estate Research Corporation, 1971.

Ellul, Jacques. *Propaganda: The Formation of Men's Attitudes.* New York: Knopf, 1965.

Elmore, Richard F. "The Politics and Administration of an Educational Experiment: The Case of Follow Through." Special Qualifying Paper. Cambridge, Massachusetts: Harvard University Graduate School of Education, 1972.

Elmore, Richard F. "Design of the Follow Through Experiment." In: Alice M. Rivlin and P. Michael Timpane (eds.), *Planned Variation in Education: Should We Give Up or Try Harder?* Washington, D.C.: The Brookings Institution, 1975, 23–46.

Floden, Margret B. (Buchmann). "Some Remarks on Social Experimentation." Unpublished paper. Stanford University, 1974.

Gilbert, John P., Richard J. Light, and Frederick Mosteller. "Assessing Social Innovations: An Empirical Base for Policy." In: Carl A. Bennett and Arthur A. Lumsdaine (eds.), *Evaluation and Experiment.* San Francisco: Academic Press, 1976.

Gramlich, Edward M. and Patricia P. Koshel. *Educational Performance Contracting: An Evaluation of an Experiment.* Washington, D.C.: The Brookings Institution, 1975.

Hitch, Charles, J. *Decision making for Defense.* Berkeley: University of California Press, 1970.

Horowitz, Irving Louis and James Everett Katz. *Social Science and Public Policy in the United States.* New York: Praeger Publishers, 1975.

March, James and Herbert Simon. *Organizations.* New York: John Wiley & Sons, 1958.

McLaughlin, Milbrey W. *Evaluation and Reform.* Cambridge, Massachusetts: Ballinger Publishing Co., 1975.

Orlans, Harold. "The Political Uses of Social Research." *American Academy of Political and Social Scientists* 394 (1971), 28–35.

Popham, W. James. *Educational Evaluation.* Englewood Cliffs: Prentice-Hall, 1975.

Provus, Malcolm M. *Discrepancy Evaluation.* Berkeley: McCutchan, 1971.

Riecken, H.W. and R.F. Boruch (eds.). *Social Experimentation.* New York: Academic Press, 1975.

Rivlin, Alice M. *Systematic Thinking for Social Action.* Washington, D.C.: The Brookings Institution, 1971.

Rivlin, Alice M. and P. Michael Timpane. *Planned Variation in Education: Should We Give Up or Try Harder?* Washington, D.C.: The Brookings Institution, 1975.

Schultze, Charles L. *The Politics and Economics of Public Spending.* Washington, D.C.: The Brookings Institution, 1968.

Smith, Eugene R. and Ralph W. Tyler. *Appraising and Recording Educational Progress.* New York: Harper and Brothers, 1942.

Speizman, William. "Evaluation: An Evaluation from a Sociological Perspective." In: C. Wayne Gordon (ed.), *Uses of the Sociology of Education.* Seventy-third Yearbook of the National Society for the Study of Education. Part II. Chicago: University of Chicago Press, 1974, 192–210.

Stake, R.E. "The Countenance of Educational Evaluation." *Teachers' College Record* 68 (1967), 523–40.

Steinbruner, John D. *The Cybernetic Theory of Decision: New Dimensions of Political Analysis*. Princeton: Princeton University Press, 1974.

Stufflebeam, Daniel L. et al. *Educational Evaluation and Decision Making*. Ithaca, Illinois: F.E. Peacock, 1971.

Truman, David B. *The Governmental Process: Political Interests and Public Opinion*. New York: Knopf, 1951.

Williams, Walter and John Evans. ''The Politics of Evaluation: The Case of Head Start.'' *The American Academy of Political and Social Science Annals*. 385 (1969), 118–32.

11 THE USE OF JUDICIAL EVALUATION METHODS IN THE FORMULATION OF EDUCATIONAL POLICY

Robert L. Wolf

More than ever before in our nation's history, the spirit of consumerism and participation has taken hold. Recently, in California, the people expressed their sentiment with the passage of Proposition 13. Only now, after the attending emotionalism has subsided, are the cold, disheartening facts and consequences becoming evident. Clearly, the vote was based more on frustration than on informed understanding of what the law would actually accomplish.

Something akin to what prompted Proposition 13 in California is being witnessed throughout educational institutions in America. The desire of the public to participate in educational policy formulation has been increasing steadily over the past decade. Unfortunately, manifestations of this desire have often come in the form of confrontational politics in which groups, both inside and outside the system, vie for privilege and control. While the focus of this article is not on school governance per se, it is worth noting that there is growing dissatisfaction among professional educators and the public at large about how the schools are run. The frightening increase in the number of teacher strikes alone attests to the fact that a crisis is brewing.

Wolf, Robert L. "The Use of Judicial Evaluation Methods in the Formulation of Education Policy." *Educational Evaluation and Policy Analysis*, no. 3, 1 (May–June 1979), 19–28. Copyright 1979, American Educational Research Association, Washington, D.C. Reprinted with permission.

The effectiveness of any educational enterprise is seriously undermined in the context of ongoing confrontational activity. Teacher strikes, as noted, are occurring with greater frequency across the nation and are staged most often on the grounds of "economic deprivation." In my view, however, this argument camouflages a more serious complaint, namely a *withholding of accessibility*. And this same withholding of accessibility applies to the general public as well. The result is a pervasive cynicism that weakens the educational process and ultimately undermines the possibility of a partnership between provider and consumer. Evidence suggests that parents, teachers, taxpayers, and vested interest groups within the community are being locked out of the decision- and policy-making process (Wolf, 1978a). Given the seriousness of this allegation, ameliorative strategies are not only indicated, but their initiation is imperative. What form positive and productive participation will take in policy formulation and decision making is, I believe, one of the most challenging of issues facing American educators today.

This issue is compounded, however, by the fact that evaluation studies commissioned at local, state, and national levels to inform policy decisions are often misleading, irrelevant, or totally inappropriate. The public has been invited to participate but too often only as a token gesture. And where technical input has been solicited, it is, in many instances, misguided. What is needed most are mechanisms that allow for both meaningful evaluation efforts and broad-scale participation to facilitate policy determination, particularly policy that is relevant to the needs of persons who will be directly impacted by it. Responsive evaluation strategies that involve broad participation are, therefore, viewed as one way to avoid Proposition 13-like confrontations in the future. The articulation of an evaluation method that allows for the systematic and legitimate involvement of parents, teachers, citizen groups, taxpayers, school board members, students, and administrators and at the same time helps to inform responsive policy is the purpose of this essay.

Policy and Evaluation

It is close to being true that policy is decision making set in stone — the transformation from due process to law. Most policy studies, particularly in education, occur *after* policy has been initiated and implemented. While these kinds of studies are important in understanding the impact or effects of policy, they do little to guide or inform new policy initiatives. In fact, the methodology is often so restrictive that many important questions regarding policy impact go unanswered and often are not raised in the first place. It is my view that methodological reform is needed not only to study policy, but, more importantly, to help inform it. At this juncture in our social history, methods are urgently needed to involve broad participation in policy making. Evaluating possible policy alternatives in advance of the formulation of policy becomes critical. In other words, evaluation efforts that help *form* policy are important, more so than evaluation efforts that *study* policy effects post facto. Recognizing that people want to be involved in the determination of policies that affect their lives, studies that lead to policy formulation seem not only appropriate but increasingly attractive as an alternative. In fact, the concept of *policy-analysis studies* may need to be supplanted by the more participatory concept of *policy-formulation studies* if inquiry and reason are to survive in these consumer-oriented times.

Given this view, it seems unlikely that conventional study methods that rely so heavily on esoteric processes, including hypothesis testing and statistical inference, will provide the means to either understand or change the circumstances under consideration. Although conventional strategies may be appropriate for some particular evaluation questions, using them in the context of trying to comprehend the broad impact of various educational processes seems untenable. Specifically, when a decision-making body contemplates the formulation of policy or the evaluation of potential policy positions, it is essential that the perceptions of persons affected by the existing policy and/or emerging policy be analyzed.

Perhaps a brief discussion of what constitutes a policy-level problem is in order. Professor Dale Mann, a leading expert on educational policy, defines policy concerns as:

1. public in nature;
2. very consequential, i.e., issues having both importance and impact;
3. complex, i.e., issues embedded in political, economic, psychological, social, and moral components;
4. dominated by uncertainty, i.e., issues, and/or contemporary manifestations of past dilemmas; and
5. complicated by differing and competing interests (Mann, 1975). If these assumptions are correct, then many educational studies are, in essence, policy studies and, therefore, demand responsive evaluation methods.

One such responsive approach is the Judicial Evaluation Method (JEM) that I have been developing and refining over the past several years (Wolf, 1973, 1974a, b; 1975; Wolf & Tymitz, 1977a, b; Wolf, 1978a, b). This method provides a means for all parties (parents, children, school personnel at all levels, taxpayers, and community groups) to participate meaningfully throughout all phases of the evaluation process and in a variety of capacities. The remainder of this paper identifies conceptual and operational features of the JEM and illustrates its application to policy formulation studies at the local and national levels through two brief case examples.

The Judicial Evaluation Method

Elsewhere (Wolf, 1978b), I have carefully described and analyzed the development of the JEM, discussed its various implementations, and suggested new applications in the context of evaluation reform. While that discussion is too lengthy to reiterate, let it suffice to say that the law, as a metaphor, offers many important concepts (fact-finding, adversarial proceedings, cross-examination, evidentiary rules and procedures, structured deliberations, etc.) that when adapted to evaluation efforts add certain dimensionality lacking in more conventional forms of social inquiry. In contrast to more *scientific* methodologies, which generally exclude human testimony and judgment in the spirit of seeking objectivity, the *legal* model places a premium on these forms of evidence. In fact, human testimony is the cornerstone of evidence used in any legal proceeding. Testimony must be understood within the context of facts and situations explored by the parties at trial. The ultimate evidence, then, which guides deliberation and judgment, includes not only the *facts* but a wide variety of perceptions, opinions, biases, and speculations, all within a context of values and beliefs. Oftentimes the more subjective forms of evidence help put the facts into proper perspective.

The JEM was conceptualized in the early 1970s as a method which would, at least in part, function for persons needing to reach some decision in education as the judge in a courtroom does for jurors; that is, it would establish systematic procedures for inquiry and set forth criteria for classifying, evaluating, and presenting evidence in a clear, cogent, and reasonable manner. By adapting a modified set of legal procedures, I believed that educational evaluators would tend to rely more on human testimony and be better able to develop a clearer understanding of the range of issues involved in their inquiry. Perhaps the most significant aspect of the judicial metaphor, as I see it, is that the court's mode of inquiry is educative. The decision-making group (the jury) is instructed, during the course of the trial, as to how to use the evidence, weigh it accordingly, and render sound judgments based on its presentations. At its conception, the JEM was intended as a means for translating the appropriate legal metaphors into social-inquiry terms. My intention was not to replicate legal procedures in educational evaluation, but rather to use the metaphors of law in developing appropriate and meaningful evaluation concepts and procedures.

The JEM has been implemented in a variety of educational contexts over the past half decade (see the recent review by Wolf, 1978b), thus providing for major reconsiderations of the procedures and the substantive aspects of the approach. It was discovered several years ago that an in-depth investigation was critical in the implementation of the JEM and thus stimulated the development of a new methodological strategy called *naturalistic inquiry* that my colleagues and I at Indiana University have been refining during the last few years. This new method has been gaining popularity in its own right (Wolf & Tymitz, 1976; 1977a, b; Guba, 1978; Wolf, 1978b).

In order to conduct the most in-depth *judicial* inquiry possible and to prepare a full and complete argument for each issue being evaluated, investigators need to become familiar with a wide range of naturalistic inquiry techniques (Wolf, 1978*a*). No case can be built without evidence, and no evidencee can be identified, examined, and amassed without carefully executed in-depth interviews, observations, site analyses, document review (including both quantitative and qualitative information), and evaluation of existing data summaries. Judicial procedures rely heavily on the ability of each evaluation team to conduct broad, responsive, naturalistic exploration.

The development, refinement, and adaptation of these rigorous field techniques has made the JEM particularly unique. The method has now combined intensive field investigation with the public display of a wide range of evaluation evidence. Moreover, the JEM, particularly when applied to policy-related circumstances, demands that persons affected by existing or emerging policy be intimately involved in the inquiry process. This involvement ensures that the method is not only rigorous but responsive as well.

Prior to discussing the operational stages of the JEM, one final comment is offered. During the last five years, the JEM has been both applied and critiqued by others (Levine, 1976; Worthen & Owens, 1978; Popham & Carlson, 1977; Thurston, 1978). It has been subjected to more careful scrutiny than perhaps most evaluation methods receive. In some instances, it has been unduly lauded, but too often it has been misapplied and misunderstood. The power of the judicial metaphor, at least for me, is that it is aimed at *judicious* practice. Oftentimes, however, the metaphor has been sufficiently bastardized so as to produce less than desirable results. The JEM is *not* an adversarial debate as such, and I have consistently resisted the tendency to refer to it as *adversary evaluation* as others do. As stated earlier, the metaphors of law are just that — metaphors. As metaphors they offer important insight as to how meaningful, judicious evaluation can be conducted in education. Once the concepts are taken too literally, the object of judicial evaluation then becomes *winning*. This is precisely *not* what the JEM strives for. The goal, rather, is directed toward clarification and understanding of the complexity involved in educational programs and the subsequent offering of recommendations that can inform responsive action.

The remainder of this paper will present the operational stages of the JEM when applied to policy-formulation activities, and describe two case examples of its implementation, one in a national policy-study effort and the other within a local school community.

Stages of JEM in Policy Formulation

Having implemented the JEM in a variety of socio-educational settings, four well-defined stages can now be identified. They are the issue generation stage; the issue selection stage; the preparation of arguments stage; and the public hearing (Clarification Forum) stage.

Stage 1: Issue Generation.   This stage is the exploratory phase of the inquiry, designed to identify as broad a range of issues as possible. A pool of issues emerges out of the content of interviews, through direct observations and source documents. These preliminary data help to shape the course of the inquiry through succeeding stages. The strategies embodied in the naturalistic inquiry paradigm predominate this stage of the process.

Stage 2: Issue Selection.   During this stage, the array of issues pooled is reduced to a manageable size for presentation at the Clarification Forum. Issue selection is sensitive to the audience's information needs and involves delineation of the most salient issues. Extensive analysis of a full range of issues occurs as does a critique of logical inferences relevant to the substantiation of those issues. Because aspects of issues may change over time, frequent analysis for relevance and interpretation is essential. It is important to note that issues that are not selected for presentation in the forum remain intact and are included in the final documentation of the policy-formulation study. Again, the strategies of naturalistic inquiry are extensively employed.

Stage 3: Preparation of Arguments.   This stage involves building cases and preparing final arguments for case presentation. Specific points of contention are developed around each issue so that case presenters may pose distinctively different perspectives. At this juncture, witnesses are selected and re-interviewed relative to their anticipated testimony. Documents and transcripts are analyzed to refine lines of arguments and to develop evidence for the hearings. It is to be noted that arguments are not designed to provoke confrontation. The aim is that each side be given the opportunity to present opposing views, thus providing differing perspectives on complex issues. It is important to note that during this stage both teams share their information and respective plans of action. Since the overall process is aimed at clarification and responsive policy formulation, sharing of insights becomes imperative.

Stage 4: Clarification Forum.   In this final stage of the inquiry, a public presentation of the data is made. The format of the hearings *approximates* that of a court of law. A panel comprised of policymakers, citizens, etc., is convened to hear the evidence. Case presenters make their cases through witnesses selected to represent their views relative to a given issue. Direct, cross, re-direct, and re-cross examination of all the witnesses are engaged in; and, as in a court of law, opening and closing arguments are presented. Based on the evidence presented, the panel deliberates and makes its recommendations.

Key Roles in Implementing the JEM

In implementing the four stages of the JEM, several key roles have been identified: investigative teams, the case analyst, the case presenter, the forum moderator, the clarification panel, and the panel facilitator.

Investigative Teams. Each issue to be "adjudicated" is investigated by two teams directed to explore the different perspectives on a particular issue. The duties of the investigator include identifying potential witnesses; conducting in-depth interviews; preparing narrative syntheses for all interviews; and identifying documents, artifacts, and other evidence. Essentially, the teams are responsible for building comprehensive cases and for developing challenges to the case proposed by the other team.

Case Analyst. This person serves as the investigative team supervisor and is responsible for overseeing all activities of a given team. Specifically, the case analyst identifies and screens potential witnesses, conducts in-depth interviews, debriefs team members, and presents interim reports on the procedural and substantive status of interviews and arguments. Analysts continually interact with each other to share information and plan for the Clarification Forum.

Case Presenter. Case presenters have the responsibility of making the actual arguments at the Clarification Forum. In the form and style of "attorneys for the prosecution" and "attorneys for the defense," case presenters argue the different positions on any given issue. Arguments are made through the testimony of witnesses and in opening and closing statements. Skillful direct and cross examination of witnesses is critical in this public presentation of the data. (Most of the implementation efforts by others, when using the JEM, have failed to include this critical examination of witnesses.)

Forum Moderator. The forum moderator enforces the rules of evidence and procedure and directs the scheduled flow of events as the forum proceeds. The moderator also assists the clarification panel to judge the adequacy of the evidence presented and clarifies points of contention. The moderator rules on objections during the course of witness examination and also instructs the panel as to how to weigh evidence and how to structure its deliberations.

Clarification Panel. The clarification panel is composed of persons interested in and perhaps experienced in the particular policy question under consideration, but not necessarily responsible for its formulation and/or implementation. The composition of the panel varies, but it is likely to represent groups such as school personnel, parents, advocacy groups, state and federal educational agencies, and the like. The panel is charged with considering the evidence presented. Panel members are afforded the opportunity to ask questions of the witnesses for purposes of clarification during the course of the public proceedings. Upon completion of their deliberations, the panel presents a written statement of their recommendations. The deliberation period is not public, although a stenographer may record the session to capture the essence of what is being said. However, all statements remain anonymous.

Panel Facilitator.   The panel facilitator is a person familiar with the judicial approach, who helps the panel meet its responsibilities. The role involves clarifying points of confusion during the deliberation session and helping the panel weigh evidence. In essence, the role is an extension of the forum moderator's function and is provided exclusively for the clarification panel.

Applications of the Model

Employing the JEM in the context of policy-formulation studies is a complex and complicated task. The method has been recently applied in a prepolicy formulation study on the national level and also in a local-school community. Each example will be briefly reported and analyzed.

Example 1:   A National Policy Study of P.L. 94–142

Although the judicial inquiry strategy has been introduced previously as an evaluation paradigm in several large scale implementations (Wolf, 1975), this study served as the prime adaptation to policy planning and analysis. In brief, the effort involved the examination and clarification of individual and organizational expectations, perceptions, practices, and concerns related to implementation of Public Law 94–142, the Education for All Handicapped Children Act (signed by President Ford on November 29, 1975, and initiated on October 1, 1977).

Analogous to a civil rights act for handicapped children, P.L. 94–142 is aimed at assuring that all handicapped children have available to them a free and appropriate education. The law, through a variety of specific requirements, mandates that the instruction and services offered by the public schools must emphasize special education designed to meet the needs of each child.

The Bureau of Education for the Handicapped (BEH) has been charged with assuring compliance with the law as well as providing technical assistance to local and state agencies in fulfilling their respective roles. Given the complexity of the law and the responsibility that the BEH has for formulating policy to guide implementation and to assess effectiveness, the study was created to provide a context for federal, state, and local education agencies to examine and clarify expectations, practices, and concerns relative to P.L. 94–142.

Specifically, the policy formulation study was designed to identify the concerns of those responsible for and influenced by the implementation of the law; facilitate broad understanding of the law and how its components could be implemented across state and local agencies; and provide an opportunity for fair and rational discussion of the issues related to implementation of the law.

The JEM was selected because it offered a useful mechanism for collecting, synthesizing, presenting, and judging in-depth information related to people's beliefs, concerns, and attitudes regarding potentially controversial issues. The method also permitted meaningful input by persons ultimately affected by federal, state, and local policy formulations pursuant to the law's implementation. During the one-year investigation from October 1976 to September 1977, the statements of hundreds of parents, teachers, administrators, state educational officials, advocacy group members, congressional staff, professional experts, and handicapped children led to clarification sessions in four selected states.

Staff.   The staff for this study included federal administrative coordinators from BEH and state coordinators responsible for logistics and information collection, synthesis, and dissemination. I was responsible for the methodological design, staff training, and continuous monitoring and technical facilitation. Two case analysts were identified for each state; each analyst supervised a team of investigators. A panel facilitator and two forum moderators were also used.

Issue Generation and Selection.   Three issues were finally selected following several months of intensive interviews and exchange of findings among the state coordinators. Each issue was stated so that dichotomous arguments could be made. The three issues were:

1. use of procedural documents for monitoring purposes will limit/will not limit other potential uses;
2. standardization of the mandated procedures will facilitate/will not facilitate the implementation of the federal requirements; and
3. the impact of the federal requirements will be to increase/decrease the quality of education of handicapped children.

Case Building.   Several hundred persons within each state were interviewed during the preliminary case-building phase, in which potential witnesses were identified and the saliency of issues confirmed. The final selection of witnesses occurred after four additional rounds of interviews.

The Clarification Forum.   The four Clarification Forums were conducted during May 1977. Each state's forum lasted three days. Recommendations of the clarification panel were presented in a written document.

Outcome.   The JEM produced a prodigious amount of qualitative information, all of which was analyzed, synthesized, and presented in state reports. Each Forum attracted wide attention and served as an important communication vehicle. Most significantly, the findings and recommendations by the Clarification Forums were used in drafting the final Federal Regulations of P.L. 94–142, issued in August 1977.

Example 2:   A Study of Policy Formulation in a Local School District

In this application, the JEM involved community-wide participation in exploring issues concerning public school governance in a central Indiana School District (Wolf, 1978*a*). The study's purpose was two-fold. First, it was designed to examine the feasibility of the method on a community-wide basis. Second, the study was intended to learn about how public schools are governed and to make suggestions for policy alternatives. The project was supported by a grant from the Lilly Endowment.

Methods.   The same operational stages described in the preceding section on the national study of P.L. 94–142 were employed in this local effort, i.e., issue generation, issue selection, preparation of arguments, and a Clarification Forum. The study was widely publicized by the local media, and citizens in the community were eager to participate, along with school personnel and students. After several months of field research by investigative teams (in-depth interviewing of students, teachers, parents, school administrators, etc.; a perusal of a full range of relevant resource documents; etc.), a Clarification Forum was held, spanning three consecutive evenings, which resulted in the development of a detailed set of recommendations by the clarification panel (comprised exclusively of citizens from the community). These recommendations were submitted to the school superintendent and local school board for their consideration. Local news media also presented the recommendations to the public.

Outcomes.   While the full impact of this study is not yet known, one fact is unassailable. The JEM is a viable mechanism for helping a wide variety of persons in local communities take an active role in exploring school-related issues and participate in school-policy formulation. Since the forum, the chamber of commerce, the school board, representatives of the central administration, and other interested groups and individuals have met to discuss the policy recommendations. Out of the eleven recommendations issued by the clarification panel in April 1978, seven have already been adopted. Informal interviews conducted with community leaders, parents, and school personnel after the project ended suggest that the public nature of the process and the fact that different groups participated equally legitimized the policy recommendations and accounted for their wide acceptance. Other school districts in the state have since expressed their interest in participating in community-wide policy formulation efforts.

In both examples cited above, the JEM has demonstrated an impact on the policy formulation process. This is particularly noteworthy because in the past many evaluation approaches have failed to be instrumental in the determination of educational policy. If the components of the JEM are viewed as helpful to the policy formulation process by a range of persons involved in and/or affected by that process, then hope is offered in bridging the gap between evaluation and policy that has plagued past evaluation efforts. This is true at both state and national levels, as well as across local communities. In the final section of this paper, the JEM will be analyzed with particular emphasis on its role in policy formulation. Additionally, specific methodological insights will be offered.

Further Considerations of the JEM in Policy Formulation

The discussion below will again focus upon the operational stages of the JEM, but will do so this time as a means of illuminating and clarifying the role that each stage serves in the policy formulation process. This presentation is based upon the experience and insights gained through the implementation of the two studies discussed earlier. The issue stages, the case building, and the Clarification Forum will each be treated separately.

Issue Stages

As stated, both the issue-generation and issue-selection stages are unique to this inquiry mode. Many policy studies begin with a preconceived set of questions that create a study focus potentially irrelevant or insensitive to the perceptions of those involved in or affected by the educational processes in question. In this sense, such studies may be methodologically sound (according to the criteria used to judge conventional evaluation-policy studies), but conceptually and substantively inappropriate.

A major assumption underlying the JEM's application to policy formulation is that policy studies should focus on issues that are responsive to the needs, beliefs, aspirations, concerns, and perceptions of the people involved. This emphasis places great demands upon the initial fact-finding phase of the investigation. In both of the studies cited in this paper, the issue-generation and selection stages have been particularly vulnerable for a variety of methodological and political reasons. The sensitive nature of the interaction required by the JEM between the investigator and individual respondents demands a level of skill beyond those typically demonstrated by evaluators employing more conventional methods. Essentially, the issue-framing process attempts to ascertain what realities exist in people's minds regarding certain socio-educational matters. Of importance here is that it is far more difficult to identify issues than it is to have people respond to issues that are already formulated. Nothing less than this kind of issue-identification process will suffice, however, if the JEM is to satisfy its requirement for responsiveness. This is particularly true in policy-related applications.

Methodologically speaking, the scope of the initial interview sample is critical. Here, the concern is not of randomness or representativeness; but, rather, for both political and substantive reasons, it is imperative that the investigator identify *key* informants who have a sense as to the critical issues and concerns that will form and guide the policy review. The more skilled and experienced the investigator, the more that investigator will be able to move beyond the expected contacts and uncover a new and expanding variety of persons to be interviewed.

Even when the issues are generated and delimited, the challenge is to state them in an appropriate manner. The language and construction used is critical, for issue statements must be credible and legitimate to those whose input helped shape them. It is essential that respondents in the initial fact-finding interviews recognize that the tentative issue statement reflects their views.

When issues are being selected for presentation in the Clarification Forum, care must be taken to frame those issues so as to promote a dialectical exchange. While the forum is not designed to be contentious, it is designed to present arguments around a common set of issues. A critical point in the evolution of the JEM's implementation strategies occurred when it was recognized that an operational definition of the term *issue* was needed, as well as a set of procedures for final issue selection. It was determined that an issue was a statement or proposition upon which ordinary persons could disagree and thus establish arguments around points of disagreement. Operationally, however, most people do not speak in terms of issues (as defined here). People voice concern, articulate problems, make suggestions, and offer congratulations. These praises, concerns, suggestions, etc. all count as evidence. They need to be recorded, documented, analyzed, and even presented at the forum through the testimony of persons who first revealed such comments. But these data must always be presented in the context of a specific issue. The issues become the focal points for the presentation of opposing arguments, which in turn are comprised of specific concerns. At first it was believed that issues could only reflect extremely dichotomized positions, i.e., program strengths versus weaknesses, go or no-go decisions, etc. Over the years, however, it was realized that any legitimate differing of positions around a central statement constituted an issue worthy of consideration. Obviously, the issues of greatest saliency to those ultimately involved in or affected by the policy decisions in question should be the ones upon which to focus. It is important to note that when the final set of issues are agreed upon, they are stated in a manner that provokes reasoned and reasonable discussion but which is void of adversarial contest. Arguments that are contrived for the sake of argument only serve to cloud an issue and must be carefully avoided. In policy formulation studies, it is especially important to establish positions based upon real differences.

Case Building

Case building provides the critical link between the data collection and analysis and the public presentation of the evidence and arguments. How, and how well, arguments are constructed and presented will determine what the audience learns at the public Clarification Forum and what the clarification panel ultimately sees fit to recommend. Poorly contrived arguments can only serve to distort the evidence and undermine the possibility of a powerful set of panel recommendations. Again, staff expertise and experience are essential during this investigative-analytical stage of the process.

One particular concern during the case-building phase is evidence. Without strong, cogent arguments accompanied by relevant and clear supporting evidence, the Clarification Forum potentially becomes a "paper tiger." The most difficult challenge of the entire process is to have the clarification panel produce a set of policy recommendations that are specific enough to be both operational and helpful. In order for the panel to produce such recommendations, the arguments and evidence must likewise be detailed and specific. In the final analysis, the burden rests with the investigative teams who, through attention to necessary details, conduct inquiries which will prove useful. While much has been accomplished during the recent implementations of the JEM that helped establish the validity and reliability of the data being collected, it has been observed that the more expert the field investigators, the greater the potential for an information-rich forum and a clear, cogent, specific set of policy recommendations.

The Clarification Forum

As stated, the Clarification Forum is the culminating event of the entire investigative process. While most of the salient evidence is presented during this phase, information not specifically relevant to the agreed-upon issues, but nonetheless important, is documented through more conventional means.

There is a system of checks and balances that operates in the Clarification Forum. If the cross-examination by the case analyst is weak, then either the forum moderator or the panel facilitator assumes responsibility for deeper examination. Likewise, if the panel fails to ask obvious questions, the forum moderator or the case analysts can intervene to acquire the needed information. This system helps to assure that the maximum amount of information possible is solicited from the witnesses. The more information gleaned, the better able the panel is to make informed and responsible recommendations. (Experience suggests that a training session for the panel in the examination of witnesses and deliberation procedures enhances their role greatly.)

Special Staffing Problems

The success of the JEM depends heavily upon an exceptionally competent staff experienced in interview and observation techniques. This is particularly true when dealing with politically sensitive policy studies, such as the ones presented here.

Because of the many subtleties inherent in the application of the JEM and because routinized procedures are rarely indicated, staff must possess a special flair for ingenuity and a high tolerance for ambiguity not often required by other inquiry approaches. It is difficult to teach the needed skills. The worker in this method must be sensitive, perceptive, analytical, and dedicated. A staff member must also be a businessperson, in that the entire process rests on the negotiation and maintenance of a full range of informal contracts. School personnel do not cooperate unless they are *contracted* to do so; witnesses do not testify unless they have been *contracted* to do so.

The field worker who collects the data is the same person who joins with colleagues to define, construct, and delineate issues and concerns. Now the challenge is for the businessperson-journalistic reporter to become epistemologist-scientist. Persons with the range of skills needed and the ability to shift quickly through a range of diverse demands are indeed difficult to find.

Conclusion

In the final analysis, I believe that the use of the JEM offers great promise. Policy formulation should always be a matter of public debate, a forum where a variety of views are attended to and legitimized. In both of the studies cited in this article, many viewpoints were solicited and honored. After all, no policy is valuable if it is not viewed as credible by those who are to be influenced. Because these studies were framed in a public context and because people were asked to contribute *their* insights, it is believed that policy so formulated will be viewed as being not only credible but supportable. The JEM provides an opportunity for broad public participation in dealing with controversial, ambiguous, and complex sets of issues. In providing such an opportunity, the framework extends beyond what has been traditionally accomplished and offers a hopeful mechanism for policy making in the future.

References

Guba, E. *Toward a methodology of naturalistic inquiry in educational evaluation.* CSE Monograph Series in Evaluation, no. 8. University of California at Los Angeles, 1978.

Levine, M. "Experiences in adapting the jury trial to the problem of educational program evaluation." Unpublished manuscript, State University of New York at Buffalo, 1976.

Mann, D. *Policy decisions in education: An introduction to calculation and control.* New York: Teacher's College Press, 1975.

Popham, W.J., and Carlson, D. "Deep dark deficits of the adversary evaluation model." *Educational Researcher,* no. 6, 6 (1977), 3–6.

Thurston, P. "Revitalizing adversary evaluation: Deep dark deficits or muddled mistaken musings." *Educational Researcher,* no. 7, 7 (1978), 3–8.

Wolf, R.L. "The application of judicial concepts to educational evaluation." Unpublished doctoral dissertation, University of Illinois, 1973.

Wolf, R.L. *Evidence and Evaluation: The metaphors of law.* Paper presented at the annual meeting of the American Educational Research Association, 1974*a*.

Wolf, R.L. "Trial by jury." *The Phi Delta Kappan,* November 1974*b*.

Wolf, R.L. "Operationalizing responsive evaluation." Unpublished manuscript, Indiana Center for Evaluation, 1975.

Wolf, R.L. *Studying school governance through judicial evaluation procedures.* Bloomington, Indiana: Indiana Center for Evaluation, 1978*a*.

Wolf, R.L. *Judicial metaphors in education: Past, present and future.* 1978*b*.

Wolf, R.L. and Tymitz, B.L. "Ethnography and reading: Matching inquiry mode to process." *Reading Research Quarterly,* September 1976.

Wolf, R.L. and Tymitz, B.L. *Enhancing policy formulation through naturalistic/judicial inquiry procedures: A study of the individual education program component of public law 94–142.* Bloomington, Indiana: Indiana Center for Evaluation, 1977*a*.

Wolf, R.L. and Tymitz, B.L. "Framing issues in naturalistic/judicial inquiry." Unpublished manuscript, Indiana Center for Evaluation, 1977*b*.

Worthen, B.R. and Owens, T.R. "Adversary evaluation and the school psychologist." Unpublished monograph, Portland, Oregon: Northwest Regional Educational Laboratory, January 1978.

12 DEEP DARK DEFICITS OF THE ADVERSARY EVALUATION MODEL[1]

W. James Popham and Dale Carlson

As a spectator attraction, competition is hard to beat. Whether it's a courtroom drama or a sporting event, we thrill as the contest totters in favor of one side, then the other. Perhaps it's the uncertainty of the outcome that fascinates us. But whatever the appeal, it's quite clear that ancient folks, like present-day ones, got genuinely excited by competitive events. The athletic contests of antiquity, whether Greek, Roman, or Mayan, were capable of drawing standing-room-only audiences.

It is not surprising, therefore, that when people recently started touting the adversary model as a novel approach to educational evaluation, many of us were enthralled. After all, this would be a chance to pick up all the dramatic dividends of a competitive event and, if the legal folklore is to be believed, to end up with an objective evaluation in which both sides of a case are most forcefully presented. Oh yes, the adversary evaluation model was quite alluring.

Adversarying under Palm Trees

In spring, 1976, the writers were invited to participate in an adversary evaluation project being directed by the Northwest Regional Educational Laboratory

Popham, W. James and Carlson, Dale. "Deep Dark Deficits of the Adversary Evaluation Model." *Educational Researcher,* (June 1977), 3–6. Copyright 1977, American Educational Research Association, Washington, D.C. Reprinted with permission.

(NWREL) for the state of Hawaii. The focus of the evaluation was a large-scale, team-teaching program for K-3 classes in Hawaii, a program in which three teachers worked with two classrooms full of children, hence the designation: The Hawaii 3-on-2 Program.

Both of us were intrigued by the adversary evaluation model and wanted to learn more about it. And if we were going to learn about the adversary approach, then careful analysis (three seconds) suggested that Hawaii would be a more suitable place to acquire such knowledge than, say, equatorial Africa, Antarctica, or just about any place else we could think of. Adversarying in Hawaii was an offer we just couldn't turn down.

Thus, for the better part of a year, we were intermittently involved in carrying out an adversary evaluation. We were two members of a four-person Advocate Team, the team which by coin-toss ended up defending the raptures of the Hawaii 3-on-2 Program. Another fourperson team, designated as the *Adversary Team,* was charged with attacking it. Staff members from NWREL served as arbiters. A complete report of the evaluation effort is available elsewhere.[2]

The Cream Begins to Curdle

During the early stages of the evaluation, both of us behaved like kittens with bowls full of cream. We were caught up with the glitter of the adversary approach even as we worked out ground rules with our colleagues, and we anticipated the future give-and-take of the adversarial contest. It seemed, further, like an excellent vehicle for setting forth two partisan but opposing views of the program we were evaluating. Everything was peachy.

But as the months went wandering by and we became more and more conversant with the adversary evaluation model, either our cream began to curdle or we sensed the incongruity of behaving like middle-aged kittens. Now, the evaluation behind us, we want to register downright skepticism regarding the adversary evaluation model, at least insofar as it is applied to education. Its deficits are deep in the sense that they may render the approach essentially inappropriate for any significant applications. Its deficits are dark in the sense that it's hard to detect some of these weaknesses unless you've actually participated in an adversarial evaluative effort and attempted self-consciously to appraise what was going on.

We wish to set forth, therefore, the set of weaknesses which we believe are present in most adversary evaluation approaches. Along the way, we will attempt to offer a few suggestions, where warranted, for ameliorating certain of the weaknesses.

Some of the deficits to be discussed in the following paragraphs, obviously, represent more serious difficulties than others. Some, it appears, can be taken care of with either modest or serious effort. Some, in our estimate, are sufficiently formidable that they render the adversary approach ineffectual for educational evaluators.

Because the typical ingredients of adversary evaluation models have been described elsewhere, they will not be recounted here. For those unfamiliar with the adversary approach, an examination of these sources is recommended.[3] Clearly, there are all sorts of variations in the actual way that an adversary evaluation study is carried out.

Deficit Number One: Disparity in Proponent Prowess

If an adversary evaluation model is to function effectively, it is assumed that both sides of an issue will be satisfactorily presented for the consideration of decision-makers. This is far easier to assume than to accomplish. And, of course, if one side of a proposition is not adequately defended, then the decisionmakers may erroneously opt for the other side merely because it appears more compelling.

All too often we see instances in our nation's legal enterprise where one would have to be naive to contend that equality of justice is present. Whereas affluent defendants can have an attorney such as Melvin Belli or F. Lee Bailey, poverty-stricken defendants may be obliged to accept a public defender fresh out of law school. And, notwithstanding a biblical exception or two, most David-Goliath contests end up in favor of the big fellow.

In the conduct of adversary educational evaluations, it is all too likely that there will also be a disparity in the skill of the two competing teams (or individuals). The danger, of course, is that the effective team may end up defending the weak side of the case, yet do it so well that the decisionmakers are won over.

Although we all recognize that this happens in the real world, somehow the occasional injustice that stems from mismatched lawyers seems less outrageous than when an incorrect educational decision is made because of a mismatch in adversary skills. In the courtroom, one or two people at most are usually wronged. That's terrible, but we recognize that systems operated by human beings will have their share of failures. We have become inured to an occasional miscarriage of justice. Yet, when the matter at hand is an educational decision that can influence the formative years of essentially unprotected children, all of a sudden the stakes are perceived as much higher. Injustice is unacceptable whenever it occurs, but when it occurs with large numbers of young children, it seems genuinely intolerable.

In the adversary evaluation of the Hawaii 3-on-2 Program referred to earlier, the writers found themselves assigned (via a coin-flip) to defend the merits of a program which we became increasingly convinced was not a cost/effective investment for the taxpayers of Hawaii. Primary-grade children, we came to believe, were being shortchanged because a program that cost about $10,000,000 annually was not yielding its promised results. But there we were — obliged to defend it. What would happen if we did an effective job of convincing the Hawaii decisionmakers, so convincing that they opted to maintain the 3-on-2 program in its present form? Our team might win the adversary contest, but the children of Hawaii would experience a decisive loss.

Yet, should we harness our zeal in trying to defend the 3-on-2 program? Obviously not, since the adversary model would then lose its purported advantage of fully setting forth both sides of a case.

Remedy. In order to cope with this profound weakness of the adversary evaluation model, it is our belief that procedures will have to be employed whereby each adversary team (individual) argues *both* sides of the case at hand. By having each team prepare a pair of reports, one pro and one con, the decisionmakers would be able to consider two sets of positive and two sets of negative arguments. The more capable team should be able to do a better job defending the more defensible side of the issue.

While this does involve double work for the adversary teams, it should pose no insurmountable intellectual problems. College and high school debaters constantly shift sides of an issue as they wind their way through each year's debate tournaments. If anything, by undertaking to defend both sides of an issue, members of an adversary team should experience less ethical qualms because they can do their best job in defending both the "wrong" and "right" sides of a case.

Deficit Number Two: Fallible Arbiters

Anyone familiar with our courts will instantly concede that judges vary in their abilities. Some people who sit on the bench are better suited to dusting or polishing it. But, thankfully, when a judge rules improperly in a trial, that case can be appealed to a higher court where such errors can be rectified.

We don't have an appeals court when we carry out adversary evaluations. If the people coordinating the overall conduct of the evaluation muck up, where is an adversary team to turn? Oh, resigning from the project is always possible, but that hardly seems appropriate in many instances. And merely registering formal protests doesn't do the job if the arbiters rule against you. The situation can become really sticky at times. Let's illustrate.

In the evaluation of the Hawaii 3-on-2 Program, the writers were obliged to defend 3-on-2. We were certain that if standardized achievement tests were used, there would be no significant differences in favor of the 3-on-2 pupils. Previous evaluations of 3-on-2 had turned out that way. Standardized achievement tests almost invariably result in no significant differences. Why should anything be different in this case? Yet, even though we realized that standardized achievement tests would be used in the 3-on-2 evaluation, for surely our adversary colleagues would insist that they be used, we were prepared to argue against their appropriateness.

In the early stages of the evaluation, as the adversary teams and the arbiters worked out procedural details of the evaluation, one of the ground rules agreed to was that both teams would collaboratively work out the design for the study, then agree not to subsequently criticize that design. It seemed a sensible ground rule.

But our team did not interpret that ground rule to preclude the possibility of criticizing the tests themselves, whereas the arbiters assumed that the "design" included the measuring instruments used. It was an instance of the kind of misunderstanding that often pops up when dealing with such matters. But had the arbiters imposed their interpretation on us, rigidly insisting that we could not attack the testing devices, our case would have been badly damaged. (It was weak enough in any event.) What should we have done?

As it turned out, the arbiters exercised good judgment (in our view) and allowed us to question the suitability of the tests. Yet, there are innumerable points along the way where unwise arbiter decisions can improperly influence the case in one direction or the other. This is particularly true in an embryonic arena where no set of tested ground rules exists for the conduct of such evaluations.

Remedy. Other than striving to secure saint-like individuals to serve as arbiters, we do not have a handy solution to cope with this problem. All of the remedy tactics we considered turned out to be patently inefficient or too elaborate to be practical.

Deficit Number Three: Excessive Confidence in the Model's Potency

Faced with problems that appear insoluble, people often seek solutions from technologies they don't understand very well. We tend to ascribe unwarranted potency to disciplines that we don't comprehend. Perhaps we think: "If a field is so complex that *I* don't understand it, it must be worthwhile." Surely the deference of many educational practitioners toward statisticians is prompted by the fact that few practitioners have ever ginned up a geometric mean or fondled a canonical correlation coefficient.

Perhaps this same mentality is operative when we assume that adversary evaluation approaches will lead us out of evaluative imprecision and directly into a world of improved decisions. Leon Lipson of the Yale Law School puts it succinctly as he comments on a proposed science court, a scheme analogous to the adversary evaluation model:

> . . . the proposal overestimates the power and efficacy of the adversary process as a means of finding a truth — even current, provisional, working, technical truth — that the "loser" will concede to be truth.[4]

Lipson observes that the recent initiatives to throw a variety of controversies into the mode of quasi-judicial resolution generally came from those whose experience with the law is limited. He concludes his appraisal of such proposals cogently:

> The proposal, in sum, rests upon the wistful hope that conflict conducted in the public view on difficult technical and scientific aspects of controversial issues can be leached of its political juices. Do we have to spend years, and millions, to relearn the folly of such a hope? Over the last few years, experts and laymen have found other and better ways of communicating with one another, in a variety of official and unofficial forums. The proposal for a science court appears to be not so much a useful addition to the spectrum of working devices as a quaint fantasy of technical closure in circumstances of disagreement over policies.[5]

Remedy. While there is no certain way to bridle the enthusiasm of recent converts, we must recognize that much of the drum-pounding for the adversary evaluation model is emanating from educators who, as Lipson observes, have limited experiencee with the legal discipline from which it is derived. To balance the well-intentioned zeal of adversary model devotees, we must add occasional dashes of reality to their ''quaint fantasy.''

Deficit Number Four: Difficulties in Framing the Proposition in a Manner Amenable to Adversary Resolution

Drawing on our familiarity with the courtroom contest, we too readily assume that educational issues can be cast in such a way that an advocate-adversary conflict will yield suitable guidance for decisionmakers. But the decision options facing educational policymakers are often more complicated than can be readily encompassed in the framework of a simple guilty/innocent, winner/loser, or go/no-go adversary contest.

As we became more and more conversant with the intricacies, both educational and political, of the Hawaii 3-on-2 Program, we realized that Hawaii's decisionmakers should not be forced to deal with a simple save-it-or-scrap-it choice. Middle-ground positions were more sensible. Half-way measures, in this instance, probably made more sense. But there we were, obliged to do battle with our adversary colleagues on the unembellished question of whether to maintain or terminate the 3-on-2 program. Most issues facing educational decisionmakers are more similar to the myriad-option 3-on-2 cases than they are to the guilty/innocent courtroom model.

Remedy. Apply the adversary evaluation model exclusively to those educational situations in which it is thoroughly clear that only a binary choice faces decisionmakers and in which the two decision options are in direct opposition to one another.

Deficit Number Five: A Cat's-Paw for Biased Decisionmakers

Although in the abstract we can think of the adversary evaluation model as a crucible from which truth obligingly bubbles forth, in the hands of an unprincipled decisionmaker, the model can serve a more devious function. Let's say you're a college president who secretly wishes to eliminate a small Germanic languages department so as to use the freed-up financial resources for other purposes. Now, if you commission an adversary evaluation of the merits of saving or squashing the Germanic languages department, you know that you'll get an argument on both sides of the issue. All you have to do is sit back, then assert that you were reluctantly persuaded by the arguments in favor of abolishing the department. For you, it's a no-lose situation. Who's to say you weren't, quite properly, persuaded by the team advocating abolition?

Although it is surely not the case that most educational decisionmakers are unscrupulous or that every time an adversary model is employed a biased decisionmaker is using it as a ploy to support a prejudgment, we must recognize that this possibility exists.

Remedy. We can proffer no way of heading off this misuse of the adversary model, other than by requiring potentially evil decisionmakers to take an extension course in ethics — and it would have to be awfully well taught. A screening test to detect latent unscrupulousness in decisionmakers should be developed without delay.

Deficit Number Six: Excessive Costs

It is difficult to conceive of an adversary evaluation project that would cost no more than a conventional evaluation study. The costs of doing an adversary study properly are typically double, at least, the cost of an ordinary evaluation study because two teams and a coordination/arbitration staff are required. Besides the raw staffing requirements, there typically will be a greater demand for data because the two teams will often grasp at straws, any old straws, in an effort to bolster their cases.

In the Hawaii 3-on-2 Program evaluation, for example, we attempted to secure various sorts of attitudinal data from teachers and pupils which had only a very slight chance of turning out in our favor. Yet, because we were obliged to defend a case in which there were no supporting student-performance data, we were desperate. Had we been approaching the evaluation task in a more conventional fashion, it is unlikely that we would have carried out these fishing excursions.

In addition, surely because there are yet no definitive guidelines for the conduct of adversary evaluations, there is an alarming amount of time expended on ground rule clarification, re-clarification, and reconsideration. We spent an inordinate chunk of our time in the Hawaii evaluation trying to work through the various aspects of our operating procedures. This was necessary, to be sure, since we really were obliged to settle these details; but the resolution of procedural matters does bump up the cost of an adversary evaluation effort.

For instance, in December 1976, both 3-on-2 adversary teams met in Portland for a three-day meeting to exchange our initial reports (for the first time) and to prepare initial drafts of rebuttal statements. Of the *three* working days, we spent about *two* days dealing with procedural matters regarding the initial reports and how to handle the reporting formats planned for the following month in Hawaii. While two-thirds of our working time may have been needed for procedural matters, such wrangling obviously increases the cost of the enterprise.

And if, in an effort to reduce the disparity in adversary team prowess, anyone followed our earlier suggestion to have both teams prepare a report on each side of the case, the costs would multiply even further. Clearly, conducting adversary evaluations is costly business.

Remedy.   Only entertain the thought of an adversary evaluation approach when you can afford it. Note that we did *not* say only use an adversary evaluation approach when the issue is important enough to warrant the extra costs. The entire trust of this paper has been to suggest that the adversary model is not an expensive but more effective model to be trotted out only when the stakes are high enough. The higher the stakes, the more queasy we become about becoming adversarial. All we are saying here is, if you can't afford to spend the extra dollars in your evaluation, don't go the adversary route.

Retrospect

When the writers accepted the assignment to work on the Hawaii 3-on-2 Program evaluation, we did so chiefly to learn more about the adversary model. We did not enter into this activity with the thought that we were going to end up disliking the model. Indeed, we both thought we were going to learn more about its intricacies so we could apply it to future evaluations. As the foregoing analysis suggests, our romance with the adversary model soon faded into neutrality, then downright negativism.

What will happen to the adversary evaluation model in the next few years? Well, it's sure to have a champion or two who, considering it their personal hobbyhorse, will push it for all it's worth. What we've been trying to say, however, is that it's not worth much. The adversary evaluation model brings with it not only a few real (and many imaginary) dividends; it brings also far too many deficits.

Notes

1. Adapted from a paper presented as part of a symposium. ''The Adversary Evaluation Model: A Second Look.'' Annual Meeting of the American Educational Research Association, New York, April 4–8, 1977.

2. Northwest Regional Educational Laboratory. *3-on-2 Evaluation Report, 1976–77.* vols. I, II, and III. Portland, Oregon: January 1977.

3. For example, see Wolf, Robert L ''Trial by jury: A new evaluation method.'' *Phi Delta Kappan,* no. 3, 57 (November 1975), 185–87; Owens, Thomas. ''Educational evaluation by adversary proceeding.'' In: Ernest House (ed.), *School evaluation: The politics and process.* Berkeley, California: McCutchan, 1973; Levine, Murray. ''Scientific method and the adversary model.'' *American Psychologist,* September 1974, 666–77; or Kourilsky, Marilyn. ''An adversary model for educational evaluation.'' *Evaluation Comment,* no. 2, 4 (1974).

4. Lipson, Leon. ''Technical issues and adversary process.'' Letter to the editor, *Science,* 194 (1976), 890.

5. Lipson, 1976, p. 890.

13 THE CLARIFICATION HEARING:
A Personal View of the Process
George F. Madaus

It was early morning of the second day of the Clarification Hearings in Washington, D.C. I was seated in front of the makeup table cluttered with bottles, tins, and brushes of all sorts, my new TV-compatible suit and blue shirt carefully protected by a bib. As the makeup artist was applying a brown fluid to my face (and undoubtedly wishing she had the skills of a plastic surgeon), Bob Ebel happened by the door. Seeing Bob, the incongruity of the situation hit me. How did I and a number of my colleagues in the next room waiting their turn in front of the lightbulb-studded mirror, get involved in this alien world? While I had my doubts from the beginning, Bob's appearance triggered the realization that 11 months earlier, when I agreed to serve as team leader for the negative side in the Clarification Hearings on Minimum Competency Testing (MCT), I really had no idea what I had let myself in for. I was again brought up short about the implications of the whole process and my part in it two weeks ago after viewing,

Madaus, George F. "The Clarification Hearing: A Personal View of the Process." *Educational Researcher*, (January 1982), 4–11. Copyright 1982, American Educational Research Association, Washington, D.C. Reprinted with permission.

The following chapter represents the author's perceptions and suggestions about the process — a modified judicial evaluation model — used in the National Clarification Hearings on Minimum Competency Testing.

along with students and colleagues here at Boston College, the edited version of the hearings on public television. In what follows I have attempted to describe my reactions and feelings, both positive and negative, to various aspects of the process leading up to the hearings, the hearing itself, and the final TV product developed by Maryland Public Broadcasting (MPB).

I will not get into the specifics of either case except where it might illustrate a more general point about the process itself. This paper does not rehash the pros or cons of MCT. Interested readers can find the outline of both cases in the *Phi Delta Kappan,* October 1981 issue, and the tapes of the full 24 hours of hearings and the three hour edited version are readily available.

Instead of specifics about MCT, I will concentrate on the strengths and weaknesses — as I see them — of the clarification process itself — as I experienced it. Further, in a more general sense, I have set down my reflections about the strengths and weaknesses of using a modified judicial evaluation model at the national level to illuminate and clarify education issues.

The Model

We employed a modified version of the adversary of judicial evaluation model (JEM). The principal modification was the elimination of a jury or panel whose purpose was to hand down a decision or make recommendations about the object being evaluated. There were very good reasons for this deletion. By eliminating a ''verdict'' or a set of recommendations, NIE avoided the unpleasantness and controversy that would have certainly followed on a federally sponsored panel declaring one side or the other the ''winner,'' or promulgating a set of recom- mendations on how to structure a MCT program. If the verdict or recommenda- tions favored the negative side, it would have surely unleashed a raft of criticism and complaints about unwarranted federal intervention in state programs. If the pro side was the beneficiary, then NIE would have had to deal with the enmity of those advocacy groups opposed to MCT. By eliminating the panel or jury component from the Clarification Hearing process, NIE avoided this no-win situation. ''Winning'' or ''losing'' was left to the eyes of the beholders: *de gustibus non est desputandum.*

This modification, made in August, took on added significance after the November election. The Clarification Hearing mode was viewed as an acceptable, nonintrusive federal presence in education; it provided information to state and local policymakers which they could use or ignore as they saw fit.

From the beginning, NIE insisted that we were engaged in a clarification process; our task was to illuminate the issues surrounding MCT. Winning and competition between the teams were not to be part of the process leading to the hearing. Therefore, one of my main criterion in evaluating the clarification hearing model is the extent to which I feel it effectively and efficiently clarifies and illuminates issues.

The Audience and the Model

From the outset, the plan was to make the videotaped proceedings of the hearing, along with written transcripts, available to interested policymakers at all levels. These products were to help inform their decisions concerning the design or modification of MCT programs. Initially, there were no plans to produce a television program to be aired nationally by the Public Broadcasting System (PBS), but this feature was added to the process in the late fall.

Staying with the original, more limited goal for a moment, one must ask how reasonable it is to expect policymakers, or even their surrogates, to view the full 24 hours of proceedings? I thought then, and nothing has happened to change my mind since, that it was preposterous to expect legislators or board members to find the time to view unexpurgated tapes.

The next question was: How reasonable is it to extract a one or two hour executive summary tape, which policymakers might be more apt to view and which truly reflects the complexity of the issues? I did not know the answer to this question initially. However, after viewing the three hour edited version of the tapes, I feel that altogether too much clarity and illumination is lost through the editing process. These doubts about the validity of the summary tapes are not a reflection on the work done by MPB. Based on material recommended by both teams, producer Frank Batavick did a superb job of putting together the edited version for the series, "Who's Keeping Score?" The difficulty is that you necessarily do violence to a carefully constructed, 12 hour case when you are forced to reduce the testimony and evidence to 75 minutes.

This leads me to my next question: Why go through 24 hours of exhausting hearings if the product that will receive the widest circulation and viewing is a three hour summary tape? If I had been cleverer, perhaps I could have structured each witness' testimony so that a piece could have been lifted intact for the expurgated version. But had I been that shrewd, why bother with the rest? Unlike a real trial, we were not building a record for an appeal.

Here I also must record my pessimism about the possibility of policymakers taking the time to read a more traditional, written evaluation of MCT. In hindsight — and I would caution the reader that mine is not always 20/20 — I think that the TV medium has the potential of reaching and affecting more policymakers than does our more traditional evaluation reports. However, I also feel that the clarification hearing mode does not exploit the potential of that medium to reach and educate viewers. I am convinced now that the expertise of the participants, the TV time allocated to the project, and the funds expended for the series, "Who's Keeping Score?" would have been better used to produce a three- or four-part documentary on MCT — not a flashy but shallow, commercial-type documentary, but one of more substance and visual power, perhaps a NOVA or Cosmos-type product.

If such a four hour documentary had been our goal at the outset, the two teams could have worked cooperatively with the TV experts to put together a TV production that could have more effectively exploited the medium in presenting the pros and cons of MCT. Such a series would have been a more effective, efficient, and dramatic way to illuminate the issues than the static question-and-answer format employed in the hearings. Also, more public television outlets might have picked up the product, than have to the date elected to show "Who's Keeping Score?"

When NIE informed us of the decision to involve MPB in producing a series of three one-hour excerpts for each day of the hearing, to be aired on public television and to be preceded by a one hour documentary produced solely by MPB with very little input from the team, the whole enterprise was transformed. We had a new audience, the general public or that segment of it that watched PBS. We were repeatedly admonished not to alter our efforts to continue as before; nonetheless, the spectre of the nationally aired product had considerable psychological impact. We certainly sensed that the process had been changed, but we did not appreciate until after the editing process to what extent the medium had altered the process. The announcement did change the way we chose some of our witnesses. For example we wanted some witnesses who would be recognized as creditable by a more general audience than the education, testing/research communities. We also asked the question: "How will this witness come across on TV?"

Presented with NIE's decision to seek funds for the public broadcasting component, our team requested that part of that budget include a TV expert for each team. This request, like several others, was ignored. However, if a similar process is ever repeated, it is crucial that each team have a TV person working closely with it to help the team utilize the power of the medium in presenting their case. Of course, such an addition adds to the cost.

If I had it to do again — God forbid — and the hearing mode was still the vehicle, then I would want to rehearse witnesses before a TV consultant and a small panel of lay people. The lay panel could provide feedback on whether technical points were properly translated and presented and whether the material and testimony were understood. Some evidence and testimony that I understood because of my background were clear neither to educators without a research background nor to those outside the field. The extent of this problem was not evident to me until the hearing and the editing process. A lay panel watching a rehearsal of the evidence and testimony would have helped us avoid this problem. But again, this would have added to the cost of the project and necessitated cooperation on the part of the witness that might not always be forthcoming from busy public personalities.

A TV consultant could offer advice on how the witness might better come across on TV. For example, two witnesses read a great deal of their testimony. If you read the transcript the testimony is very powerful. However, it does not make for good TV viewing; eye contact was not maintained and the testimony lost spontaneity. Perhaps I should have anticipated this problem, but I did not.

More importantly, the TV consultant would have been invaluable in helping us better utilize the visual medium to present some of our evidence and technical arguments. Technical matters are difficult to present to a general audience through the question-and-answer format of the JEM. While both teams used graphics to illustrate material, these were static renditions of drawings supplied by the teams. Nonstatic graphics, such as those seen on Wall Street Week, and other visual devices, such as short film clips or animations could have helped to make some of the arguments more understandable to a general audience. Here again, there are budget implications. The TV person could also have helped us to anticipate the editing process in structuring the testimony of each witness. In short, if you are going to reach a large audience to clarify an educational issue by using TV, don't go into the process with one hand tied behind your back. While I knew a fair bit about the issues surrounding MCT, I knew nothing about the medium.

The Issue and the Model

My perception is that NIE was very happy with the Clarification Hearing. The hearings and NIE's effort were received favorably by the public. The process resulted in a NIE-sponsored product that may be seen by a very large audience of both professional educators and lay people, depending on how many PBS affiliates choose to air it. The hearings were seen as an acceptable federal presence in education — informative but not intrusive. I have heard since that NIE was considering using the model with other issues and this gives me pause. Care needs to be taken in using the clarification hearing model with some issues.

In some respects, NIE was lucky that MCT was the subject of the first national use of the Clarification Hearing model, lucky in the sense that MCT is not a highly divisive issue encompassing deeply felt ideological or value-rooted positions. Moreover, it is not a burning issue in the minds of the public. You do not see bumper stickers that say, "Toot if you're against MCT." You are not accosted in airports by people with signs that say, "A Little MCT Never Hurt Anyone." Further, the possible positive and negative effects of MCT are rather easy to document, and technical issues of testing are fairly straightforward.

I have serious reservations, however, about using the model for highly divisive issues, such as busing or abortion. I also have my doubts whether it should be used for clarifying the issues surrounding bilingual education. I think that a federally sponsored Clarification Hearing on such ideologically based issues, which affect deeply held beliefs on both sides, could cause great mischief. The composition of the two teams and the selection of the hearing officer could touch off protests from groups on the right and left of the issue. Cooperation and data-sharing would be difficult. I would anticipate severe and bitter fights over the admissability of evidence and witness testimony.

Thus, while I feel that the clarification model or some variant on it has the potential to illuminate a number of issues for various stakeholders and publics not reached through more traditional evaluations, I think the issue needs to be chosen with care, particularly if federal funds are involved.

The Team

The first task I faced after agreeing to be the team leader for the con, or negative, team was to build a team. This is a crucial step in the process. In choosing team members, I tried to select peers who could serve an outreach function to the various constituencies concerned about MCT. I was blessed with a superb team. Ours was truly a team effort from beginning to end.[1]

Unfortunately because of budget limitations, we met as a team only twice prior to the hearing. The first occasion was a meeting in Washington to orient both teams. Our second meeting in January was devoted to the development of strategy for case building and identifying potential witnesses and groups to contact. While subsets of the team met from time to time, the whole team never came together again until the hearing. Further, the budget did not cover very much in the way of the team members' time once the days for the two meetings, the hearings, and the editing were deducted. If the model is ever used again, the budget should accommodate at least three or four team meetings prior to the hearing and sufficient funds to cover the team members' work during the case-building process. There was altogether too much "contributed service" on the part of generous team members. Both teams should come together for the two final data-sharing sessions and for both sessions with the hearing officer. Once again, these recommendations would increase the cost of the project. However, it does little good to have an excellent team but not be able to optimally utilize their talent.

There were disagreements on some details of strategy and on a few issues, and there was one that is worth recounting. What part should team members play at the actual hearing? Originally, I was not comfortable with handling all the direct and cross-examination myself. I felt that each team member, if he or she wished, should participate to some extent in both of these functions. Some team members disagreed. They felt that if all eight of us were directly involved in examining witnesses it would be confusing to the TV audience viewing the edited copies (another example of how the spectre of the TV production influenced us). Further, there was some sentiment that the direct and cross-examination should be handled by someone with trial experience. However, most of us felt that if the JEM was to work, non-lawyers should be able to handle those functions. After polling the team, it was agreed that the task of direct and cross-examination would be split between Diana Pullin and myself. Instinctively, I was troubled by the decision. A few weeks before the hearing, I reconsidered, after one team member asked what the team would do during the hearing other than sit and take notes. At the 11th hour I decided that all team members would participate in either the direct examination and/or cross-examination of witnesses. I would recommend this course to anyone using the model. People in the audience and those who viewed the TV version commented on the team participation and involvement. We looked and acted like a team. Those who originally had reservations also agreed that this involvement was beneficial.

Budget

One serious reservation about applying the JEM on a national scale is the cost. Each team had a budget of $107,000 with which to work. An additional $100,000 went to a subcontractor for project management and for the hearing. About $250,000 (I do not know the exact amount) went to MPB for the TV component.

One hundred thousand dollars is simply not sufficient to do the job correctly. Travel for the team to meet before, during, and after the hearing, and for data-sharing and meeting with the hearing officer; travel for 30 witnesses to come to Washington, and for case development — all this took a large chunk out of the budget. In keeping a daily log of my activities, I found the job to be nearly a full-time one from December through July, although I was budgeted for one quarter time. As I mentioned earlier, the budget for team members was stingy and only their generosity made some of the work possible.

The budget did not permit us to do research, as originally planned, nor did it permit a first-hand investigation of the sites chosen by the opposing team. On the first point, we had to rely pretty much on what was out there, and much of that was simply testimony or hearsay. There were a number of issues on which we would have liked to have gathered data, but we could not because of the costs. Bob Linn did the analysis of extant data tapes to illustrate points about the cut score, measurement error, and item bias, but that was the extent of our original research. For the rest we collated the data, testimony, and hearsay that we found, primarily by mail and phone.

Not being able to visit the opposing team's sites was a major disadvantage. While we had a very broad outline of what each of their witnesses was going to say, the best we could do was to call them or contact individuals who might help us develop a line of cross-examination. This approach was not very beneficial. Our cross-examination was by far the weakest aspect of our case. However, if we had

had the funds to go to each site and could have gotten the necessary cooperation to interview and observe for a week or so, I am confident that we could have turned up rebuttal witnesses or at least better lines of cross-examination. Whether those rebuttal witnesses would have felt free to testify is another matter to which I will return.

A national Clarification Hearing is not cheap, and the funds expended on this project do not reflect what is needed to do the job adequately. I have already made a number of suggestions that would increase the costs. As Jim Popham said to me at one point, it's a matter of a 15-watt bulb for illumination instead of 100 watts. The basic question is whether additional wattage can be justified through a cost-benefit analysis.

Time

One major difference between the JEM and the actual judicial process is that the JEM has sharp time limits, for practical reasons, related to budget and audience. Direct, cross, redirect, and recross are all constrained by a fixed time limit.

A good deal of witness preparation involved timing. A major decision we had to make was how much of our time should be allocated to direct and how much to cross-examination. At one point, we felt that we would cross-examine only a few witnesses husbanding our time for our case in chief. Eventually I think we cross-examined all but two witnesses. However, in editing the tape for "Who's Keeping Score?" we selected very little cross-examination, using our precious 75 minutes for direct testimony.

We employed two stop watches to keep track of time. The cross-examination of one witness was progressing very well, but we were forced to cut it short because we had gone over our allotted time. Another five to ten minutes and we might have made some very telling points. Whether they would have been included in the edited version is another question. If we had turned up a witness to directly rebut a pro witness, we would have been faced with an interesting time trade-off between rebuttal and direct testimony.

Considerations related to time influenced the kind of case we chose to develop. There were two strategies. The first was to develop only a few points and have all witnesses hammer repeatedly at the same theme. The pro team selected this strategy, and it was very effective. It is easier for the audience to follow the more limited arguments, and repetition hammers the point home.

The second strategy, and the one we followed, was dubbed by Wade Henderson as "the death by a thousand cuts." We felt that in addition to the three issues there were a number of important contentions that also had to be developed — for example, the technical limitation of tests when used for certification — if the issues surrounding MCT were to be truly clarified and illuminated. Further, as far as possible, the views of various concerned groups had to be represented. This involved allocating time across many points and constituencies.

I did not have a good solution to the problem of the time constraints associated with the model. However, two teams jointly developing a documentary with a TV crew, I feel, would have been able to clarify the issues and contentions more effectively and efficiently with less time than was needed for the three days of hearings.

The Negative or Con Label

The label *con* or negative team was a difficult burden to carry for a number of reasons. First, being against competency testing is akin to being against motherhood. The adjective *competency* in front of the noun *test* puts the opposition in a difficult position. Second, it is always difficult to argue against the status quo, not to mention trying to prove a negative. Certainly our side was the more threatening one to established programs. This, in turn, made it difficult to gain entry to programs or to obtain data we wanted to investigate. Why should an administrator collaborate on a process that might involve dirty linen appearing on national television?

Third, we repeatedly had to emphasize that our team was not anti-testing or against standards. Fourth, we felt that we had to spend part of our time and resources presenting an alternative to MCT. In short, I felt our side had to carry a heavier burden of proof.

Perhaps the most difficult aspect of the negative label was trying to get school people to testify. Very often we were told of problems endemic to MCT, but the person did not feel free to testify because either district or state administrators were sold on the program. For a while we even wrestled with ways witnesses might remain anonymous. We were very explicit in warning people that there might be a backlash associated with their public appearances. Further, we decided not to have students relate their problems with MCT, because they might later be embarrassed by their TV appearance.

If the goal is to clarify and illuminate issues through TV, then using the documentary approach might help to lessen the problem and the difficulties associated with the negative or con label. In fact, using such an approach might involve only one team with different views represented.

Project Management

Future uses of the model should involve one major change. After providing the funds directly to the teams, rather than going through the red tape of monthly billings to a third-party contractor, the funding agency should withdraw from the management of the project. Day-to-day project management should be in the hands of the hearing officer and his or her staff. Alternately analogous to a court-appointed monitor, an independent group or individual appointed by the hearing officer could manage the mechanics of the project. The funding agency should not be involved in directly telling or even suggesting to a team what it thinks the team should or should not do; nor should the agency intervene with its view of what should be, in debates or arguments between the two teams. Such disagreements should be adjudicated by the hearing officer, or a designate, without either the explicit or implicit intrusion of views on the part of the funding agency staff.

At the very least, the whole issue of the funding agency's role in the process needs more discussion. The JEM is held out as one that presents an opportunity for impartial pursuit of the "truth." When the funding agency or its representatives have an implicit or explicit agenda of their own related either to the substantive area being evaluated or concerns about backlash that might ensue, then it is no longer an impartial party in the process.

The Issues

A key ingredient in the process is the framing of the issues and the definitions of key terms. This is a place where I felt we went awry. Both sides thought that they understood the boundaries of the debate and the terms as defined. It turned out that they meant different things to the two teams. For example, we thought we were debating programs where, if a pupil did not pass a test, he or she was not promoted, could not graduate, or was automatically put in a remedial program. After examining them, we felt that the South Carolina and Detroit programs did not fit these parameters. In South Carolina, they do not use the test results as a sole or primary determiner for promotion or graduation. Further, the state's regulations forbid using the test score alone to classify students for remediation. In Detroit, pupils who fail the test still receive a regular diploma, but if they pass they receive an endorsed diploma. There was a heated, even bitter, debate over the inclusion or exclusion of these two sites. In the case of Detroit, the pro team considered the endorsed diploma a form of classification. We were not aware of this variant when we agreed to the definition of classification, and hence we objected. We did not know if we were opposed to endorsed diplomas. In the case of South Carolina, they argued that the test information was part of a classification procedure. We argued that it did not fit the sole or primary determiner criterion. The point is not to revisit these arguments but to recommend that a fuller discussion of the boundaries of the debate and definition of key terms should include specific reference to the actual sites to be used. This type of discussion, moreover, should not be put off but should come very early in the data-sharing process.

Data Sharing

Data-sharing is a key component in the JEM. Unfortunately, there were weaknesses in this process, part of the problem being related to distance. The training tape showed a project at the University of Indiana, where the two teams were on the same campus and worked closely together. It is very difficult to collaborate when you are 3,000 miles apart, and only a small portion of your time is supposedly covered by the contract. True, we did have meetings in which we were able to share data, but discussions of the TV process ate into the available time, and there were not a lot of data to share until about 10 weeks or so before the hearings. Rather than inundating the other team with all the material and leads we were following, it was agreed that we would wait until the case was more or less firm before sending essential material. This was to keep the reading down to an acceptable level.

I do not know exactly how to overcome these problems except to say that the teams need more, or at least longer, joint meetings in which the actual evidence, testimony and cross-examination of each witness are discussed in detail. Exposing your hand completely at a joint meeting, like a dummy hand in bridge, is a difficult concept psychologically when deep down you often feel you're in a poker game. A joint effort at building a TV documentary might alleviate this problem. Another interesting variant might be to have one team develop and present both sides of the case.

The Hearing

The hearing itself was both stimulating and exhausting. Eight hours a day of hearings for three days, coupled with nightly preparation, is a fatiguing experience. Before the hearing, some sort of introduction to the TV cameras is needed. Also, during the hearing a TV monitor should be provided for each team to give the team feedback on such basic matters as eye contact, posture, positioning and delivery.

On the hearing mode itself, I think once you eliminate the panel, decide to televise the proceedings, and are not evaluating a particular program with its direct acquiescence and cooperation, then, at least on a national scale, the hearing format is not the most efficient or effective way to clarify or illuminate issues. The hearing mode is probably effective and efficient at the state or local level when you are assured that the stakeholders to the evaluation will be in attendance and when a panel is constituted to make recommendations about a program that has agreed to this form of evaluation. Furthermore, limiting the hearing to the state or local level greatly reduces costs.

An interesting variant in the present model would be to have the two teams come together after the hearings to cooperatively make recommendations to design a MCT program, taking into account evidence and testimony introduced at the hearing.

The Hearing Officer

This project was indeed fortunate to have as its hearing officer Barbara Jordan, who was very ably assisted in her task by Paul Kelley of the University of Texas. There were at least two possible roles for the hearing officer. The first, and the one Professor Jordan chose, was that of neutral arbitrator: She set the stage for the hearings by describing the process, purpose, and procedures; she introduced witnesses, ruled on objections, and acted as a referee. The second option was for the hearing officer to intervene directly by questioning witnesses. A minor problem with this second option was the already tight time constraints built into the process. A more troubling problem would have been that questions put by a nationally respected hearing officer could tip a case in favor of one side or another. The tone of the questioning might implicitly signal to the viewing audience a "decision" by the hearing officer in favor of one side. This would negate the benefits of eliminating the jury or panel from the proceedings. For this reason, I would recommend the first role as the most appropriate one when the model is used in a national context.

The Product

After the hearings, each team had the job of editing their four hours of each day's proceedings down to 25 minutes. Several things became apparent immediately. First, the written transcript was not a particularly good guide for editing; material that read well did not necessarily view well. Second, our evaluation of witnesses made at the hearings did not necessarily hold up when we saw the tapes. It was very difficult to edit 15 or 20 minutes of testimony down to two or three. Basically, this involved making sure that all of our arguments were covered by quick snippets. This, in turn, resulted in a final product that lacked depth and clarity. We were forced to ask "Why three days of hearings if the most widely disseminated product is a bastardized version?"

There is a wealth of material in the full 24 hours of tapes, which could be excerpted to develop into short tapes for specific audiences dealing with focused issues. For example, tapes dealing with all of the evidence and testimony concerning MCT and the handicapped would make excellent viewing for concerned groups and for pre- and in-service teachers. Similarly, the testimony on reading or on technical issues could be excerpted for teaching purposes. These potential spin-off tapes for special audiences or for pre- or in-service teaching could be a very desirable side effect associated with the full three days of hearings.

Conclusion

The model, with its public television component, has the potential to reach and educate audiences that would not ordinarily be reached through more traditional evaluation reports. Research on the model, or variants of it, should be pursued. Evaluations of the process now in progress should shed additional light on the model's strengths and weaknesses.

At the local and state level, with a specific program that agrees to the process, the model may be very useful, although it might tax the attention span and retention powers of the audience. When the model is used nationally, costs go up substantially, and the issue to which the model is applied must be chosen with care. Further, a panel to hand down a verdict is probably not desirable. More importantly, if the purpose is to clarify and illuminate issues for the general public and for various stakeholders through the television medium, then the question-and-answer, basically aural mode of the model may not be the most effective or efficient use of available time. Going through three days of intensive hearings using the question-and-answer format and then editing out 90 percent of the proceedings makes little sense to me. Rather, it would be better to start out with the final product in mind and utilize the medium and its technology to its best advantage.

My experience with the Clarification Hearing was like my experience in the Army. After it was over and I was out, I was glad I had the experience. I had learned all kinds of new things and met some wonderful people, but no way would I re-up.

Note

1. The team members, who helped to develop arguments, located and prepared witnesses, helped with both direct and cross-examination of witnesses during the hearing, and assisted in the editing of the TV tapes, were: James Breeden, Senior Manager, Office of Planning and Policy, Boston Public Schools; Sandra Drew, Chicano Education Project, Denver, CO; Norman Goldman, Director of Instruction, New Jersey Education Association, Trenton; Walter Haney, National Consortium on Testing, Huron Institute, Cambridge, MA; Wade Henderson, Executive Director, Fund for Public Education, Council on Legal Education Opportunities, American Bar Association, Washington, D.C.; Robert Linn, Chairman, Department of Educational Psychology, University of Illinois at Urbana-Champaign; Renee Montoya, Chicano Education Project, Denver; and Diana Pullin, Staff Attorney, Center for Law and Education, Washington, D.C. While not a member of the team, Simon Clyne of Boston College was invaluable as an administrative assistant to the team.

14 EVALUATION IDEOLOGIES
Michael Scriven

New disciplines are often wracked by ideological disputes. In this respect, evaluation is no different from some of the other new entries in the disciplinary sweepstakes — in recent decades these include sociobiology, computer science, feminist theory, non-formal logic, serious parapsychology, ethnic and policy studies, ecobiology, molecular biology, structural linguistics, computerized mathematics, physiological and cognitive psychology, psychohistory, and others. There is nothing new about this, as some reflection on the history of evolutionary theory and astronomy will remind us. But it is hard to achieve perspective on any revolution of which we are part. The proliferation of evaluation models is a sign of the ferment of the field and the seriousness of the methodological problems which evaluation encounters. In this sense, it is a hopeful sign. But it makes a balanced overview very hard to achieve; one might as well try to describe the "typical animal" or the "ideal animal" in a zoo.

Evaluation is a peculiarly self-referent subject. In this respect, it is like the sociology of science; that is, the sociology of science includes the sociology of the sociology of science and, hence, is self-referent. Similarly, systematic objective evaluation — the kind with which the discipline is concerned — is not restricted to the evaluation of microscopes. If it were, it would not include itself. But evaluation applies to the process and products of all serious human endeavor and hence to evaluation. The application of evaluation to itself is sometimes called

229

meta evaluation, and it has generated the standards for educational program evaluation that are summarized and discussed elsewhere in this book.

Just as it is especially disappointing that the sociology of science — a subject older than this century and dedicated to a self-referent activity — was almost blind to the sexist bias in science, no doubt because that bias pervaded sociology of science as well as other branches of science, so it is depressing to notice the extent to which certain prejudices continue to shape the practice of evaluation. I have no doubt that many more apply than I shall mention here — Ernest House has warned us about some others in *Evaluating With Validity* (Sage, 1980) — but the ones discussed here may constitute a useful start for creating the kind of anxiety and self-scrutiny that will uncover the rest. Later in the paper, I critique standard evaluation processes in the light of these biases, and I also talk about methods and models which avoid them.

These ideologies or fundamental biases that have pervaded much of evaluation include:

1. The Separatist Ideology. "I am an evaluator, you are a subject, she is an object" — i.e., the denial or rejection of self-reference, less kindly described as a kind of criticism. This is most clearly seen in the failure of evaluators to turn their attention to the procedures by which they are themselves evaluated as — and which they use to evaluate others — members of the scientific community. The most scandalous of these procedures include peer review — for research funding or personnel decisions — by uncalibrated, unvalidated, and un-followed-up review panels. It was easy to get away with this as long as evaluation was treated as meaning first of all the evaluation of students (when the word *evaluation* occurs in the title of a book published before 1960, it almost invariably refers to the practices of student performance assessment), and then program evaluation. Program evaluation is not self-referent, since evaluating a program does not itself constitute a programmatic activity. This may have been one of the reasons for the almost phobic intensity of the focus on program evaluation, though undoubtedly another reason was that the funding lay in that direction. In any case, we see here an unhealthy example of parasitism; the constricted notion of what evaluation was all about fed on the improper practices in everyday scholarly operations, from the allocation of funds to the selection of personnel. I postulate as the psychological dynamics behind this kind of error, which would be hard to explain unless there was a deep motivation for it, the existence of something which I will call *valuephobia,* a pervasive fear of being evaluated, which I take to be a part of the general human condition — with rare exceptions — and to apply to scientists very generally, evaluators amongst them. We have frequently seen examples of "going native," the phenomenon of field evaluators posted at program sites who are unable to withstand the social tensions of that role and succumb to the pressure of need-affiliation, joining the staff in point of view and commitment. Often one finds that within a year, staff evaluators begin to develop significant blindnesses to obvious weaknesses in the program which they are supposed to be evaluating — weaknesses that they would never have overlooked when they first came in. Going native may be an empathic response to valuephobia of the staff under one's evaluative eye, or it may be motivated by the anti-evaluative backlash from that staff.

Thus, the phenomenon of the unscientific scientist, psychologically comprehensible in terms of epidemic valuephobia, represents a simple distortion of scientific inquiry — separatism — which misrepresents it as requiring a permanent role separation between the observer and the observed. In fact, though objectivity is hardest to achieve in self-reference, it is an ideal towards which we must strive, and which we do commonly recognize as part of the obligation of professionalism. Moreover, though claims to achieve it should be viewed with suspicion, there are many ways to approach it. So the first ideology that affects evaluation, driven by valuephobia, is the ideology of the separation of subject and object in an inappropriate way.

2. The Positivist Ideology. The various phases in the development of evaluation proceeded against a most important backdrop of a great ideological battle in the philosophy of science, indeed in philosophy as a whole. This was the battle between the positivists and their opponents, originally the idealists and later many others. Right though the positivists were to attempt a drastic reduction in the cant and circumstance of much then-current philosophy, they over-corrected heavily, and we are still a long way from recovering our equilibrium along with a sense of the possibility of objectivity in ethics and other domains of value inquiry such as evaluation.

Since it is obvious from a cursory review of the contents of scientific works that they are frequently highly evaluative and that the evaluations in them are frequently and carefully rendered highly objective by analysis and documentation (I particularly have in mind evaluations of experimental designs, scientific instruments, the contributions of other scientists, and alternative explanations of the data), it is somewhat bizarre that science of the twentieth century represented itself as value-free. Again, one must consider the possibility that this was an ideology generated to reduce valuephobic anxieties. Surely it is necessary to reach for psychological explanations of such glaring discrepancies as that between the assertion that no evaluative judgments can be made with scientific objectivity and the ease with which evaluative judgments about the performance of students were produced by the very instructors who had just banned them from the domain of objectivity. Thus, both in their pedagogical practice and their professional publications, scientists acted as evaluators who were prepared to back up their evaluations as objective and appropriate, yet who denied the possibility of any such process within the field of their expertise. Since the field of expertise of an educational psychologist includes the practice of grading educational efforts, those academics were guilty of the most direct inconsistency.

Thus, while the separatist ideology or bias rejects the self-referent nature of science or evaluation, the positivist ideology rejects the evaluative nature of science. Both involve inconsistencies between professed philosophy and professional practice, and both have constricted the growth of evaluation severely, since it violates both taboos. One has only to observe the vehemence with which many scientists attack the idea of student evaluation of their teaching on *a priori* grounds without the faintest consideration of whether there is scientific evidence for its validity (see the January 1983 correspondent columns of the *Chronicle of Higher Education*) to see the separatist ideology at work; and the rejection slips which accompanied submissions of articles about evaluation to social science journals prior to the mid-1960s amply demonstrate the power of the positivist ideology, the value-free component of which was often and misleadingly called "empiricism." The wolfdog of evaluation is acceptable as a method of controlling the peasants, but it must not be allowed into the castle — that is the message which each of these ideologies represents, in its own way.

3. The Managerial Ideology.   When program evaluation began to emerge, who commissioned it? Program instigators and managers, legislators and program directors. And whose programs were being evaluated? Programs initiated by the same legislators and managers. It is hardly surprising that a bias emerged from this situation. In the baldest economic terms, the situation could often be represented in the following way: someone looking for work as an evaluator (e.g., bidding on an evaluation contract) knew that they could not in the long run survive from the income from one contract. It followed that it was in their long-term self interest to be doing work that would be attractive to the agency letting the contract. Since that agency was typically also the agency responsible for the program, it also followed the evaluators understood that favorable reports were more likely to be viewed as good news than unfavorable ones. Absent extreme precautions, such as radical separation of the evaluation office from the program offices and direct reporting/ promotion, etc. of the evaluators by the chief-of-staff, on a highly professional basis, there was a strong predisposition towards favorable evaluations. It is extremely noticeable that when the General Accounting Office or the Congressional Budget Office or the Audit Agency or the Inspector General's Office — all of which are well-insulated evaluation shops — do evaluations of federal programs, the results are very much more critical than those done by allegedly independent contractors, when the contract is let by the agency itself. Even these "internal-external" evaluation shops — the General Accounting Office for example — are not immune to the bias of ultimate shared self interest, since all are agents of a government that wants to look good; but there is a great difference in degree. When we move further down the spectrum, to the usual situation in a school district where the Title I evaluator may be on the staff of the Title I project manager, the pressures toward a favorable report become extreme. Everyone knows of cases where the project manager simply removes the critical paragraphs from the evaluator's report and sends it on upstairs as a co-authored evaluation.

The managerial ideology went far beyond a simple conflict-of-interest bias, though that reaches so far that perhaps only the appointment of lifetime evaluators, following the standard legislative model of the appointment of superior court justices, could be taken seriously as a countermeasure that showed the society to be fully aware of the problem. The managerial ideology generated a major conceptual scheme, which pervasively contaminates almost all contemporary program evaluations. This is the achievement or success model for evaluation, translated to the view that program evaluation consists of identifying the goals of programs and determining whether they have been met. Relevant though that is to the concerns of the manager, it is of no interest at all to the consumer. The road to hell is paved with good intentions, and the road to environmental desolation is paved with successful programs of pest eradication. The distinction between intended effects and side effects is of no possible concern to the consumer, who is benefitted or damaged by them alike, and consumer-oriented evaluation is, on the whole, considerably more important than manager-oriented evaluation. Although goals and objectives are considerably overrated as aids to good management, resulting in the absurdities of detailed daily lesson plans which may inhibit good teaching more than they facilitate it, there is at least some argument for them in a planning context. There is no argument for them in the evaluation context, *except* for providing managerial feedback and for providing meta-managers with some index of the success of their subordinates in projecting reasonable goals.

Once again, we can find here the cavalier disregard of one's own behavior so characteristic of the separatist syndrome. The very program manager who thinks that goal-free evaluation is either absurd or obscene or illegal, walks straight into the local automobile dealership and proceeds to evaluate the products there without the slightest inclination to request a statement of objectives from the General Motors design team that labored long and hard to produce them. Nor will any reference to such goals be found in *Consumer Reports,* widely read by scientists who loudly proclaim the impossibility of objective empirical evaluation and by managers who proclaim the impossibility of goal-free evaluation.

Consumer Reports is an irrefutable counter-example to the paradigm of goal-achievement program evaluation. The coterie of program managers and their consultants work up many rationalizations to keep program evaluation separate from product evaluation ("people aren't products," etc.), lest the obvious incongruity between the goal-based paradigm they espouse and the needs-based paradigm they employ in their own affairs should become too apparent. It is a phenomenon of some significance that for 15 years all books about the "new discipline of program evaluation" were entitled *evaluation,* talked about evaluation, and turned out to only deal with program evaluation. Not only did they thereby ignore product evaluation, the one kind of evaluation for which we had many decades of thoroughly reliable development; but they also ignored personnel evaluation, an extraordinary achievement since no serious program evaluation can be done without looking at the treatment of personnel in the program, i.e., at personnel evaluation. Now the treatment of personnel involves considerations of justice — that is, ethics — as well as some other quite sophisticated methodological issues, and it comes perilously close to home since it involves the evaluation of people — and even program managers are people.

So we find valuephobia once more leading to extraordinary global and logistical maneuvers designed — unconsciously, no doubt — to screen off the ethics and the personnel evaluation as if somehow they could be avoided in the course of program evaluation. If they were brought in, of course, then we would have to face the possibility that managers had to be evaluated, that the goals of programs were just as evaluable as their impacts, and that even ethics itself had to be faced as a legitimate part of serious comprehensive program evaluation. In particular, affirmative action issues could not be treated as merely part of the legal background of program evaluation. They would have to be dealt with as serious issues with respect to which correct answers have to be discovered — or else most programs could not be given a clean bill of health.

The managerial ideology dovetailed very nicely with the positivist ideology, because treating a program as equivalent to its success in achieving its goals was a wonderful way of avoiding having to make any value judgments. It merely passed the value judgment buck along to the program managers, accepting their determination of goals as the presupposition of the investigation. ''You tell us what counts as a good outcome, and we (scientists) will tell you whether you got it'' was the posture, and it was a very attractive one for the valuephobe. The manager, in turn, could often pass the buck back to a legislature, and they — if they so desired — could always blame the public. Goal-achievement evaluation was thus a smokescreen under which it was possible for adherents of value-free dogma to come out of the woodwork and start working on some rather well-financed evaluation contracts. They were not, they said, violating the taboo on making scientific value judgments; they were just investigating the success of a means to a given end. They were also, thereby, committed to connivance-without-cavil in some pretty unattractive programs, including the efforts of the CIA in Central and South America as well as Southeast Asia. When the radical left of the sixties turned up these activities, it concluded that such behavior showed that science was not in fact value-free. All it showed was that scientists were not value-free, a conclusion which no one had ever denied. Although badly bitten over the politics of these exposés, establishment social scientists rightly regarded them as irrelevant to the fundamental logical propriety of the value-free position. For that position maintained only that scientific evidence could not substantiate evaluative judgments, and it never involved the claim that science could not be used for good or ill, by scientists or others. I have mentioned above, and argued in greater detail elsewhere, that the fundamental logical position — that science cannot substantiate value judgments — was completely wrong, and indeed obviously wrong; it is for this error that the social scientists must be condemned, and it was this positivist error that led to the managerial error. For only if one believed oneself incapable of disciplined and scientific investigation of value claims could one so readily adopt, without careful scrutiny, the shoddy value premises of the counterinsurgency programs.

Substantial branches of the federal government are in fact concerned with product evaluation — perhaps the Federal Drug Administration is the most conspicuous example. The very methodology that they employed was one which placed an absolutely minimal emphasis upon the achievement of the goals or objectives of the manufacturers or vendors of the product; there was never much doubt that if something came through the doors of the FDA labeled "post-anesthetic analgesic," it would reduce post-operative pain. The problem was always focussed on the side effects. Now one can hardly evaluate side effects by asking whether they represent the achievement of the intended effects, to which they are by definition irrelevant. So what does one use in evaluating side effects? One uses the needs of the patient — or client, or consumer, or user, or student. Thus, in order to evaluate side effects, which one cannot avoid doing if one is to do responsible program or product evaluation, one must have some kind of needs assessment in hand. But if one has some kind of needs assessment in hand, then one can use it to evaluate all effects, whether intended or not. Indeed, it is exactly the appropriate device for doing so. Consequently, one can completely by-pass the reference to goals. Programs, like products should be evaluated by matching their effects against the needs of those whom they affect. And that is what the doctrine of "goal-free evaluation" recommends.

What happens in the managerial ideology is of course that one presupposes the goals of the program were based upon an infallible and eternally valid needs assessment, so that one can use the goals as a surrogate for needs. Unfortunately, that leaves the side effects out of consideration; and it is of course ludicrous to assume either that managers (or those who employ them) always do needs assessment, or always do valid needs assessments, or that any such needs assessments, even if done and valid, will *still* be valid years later when the time has come to evaluate the program. Needs change, not only because we come to recognize new ones, but because programs come and go, population demographics change, the state of the economy varies, and the extent to which needs have been already met varies. Hence up-to-date needs assessment — or something equivalent to this, such as the functional analysis that is often a surrogate for needs assessment in the case of product evaluation — is an essential part of any serious evaluation.

The managerial ideology has another extremely unfortunate error built into it. Not only does it ignore the consumer's point of view, disregard side effects and the justice of the delivery process, but it also pays little attention to a special concern of the taxpayer. One often hears managers arguing that their programs should only be evaluated on the basis of whether the program goals were achieved, "because that is all that they undertook to do." The evaluation point of view is not concerned solely with — and frequently not at all concerned with — the narrow legal obligations of managers, but also with their ethical obligations, and — transcending the managers altogether — the true merit or worth or value of the program itself. Now *that* raises such questions as whether the same results could have been achieved for less money via another approach, or even for considerably less money using this approach, despite the fact that the contract was completed within the allowed budget.

It is of great significance that the whole question of serious cost analysis was virtually unknown to academic circles until quite recently and that even now it is not part of the standard training of social scientists within the applied fields. Those of us in evaluation who have pushed hard for cost analysis as an equal partner in the team of evaluation methodologies, recall vividly that the notion of cost effectiveness originated not in the academy, but with the Army Corps of Engineers. And cost analysis is by no means conceptually clear to this day; the standard references contradict each other even on the definition of cost (Scriven, 1983).

The effective use of the money available on the project for which it was allocated is one dimension of cost effectiveness; another dimension involves opportunity costs, that is, the comparison of this particular way of expending the resources with other ways that would have achieved similar or better results. This second dimension in cost analysis raises the awkward spectres of a series of "ghosts at the banquet," the ghosts of all the alternative possibilities that were not realized. Should the evaluator have to evaluate not just the program under evaluation, but all the alternatives to it? The cost of such evaluations would be unrealistically great. But if no evaluation is done of the critical competitors — the most important alternatives — then one can never say that the expenditure on the present project was justified. And that conclusion, that the project represented the best or even a justifiable expenditure, is precisely the type of conclusion that many clients for evaluations request, or need even if they do not request it. In particular, it is part of the evaluation imperative to address that question unless there are specific reasons for avoiding it, since it is the question that directly concerns society as a whole rather than special interests of the funding agency and the managers and staff of the program.

So, it is clear that the managerial bias furthered an ideology that omitted a number of important dimensions of the most important kind of evaluation — the systematic and objective determination of worth or value. It is also clear that there are procedures available to reverse this bias and move towards needs-based rather than goal-based evaluation, to what we might call consumer-oriented rather than manager-oriented evaluation. These methodologies include a full range of techniques of cost analysis, including techniques for the analysis of opportunity costs and non-money costs; the provision of opportunities for those who are evaluated to respond to the drafts of the evaluation before it is given to the client officially; and the procedures of goal-free evaluation.

The latter approach not only represents a counterveiling methodology, but a useful methodological simplification, because the practical task of identifying the true "goals of the program" is often completely beyond reasonable solution. One may dig into the historical transcripts — the General Accounting Office goes back to the discussions in committee hearings prior to the formation of legislation — but one then faces the fact that the working goals of the program change with the experience of program delivery. Should one then use the goals of the senior staff members; of the firing-line staff; of the responsible individuals in the funding agencies; or all of the above at the beginning of the evaluation, or during the evaluation, etc., etc.? The problems of converting these goals, expressed inform-ally or rhetorically, into behavioral objectives; of avoiding or resolving inconsis-tencies in them; of handling the prioritizing of them; of dealing with clear cases of mistaken empirical assumptions in them; and so on, still remain to be solved. Goals are often best seen as inspirational devices — they make poor foundations for analysis.

It is also important to note that for the evaluators to be aware of the goals of the program is for them to be given a strong perceptual bias in a particular direction, which, in conjunction with whatever positive or negative effect they possess for the program, unleashes the possibility of a distorted perception of the results. It is entirely typical for evaluators to look mainly in the direction of the intended results, because they know that the client is particularly interested in that direction; they know that not doing a thorough job in that direction will count against them for future contracts or employment, and they know that they typically will be completely off the hook as far as the client is concerned if they report only on results in that general area. The possibility of this kind of "lazy evaluation" thus opens up, and it is all too often enough to keep one busy without a serious search for side effects. When the field staff do not know the goals of the program, except in the most obvious and general sense, and are only allowed to talk to the program's clients rather than program staff, then they are much more likely to pick up other effects. For one thing, they are on their mettle with no clues; for another, they begin to identify with the recipients and that is a much more appropriate identification — if one has to be made — than with the program staff, not only methodologically (since it generates a new set of biases that can offset the managerial ones), but also ethically. After all, the program staff existed only to serve the recipients, not the other way around. It is therefore extremely unfortunate if evaluators spend most of their time talking to program staff and relatively less of their time talking to program clientele. Social linkages created by these contacts are another source of bias in addition to the perceptual bias in knowing the goals.

There is no need for program evaluation to be done on a wholly goal-free or wholly goal-based commitment. A mixture of the two — with some staff aware of goals and others, isolated from the first group, not aware of them — often works very well. A mode reversal is also possible, with the staff beginning their work in ignorance of the goals and proceeding as far as the preliminary report in writing;

then being informed about the goals, and proceeding through such further work as may appear necessary at that point. So one can often eat one's cake and have it, if one does it in the right order. Goal-free evaluation roughly corresponds to double-blind design in the medical field, and for those same reasons is to be deemed advantageous where possible. It is not, in general, more expensive, though it will certainly be so in some cases, and it will be less expensive in other cases — especially since the cost of disruption of staff and services (so often not counted into the cost of evaluation) is largely eliminated.

Given that evaluation is an essential part of quality control, one learns something extremely important from the discovery that the very term *evaluation* is such anathema in many quarters — for example, in large parts of the federal government system — that people go to great lengths to use other language such as *assessment* or *policy analysis* to cover precisely an evaluation process. It is clear that valuephobia, given the educational background and professional commitment of most people working in the human services area, is far more powerful than their commitment to quality. While it may well be true that evaluation is often performed extremely badly, that it may be a damaging activity for worthwhile programs and involve a risk of unfair treatment for worthy people, that hardly justifies the extraordinary defensive maneuvering that goes on in order to avoid it or its impact. The interest in quality control that the Japanese have shown with the institution of Quality Circles has been widely remarked, but a much deeper and more serious deficiency underlies the fact that Quality Circles, invented here, were disregarded until Japan took them up. Valuephobia runs deep.

Another example: there is no such thing as professionalism without a commitment to evaluation of whatever it is that one supervises or produces — and to self-evaluation as well. Yet few professional schools have even the most superficial curriculum commitment to evaluation training of any kind, let alone of professionals.

At the very least, one would expect to find some willingness among managers to treat investment in evaluation on a straight investment basis; since it is clear that it makes claims to pay off in much the same way as any kind of management consulting pays off, or indeed in the way in which computerization pays off, managers who were seriously oriented towards quality consideration would certainly run up some experimental evidence as to the extent to which evaluation by certain evaluators, done in certain ways, etc., pays off or does not pay off. While most program evaluation may be too biased and superficial to be worth following up, it is patently obvious that good product evaluation and good personnel evaluation can pay off very many times over. There are also a number of clear cases where large-scale program evaluation has paid off by factors between 10 and 100. (The doctrine that evaluation should more than pay for itself, on the average, is a meta evaluation criterion of merit and has been referred to as the doctrine of cost-free evaluation.) Thus, the managerial bias is carried to the extreme of a very self-serving indulgence in valuephobia.

4. The Relativist Ideology. Whereas the positivists were committed to the view that there was some kind of definite external world about which we learned through our senses and through experiments, more recent philosophy of science has tended to move away from this "realistic" or "external world" commitment towards the view that everyone has his or her own reality, all equally legitimate. And evaluation has been very much influenced by this movement in the philosophy of science. Throughout this book, in articles by the most distinguished workers in evaluation, one finds not only a shying away from the notion of objective determination of worth — as in Cronbach's aversion to summative evaluation — but also a shying away from even the notion of objectively correct descriptions of programs. Multiple perspectives, yes; multiple realities, no. While it is in my view perfectly appropriate to respond to the obvious need for multiple perspectives and multiple levels of description by abandoning any naive assumption about the existence of a single correct description of objects in the external world (including programs), it is equally mistaken to overreact in the direction of solipsism or relativism. The relativist ideology or bias is, in my view, a case of such overreaction; it is often to be recognized by the emphasis placed by its supporters upon the impossibility of establishing "the truth," or "the existence of a correct view of the world," and so on. If it were really the case that there is no objective superiority of some descriptions above others, then there could be no discipline of physics any more than evaluation. The concept of relativism is self-refuting; if everything is relative, then the assertion that everything is relative cannot itself be known to be true. So, although we may reject the existence of a single correct description, we should not abandon the idea that there is an objective reality, though it may be a very rich one that cannot be *exhaustively* described. It may even be one which can only be described in a non-misleading way by giving descriptions which are relativised to each audience; we may concede all this, and yet insist that in many cases there is such a thing as a correct — though not a unique — description (given a certain audience and level) by contrast with a number of incorrect descriptions. Indeed, these descriptions may involve descriptions of the merit, worth, or value of parts or aspects of the entity being investigated.

It has been argued above that the very core of science, as of other disciplines, is committed to the objectivity of evaluation — in fact, if one could not distinguish good from bad scientific explanations, one could not be said to be a scientist at all — and there is thus no shame or indeed any further commitment involved in treating evaluation as an objective discipline. The fact that ethical issues must also be handled raises the question of the status of objectivity in that subfield of evaluation; but whatever decision one comes to there, one cannot weaken the resolve with which one must address the search for the best and the better and the ideal when evaluating all aspects of a program other than the ethical. Programs are simply very complicated institutions, but they are no more complicated than theories or even experimental designs, which we have no hesitation in evaluating by strictly scientific criteria. It is a modest enough — and surely a scientific — suggestion that we should evaluate programs in terms of their latent rather than their alleged function.

Thus, I see the re-emergence of relativism as the latest and most serious bias in evaluation methodology, because it comes from the evaluators themselves. It is quite easy to show that those who support it officially actually disregard it in their common practice. Just as managers act as goal-free evaluators of consumer goods, so relativists act as objectivists in their grading of their students or of the interpretations by their colleagues of certain experimental results. This inconsistency between practice and philosophy is a sure sign of the immaturity of this field at the present moment. There are many other such signs, and in the ensuing paragraphs we will call attention to a few standard evaluation practices that violate some of the most obvious criteria for systematic evaluation — and yet have not been universally condemned by professional associations of evaluators and often are not even seen as particularly relevant to the narrowly conceived business of program evaluation. In the course of discussing these examples, albeit very briefly, we will also take the opportunity to introduce one or two conceptual distinctions that clarify practices and malpractices as well as referring to the four fallacious ideologies that we have outlined above.

The Social Science Model. This set of four fallacious ideologies often seems to congeal into something that could be called the traditional social science model of evaluation. Since we are here proposing a set of alternative positions or ideologies, which we will elaborate in modest detail below, it can be argued that we are proposing an alternative and more appropriate model for the social sciences. Thus, if this argument is correct, evaluation should lead us to a considerable sophistication of the rather primitive philosophy of science that has been associated with the social sciences, and one might sum this up by saying that evaluation turns out to be a better model for the social sciences than they have proved to be for it. Taking this view seriously, one looks more carefully at the publications in the traditional social science journals and sees many ways in which these could be increased in their value, to science and to society, if a range of further questions were to be addressed about them, both at the design level and the meta level. So there is a second goal for this paper, the commitment to substantial reform of the ideology and hence the practice of the social sciences and not just of evaluation.

The examples that follow come from educational experience, not just because we are all familiar with such cases, but because it may be that the largest payoff from improvement in evaluation can be achieved if reforms in educational evaluation take place — by contrast with reforms in the administration of criminal justice or other human services. The examples chosen scarcely exhaust the area; we could have focussed solely on the kind of evaluation that underlies the current mania about computers, e.g., the absence of serious needs assessment behind the push for teaching BASIC as "computer literacy." But we focus on older sins.

The Evaluation of Student Work. In this most common of all educational experiences, we find example after example of methodological misconceptions and misdirections, which clearly show how well segregated our intellectual efforts were from our pedagogical practices. It is only as the discipline of evaluation has grown to some degree of autonomy and as external social pressures have forced us to re-examine the evaluation of students that we have come to raise our eyebrows over practices which many of our most intelligent and best-trained social scientists had set up and nurtured for decades.

We will not here rehearse the whole sorry story of the abuses of norm-referenced testing and the gradually improving mix with criterion-referenced testing that is emerging. As the fights over minimum competency achievement tests for graduation or promotion, over the definition of test bias, over the concept of instructional validity, and about other issues are reaching a more mature level of discussion, assisted by the courts and public opinion as well as the scholars, we are seeing the development of evaluation by contrast with mere testing. We will here simply comment on a basic logical point that has not been treated with appropriate respect in the literature on measurement, but which becomes crucial as we attempt to develop the logic of evaluation in any consistent and comprehensive way. The basic logical relations in evaluation seem to be four in number: grading, ranking, scoring, and apportioning. The following definitions are partly stipulative, but involve very little straightening out, being mainly a reflection of the implicit logic of the common terms. *Grading* is the allocation of objects to a set of classes that are ordered by merit or worth; the number of classes usually being small compared to the number of entities graded, and the description of each class being given in terms that refer to some external standards of merit or worth, i.e., not simply to relative position. *Ranking* is the allocation of individuals to some position in an ordering, usually one where the number of positions is equal to or almost equal to the number of individuals; the order being by merit or worth. *Scoring* is the most elaborate standard mensurable approach associated with evaluation; it involves the ascription of a quantitative measure of merit or worth to each individual in the group being evaluated. And *apportioning* is the process of allocating a finite valuable resource in varying amounts to each individual as a means of expressing an assessment of merit or worth. Certain obvious connections and lack of connection can be quickly stated. Ranking does not imply grading nor vice versa; scoring will entail a ranking but not a grading (in general); neither grading nor ranking will entail an apportioning, although apportioning can be defined in terms of a very complicated set of gradings and rankings of parts of whatever is being evaluated, whenever such parts can be identified. Both criterion-referenced and norm referenced tests require cutting scores in order to define a grading; normed tests always, and criterion referenced tests sometimes, define a ranking. The body of basic training in tests and measurement is weak on these distinctions, because of the valuephobic exclusion of explicit discussion of merit. As a result, elementary mistakes are to be found in almost every text and in many published tests, where confusions between these types of evaluation are rampant. A typical example occurs when the translation of the ratings on a five point rating scale is given as excellent; very good; average; below average; very poor. The first two of these refer to grading; the next two refer to a norm-referenced or ranking approach, and the last reverts back to a grading approach. The scale is logically unsound since the average performance of the group being rated may be very good, or poor, or anywhere else, so there are often two correct responses. The "anchors" given presuppose a more or less normal distribution *and* a coincidence of the upper reaches of the distribution with excellent performance (and correspondingly with the lower reaches), both of them are extremely implausible assumptions in most contexts of student evaluation.

The concept of grading on the curve, another symptom of valuephobia, exhibits the same distortion of the difference between grading and ranking. With typical managerial bias, it assumes that the difficulty level of the test has been set at precisely the right point so that the top ten percent (or 15 percent) which are automatically given an A will in fact deserve to be regarded as having performed not merely superior work (which is tautologically correct) but excellent work, and similarly for the other grades. If it is argued that psychologists ascribe no more significance to the A than top decile performance, then we must focus on the bottom end of the class and inquire why it should be assumed that there must always be ten percent who fail. Obviously, such an assumption is completely false in many circumstances, and, if false at that end of the distribution, the converse must be in question at the other end. And in the middle.

Of course, built into the very conception of scoring that leads to the normal distribution used in grading on the curve is precisely that identification of merit with a point in the scoring system, the commitment to an independent assessment of worth or value, that is supposedly rejected by going to grading on the curve. If one is prepared to commit oneself to the view that any point, however earned on whatever question in the test, is of equal value — the assumption without which one cannot justify scoring at all as a basis even for ranking — then one might as well commit oneself to the rather more modest assumption that one can identify a truly excellent or hopeless performance not just by its salience.

Another example of logical confusion occurs in funding decisions, where the review panel is instructed to rank or grade programs, whereas apportioning is the question at issue. (Using the wrong instructions may, however, make managerial manipulation of the results much easier.)

Teacher Evaluation. The evaluation of research has always been thought to be relatively straightforward by comparison with the evaluation of teaching; close examination of the implicit assumptions in the way research evaluation has been done has led to increasing disquiet with this in recent years, and a great deal more needs to be done towards developing reasonably objective standards for the evaluation. But the evaluation of teaching and teachers is much more of a scandal. A great deal has been written about this recently, and we will simply make two points here. First, it has rarely been remarked that there is a complete difference between an evaluation of merit and an evaluation of worth in teaching, and that these two considerations have quite different relevance to different kinds of personnel decisions. The evaluation of worth (to the institution) is an evaluation which brings in questions of the salaries in the marketplace, of the extent to which the subject matter is popular or essential to mission, of payoffs from fame (in the media sense) of the instructor and so on. None of these is involved in the evaluation of professional merit, a property of the individual and his or her performance against the standards of merit in that profession. Thus, a teacher at the college level may have the greatest merit and be of so little worth to the institution that it does not make sense to grant tenure, simply because the subject matter in which this instructor specializes no longer draws any students at all; the reverse may also be true of the great showman or grantsman who attracts income and/or students but does so without a foundation of true professional merit. Roughly speaking, initial and tenure appointments should be made on the basis of worth as well as merit, but promotions and awards should be made solely on the basis of merit.

A second interesting point that can be made about the evaluation of teachers concerns the fact that the universal procedure employed in the evaluation of primary and secondary school teachers is invalid for every possible reason. That procedure consists of visiting a very few classes, often with advance notice and using checklists or subjective judgment to determine whether appropriate practices are occurring during the visit. The sample size is too small to be of any use, even if the sample is random; the sample is not random, since the measurement process may affect the treatment; the judge is not free of significant social biases from non-classroom relationships with the teacher; the checklists are invalid; and finally the judge is completely invalidated as a detector of learning gains, which must be regarded as at least a major part of what teaching is all about. The continuance of this practice in the light of these obvious invalidities is a reflection upon the state-of-the-art of (or interest in) evaluation amongst professional administrators and teachers. It should, of course, be noted that neither unions nor management would benefit from switching to an alternative approach since neither is rewarded for the replacement of bad teachers by good ones, and indeed would be heavily punished by the emotions, costs, and struggles that would be involved in a changeover. Only the children and the taxpayer are cheated and their representatives are not yet sufficiently sophisticated to speak up about the impropriety of this process.

Apart from this generally dismal situation, there is an extremely interesting and more sophisticated point involved. Supposing that we *had* established a very reliable list of indicators of good teaching, and that we *were* able to observe teachers at work without affecting the way they teach, in a *large enough* sample of lessons. It seems that then our problems would all be solved. (In fact, we do have one such indicator, not the dozens which are widely touted; it appears that sample of lessons. It seems that then our problems would all be solved. (In fact, we do have one such indicator, not the dozens which are widely touted; it appears that "interactive time on task" is a good indicator of amount of learning.) We now come to see one of the more radical differences between formative and summative evaluation. For purposes of summative evaluation — that is, in this context, the making of personnel decisions — we cannot use statistical indicators of merit that refer to only one or some aspects of the performance. This claim of course directly contradicts the standard operating procedure in the evaluation of teachers. We cannot use such an indicator any more than we can use skin color, even when we are in possession of job-related, valid generalizations about skin color, e.g., that the crime rate is higher among blacks, and the oppression rate higher among whites. We cannot use such generalizations in the evaluation of individual cases, because, in the first place, they apply only to randomly chosen samples from the population to which they refer, and the individual in a personnel evaluation situation is by no means a random sample — we know much too much about such individuals for them to be "representative" or "typical" or "random" samples of that population. In the second place, if we do *not* know more than this about the individual in a personnel decision case, then we can and should go out and get some more evidence, evidence directly related to track record performance in this or the most similar work situation we can identify in their case history. This is scientific common sense. The ethical imperative, in addition, requires that we not use membership in a very general class as the basis for judgment about the individual; we have various terms for the associated error, for example, "guilt by association," or "stereotyping." Since there are always feasible and superior alternatives to these generalizations in personnel work, there is no justification for using them. In the case of summative teacher evaluation, the clearly superior alternative is the use of direct evidence of learning, plus appropriate standards obtained from suitable comparisons with other teachers of similar children. (Even *holistic* ratings by judges present *most of the time,* who lack the chance to acquire *social bias,* will be superior; which is to say, student evaluations of teaching.)

The various absurdly primitive attempts to use pupil performance as an indicator of teacher merit have produced an understandable backlash against this kind of approach; but when the comparisons are made with other teachers of children in the same school, where allocation to classroom is almost entirely random — or to children in similar schools serving essentially similar populations — then the difference in final achievement on a sound common test must be due to the differences in teaching ability. Minor differences are of no interest since the matching is not perfect and circumstantial variables will have some minor effects (e.g., classroom architecture, the presence of a single highly disruptive student, etc.) However, if multiple measurements of student gains are made (e.g., in an elementary school, three successive measurements across three successive terms) there is not going to be much doubt that teachers who are always two standard deviations off the mean are either genuine super-teachers or genuine failures. The courts having upheld this kind of evidence as grounds for dismissal; we should now be using it. (Where it is not available, student evaluations are the best alternative.)

Of course, even though the courts have upheld the use of comparative gain score evidence alone, it is not all that we should be gathering. We also need evidence of the quality of the content taught and not covered in the test. This is readily obtainable by inspection of materials (especially student products) by a curriculum specialist or even by a principal with experience in this area. We also need evidence about the ethicality and professionality of the teaching process. (Where student ratings are used instead of gain scores, the evaluation of all content becomes crucial.) The ethicality of the teaching process is not a matter of whether one uses negative reinforcement rather than positive reinforcement — often inappropriately regarded as cruel and unusual punishment by supervisors and principals. It is rather a matter of whether there is flagrant disregard of due process and considerations of justice, e.g., by the use of sexist or racist remarks or practices; by unfair grading practices; and by inappropriate test construction. This will best be picked up by a review of the test materials and anonymous student responses. Finally, although it is not absolutely essential, it is highly desirable to use evidence of professionality, usually best based upon a dossier submitted by the instructor. Professionalism requires self development, so evidence of advanced courses in both subject matter and method would be relevant. It requires self-evaluation; so it requires evidence that testing of one's teaching success, including (usually) the use of student evaluations, has been obtained. Both of these considerations require a steady process of experimentation, with new materials and approaches. Even a program of critical reading of new and promising literature or current research literature would be relevant to these considerations and could be documented in such a dossier.

The preceding will generate a highly satisfactory model for summative evaluation. But does it not, in one version, involve a violation of the very principles which it was set up to support? In using student evaluations, especially as our only indicator of learning, are we not using an indicator that has only a statistical correlation with merit in teaching? This is true, but this is one of the cases where a statistical indicator may be justifiable. To see why, consider an even more extreme example. Test scores by students on well-constructed scholastic achievement tests are used in order to select the entering class for colleges and graduate schools. But it is well known that such tests are not infallible indicators of what we may take to be the criterion variable — success at those colleges. If they are "merely statistical indicators," then surely we are not entitled to use them since they violate the principle of judging the individual on the basis of his or her own work rather than on the performance of people who are related by some statistical generalization to the individual being evaluated? The reader will no doubt notice two crucial differences about this case. In the first place, we *are* using the individual's own work, a comprehensive and relevant work sample, in fact. In the second place, we do not have a feasible and better alternative available, (cf., also the validity of an end-of-term course exam).

People sometimes propose that the use of the high school teachers' evaluations of the college-bound student — based, as they are, upon very extensive observation — would be superior to the use of test scores. Investigation shows that this is not usually the case, essentially because of the problem of inter-judge unreliability. In short, it is not a *systematic* alternative because there is no feasible *system* of having the same set of judges look at all candidates, so the test — which is administered in the same form to all candidates — wins on the swings of reliability what it loses on the roundabouts of inadequate work sampling. And so it is with student evaluations of teachers. Especially when the questionnaire is appropriately constructed and administered, a high score has a good positive correlation with the learning outcome. Of course we could always directly measure the learning outcomes — that is not the problem; the problem is identifying the extent to which the gains are due to teaching merit (as opposed to the textbooks, peer interaction, and intellectual or familial background), and deciding on the cutting scores that will separate good teaching performance from bad. Absent the comparative situation described earlier, our only alternative is the use of student evaluations. Now these evaluations are holistic evaluations of the particular work of the particular individual, not evaluations of part or one aspect of what the teacher does (cf., brief visits or time-on-task measures); they are probably related to learning, *and* they include allowances for other causes and for what could have been done, by contrast with what *was* done. The method is imperfect of course, but based on considerable exposure to other teachers, in the consumer's role. In short, they provide us with the comparative dimensions that we lack if we just collect gain scores. (It does not follow, by the way, that we should use a comparative *question:* ''Rate this teacher against others you have had. . . .'' That will get you a ranking — but few personnel decisions can be based on a ranking, certainly not a promotion or tenure decision. That's grading on the curve. You must ask for a grading: ''Rate this teacher A–F, where A means excellent . . . F means extremely bad.'' The student's experience with other teachers will create the range of the *feasible;* the top of that range is the locus of excellence.)

While time-on-task measurements *are* empirically related to the performance of the individual, as is skin color, the relationship is of a weaker kind, one that does not survive an increased specification of the individual's characteristics. Student evaluations are holistic of both individual and performance and, though by no means perfect, are — as far as we know and as we'd expect — superior to ratings by any other general category of judges (e.g., principals or supervisors or process experts) though we certainly need more sampling of the matrix of subject matter by age, by school environment, etc., to support this claim more substantially. Hence, we should be using them in the high school and college situation, where there are usually no comparative norms available. When comparisons *are* possible, as with multi-section freshman courses in college, it is preferable though sometimes politically impossible to set up random allocation, common tests and blind grading, and revert to the use of comparative norms.

The preceding discussion will make clear the way in which ethical considerations interact with scientific ones in personnel evaluation. It should also make clear the important distinction between holistic and what can be called analytic evaluation — one might use the terms macro evaluation and micro evaluation instead. The holistic evaluation is an evaluation of the total relevant performance, whereas the analytic evaluation evaluates some component or dimension of that performance. The evaluation of components is in some ways more useful for formative evaluation than the evaluation of dimensions, because it is likely to be easier to manipulate components than dimensions. But either may provide an adequate basis for assembling *or justifying* an overall evaluation. Counterintuitively, however, it transpires that we have clear evidence showing holistic evaluation is sometimes considerably more valid — as well as far more economical — than syntheses of micro evaluations. The problem with the analytic approach to overall evaluations is that the assembly of component scores or grades involves a weighting and combining arrangement of typically unknown validity. (See *The Evaluation of Composition Instruction*, Davis, Scriven, & Thomas, 1981). The evaluation of teaching also illustrates clearly the differences among evaluation, explanation, and remediation, so often confused in program evaluation, where the client frequently *demands* that the evaluator submit remedial recommendations as well as an overall evaluation. Attractive though that is to the client, and important though it is to do it when possible, there is often an urgent necessity to choose between sound summative evaluation and relatively unreliable and more expensive formative evaluation. It is fairly easy to evaluate teachers on the basis of their success, where one can get appropriate comparison groups set up; but it is not a consequence of the validity of this evaluation that one can give any advice whatsoever to the teachers who perform less well as to how to improve their performance. The reason for this is not only that the best approach to summative evaluation is often holistic; it is also that we lack the grounded theory to provide the appropriate explanations, since all efforts to find components of a winning style (apart from interactive time-on-task which is only marginally describable as "style") have so far failed. Absent a diagnosis of the causes of failure, whence comes a prescription?

Although the traditional approach to remediation is through explanation, the occasional success of "folk-medicine" demonstrates the *possibility* of finding remedies whose success is not inferred from a general explanatory theory, but discovered directly. And so it is with teaching; we might find that a certain kind of in-service training package is highly successful, although it does not proceed from an analysis of the causes of failure. It is thus triply wrong for a client to demand micro explanations as part of an evaluation as a route to remediation or justification. They will not necessarily lead to remediation; there are other ways to get to remediation to provide evidence for the validity of the evaluation. The latter is provided on a holistic basis, e.g., by correlational data relating evaluations by this method (or these judges) with the subsequent performance of the criterion variable. Of course, remedial suggestions are often obvious or easily uncovered from an analytic summative evaluation; but not always and the analytic approach is often not the best one.

I have already mentioned that if one approaches the evaluation of something by evaluating components or dimensions of it, which are then assembled into an overall evaluation, serious problems of validation arise about the formula used for assembly. I have discussed elsewhere the use of some traditional approaches, e.g., weighted-sum with overrides, and we have of course the well known model of cost-benefit analysis, in which we reduce costs and benefits to a single dimension and thereby convert evaluation into measurement. Much more needs to be done about the synthesis step in program evaluation; the present trends, partly because of the difficulty of this step and partly because of the influence of the relativist ideology, is towards mere "exhibiting" of performance on the multiple dimensions involved. This is simply passing the buck to the non-professional, and represents far less than the appropriate response by a professional evaluator.

Review

What is emerging from our discussion of these common evaluation practices? Two points. On the one hand, we are seeing gross errors of practice emerge under critical study, and it is not hard to see how these reflect — directly or indirectly — the ideologies or biases we have discussed. By far, the greatest influence of those ideologies is indirect in that they have discouraged recognition of the essential self-reference and evaluative nature of science; discouraged emphasis on the client's perspective; and discouraged any sustained commitment to the existence of correct versus incorrect conclusions.

The Consumerist Ideology. For many people, committed to the relativist ideology, it follows from the fact that one is attacking some ideologies that one must be supporting another. This is in error as a general conclusion, but it would be fair to say that the sum total of all the criticisms so far does add up to a point-of-view that needs to be made explicit at this point. I'll use a label for it that has been contaminated with largely irrelevant opprobrium, but still retains enough common meaning and a connotation of an ethically appropriate position; I'll say that we have been presenting a *consumerist ideology*. Consumerism is like unionism; both came into existence to represent a movement which, even from the beginning, involved some wrong activities, while representing a long overdue balancing of power and involving an essentially moral concern with people who had been left out of the reckoning. By and large, consumerism has done well by us, from the first day that Ralph Nader provided an over-simplified and in many ways unjustified analysis of the General Motors Corvair automobile, although it has brought with it some overkill pseudo-safety and pseudo-consumer protection legislation. The essential point of the consumerist ideology in evaluation is that all parties affected by something that is being evaluated should be taken into account and given at least their appropriate moral weighting — and in many cases, an appropriate opportunity for explicit participation and/or response to the evaluation process or outcome.

We can proceed quite briefly with a few more examples of bad practice still tolerated because of acceptance of the fallacious ideologies, and then conclude with a brief description of a model of evaluation methodology that can be said to unpack the consumerist ideology, just as the goal-based evaluation model unpacks the managerial ideology.

The Evaluation of Educational Institutions by Accreditation. Just as there is a completely standard model for primary or secondary teacher evaluation, so there is one for the evaluation of primary, secondary and professional schools. This model, accreditation, has a number of distinctive features, some virtues, and a number of serious weaknesses that cannot be dismissed as due to constraints on resources available for accreditation.

The distinctive features of accreditation, nearly all present in all applications of this approach, are:

1. The use of a handbook of standards, involved in several other components, beginning with
2. A self study by the institution, resulting in a report on how well they are achieving what they see as their mission; which is read by
3. A team of external assessors, usually volunteer members of the same general professional enterprise, who not only read the self-study, but also make
4. A site visit, usually for one to three days, which involves direct inspection of facilities, interviews with staff, clients, and students, plus review of prior reports, and which results in
5. A report on the institution, which usually makes various recommendations for change and for/or against accreditation (possibly with various conditions); this report is subject to
6. A review by some august panel, at which the right to appeal against the

recommendations is sometimes granted to the institution being evaluated and at which some censoring of the recommendations sometimes occurs; after which

7.   A final report and decision is issued.

Some of the desirable features here include: some use of external evaluators, self-scrutiny as a method of preparing the ground for the external suggestions and for providing a linkage group with the external assessors, a review process which gives some chance to address injustices, and a rather modest cost. Within this general framework, good evaluation could indeed be done. But it is rare to see it done.

We'll pick up only a few of the problems, more to illustrate than to provide a thorough analysis. We can conveniently group the problems under the same heading as the components.

1.   The handbook of standards is usually a mishmash ranging from the trivial to the really important, and there is usually no weighting suggested. (Sometimes there isn't even a handbook of standards.) Consequently, the bits and pieces can be assembled in more or less any way that the panel feels like assembling them, without any focus on the justification of the implicit weighting of such a synthesis. It is common for the handbook of standards to begin with some piece of rhetoric about how institutions should only be judged against their own goals, but yet we will find buried in the handbook a number of categorical standards that must be met by all institutions. This inconsistency reflects a failure to resolve the ideological tension between managerial and consumerist approaches. Managers do not want to be blamed for not doing what they did not undertake to do; on the other hand, consumers do not like to be treated badly and don't much care whether the maltreatment was unintentional or not. Ethics obviously requires that the rights of consumers be protected at least in certain respects, so that minimum standards of justice should be met by all educational institutions. It might also be argued that public institutions have some obligations to provide a service that is reasonably well-tailored to public needs, and that even private institutions — who may select more or less whomever they wish to enroll — must nevertheless provide services that are related to the needs of those whom they do enroll. (Note that the absolute standards one does encounter in these typical standards checklists are usually considerably less ethics-related than the ones just mentioned, indeed are often highly debatable; e.g., the requirement of vast libraries for graduate programs.)

2.   The self-study is frequently devoted towards a review of goals in the light of mission, and of achievements in the light of goals. This tends to involve the usual managerial biases, because of the failure to give due weight to the consumer; in particular, there is poor attention to the need to search for side effects, there is little concern with comparisons or cost-effectiveness, and usually little concern with the ethics of the process. (This of course varies considerably across the huge range of

accredited institutions, but of the many that I have seen from the medical and legal area as well as from many college and high school reports, the above seems to be a fair generalization.) Another type of weakness emerges at this point; there is rarely a professional evaluator on the internal self-study review team, and consequently many of the usual traps are fallen into, including careless ascriptions of casual efficacy to programs, misinterpretations of data about learning gains, and alleged success of graduates and so on. It is impossible to expect that there will not be some adjustment of goals to achievement — and this may sometimes be healthy — but it does provide an opportunity to duck behind goal-relativism, which is allegedly the standard by which the accrediting association will make the final judgment. Thus the managerial bias is supported by the relativist one.

3.   The team of external assessors is usually picked from volunteers, and, consequently, professional evaluators and the busiest administrative analysts and consultants are more or less automatically excluded. Professional evaluators are by no means automatically an advantage on these panels; it would be absurd for a professional evaluator to assume that they are. The only imperative is that they should sometimes be present and that careful meta-studies should be done to see if this does lead to any improvement. The idea that one can dismiss the supposed experts entirely seems naive, given the low quality of the usual reports. It must be expected that professional evaluators will have to be paid for this activity, so the price goes up; that price could be offset by reducing the size of the panel, since the indirect costs per diem and travel are quite substantial. We should find out whether some professionalism would offset some loss of numbers. There could also be systematic studies with funds from foundations, to see whether the addition of the best management consultants and evaluators will yield cost-saving suggestions that would compensate for increasing the fees to cover their costs. There would then be problems about equity as far as the still-unpaid members of the panel are concerned and serious problems about total cost. However, the quality of the evaluation reports, judged against professional evaluation standards, is so spotty that the entire process should be subject to serious scrutiny; it hardly constitutes an acceptable way in which to evaluate most of our important educational institutions.

Professionals and other busy people are not the only ones left off by the process of volunteering and subsequent selection, usually by central staff personnel. There is a strong tendency to leave radicals and other "extremists" off the panel. No doubt there are accreditation units here and there — I know of one — where this is not true; but it is certainly the general pattern, and it is a typical sign of managerial bias. If we were searching for truth, we would realize that radical perspectives often uncover the truth and can demonstrate it to the satisfaction of all panelists. And we would realize that establishment-selected judges are likely to be blind to some of the more deep-seated biases of the institution; one can see how serious this is by tracking back through old accreditation reports given during pre-feminist days. Not a sign can be seen of sensitivity to radical sexist exploitation and inappropriate passing over of women for positions which they should have received; but there were plenty of feminists around in those days, if anyone had been looking for them.

This managerial bias is of course one that will favor the institution by not uncovering the skeletons in its closet; and it is not accidental that the whole accreditation process is run by a system of fees levied on the very institutions that are accredited and which provide the personnel for the accreditation. The system is thus in a fairly straightforward way incestuous; the question is whether one can conclude that it is corrupt. To the extent it is not, we must thank the innate professional competence and commitment and integrity of the panelists, which does not entirely evaporate under the background pressure towards pro-management, pro-establishment reports. However, to jump a few steps, it is important to notice that the report by the site team will sometimes be radically censored by the review board, which has of course not been to the site, in the direction of excising many or all of its most serious criticisms or conditions. This is an unattractive situation, and one which is not widely recognized. It suggests inappropriate bias, and when we look at the procedure whereby the review boards themselves are selected, we find in many cases an even more unattractive situation. For the review panels — for example, the governing board of the regional accreditation associations in the case of schools and colleges — are often entirely self-selected and often consist almost entirely of active or retired administrators.

4.   The site visit is also not designed to capture the input of the most severe critics. Such obvious devices as setting up a suggestion box on the campus during the site visit, providing an answering machine to record comments by those who wish to call them in anonymously, or careful selection of the most severe critics of the institution from among those who are interviewed are practices that one rarely if ever encounters. Failure to adopt these practices simply shows a failure to distinguish between the need for a balanced overall final view and the need for input from the whole spectrum of consumers; both are imperative, the former does not exclude the latter, and the two are quite distinct.

So, from the use of inappropriate standards, such as the requirement of large research libraries for graduate programs instead of *access* to such libraries *or* to online databases, to the failure to enforce serious standards for the self-study (to the point where the great post-secondary institutions go through this stage without most of their faculty ever hearing that it is going on), we are dealing with grossly unprofessional evaluation. Nervousness about the incestuousness of the process is not lessened when one sees the defensive nature of the accreditation agencies' reactions to the proposal that federal or state governments should have some input to accreditation. Undesirable though this may be in various ways, a hybrid system would at least provide minimal insurance against the more outrageous examples of

"National Tobacco Research Institute" whitewashes. The extremely lax enforcement of professional standards by the medical and legal professions is a well known scandal and, although there are some professions — the psychologists are a pretty good example — which rise above this kind of managerial/separatist bias, it must be realized that the society and its legitimate government have extremely strong rights to be represented in a process which deals with the key services provided to its relatively unprotected citizenry. When we do get an occasional glimpse at the actual standards of competence in a profession — as when we see the results of competency exams on teachers, or the analysis of drug prescriptions written in a certain region — we have every right to suspect that the self-regulation process is not being done any better than one would expect, given the biases built into it. Accreditation is an excellent example of what one might with only slight cynicism call a pseudo-evaluative process, set up to give the appearance of self-regulation without having to suffer the inconvenience.

If one had to sum the whole matter up, one might call attention to the fact that in virtually no system of accreditation is there a truly serious focus on judging the institution by the performance of its graduates, which one might well argue is the only true standard. Not to look at the performance seriously, not even to do phone interviews of a random sample of graduates, not even to talk to a few employers and/or employment agencies who deal with graduates from this and others institutions; *this* is absurd.

It is scarcely surprising that in large areas of accreditation, the track record of enforcement is a farce. Among all state accreditation boards reviewing teacher preparation programs, for example, it is essentially unknown for any credential to be removed. Nor is it surprising that at one point the state of California was threatening to close down all unaccredited law schools, although some of these had a much higher success rate in getting their graduates past the bar exam than many prominent law schools in the state. And passing the bar exam is presumably one of the most important things that a law school is supposed to do for you — as far as I know, it is the only one for which we obtain a measurement. Crude measurements are not as good as refined measurements, but they beat the hell out of the judgements of those with vested interests.

Another example of crude measurement that turns out to be quite revealing is one that can be applied to the evaluation of proposals and the allocation of funds for research in the sciences, as well to the accreditation process, and it is such an obvious suggestion that the failure to implement it must be taken as a serious sign of the operation of the separatist ideology in the service of elitism. This modest proposal concerns checking the reliability of team ratings. When a review panel of peers judges that a particular proposal should be funded and another rejected, just as when a review panel judges that a particular institution should be accredited and another disaccredited (or warned, or not accredited), it seems reasonable for those affected to raise the question whether another panel drawn from the same pool of professionals would have made the same recommendation. This is of course the question of inter-judge (in this case inter-panel of judges) reliability, and until very recently no such test had ever been made (although it is the simplest and most obvious recommendation that a freshman student of one of the social sciences would make about a judgmental process of any kind that was officially regarded as subject to scientific investigation). Only separatism insulates the scientist (or other professional) from this scrutiny; and in the couple of cases where a study of inter-panel consistency has been performed, the results have not been encouraging. The North Central Association sent in two teams to have a look at the school — Colorado Springs High School — and the results demontrated not so much a lack of agreement but some important disagreements coupled with the possibilty that most of the agreements were due to shared bias. A small National Science Foundation study of the results when more than one panel, drawn from the same pool of professionals, was assigned the task of rating proposals, showed striking and substantial differences. When these relatively crude measures are the only measures we have, the only appropriate conclusion from these results must be an extremely skeptical view of the validity of the accreditation approach to program evaluation.

Ideologies and Models

Ideologies are intermediate between philosophies and models, just as models are intermediate between ideologies and methodologies. Thus more than one ideology may support a particular model; just as the relativist ideology supports Elliot Eisner's connoisseurship model, so the empiricist ideology as well as the managerial and relativist ones support goal-based evaluation models. Some subtler relations can be plausibly inferred. Recently, for example, we have seen Cronbach's group coming out strongly in favor of formative evaluation as the only legitimate kind of evaluation, by contrast with summative. In this respect, their position matches that of some staff members of the American Federation of Teachers, who are willing to support the idea of evaluation of teachers for improvement, but not the idea of quality review. Apart from logical problems with the artificial nature of this separation, it is certainly an emphasis attractive to both the positivist and the relativist ideology, because each is much more willing to tolerate the idea of improvement — with its connotations of goals and local values as the criteria — than categorical assertions about merit and worth. Few people are valuephobic about the suggestion they are less than perfect, need some improvement; but to be told they are incompetent or even far worse than others, is less palatable.

In remediating (formative evaluation), as in ranking or grading, the fundamental task is that of determining the direction of improvement of superiority, and the mere avoidance of the "cutting scores" problem that is required before you can establish grades does not avoid the logical task of establishing, i.e., justifying and evaluative assertion. Thus I see the preference for formative over summative as — from one perspective — an attempt to limit the amount of evaluative logic that one has to get into, but it does not eliminate the first and crucial step, the step that refutes both relativism and empiricism.

Relatedly, the recent tremendous emphasis on implementation and implementability as meta-evaluative criteria for the merit of evaluations can be seen as another attempt to duck the head-on confrontation with the necessity for demonstrating the *validity* of categorical value judgments, especially those involved in grading. The validity of value judgments, whether they are gradings or rankings, is what the empiricist and relativist deny; but it is a problem that must be faced, and it cannot be converted into the problem of whether the program achieves the goals of its instigators or whether an evaluation is implemented by its clients. Goal-achievement and evaluation-implementation are perfectly compatible with a categorical denial of all merit in the program or evaluation; their absence is perfectly compatible with a categorical assertion of flawless merit. In short, these proposed substitutes are not even universal correlates of the concept they seek to replace, let alone definitional components. (Perspectivism accommodates the need for multiple accounts of reality as perspectives from which we build up a true picture, not as a set of true pictures of different and inconsistent realities. The ethicist believes that objective moral evaluations are possible.)

So far we have talked very favorably about the consumerist ideology. Other strands in the position advocated here must also be recognized as implicitly supported by our criticism of the alternatives to them. These include the perspectivist and ethicist strands that stand opposed relativism and empiricism, the holistic orientation that is the alternative to reductionism (the other half of positivism), and the self-referent ideology that contrasts with separatism. We should add a word about what may seem to be the most obvious of all models for a consumerist ideologue, namely *Consumer Reports* product evaluations. While these serve as a good enough model to demonstrate failures in most of the alternatives more widely accepted in program evaluation, especially educational program evaluation, it must not be thought that the present author regards them as flawless. I have elsewhere said something about factual and logical errors and separatist bias in *Consumer Reports* ("Product Evaluation" in N. Smith, ed., *New Models of Program Evaluation,* Sage, 1981). Although *Consumer Reports* is not as good as it was and it has now accumulated even more years across which the separatist/ managerial crime of refusal to discuss its methodologies and errors in an explicit and non-defensive way has been exacerbated many times, and although there are now other consumer magazines which do considerably better work than *Consumer Reports* in particular fields, *Consumer Reports* is still a very good model for most types of product evaluation.

The Multimodel

Evaluation is a very peculiar breed of cat. The considerable charm of each of a dozen radically different models for it, well represented in this book, can only be explained by the fact that it is a chimerical, Janus-faced and volatile being. Even at the level of aphorism, one is constantly attracted by radical variations in such claims as "evaluation is one-third education and one-third art — including the arts of composition, graphics, and politics" or "evaluation should be driven one-third by the professional obligation to improvement, one-third by the society's need for quality, and one-third by the need to economize." The "Ninety-Five Theses" of the Cronbach group carry this further. Analogies with other subjects keep springing into life: architecture is one that seems particularly appealing, with its powerful combination of aesthetic component with the engineering necessities, and with the economics and needs assessment that must be taken into account before a structure can be successful. A dozen others have been advocated as paradigms, from anthropology to operations research.

But during these last few years, it is not accidental that two rather similar approaches to clarification of the practice of evaluation have emerged and gained a certain amount of support. They both represent an attempt at distilling solid principles from the models, but they also represent a kind of model in their own right. These two approaches are the *Evaluation Standards* approach, and the *Evaluation Checklist* approach, to which we will turn in a moment. It is not accidental that both are consumer-oriented; we all know the kinds of checklists that we get out of consumer magazines and which facilitate our evaluation of alternatives for purchase, and we all know the way in which professional standards are used as checklists when supposedly questionable behavior by professionals is under scrutiny. More than this practical and value-orientation is involved here, however. I think that the checklist approach — if I may use the term to cover both instantiations of what I see as essentially a similar point of view — represents a kind of model in its own right. It is not like one of the relatively simple and relatively monolithic models with which we normally associate the term. But the emergence says somethimg about the subject of evaluation, something about its complexity and its relation to other subjects; I shall call it the Multimodel, an ungainly minotaur among models. (The complex CIPP model is an important intermediate case.)

The Multimodel is multiple in a number of ways. In the first place, it commits evaluation to being *multi-field* — that is, applicable to products, proposals, personnel, plans and potentials, not just programs. Then it is *multi-disciplinary* (rather than inter-disciplinary); this means that solid economic analysis, solid ethical analysis, solid ethnographics and statistical analysis, and several other types of analysis are often required in doing a particular evaluation, and not just some standard blend of small parts of these. (Consequently, teams and consultants are often better than any soloist.) The investigations along each of these and other dimensions, some of which are devoted to entirely different disciplines, constitute a set of dimensions for an evaluation, which must eventually be integrated, since the overall type of conclusion for an evaluation (a grading, a ranking, and apportioning) is often pre-determined by the client's needs and resources. In many respects, the *multi-dimensionality* is the most crucial logical element in evaluation, because specific evaluative conclusions are only attainable through the synthesis of a number of dimensions; some involving needs assessments or other sources of value; others referring to various types of performance.

Another aspect of the multiple nature of evaluation concerns what can be called its need for *multiple perspectives* on something, even in the final report. It is often absolutely essential that different points of view on the same program or product be taken into account before any attempt at synthesis is begun, and some must be preserved to the end. The necessity here is sometimes an ethical one as well as a scientific one.

Relatedly, evaluation is a *multi-level* enterprise. When one gets a call over the phone to ask if one could possibly evaluate a certain program in an unrealistically short time-frame, it is entirely appropriate to respond that one most certainly can, indeed that one can evaluate it there and then, over the phone and without charge. One does have, after all, a considerable background of common sense and evidence about related programs which make it possible to produce an evaluation at this superficial level. We do not associate such evaluations with professionality or with high validity, but that may be a little too severe depending upon the extent of the evaluator's professional background, the similarity of the present example to other well-documented cases and the nature of the evaluative conclusion that is being requested. But if we move down from that superficial level, it is clear that there is a wide range of levels of validity/cost/credibility among which a choice must be made in order to remain within the resources of time and budget. Given certain demands for credibility, comprehensiveness, validity, and so on, there may not be a solution within the constraints of professionality, time, and budget. But more commonly there are many, and it is this that must lead one to recognize the importance of the notion of multiple levels (of analysis, evidential support, documentation) in coming to understand the nature of evaluation. One could go on; *multiple methodologies, multiple functions, multiple impacts, multiple reporting formats* — evaluation is a multiplicity of multiples.

To conclude, then, let me simply list the dimensions that must be taken into account in doing most evaluations, whether of product or program, personnel or proposals. There are certainly special features of the evaluation of — for example — teachers that do not jump out from this listing. But even the four-part checklist that I have suggested above for the evaluation of teachers can be seen to be buried in the following checklist, and indeed it can be enriched in a worthwhile way by paying more attention to some of the steps in this longer effort.

Checklists can function in different ways — there are checklists that list desiderata, and there are checklists that list necessitata. This checklist comes from the latter end of the spectrum, and it is relatively rarely that one can afford to dispense with at least a quick professional check on each of the checkpoints mentioned here. Checklists are also sometimes of a one-pass nature, and sometimes of a multiple pass, or iterative nature. Again, this is of the latter kind; one can't answer all the questions that come up under each of the early headings in adequate detail until one has studied some of the later dimensions; and, having studied them, one must come back and rewrite an earlier treatment, which will in turn force one to refine the later analysis that depends on the former. In designing and in critiquing evaluations, as well as in carrying one out, one is never quite done with this checklist.

The simple terms that I use for the title of each dimension need much unpacking, and they are there just as labels to remind the reader of a string of associated questions. More details will be found in the current edition of *Evaluation Thesaurus,* but I think enough is implied by the mere titles and the word or two that I attach to some of them to convey a sense of the case for the Multimodel. The traditional social science approach deals at most with half of these checkpoints and deals with those, in most cases, extremely superficially, as far as evaluation needs are concerned.

The Key Evaluation Checklist

1. *Description.* An infinity of descriptions is possible, of which a sub-infinity would be false, another sub-infinity irrelevant, another overlong, another overshort, and so on. Whereas relativisim infers from the fact that a large number would be perfectly satisfactory to the conclusion that there are no absolute standards here, perspectivism draws the more modest conclusion that there are a number of right answers, several of which need to be added together to give an answer that is both true and comprehensive, a fact which in no way alters the falsehood or irrelevance or redundancy of many other compound descriptions and hence the difference between right and wrong. The description with which we begin the iterative cycles through the checklist is the client's description; but what we finish up with must be the evaluator's description, and it must be based, if possible, on discussions with consumers, staff, audiences, and other stakeholders.

2. *Client.* Who is commissioning the evaluation, and in what role are they acting? (Distinguish from inventors, consumers, initiators, and so on.)

3. *Background and Context.* Of the evaluation and of whatever is being

evaluated: the hopes and fears. (This checkpoint will be set aside in the early stages of an evaluation that is to have a goal-free phase.)

4. *Resources (or strengths assessment).*   For the evaluation and for whatever is being evaluated.

5. *Consumer.*   Distinguish the targeted population from the impacted population (in a goal-based approach), and the directly impacted from the indirectly impacted.

6. *Values.*   The needs assessment, the ideals review, the relevant professional standards, expert survey, functional or conceptual analysis, and so on. The source of values for the evaluation. To be sharply distinguished from a wants assessment ("market research") unless *no relevant needs* exist.

7. *Process.*   Here we have to consider the legal, political, aesthetic, and scientific standards, some of which will have emerged from the values review, and apply them to the intrinsic nature of whatever is being evaluated.

8. *Outcomes.*   Here the traditional social, scientific, engineering, medical, etc., methodologies come into their own, except that we must treat discovering unintended outcomes as of equal importance with the search along the intended dimensions of impact.

9. *Generalizability, Exportability, Saleability.*   Across sites, staff, clients, and consumers.

10. *Costs.*   Money and non-money, direct and indirect.

11. *Comparisons.*   The selection of the "critical competitors" is often the most important act of the evaluator, since the winner may be one the client had not considered (but which is perfectly feasible).

12. *Significance.*   A synthesis of all the above.

13. *Remediation.*   There may or may not be some of these recommendations — they do not follow automatically from the conclusions of all evaluations.

14. *Report.*   As complicated as the description, with concern for timing, media, format, and presenters, to a degree quite unlike the preparation for publication of scientific results in a scientific journal.

15. *Meta evaluation.*   The reminder that evaluation is self-referent — the

requirement that one cycle the evaluation itself — its design and final
form — through the above checklist.

Conclusion

Evaluation practice is still the victim of fallacious ideologies, because we have not
applied the essential insight that evaluation is a self-referent discipline. The
plethora of evaluation models provides a fascinating perspective on the complexity
of this new subject, perhaps the keystone in the arch of disciplined intellectual
endeavor. We can only build that arch strong enough to support the huge load of
educational and social enterprises that it must bear if we come to understand its
architecture and thus the function of its keystone considerably better, and in so
doing, come to understand better everything else that we know.

References

Centra, J.A. *Determining Faculty Effectiveness.* San Francisco: Jossey-Bass, 1979.
Davis, B.G., Scriven, M., and Thomas, S. *The Evaluation of Composition Instruction.*
    Inverness, California: Edge-Press, 1981.
House, Ernest. *Evaluating with Validity.* Beverly Hills, California: Sage, 1980.
Scriven, M. "Product Evaluation." In N. Smith (ed.) *New Models of Program Evaluation.*
    Beverly Hills, California: Sage, 1981.
Scriven, M. *Evaluation Thesaurus* (3rd ed.). Inverness, California: Edge-Press, 1981.
Scriven, M. "Summative Teacher Evaluation." In J. Millman (ed.) *Handbook of Teacher
    Evaluation.* Beverly Hills, California: Sage, 1981.

15 FLEXNER, ACCREDITATION, AND EVALUATION
Robert E. Floden

Accreditations: Issues and Debates

Accreditation, the process by which an organization grants approval to an educational institution, is the central issue in several current debates among educators. The major parties in these debates are the various representatives of elementary and secondary school teachers, on the one hand, and the faculty members of schools of education, on the other. State education agencies also play an important part in these debates, but they have not been as much in the forefront as have the other two parties.

Floden, Robert E. "Flexner, Accreditation, and Evaluation." *Educational Evaluation and Policy Analysis*, no. 2, 20 (March–April 1980), 35–46. Copyright 1980, American Educational Research Association, Washington, D.C. Reprinted with permission.

The work reported herein is sponsored by the Institute for Research on Teaching, College of Education, Michigan State University. The Institute for Research on Teaching is funded primarily by the Program for Teaching and Instruction of the National Institute of Education, U.S. Department of Health, Education, and Welfare. The opinions expressed in this publication do not necessarily reflect the position, policy, or endorsement of the National Institute of Education. (Contract No. 400–76–0073.) Discussion with David Florio and Robert Koff stimulated several of the ideas in this paper. Barbara Schneider provided a thoughtful critique of a draft version.

Although a variety of issues figure in these debates, the major disagreements revolve around three questions:

1. How should the accreditation procedures be determined?
2. Who should participate in the accreditation process?
3. What are the effects of accreditation?

In the debates over these questions, reference is often made to the Flexner report (1910), a study of medical education conducted early in this century (Haberman & Stinnett, 1973; Lieberman, 1956; Orlans, 1975). In this paper, the relevance of Flexner's study to the current debates will be examined. Parallels will also be drawn between Flexner's procedures and some current issues in program evaluation.

The National Council for Accreditation of Teacher Education (NCATE) is currently responsible for the accreditation of schools of teacher education. (Not every institution educating elementary and secondary school teachers is a school. Instead, they can be departments, programs, or colleges. In this paper, all such institutions will be referred to as schools.) The two organizations that take primary responsibility for the support of the NCATE are the American Association of Colleges for Teacher Education (AACTE) and the National Education Association (NEA). The majority of members of the NCATE are representatives of either the AACTE or the NEA, and these representatives have been prominent in debates over accreditation.

The standards and techniques for accreditation of schools of teacher education have been determined by committees, comprised mainly of practicing teachers and teacher educators. The members of these committees have drawn on their own experiences and on the experience of previous accreditation committees in setting standards and criteria, which traditionally have focused on the adequacy of the physical plant and the materials available for research, the qualifications of the teaching staff, the types of courses students are required to take, and the entrance requirements for prospective students. More recently, particularly in the wake of certain legal proceedings, increased emphasis has been placed on determining the empirical relationship between accreditation standards and performance of program graduates (Dickey & Miller, 1972; Maucker, 1967; Study Commission, 1976; Zook & Haggerty, 1936). Critics of current accreditation criteria insist on the need for standards based on research and for the use of quantitative social science techniques.

The question of what groups should participate in the accreditation process has recently beeen transformed into the question of which groups will control the process (Bush & Enemark, 1975; Howsam, Corrigan, Denemark, & Nash, 1976; Orlans, 1975; Selden, 1960). The NEA has vigorously defended the position that the accreditation process should be controlled by elementary and secondary school teachers, presumably represented by the NEA (Cyphert & Zimpher, 1975; Knispel,

1975). This teachers' organization has argued that its members are most clearly aware of the needs of teachers and so are best equipped to judge whether an educational institution is working to meet those needs. The AACTE has taken an opposing position, asserting that its members have an equal, if not better, awareness of teacher needs, an awareness gained both through theoretical study of teaching and through the experiences of preparing a large number of teachers (Cyphert & Zimpher, 1975). Furthermore, teacher educators (i.e., faculty of AACTE member institutions) are the only ones with sufficient experience in the preparation of teachers to determine adequately how teacher education should be conducted.

Opinions on the question of the effects of accreditation diverge along different lines. Most representatives of both the NEA and the AACTE assume that accreditation is an effective means for controlling the quality of teacher education, though it could be made even more effective (Mayor & Swartz, 1965; Proffitt, 1975). However, some individuals see little value in the current accreditation process and would have it either drastically changed or abandoned (Knispel, 1975). The minority position is that accreditation is very expensive and has not demonstrated its effectiveness in changing or eliminating poor quality teacher education institutions. Although little evidence exists to support either position in this debate, recent findings appear to support the criticism that the process of accreditation has not proved effective (see, for example, Guba & Clark, 1976; Tyler[1]). This criticism is often coupled with the position advocating procedures supported by the weight of research evidence (Koff & Florio[2]). Since little research evidence is available to support *any* procedure, the critics would prefer to discontinue accreditation until the evidence becomes available. The supporters of accreditation uphold their position by asserting that other grounds (such as common sense) may be used to support the efficacy of accreditation, referring for evidence to the success of accreditation in other fields.

The Flexner Report

In the context of these debates on the determination of, participation in, and effects of accreditation procedures, reference is often made to the procedures used in medicine (Howsam et al., 1976; Lieberman, 1956; Orlans, 1975). These procedures are used both as examples of accreditation conducted "as it should be" and as examples of the potential value of accreditation. In both contexts, the Flexner report (1910) inevitably emerges as an exemplar of accreditation guidelines. Although Flexner's study of medical education in the United States and Canada was not accreditation in the strict sense (medical schools did not participate voluntarily), it was certainly accreditation in the broad sense — the private judgment of educational institutions.

While Flexner's report is frequently cited, it has seldom been carefully examined for solutions to current accreditation difficulties. Flexner's study was part of an effort by the American Medical Association (AMA) to reduce the number of medical schools. The AMA also hoped to bring all the remaining schools in line with a set of standards it had developed in conjunction with the Council on Medical Education of the Association of American Medical Colleges. A liaison committee of these two organizations had begun to accredit medical schools in 1907, three years before Flexner published the report in which he found 155 medical schools operating in the United States and Canada. By 1927, the number had dropped to 80.[3] Since that time, the number of schools has increased slowly, reaching 107 in 1975.

Flexner's American medical education study was sponsored by the Carnegie Foundation for the Advancement of Teaching as part of its effort to identify institutions with faculty deserving of Carnegie support. Flexner and one associate visited every existing medical school in the United States and Canada, using their observations to prepare the Carnegie report. "Bulletin Number Four," as the report is officially known, received wide publication even outside the Foundation.

> It produced an immediate and profound sensation, "making," as we say nowadays, "the front page." The medical profession and the faculties of the medical schools as well as the state boards of examiners, were absolutely flabbergasted by the pitiless exposure. We were threatened with lawsuits and, in one instance, actually sued for libel for $150,000. I received anonymous letters warning me that I should be shot if I showed myself in Chicago, whereupon I went there to make a speech before a meeting called by the Council on Medical Education and returned unharmed.

> For further details I must refer my readers to "Bulletin Number Four" itself, which is written in simple English, for I had only such knowledge of terminology as a layman could pick up in a short space of time; but such a rattling of dead bones has never been heard in this country before or since. Schools collapsed to the right and left, usually without a murmur. A number of them pooled their resources. The seven schools of my native city, which Councilman notwithstanding, I had described with the same candor employed elsewhere, were reduced to one. The fifteen schools in Chicago, which I had called "The plague spot of the country in respect to medical education," were shortly consolidated into three. (Flexner, 1960, p. 87)[4]

Flexner was an educator, but not a medical educator. He graduated from Johns Hopkins University in 1886 and taught school for four years, then established his own school in his hometown of Louisville, Kentucky. After completing his first medical education study, he went abroad to investigate the medical education provided in Great Britain and in Europe. He advised many philanthropists and founded the Institute for Advanced Studies at Princeton, New Jersey.

The reasons for Flexner's honorable mention in the current accreditation debates are obvious. He seems to have achieved a major goal of accreditation —

the elimination of inferior educational institutions. In addition, the profession of medicine has maintained a status level that all occupations covet. Flexner's study appeared to play some part in attaining this level, and accreditors aspire to duplicate his achievement in education.

Flexner's Answers to the Current Debates

The Flexner report does provide guidance for accreditation in education, with particular reference to the three questions cited earlier: How should accreditation procedures be determined? Who should participate in the accreditation process? and What are the effects of accreditation? Flexner's guidance, however, may be surprising to those who cite the report without thorough examination. In many respects, an emulation of Flexner would entail a rejection of many popular assumptions about accreditation issues. Flexner's methods are currently spurned. His participants correspond neither to the AACTE nor to the NEA; his hopes for positive effects of accreditation include additional conditions such as financial support, which find no place in the current debates.

How Should Accreditation Procedures Be Determined?

Flexner's methods were not those of quantitative social science research, but rather those of educated common sense. He dispensed with the need to examine standards of evaluation chosen by means of research on associated outcomes, by insisting that the standards were obvious. These criteria related to:

First, the entrance requirements. What were they? Were they enforced?

Second, the size and training of the faculty.

Third, the sum available from endowment and fees for the support of the institution, and what became of it.

Fourth, the quality and adequacy of the laboratories provided for the instruction of the first two years and the qualifications and training of the teachers of the so-called preclinical branches.

Fifth, and finally, the relationship between medical schools and hospitals, including particularly access to beds and freedom in the appointment by the school of hospital physicians and surgeons who automatically should become clinical teachers. (Flexner, 1960, p. 79)

Flexner did not claim support for these standards by reference to empirical studies. He saw no need for such support; if the criteria are obvious why waste time on research to prove their worth?

Similarly, Flexner was no believer in sophisticated measurement techniques, using objective instruments to determine how the schools fared with regard to these standards. Flexner spent only one day visiting a medical school and administered no objective tests. He went into the school with his eyes and ears open, looking for the "obvious" indicators of school quality. His procedure was simple, quick, and (he thought) reliable.

> It will be urged by weak schools that . . . in the time devoted to the examination of a single school it is impossible to do it justice . . . in my opinion, the objection is without force. A trained observer of wide experience can go directly to the heart of a problem of this character. The spirit, ideals, and facilities of a professional or technical school can be quickly grasped. In every instance in which further inquiry has been made, the conclusions reached by the author of the report have been sustained. (Pritchett, 1910, p. xiii)

> In half an hour or less I could sample the credentials of students filed in the dean's office, ascertain the matriculation requirements (two years of high-school, high-school graduation, two years of college work, or, finally, a college degree), and determine whether or not the standards, low or high, set forth in the school catalogue were being evaded or enforced. A few inquiries made clear whether the faculty was composed of local doctors, not already professors in some other local medical school, or the extent to which efforts had been made to obtain teachers properly trained elsewhere. A single question elicited the amount of the income of a medical school, and a slight operation in mental arithmetic showed the approximate amounts available for fulltime teachers or for distribution as "dividends" among the practicing physicians who were "professors." A stroll through the laboratories disclosed the presence or absence of apparatus, museum specimens, library, and students; and a whiff told the inside story regarding the manner in which anatomy was cultivated. Finally, the situation as respects clinical facilities was readily clarified by a few questions, directed in succession — and separately — to the dean of the school, the professors of medicine, surgery, and obstetrics, and the hospital superintendent — questions which were designed to ascertain the extent to which the school enjoyed rights or merely courtesies in the hospitals named in the school catalogue.

> In the course of a few hours a reliable estimate could be made respecting the possibilities of teaching modern medicine in almost any one of the 155 schools I visited in the United States and Canada. (Flexner, 1960, p. 79)

In choice of standards and measurement techniques, Flexner differs from prevailing trends in accreditation. Although contemporary accreditators have not been able to provide a research basis for their standards, they apologize for its absence and are anxious to provide such a basis (Maucker, 1967; Study Commission, 1976). Rather than considering common sense as an obvious criterion for justifying evaluative standards, current opinion holds that common sense is certainly second best, perhaps even inadequate in such a role. In the choice of measurement techniques, current accreditators do rely largely on college catalogs and unstructured interviews with personnel and students. But, while Flexner considered these techniques well suited to the task, they are now held in low regard.

Who Should Participate in the Accreditation Process?

Flexner would probably anger both the AACTE and the NEA with his answer to the question of who should participate in the accreditation process. The two organizations disagree on which one should have ascendency in the process, but they both assume that members of the education profession (where the profession is taken to include teacher educators) should have primary responsibility. The Flexner study has quite a different staffing policy. The individual in charge of the study — Flexner himself — was not a member of the profession whose education was studied. Henry S. Pritchett, the president of the Carnegie Foundation, made a special point of choosing someone outside medicine.

> It occurred to me that Dr. Pritchett was confusing me with my brother Simon at the Rockefeller Institute, and I called his attention to the fact that I was not a medical man and had never had my foot inside a medical school.
> He replied, ''That is precisely what I want. I think these professional schools should be studied not from the point of view of the practitioner but from the standpoint of the educator. I know your brother, so that I am not laboring under any confusion. This is a layman's job, not a job for a medical man.'' (Flexner, 1960, p. 71)

At first, Flexner's lack of specific knowledge of the field made him uncertain of his ability to conduct the study properly. Afterwards, however, he was convinced that the choice of someone outside the field was wise.

> Time and again it has been shown that an unfettered lay mind, if courageous, imaginative, and determined to master relationships, is, in the very nature of things, best suited to undertake a general survey . . . The expert has his place, to be sure; but if I were asked to suggest the most promising way to study legal education, I should seek a layman, not a professor of law; or for the sound way to investigate teacher training, the last person I should think of employing would be a professor of education. Dr. Pritchett was right: even though I might well have been the wrong choice, the proper person to study medical education was a layman with general educational experience, not a professor in a medical school. (Flexner, 1960, p. 71)

Flexner's position stands opposed to the frequently used argument that the proper accreditation of professional schools requires an inside knowledge of the profession. The AACTE and the NEA only disagree on which group has better claim to professional knowledge. Yet the Flexner report, lauded though it is, was written by a man without such professional knowledge, a man who possessed, instead, a broad general background.

What Are the Effects of Accreditation?

While Flexner opposed modern accreditors on the issue of who should participate in the accreditation process, he is in clear agreement with all parties that his study was uniquely influential. Although credit for the decline in the number of medical schools is claimed, with some justification, by other organizations, no one denies that Flexner was largely responsible for the speed with which the schools disappeared. Few quarrel with Flexner when he asserts that the schools that disappeared were largely inferior to those that remained.

Flexner distinguishes himself by emphasizing the context within which accreditation studies can have a positive effect. In recent debates, both those who claim accreditation has a positive effect and those who claim it has little or no effect have placed little weight on the factors influencing effectiveness. Flexner, on the other hand, was particularly sensitive to these issues and worked to create a situation where the improvements suggested by his study would be carried out.

In particular, Flexner recognized the importance of money. Obvious though the importance of money for improvements may seem, it is an area often neglected in accreditation. Changes of any substance require money. Inertia, particularly in academic institutions, is a large obstacle to change. Any change which also involves financial sacrifice is not likely to occur.

Flexner not only said that institutions needed money to make improvements, he also aided the institutions in obtaining funds. Flexner engineered the disbursement to medical schools of over $50 million of Rockefeller money. The Rockefeller contributions inspired further contributions of more than ten times that amount.

The importance of proper support for suggested changes seems to be ignored in contemporary accreditation debates. Those who argue the value of accreditation imply that needed changes will take place regardless of other factors. Those disappointed by accreditation's apparent lack of impact often lay the blame on accreditation, not recognizing that the process itself can hardly be expected to produce improvements when adverse conditions exist.

If accreditors instruct an institution to make particular changes, three options are open. First, officials may amass the necessary funds and make the changes. Second, they may decide the changes cannot be made and close their doors. Third, they may decide not to worry about what the accreditors say and make no changes. If an institution exercises either of the first two options, the aims of accreditation have been realized. When the third option is taken, the process of accreditation has failed to achieve its main purpose.

In Flexner's study, many schools were so obviously inadequate that public opinion removed the third option. For many of the better schools, Flexner provided funds to allow necessary improvements. In both cases, Flexner's accreditation procedures were successful.

In the case of schools of teacher education accreditations, on the other hand, the third option is far more often taken. Two factors contribute to this. First, few schools of teacher education are as obviously deficient as inferior medical schools. In addition, Flexner's common sense criteria were readily accepted by the public as minimum standards for medical education and demonstrated failure to meet those standards was condemned. Few schools of teacher education are so obviously deficient that they would be forced to close by the weight of public opinion.[5]

Secondly, funds for program improvement are not as readily available to schools of teacher education as Flexner made them to medical schools. Thus, many schools which acknowledge the need for improvement are unable to act because of adverse financial conditions. Failings in accreditation of schools of teacher education may be partly explained by the absence of clearly inadequate schools and the absence of funding for improvements.

Flexner, though rated highly for his work on *Carnegie Bulletin Number Four,* seems at odds with current opinions on all three accreditation issues. On the question of choice of standards and methods, he lauds common sense and simple observation above current emphasis on objective social science. On the choice of accreditation personnel, he supports the use of generally educated layman, rather than choosing anyone with professional knowledge of the field. Finally, in the area of effects of accreditation, Flexner acknowledges his own success, but emphasizes the importance of factors no longer carefully considered — chiefly the provision of financial support for recommended changes.

Accreditation and Program Evaluation

Although Flexner stands opposed to those discussing accreditation, he would probably sympathize with many of the recent positions taken by members of a closely related field — program evaluation. Even though accreditation can be thought of as a part of program evaluation, discussions of accreditation and discussions of program evaluation seem totally separate (a notable exception is the important work in both fields conducted by Orlans, 1971, 1975). Those discussing accreditation often cite Flexner but seldom concur with his positions; those discussing evaluation seldom cite Flexner but often support his positions.

Although the majority of program evaluators lean toward the methods of objective social science, two influential members of the evaluation community have recently advocated the use of common sense and unstructured observation. In major presentations at the 1974 meeting of the American Psychological Association, Donald T. Campbell and Lee J. Cronbach partially reversed their earlier positions to advocate a return to nonquantitative methods of evaluation (Cronbach, 1975; Campbell[6]).

Campbell argues that common sense is, in many respects, the basis of all other knowledge and must take a central position among the various ways of evaluating any program. Common sense knowledge pervades all knowledge, even that of quantitative social science. Although Campbell does not reject quantitative evaluation methods, he does not believe that common sense as an evaluative tool should be rejected unless some other procedure is demonstrably better. Too many modern evaluators have adopted quantitative methods and rejected common sense without demonstrating that common sense has been surpassed in effectiveness. Campbell advocates a renewed emphasis on common sense knowledge and qualitative methods:

> I have sought to remind my quantitative colleagues that in the successful laboratory sciences, quantification both builds upon and is cross-validated by, the scientist's pervasive qualitative knowledge. The conditions of mass-produced quantitative social science in program evaluation are such that much of this qualitative base is apt to be lost. If we are to be truly scientific, we must re-establish this qualitative grounding of the quantitative in action research. (p. 30)

Cronbach (1957) was one of the first to point out that an educational treatment may not have the same effect on all individuals. His influential paper led to a wide variety of research on the differential effects on individuals of varying aptitude (aptitude-treatment interaction, or ATI, studies). When he reviewed 20 years of ATI research (1975), he found that the number of such variations in treatment effects was enormous. When the effect of the treatment depends on so many qualities of the individual, it becomes difficult, if not impossible, to speak of some single treatment effect. Rather, one must give a detailed description of the individuals to whom the treatment was given in order to incorporate all the individual differences affecting the treatment effect produced. A detailed description of the individuals treated and the effects on each of those individuals must be produced, rather than conducting an experiment to investigate a single treatment effect. The problem is compounded by changes in treatment effects over time. Cronbach (1975) concludes that the difficulties in finding generalizable evaluative results by quantitative methods may be insurmountable. One suggestion for salvaging useful knowledge from program evaluations is to attempt to capture complexity by increasing emphasis on simple observation and reporting.

> The two scientific disciplines — experimental control and systematic correlation — answer formal questions stated in advance. Intensive local observation goes beyond discipline to an open-eyed, open-minded appreciation of the surprises Nature deposits in the investigative net. This kind of interpretation is historical more than scientific. I suspect that if the psychologist were to read more widely in history, ethnology, and the centuries of humanistic writings on man and society, he would be better prepared for this part of his work. (Cronbach, 1975, p. 125)

Supporters of ethnographic methods in education research go beyond Campbell and Cronbach to advocate the primacy of common sense and unstructured observation. These techniques, traditionally used in anthropological studies of primitive cultures, have recently been applied in evaluation and research studies (Cusick, 1973; Wilson, 1977; Wolcott, 1973[7]) Ethnographers argue for these techniques both from successes in anthropology and from the philosophical position that human interaction cannot be described in objective terms of time and motion but must also include reference to the meanings that the humans attach to their actions (Natanson, 1963; Winch, 1958).

Although Flexner advocated the use of common sense, his reasons differ from those of Campbell, Cronbach, and the ethnographers. Flexner reasoned that common sense was adequate to the job; he was not rejecting any alternative approaches since, at the time, there were none. Flexner's work was conducted before quantitative measurement had invaded, eventually to dominate, social science. He could not be expected to defend common sense against criticisms not yet voiced. Of all the supporters of common sense as a valid evaluative method, Campbell comes closest to Flexner's rationale when he emphasizes the dependence of *all* observation, measurement, and evaluation on common sense.

Viewed in another way, Flexner holds a position that is quite modern in its naive reliance on common sense. Popper (1972), for example, repudiates many forms of skepticism through his acceptance of a position of realism. This position is one of common sense (as Popper admits), and its defense against opposing positions is not to point out their flaws but to accept what common sense indicates until good reason has been given for rejection. A demonstration that common sense might be wrong is not sufficient reason to abandon it, unless an alternative is proposed that will serve better than common sense in all situations. Quantitative social science has never provided such an alternative but has merely indicated the possibility of error when relying on common sense.

The return to the use of common sense can be seen as the reinstatement of a valid evaluative tool, rather than as the introduction of any new merits of the method. It is not that the use of common sense has been shown to be better than other procedures, but that its new competitors were oversold and are now being more accurately assessed.

Flexner's position on the personnel to be involved in accreditation is both supported and supplemented by a number of works on the methods of evaluation. The distinction between internal and external evaluators captures much of the difference between Flexner and those advocating professional participation in the accreditation process. An internal evaluator is closely associated with the program under consideration, paralleling the accreditor who is a member of the profession he is evaluating. An external evaluator is not associated with the professional program and corresponds to Flexner's layman.

Although the analogy is not perfect, most of the points made about internal and external evaluators will apply to the distinction Flexner makes between laymen and members of the profession participating in accreditation. Internal evaluators have the advantage of greater knowledge of the professional program they are evaluating (Agarwala-Rogers, 1977; Freeman, 1977). They have prolonged experience and can understand the program's complexity. In addition, they are familiar, perhaps causing program staff members to be more open with them.

Program directors are likely to listen sympathetically to suggestions for program changes because they know that the evaluators understand program operations.

Similarly, the accreditor who is a member of the profession being assessed has the advantage of detailed knowledge. The accreditor will probably be treated by those being studied as "one of us." Recommendations made may carry added weight since they come from one who appreciates the complexities of the profession.

Sympathy with the program may put internal evaluators at a disadvantage, however, since they may overlook obvious problems. Their familiarity with the program may lead them to take controversial procedures and goals for granted. Internal evaluators may be unwilling to make serious criticisms, either because those to be criticized are superiors and friends or because their association with the program brings their criticisms back upon themselves (Freeman, 1977; Scriven, 1976; Tumin, 1975). Internal evaluators also often lack the power to enforce their suggested changes.

Similar disadvantages apply to accreditors drawn from the ranks of the profession which is to be evaluated. Socialization into the profession leads them to take questionable practices for granted. Professional ties to other members of the profession may weaken or eliminate criticism, and the accreditor may feel that criticism of the program reflects on him or her as a member of the profession. Finally, the accreditor holds little power to enforce changes.

The case of external evaluators and lay accreditors is just the reverse; all the advantages noted above are disadvantages, and all the disadvantages, advantages. Flexner explicitly considered the most serious disadvantage in the use of lay accreditors as that of lack of understanding of the profession. While acknowleding this potential weakness, he asserted that general knowledge was sufficient for the study of an educational institution. More detailed professional knowledge, he argued, would have effected only marginal improvement in the accreditation study at the expense of impartiality. Flexner (1960) even refused the offer extended by the American Medical Association to assist him via the establishment of an advisory board of physicians. Flexner was aware that a member of the profession acting as an accreditor might have some advantages over a layman (although it is not clear whether he has considered all the advantages cited above), but he strongly preferred lay accreditors for all his accreditation studies.

The seeming success of Flexner's study might be attributed to political forces already moving at the time to eliminate inferior medical schools. Flexner, of course, challenged that position, and rightfully so. Although the number of medical schools had begun to decline prior to Flexner's study, the trend fails to account for the dramatic decrease after 1910.

Many discussions of the impact of recent program evaluations have been attempts to explain their apparent failure. Evaluators have often felt that their studies were ignored (Gramlich & Koshel, 1975; Williams & Evans, 1969). The literature explaining this apparent failure follows two main themes. First, evaluation results are only used when they fit the decisions officials have already made (Orlans, 1971; Williams & Evans, 1969). An evaluation that criticizes a politically unpopular program will be used to justify dismantling the program. Otherwise, evaluation reports will be quietly filed and forgotten. Seemingly unsuccessful accreditation programs may have received similar reactions. The analogy to program evaluation is not strong here, since the medical school case lacks a corresponding central body with power to discontinue programs.

Second, the evaluations may have only failed outwardly. Cohen and Garet (1975) have argued that evaluations influence policy decisions by causing changes in beliefs about the programs evaluated. Evaluations appear to fail only if a narrow set of decisions is considered. Floden and Weiner (1978) suggest that evaluations may serve many functions beyond the provision of information for specific policy decisions. The functions include an increase in the reflective thinking of program staff, a smoothing of the process of social change, and an increase in general feelings of well-being. None of these arguments appears in the accreditation literature. An application of these evaluative approaches may add worthwhile dimensions to the appraisal of accreditation.

The contemporary literature which best reflects Flexner's particular emphasis on context, particularly fiscal context, is probably found not in evaluation, but in the related area of organization theory. Organization theorists are often cited when evaluators are explaining particular results of evaluations and are identifying ways to increase the likelihood of evaluation use. A basic tenet of the writings of organizational theorists is that organizations resist change and, hence, must be put under pressure before change will occur. The response to change may be a re-examination leading to the best possible changes; organizations are more likely, however, to make the minimal adjustment that will alleviate the pressure (Cyert & March, 1963; March & Simon, 1958; Steinbruner, 1974). Flexner (1960) recognized this problem and often grew impatient with the creeping pace of instructional decisionmaking. His solution, as indicated earlier, was to smooth the way for change by providing money for adjustments. In general, Flexner was aware that the context of an accreditation study would influence its impact. He seems to have been less aware of the variety of contextual variables and outcomes than are current writers in accreditation. Accreditation debates would benefit from an examination of current evaluation discussions foreshadowed by Flexner.

Current Implications of the Flexner Report

Flexner is often cited in accreditation literature as someone who made accreditation work. Those who cite him have generally failed, however, to examine how

Flexner got accreditation to work and how his procedures may have application today. Much of what Flexner did is being rediscovered in modern evaluation literature, often without reference to Flexner. Accreditors can learn from Flexner and from the modernizations of his views found in program evaluation literature.

If one takes Flexner's work as a model, the criteria by which accreditation standards and methods are chosen shifts from an emphasis on objective social science to an emphasis on common sense and unstructured observation. This may represent a great shift in aspirations and the way in which current practice is perceived. It is a mistake to demand that the standards and methods of teacher education be validated by empirical research on student performance; common sense is enough. On this stand, Flexner would receive support from a number of contemporary evaluation leaders.

In addition, Flexner would seek to end the debate over whether the NEA or the AACTE should control the accreditation process by declaring that neither should. Rather, he would probably give control to a board made up of laymen. He might try to remove teachers and teacher educators from the process altogether. Although he would receive support from current evaluators in this move, other evaluators would be quick to point out the possible disadvantages of this approach.

Flexner would also show no surprise at claims of accreditation's failure. He would point out that change is not likely to occur unless the change is made possible by mobilizing public opinion and providing financial support. Some evaluators (Campbell, 1969; Ross & Cronbach, 1976; Tumin, 1975; Weiss, 1972) would support Flexner in this stance, expanding on his position to indicate other influencing variables as well as other indicators of accreditation success.

In summary, accreditors might learn from Flexner and program evaluators that they should abandon attempts to make accreditation procedures more "scientific," instead, turning control of the process over to laymen and devoting their energies to raising money for changes indicated by the resultant accreditation studies. Perhaps then their hopes for a Flexner report in education may be realized.

Final Notes

The success of the Flexner report must be at least partially attributed to the man himself. He had a dynamic writing style that dramatically presented the schools as he saw them, a knack for raising funds for his projects, and a good sense of timing. Although the *Carnegie Bulletin Number Four* is the achievement with which he is most often associated, the breadth of his other achievements reinforce the impression that he was a remarkable individual. It is unlikely that anyone else could have had his impact on medical education.

Even Flexner might have a difficult time duplicating his feat in the field of teacher education. It is not as easy to come by $50 million as it seems to have been in the first quarter of this century, and money does not buy nearly as much now as it did then. While schools of teacher education may not require as expensive a physical plant as that of a medical school, an institutional change of comparable scope to that inspired by Flexner would still be incredibly costly.

Furthermore, it is difficult to believe that any of the schools of teacher education operating today are as strikingly inadequate as those Flexner portrayed in his report. Perhaps Flexner could write a description of a school of teacher education that would stir the public as his Carnegie report did, but that possibility seems remote. Yet even if it is unreasonable to anticipate a Flexner report on teacher education, it may not be unreasonable to expect some positive effects of accreditation. Following the example of Flexner and current evaluation trends may be a better way to achieve those effects than any of the options presently under consideration.

Notes

1. Tyler, R.W. *Research on the politics of institutional accreditation.* Paper presented at the annual meeting of the American Educational Research Association, New York, April 1977.

2. Koff, R., & Florio, D. "Educational policy and accrediting schools of education." Unpublished manuscript. Chicago, April, 1977.

3. Though discussions in teacher education assume that Flexner's report produced the drop in the number of schools, recent evidence indicates that the drop might have occurred for other reasons.

4. Flexner's autobiography, *I Remember,* was originally published in 1940. A revised edition was published in 1960.

5. The following is the description of one school as taken from Flexner's (1910) report: California Medical College, Eclectic, Organized at Oakland in 1879, this school has led a roving and precarious existence in the meanwhile. Entrance requirement: Nominal. Attendance: 9, of whom 7 are from California. Teaching staff: 27, of whom 26 are professors. Resources available for maintenance: Fees, amounting to $1060 (estimated). Laboratory facilities: the school occupies a few neglected rooms on the second floor of a 50-foot building. Its so-called equipment is dirty and disorderly beyond description. Its outfit in anatomy consists of a small box of bones and the dried-up, filthy fragments of a single cadaver. A few bottles of reagents constitute the chemical laboratory. A cold and rusty incubator, a single microscope, and a few unlabeled wet specimens, etc., form the so-called equipment for pathology and bacteriology. Clinical facilities: there is no dispensary and no access to the County Hospital. The School is a disgrace to the state whose laws permit its existence. Date of visit: May 1909. (p. 190).

6. Campbell, D.T. *Qualitative knowing in action research.* Kurt Lewin Award Address, Society for the Psychological Study of Social Issues, meeting with the American Psychological Association, New Orleans, September 1974.

7. Wolcott, H. *The use of anthropological models in the organization and analysis of a field study.* Paper presented at the Institute for Research on Teaching, February 1977.

References

Agarwala-Rogers, R. "Why is evaluation research not utilized?" In: M. Guttentag and S. Saar (eds.), *Evaluation studies review annual* Vol. 2. Beverly Hills, California: Sage Publications, 1977.

Bush, R.N. and Enemark, P. "Control and responsibility in teacher education." In: K. Ryan, (ed.), *Teacher education: The seventy-fourth yearbook of the National Society for the Study of Education.* Part II. Chicago: University of Chicago Press, 1975.

Campbell, D.T. "Reforms as experiments." *American Psychologist,* 24 (1969), 409–29.

Cohen, D. and Garet, M. "Reforming educational policy with applied social research." *Harvard Educational Review,* 45 (1975), 17–43.

Cronbach, L.J. "The two disciplines on scientific psychology." *American Psychologist,* 12 (1957), 671–84.

Cronbach, L.J. "Beyond the two disciplines of scientific psychology." *American Psychologist,* 30 (1975), 116–27.

Cusick, P. *Inside high school.* New York: Holt, Rinehart, & Winston, 1973.

Cyert, R.M. and March, J.G. *A behavioral theory of the firm.* Englewood Cliffs, New Jersey: Prentice-Hall, 1963.

Cyphert, F. and Zimpher, N.L. "The governance of teacher education accreditation: A higher education perspective." In: *Accreditation issues in teacher education.* Washington, D.C.: 1975. ERIC Document Reproduction Service no. ED 107 643.

Dickey, F.G. and Miller, J.W. *A current perspective on accreditation.* Washington, D.C.: American Association for Higher Education, 1972.

Flexner, A. *Medical education in the United States and Canada.* Bulletin no. 4. New York: Carnegie Foundation for the Advancement of Teaching, 1910.

Flexner, A. *Abraham Flexner: An autobiography.* New York: Simon and Schuster, 1960.

Floden, R.E. and Weiner, S.S. "Rationality to ritual: The multiple roles of evaluation in governmental process." *Policy Sciences,* 9 (1978), 9–18.

Freeman, H.F. "The present status of evaluation research." In: M. Guttentag and S. Saar (eds.), *Evaluation studies review annual,* vol. 2. Beverly Hills, California: Sage Publications, 1977.

Gramlich, E.M. and Koshel, P.P. *Educational performance contracting: An evaluation of an experiment.* Washington, D.C.: The Brookings Institution, 1975.

Guba, E.G. and Clark D.L. *Contemporary scenarios of knowledge production and utilization in schools, colleges, and departments of education.* Bloomington, Indiana: Research on Institutions of Teacher Education, 1976. ERIC Document Reproduction Service no. ED 139 809.

Haberman, M. and Stinnett, T.M. *Teacher Education and the new profession of teaching.* Berkeley, California: McCutchan, 1973.

Howsam, R.B., Corrigan, D.C., Denemark, G.W., and Nash, R.J. *Educating a profession.* Washington, D.C.: American Association of Colleges for Teacher Education, 1976.

Knispel, M. "Issues in accreditation." In: *Accreditation issues in teacher education.* Washington, D.C.: 1975. ERIC Document Reproduction Service no. ED 107 643.

Lieberman, M. *Education as a profession.* Englewood Cliffs, New Jersey: Prentice-Hall, Inc., 1956.

March, J.G. and Simon, H.A. *Organizations.* New York: Wiley, 1958.

Maucker, J.W. "Imperatives for excellence in teacher education: An excerpt from the third Charles W. Hunt Lecture." In: Karl Massonari (ed.), *Evaluative criteria for accrediting teacher education: A source book on selected issues.* Washington, D.C.: The American Association of Colleges for Teacher Education, 1967.

Mayor, J.R. and Swartz, W.G. *Accreditation in teacher education: Its influence on higher education*. Washington, D.C.: National Commission on Accrediting, 1965.

Natanson, M. (ed.). *Philosophy of the social sciences: A reader*. New York: Random House, 1963.

Orlans, H. "The political uses of social research." *American Academy of Political and Social Science Annals,* 394 (1971), 28–35.

Orlans, H. *Private accreditation and public eligibility*. Lexington, Massachusetts: D.C. Heath, 1975.

Popper, K. *Objective Knowledge: An evolutionary approach*. Oxford: Oxford University Press, 1972.

Pritchett, H.S. "Introduction." In: A. Flexner (ed.), *Medical education in the United States and Canada,* Bulletin no. four. New York: Carnegie Foundation for the Advancement of Teaching, 1910.

Proffitt, J.R. "Accreditation from the federal perspective." In: *Accreditation issues in teacher education*. Washington, D.C.: 1975. ERIC Document Reproduction Service no. ED 107 643.

Ross, L. and Cronbach, L.J. (eds.). "Handbook of evaluation research: Essay review by a task force of the Stanford Evaluation Consortium" *Educational Researcher,* 5 (1976), 9–19.

Scriven, M. "Evaluation bias and its control." *Evaluation Studies Review Annual,* 1 (1976), 101–118.

Selden, W.K. *Accreditation: A struggle over standards in higher education*. New York: Harper and Brothers, 1960.

Steinbruner, J.D. *The cybernetic theory of decision: New dimensions of political analysis*. Princeton, New Jersey: Princeton University Press. 1974.

Study Commission on Undergraduate Education and the Education of Teachers. *Teacher education in the United States: The responsibility gap*. Lincoln, Nebraska: University of Nebraska Press, 1976.

Tumin, M.M. "Politics and evaluation." In: S.B. Anderson, S. Ball, R.T. Murphy, and Associates (eds.), *Encyclopedia of educational evaluation*. San Francisco: Jossey-Bass, 1975.

Weiss, C. *Evaluation research: Methods of assessing program effectiveness*. Englewood Cliffs, New Jersey: Prentice-Hall, 1972.

Williams, W. and Evans, J. "The politics of evaluation: The case of Head Start." *The American Academy of Political and Social Science Annals,* 385 (1969), 118–32.

Wilson, S. "The use of ethnographic techniques in educational research." *Review of Educational Research,* 47 (1977), 245–66.

Winch, P. *The idea of social science and its relation to philosophy*. New York: Humanities Press, 1958.

Wolcott, H. *Man in the principal's office*. New York: Holt, Rinehart, & Winston, 1973.

Zook, G.F. and Haggerty, M.E. In: *The evaluation of higher institutions; Principles of accrediting higher institutions,* Vol. 1. Chicago: The University of Chicago Press, 1936.

16 THE CASE STUDY METHOD IN SOCIAL INQUIRY[1]

Robert E. Stake

It is widely believed that case studies are useful in the study of human affairs because they are down-to-earth and attention-holding but that they are not a suitable basis for generalization. In this paper, I claim that case studies will often be the preferred method of research because they may be epistemologically in harmony with the reader's experience and thus to that person a natural basis for generalization.

Experience.   We expect an inquiry to be carried out so that certain audiences will benefit — not just to swell the archives, but to help persons toward further understandings. If the readers of our reports are the persons who populate our houses, schools, governments, and industries, and if we are to help them understand social problems and social programs, we must perceive and communicate (see Bohm, 1974; Schön, 1977) in a way that accommodates their present understandings.[2] Those people have arrived at their understandings mostly through direct and vicarious experience.

Stake, Robert E. "The Case Study Method in Social Inquiry." *Educational Researcher* (February 1978), 5–8. Copyright 1978, American Educational Research Association, Washington, D.C. Reprinted with permission.

And those readers who are most learned and specialized in their disciplines are little different. Though they write and talk with special languages, their own understandings of human affairs are the most part attained and amended through personal experience. I believe that it is reasonable to conclude that one of the more effective means of adding to understanding for all readers will be by approximating through the words and illustrations of our reports the natural experience acquired in ordinary personal involvement.

At the turn of the century, German philosopher Wilhelm Dilthey (1910) claimed that more objective and "scientific" studies did not do the best job of acquainting man with himself.

> Only from his actions, his fixed utterances, his effects upon others, can man learn about himself; thus he learns to know himself only by the round-about way of understanding. What we once were, how we developed and became what we are, we learn from the way in which we acted, the plans which we once adopted, the way in which we made ourselves felt in our vocation, from old dead letters, from judgments on which were spoken long ago....we understand ourselves and others only when we transfer our own lived experience into every kind of expession of our own and other people's lives.

He distinguished between the human studies and the other kinds of studies.

> The human studies are thus founded on this relation between lived experience, expression, and understanding. Here for the first time we reach a quite clear criterion by which the delimitation of the human studies can be definitively carried out. A study belongs to the human studies only if its object becomes accessible to us through the attitude which is founded on the relation between life, expression, and understanding.

Dilthey was not urging us merely to pay more attention to humanistic values or to put more affective variables into our equations. He was saying that our methods of studying human affairs need to capitalize upon the natural powers of people to experience and understand.

Knowledge.   In statements fundamental to the epistemology of social inquiry, Polanyi[3] distinguished between propositional and tacit knowledge. Propositional knowledge — the knowledge of both reason and gossip — was seen to be composed of all interpersonally sharable statements, most of which for most people are observations of objects and events. Tacit knowledge may also dwell on objects and events, but it is knowledge gained from experience with them, experience with propositions about them, and rumination.

> Through reason man observes himself; but he knows himself only through consciousness. (Tolstoy, *War and Peace* , 1869)

Tacit knowledge is all that is remembered somehow, minus that which is remembered in the form of words, symbols, or other rhetorical forms. It is that which permits us to recognize faces, to comprehend metaphors, and to "know ourselves." Tacit knowledge includes a multitude of unexpressible associations, which give rise to new meanings, new ideas, and new applications of the old. Polanyi recognized that each person, expert or novice, has great stores of tacit knowledge with which to build new understandings.

It is a common belief that these ordinary understandings, both new and old, are merely the pieces from which mighty explanations are made. And that explanation is the grandest of understandings. But explanation and understanding are perhaps not so intimately interwoven.

> Practically every explanation, be it casual or teleological or of some other kind, can be said to further our understanding of things. But "understanding" also has a psychological ring which "explanation" has not. This psychological feature was emphasized by several of the nineteen-century antipositivist methodologists, perhaps most forcefully by Simmel who thought that understanding as a method characteristic of the humanities is a form of *empathy* or re-creation in the mind of the scholar of the mental atmosphere, the thoughts and feelings and motivations, of the objects of his study.
>
> . . . Understanding is also connected with *intentionality* in a way that explanation is not. One understands the aims and purposes of an agent, the meaning of a sign or symbol, and the significance of a social institution or religious rite. This intentionalistic…dimension of understanding has come to play a prominent role in more recent methodological discussion (Von Wright, 1971).

Explanation belongs more to propositional knowledge, understanding more to tacit.

Philosophers of the positivist school, Carl Hempel and Karl Popper particularly, have posited that propositional statements of lawful relationship are the closest approximations of *Truth* — whether we are talking about physical matter or human. They would have us speak of attributes and constructs, such as energy and mass or work-ethic and masculinity, and the relationships among them. Antipositivists such as Dilthey, Von Wright, and William Dray have claimed that *Truth* in the fields of human affairs is better approximated by statements that are rich with the sense of human encounter: To speak not of underlying attributes, objective observables, and universal forces, but of perceptions and understanding that come from immersion in and holistic regard for the phenomena.

In American research circles, most methodologists have been of positivistic persuasion. The more episodic, subjective procedures, common to the case study, have been considered weaker than the experimental or correlational studies for explaining things.

When explanation, propositional knowledge, and law are the aims of an inquiry, the case study will often be at a disadvantage. When the aims are understanding, extension of experience, and increase in conviction in that which is known, the disadvantage disappears.

Generalization. The scientist and the humanist scholar alike search for laws that tell of order in their disciplines. But so do all other persons look for regularity and system in their experience. Predictable covariation is to be found in all phenomena. In 1620, Francis Bacon said:

> There are and can be only be two ways of searching and discovering truth. The one flies from the senses and particulars to the most general axioms . . . this is now the fashion. The other derives axioms from the senses and particulars, rising by the gradual and unbroken ascent, so that it arrives at the most general axioms last of all. This is the true way, but as yet untried.

He claimed that *Truth* lies in the most general of axioms, a far and labored trek from experience.[4]

Another point of view holds that *Truth* lies in particulars. William Blake (1808) offered these intemperate words:

> To generalize is to be an idiot. To particularize is the lone distinction of merit. General knowledges are those that idiots possess.

Generalization may not be all that despicable, but particularization does deserve praise. To know particulars fleetingly, of course, is to know next to nothing. What becomes useful understanding is a full and thorough knowledge of the particular, recognizing it also in new and foreign contexts.

That knowledge is a form of generalization, too, not scientific induction but *naturalistic generalization* , arrived at by recognizing the similarities of objects and issues in and out of context and by sensing the natural covariations of happenings. To generalize this way is to be both intuitive and empirical, and not idiotic.

Naturalistic generalizations develop within a person as a product of experience. They derive fron the tacit knowledge of how things are, why they are, how people feel about them, and how these things are likely to be later or in other places with which this person is familiar. They seldom take the form of predictions but lead regularly to expectation. They guide action, in fact they are inseparable from action (Kemmis, 1974). These generalizations may become verbalized, passing of course from tacit knowledge to propositional; but they have not yet passed the empirical and logical tests that characterize formal (scholarly, scientific) generalizations.

Sociologist Howard Becker[5] spoke of an irreducible conflict between sociological perspective and the perspective of everyday life. Which is superior? It depends on the circumstance, of course. For publishing in the sociological journals, the scientific perspective is better; but for reporting to lay audiences and for studying lay problems, the lay perspective will often be superior. And frequently that everyday-life perspective will be superior for discourse among scholars, for they too often share among themselves more of ordinary experience than of special conceptualization. The special is often too special. It is foolish to presume that a more scholarly report will be the more effective.

The other generalizations, i.e., rationalistic, propositional, law-like generalizations, can be useful for understanding a particular situation. And they can be hurtful. Obviously, bad laws foster misunderstandings; and abstract statements of law distract attention from direct experience. Good generalizations aid the understanding of good general conditions, but good generalizations can lead one to see phenomena more simplistically than one should.

It is the legitimate aim of many scholarly studies to discover or validate laws; but the aim of the practical arts is to get things done. The better generalizations often are those more parochial, those more personal. In fields such as education and social work, where few laws have been validated and where inquiry can be directed toward gathering information that has use other than for the cultivation of laws, a persistent attention to laws is pedantic.

Cases.   The object (target) of a social inquiry is seldom an individual person or enterprise. Unfortunately, it is such single objects that are usually thought of as "cases." A case is often thought of as a constituent member of a target population. And since single members poorly represent whole populations, the case study is seen to be a poor basis for generalization.

Often, however, the situaton is one in which there is a need for generalization about that particular case or generalization to a similar case rather than generalization to a population of cases. Then the demands for typicality and representativeness yield to needs for assurance that the target case is properly described. As readers recognize essential similarities to cases of interest to them, they establish the basis for naturalistic generalization.

The case need not be a person or enterprise.It can be whatever *bounded system* (to use Louis Smith's term) is of interest. An institution, a program, a responsibility, a collection, or a population can be the case. This is not to trivialize the notion of case but to note the generality of the case study method in preparation for noting its distinctiveness.

It is distinctive in the first place by giving great prominence to what is and what is not "the case" — the boundaries are kept in focus. What is happening and deemed important within those boundaries (the emic) is considered vital and usually determines what the study is about, as contrasted with other kinds of studies where hypotheses or issues previously targeted by the investigators (the etic) usually determine the content of the study.

Case studies can be used to test hypotheses, particulary to examine a single exception that shows the hypothesis to be false. Case studies can be highly statistical; institutional research and vocational counseling case studies often are. But in the social science literature, most case studies feature: descriptions that are complex, holistic, and involving a myriad of not highly isolated variables; data that are likely to be gathered at least partly by personalistic observation; and a writing style that is informal, perhaps narrative, possibly with verbatim quotation, illustration, and even allusion and metaphor. Comparisons are implicit rather than explicit. Themes and hypotheses may be important, but they remain subordinate to the understanding of the case.[6]

Although case studies have been used by anthropologists, psychoanalysts, and many others as a method of exploration preliminary to theory development,[7] the characteristics of the method are usually more suited to expansionist than reductionist pursuits. Theory building is the search for essences, pervasive and determining ingredients, and the makings of laws. The case study, however, proliferates rather than narrows. One is left with more to pay attention to rather than less. The case study attends to the idiosyncratic more than to the pervasive.[8] The fact that it has been useful in theory building does not mean that that is its best use.

Its best use appears to me to be for adding to existing experience and humanistic understanding. Its characteristics match the "readinesses" people have for added experience. As Von Wright and others stressed, intentionality and empathy are central to the comprehension of social problems, but so also is information that is holistic and episodic. The discourse of persons struggling to increase their understanding of social matters features and solicits these qualities. And these qualities match nicely the characteristics of the case study.[9]

The study of human problems is the work of scientists, novelists, journalists, everybody, of course — but especially historians. The historian Herbert Butterfield (1951) recognized the centrality of experiential data and said:

> . . . the only understanding we ever reach in history is but a refinement, more or less subtle and sensitive, of the difficult — and sometimes deceptive — process of imagining oneself in another person's place.

Case studies are likely to continue to be popular because of their style and to be useful for exploration for those who search for explanatory laws. And, moreover, because of the universality and importance of experiential understanding, and because of their compatability with such understanding, case studies can be expected to continue to have an epistemological advantage over other inquiry methods as a basis for naturalistic generalization. Unlike Bacon's "true way" of discovering *Truth*, this method *has been* tried and found to be a direct and satisfying way of adding to experience and improving understanding.

Notes

1.   Written at the Centre for Applied Research in Education, University of East Anglia, as part of an assignment for the Organization for Economic Cooperation and Development, Paris.

2.   In this paper, I am writing about the formal inquiry to be done by people, on or off the campus, who are subject to great rewards for scholarly work and knowledge production and to lesser rewards for professional support and problem solving. In the USA, there are few civil service or applied research agencies which validate their inquiries according to its service value more than to its "internal and external validities," as defined by Campbell and Stanley (1966). I see it as unfortunately necessary to overstate the distinction between academic research and practical inquiry as a step toward improving

and legitimizing inquiries that are needed for understanding and problem solving but which are unlikely to produce vouchsafed generalizations

3. I am indebted to statements by Harry Broudy (1972) and Andrew Ortony (1975) for helping me understand the educational relevance of the writing of Polanyi.

4. But he noted that at least before 1620 *that* was not the way humans reached understanding.

5. Howard Becker (1964). Important ideas about the special use of case study as precursor to theoretical study are found in his "Problems of Inference and Proof in Participant Observation," (1958).

6. This is not to say that all case studies are as described here. Medical "write-ups," for example, are very different. But these characteristics are commonly expected and little different than those specified by Louis Smith (1973), for example, to be: credible, holistic, particularistic, individualizable, process-oriented, ego-involving, and blending of behavioral and phenomenological methodologies.

7. In Julian Simon, (1969), for example.

8. Barry MacDonald and Rob Walker have made the strongest case I know for using idiosyncratic instances to create understanding of more general matters, as in "Case Study and the Social Philosophy of Educational Research" (1975).

9. It would be of interest to get empirical data on the perceived utility of case studies. It can be presumed, I fear, that some respondents, having heard objections to the case study method from such authorities as Julian Stanley and Donald Campbell and thinking more of political value, than informational value, would underrate their utility for understanding and generalization.

References

Bacon, Sir Frances. *Novum Organum,* 1620.

Becker, Howard S. "Problems in the publication field studies." In: Arthur J. Vidich, Joseph Bensman, and Maurice R. Stein (eds.) *Reflections on Community Studies.* New York: John Wiley, 1964, p. 273.

Becker, Howard S. "Problems of inference and proof in participant observation. *American Sociological Review,* 59 (1958), 652–60.

Blake, William. *Annotations to Sir Joshua Reynold's "Disclosures,"* 1808.

Bohm, David. "Science as perception — communication." In F. Suppe (ed.), *The Structure of Scientific Theories.* Urbana: University of Illinois Press, 1974.

Broudy, Harry S. "The life uses of schooling as a field for research." In: L.G. Thomas (ed.), *Philosophical redirection of educational research.* 71st Yearbook of NSSE, Part I, Chapter IX, 1972.

Butterfield, Sir Herbert. *History and human relations.* London: Collins, 1951.

Campbell, Donald T., and Stanley, Julian C. *Experimental and quasi-experimental designs for research.* Chicago: Rand McNally, 1966.

Dilthey, Wilhelm. "The construction of the historical world of the human studies" (Der Aufbauder Welt in den Geisteswissenschaften. 1910) *Gesammelte Schriften* I-VII Leipzig: B.G. Teubner, 1914–1927.

Dray, William H. *Laws and explanation in history.* Oxford University Press, 1957.

Hampel, Carl G. "The function of general laws in history." *Journal of Philosophy,* 39 (1942).

Kemmis, Stephen. *An ecological perspective on innovation.* Urbana: University of Illinois College of Education, 1974. (mimeo).

MacDonald, Barry, and Walker, Rob. "Case study and the social philosophy of educational research." *Cambridge Journal of Education*, no. 1, 5 (1975).

Ortony, Andrew. *Knowledge, language and thinking*. Urbana: University of Illinois College of Education, 1975. (mimeo).

Polanyi, Michael. *Personal knowledge*. New York: Harper & Row, 1958.

Popper, Karl. *The poverty of historicism*. London: Routledge and Kegan Paul, 1957.

Schön, Donald A. *Metaphor and the social conscience*. Paper delivered at the Conference on Metaphor and Thought, University of Illinois, September 1977.

Simon, Julian L. *Basic research methods in social science: The art of empirical investigation*. New York: Random House, 1969.

Smith, Louis. *An aesthetic education workshop for administrators: Some implications for a theory of case studies*. Paper presented at AERA, Chicago, 1974.

Tolstoy, Leo. *War and Peace*. 1869.

Von Wright, Georg Henrik. *Explanation and understanding*. London: Routledge and Kegan Paul, 1971.

17 PROGRAM EVALUATION, PARTICULARLY RESPONSIVE EVALUATION

Robert E. Stake

I am pleased to have this opportunity to talk about some recent developments in the methodology of program evaluation and about what I call *responsive evaluation*.

I feel fortunate to have not only these two days but also some seven months to think about these things. My hosts here at the Göteborg Institute of Educational Research have been most hospitable, but generous also in hearing me out, pointing my head in still another way, weighing the merit of our several notions, and offering occasionally the luxury of a passionate argument.

When Erik or Hans or Sverker or Ulf and I agree, we are struck by the fact that the world is but one world, and the problems of education are universal. When we disagree, they are quick to suggest that the peculiar conditions of education in America have caused me to make peculiar assumptions and perhaps even warped my powers of reasoning. I am sure that some of you here today will share those findings. What I have to say is not only that we in educational research need to be doing some things we have not been doing, but that in doing what we have been doing we are in fact part of the problem.

Our main attention will be on program evaluation. A program may be strictly or loosely defined. It might be as large as all the teacher training in the United States

Stake, Robert E. "Program Evaluation, Particularly Responsive Evaluation." Paper presented at conference on *New Trends in Evaluation,* Göteborg, Sweden, October 1973. Reprinted with permission.

or it might be as small as a field trip for the pupils of one classroom. The evaluation circumstances will be these: that someone is commissioned in some way to evaluate a program, probably an ongoing program; that he has some clients or audiences to be of assistance to — usually including the educators responsible for the program; and that he has the responsibility for preparing communications with these audiences.

In 1965, Lee Cronbach, then president of the American Educational Research Association (AERA), asked me to chair a committee to prepare a set of standards for evaluation studies, perhaps like the *Standards for Educational and Psychological Tests and Manuals,* compiled by John French and Bill Michael and published in 1966 by the American Psychological Association. Lee Cronbach, Bob Heath, Tom Hastings, Hulda Grobman, and other educational researchers have worked with many of the U.S. curriculum-reform projects in the 1950s and early 1960s, and have recognized the difficulty of evaluating curricula and the great need for guidance on the design of evaluation studies.

Our committee reported that it was too early to decide upon a particular method or set of criteria for evaluating educational programs, that what educational researchers needed was a period of field work and discussion to gain more experience in how evaluative studies could be done. Ben Bloom, successor to Lee Cronbach in the presidency of the AERA, got the AERA to sponsor a monograph series on curriculum evaluation for the purpose we recommended. The seven volumes completed under AERA sponsorship are shown in the Reference section. The series in effect will continue under sponsorship of the University of California-Los Angeles (UCLA) Center for the Study of Evaluation, whose director, Marv Alkin, was a guest professor here at this Institute for Educational Research two years ago. I think this monograph series can take a good share of the credit, or blame, for the fact that, by count, over 200 sessions at the 1973 AERA annual meeting programs were directly related to the methods and results of program-evaluation studies.

There were two primary models for program evaluation in 1965, and there are two today. One is the informal study, perhaps a self-study, usually using information already available, relying on the insights of professional persons and respected authorities. It is the approach of regional accrediting associations for secondary schools and colleges in the United States and is exemplified by the Flexner report (1916) of medical education in the USA and by the Coleman report (1966) of equality of educational opportunity. In *Nine Approaches to Educational Evaluation* (see Appendix A), I have ever so briefly described this and other models; this one is referred to there as the *Institutional Self-Study by Staff Approach*. Most educators are partial to this evaluation model, more so if they can specify who the panel members or examiners are. Researchers do not like it because it relies so much on second-hand information. But there is much good about the model.

Most researchers have preferred the other model, the pretest/post-test model, what I have referred to on the *Nine Approaches* sheet at *Student Gain by Testing Approach*. It often uses prespecified statements of behavioral objectives — such as are available from Jim Popham's Instructional Objectives Exchange — and is nicely represented by Tyler's (1942) "Eight-Year Study," Husen's (1967) *International Study of Achievement in Mathematics,* and the National Assessment of Educational Progress. The focus of attention with this model is primarily on student performance.

Several of us have proposed other models. In a 1963 article, Cronbach advocates having evaluation studies considered applied research on instruction, to learn what could be learned in general about curriculum development, as was done in Hilda Taba's Social Studies Curriculum Project. Mike Scriven (1967) strongly criticized Cronbach's choice in AERA Monograph no. 1, stating that it was time to give consumers (purchasing agents, taxpayers, and parents) information on how good each existing curriculum is. To this end, Kenneth Komoski established in New York City an Educational Products Information Exchange, which has reviewed equipment, books, and teaching aids but has to this day still not caught the buyer's eye.

Dan Stufflebeam was one who recognized that the designs preferred by researchers did not focus on the variables that educational administrators have control over. With support from Egon Guba, Dave Clark, Bill Gephart, and others (1971), he proposed a model for evaluation that emphasized the particular decisions that a program manager will face. Data-gathering would include data on context, input, process, and product; but analyses would relate those things to the immediate management of the program. Though Mike Scriven criticized this design, too, saying that it had too much bias toward the concerns and the values of the educational establishment, this Stufflebeam CIPP model was popular in the U.S. Office of Education for several years. Gradually, it fell into disfavor not because it was a bad model, but partly because managers were unable or unwilling to *examine their own* operations as part of the evaluation. Actually, no evaluation model could have succeeded. A major obstacle was a federal directive, which said that no federal office could spend its funds to evaluate its own work; that that could only be done by an office higher up. Perhaps the best examples of evaluation reports following this approach are those done in the Pittsburgh schools by Mal Provus and Esther Kresh.

Before I describe the approach that I have been working on — which I hope will someday challenge the two major models — I will mention several relatively recent developments in the evaluation business.

It is recognized, particularly by Mike Scriven and Ernie House, that co-option is a problem, that the rewards to an evaluator for producing a favorable evaluation report often greatly outweigh the rewards for producing an unfavorable report. I do not know of any evaluators who falsify their reports, but I do know many who consciously or unconsciously choose to emphasize the objectives of the program staff and to concentrate on the issues and variables most likely to show where the program is successful. I often do this myself. Thus, the matter of *meta evaluation,* providing a quality control for the evaluation activities, has become an increasing concern.

Early in his first term of office, President Nixon created a modest Experimental Schools Program, a program of five-year funding for three carefully selected high schools (from all those in the whole country) and the elementary schools that feed students into them. Three more have been chosen each year, according to their proposal to take advantage of a broad array of knowledge and technical developments and to show how good a school can be. The evaluation responsibility was designed to be allocated at three separate levels, one *internal* at the local-school level; one *external* at the local-school level (i.e., in the community attending to the working of the local school but not controlled by it); and a third at the national level, synthesizing results from the local projects and evaluating the organization and effects of the Experimental Schools Program as a whole. Many obstacles and hostilities hampered the work of the first two evaluation teams, and work at the third level — according to Egon Guba, who did a feasibility study — was seen to be so likely to fail that it probably should be carried no further.

Mike Scriven has made several suggestions for meta evaluation, one most widely circulated based on abstinence, called *goal-free evaluation.* Sixten Marklund has jokingly called it "aimless evaluation." But it is a serious notion, not to ignore all idea of goals with the program sponsors or staff. The evaluator, perhaps with the help of colleagues and consultants, then is expected to recognize manifest goals and accomplishments of the program as he works it in the field. Again, with the concern for the consumer of education, Scriven has argued that what is intended is not important, that the program is a failure if its results are so subtle that they do not penetrate the awareness of an alert evaluator. Personally, I fault Scriven for expecting us evaluators to be as sensitive, rational, and alert as his designs for evaluation require. I sometimes think that Mike Scriven designs evaluation studies that perhaps only Mike Scriven is capable of carrying out.

Another interesting development is the use of adversarial procedures in obtaining evidence of program quality and, especially, in presenting it to decisionmakers. Tom Owens, Murray Levine, and Marilyn Kourilsky have taken the initiative here. They have drawn up the work of legal theorists who claim that truth emerges when opposing forces submit their evidence to cross-examination directly before the eyes of judges and juries. Craig Gjerde, Terry Denny, and I tried something like this in our TCITY report (Stake & Gjerde, 1975) (see Appendix B for a summary of the most positive claims that might reasonably be made for the Institute we were evaluating and a summary of the most damaging charges that might reasonably be made). It was important to us to leave the issue unresolved, to let the reader decide which claim to accept, if any. But we would have served the reader better if we had each written a follow-up statement to challenge the other's claims. At any rate, this is an example of using an adversary technique in an evaluation study.

Now, in the next 45 minutes or so, I want to concentrate on the approach for evaluating educational programs presently advocated by Malcolm Parlett of the University of Edinburgh, Barry MacDonald of the University of East Anglia, Lou Smith of Washington University of St. Louis, Bob Rippey of the University of Connecticut, and myself. You have had an opportunity to read an excellent statement by Malcolm Parlett and David Hamilton (1972). Like they did, I want to emphasize the settings where learning occurs, teaching transactions, judgment data, holistic reporting, and giving assistance to educators. I should not suggest that they endorse all I will say today, but their writings for the most part are harmonious with mine.

Let me start with a basic definition, one that I got from Mike Scriven. Evaluation is an *observed value* compared to some *standard*. It is a simple ratio, but this numerator is not simple. In program evaluation, it pertains to the whole constellation of values held for the program. And the denominator is not simple, for it pertains to the complex of expectations and criteria that different people have for such a program.

The basic task for an evaluator is made barely tolerable by the fact that he or she does not have to solve this equation in some numerical way nor to obtain a descriptive summary grade, but merely needs to make a comprehensive statement of what the program is observed to be, with useful references to the satisfaction and dissatisfaction that appropriately selected people feel toward it. Any particular client may want more than this; but this satisfies the minimum concept, I think, of an evaluation study.

If you look carefully at the TCITY report, you will find no direct expression of this formula, but it is in fact the initial idea that guided us. The form of presentation was chosen to convey a message about the Twin City Institute to our readers in Minneapolis and St. Paul, rather than to be a literal manifestation of our theory of evaluation.

Our theory of evaluation emphasizes the distinction between a *preordinate* approach and a *responsive* approach. In the recent past, the major distinction being made by methodologists is that between what Scriven called *formative* and *summative* evaluation. He gave attention to the difference between developing and already-developed programs and, implicitly, to evaluation for a local audience of a program in a specific setting, as contrasted to evaluation for many audiences of a potentially generalizable program. These are important distinctions, but I find it even more important to distinguish between preordinate evaluation studies and responsive evaluation studies.

I have made the point that there are many different ways to evaluate educational programs. No one way is the right way. Some highly recommended evaluation procedures do not yield a full description nor a view of the merit and shortcoming of the program being evaluated. Some procedures ignore the pervasive questions that should be raised whenever educational programs are evaluated: Do all students benefit or only a special few? Does the program adapt to instructors with unusual qualifications? Are opportunities for aesthetic experience realized?

Some evaluation procedures are insensitive to the uniqueness of the local conditions. Some are insensitive to the quality of the learning climate provided. Each way of evaluating leaves some things de-emphasized.

I prefer to work with evaluation designs that perform a service. I expect the evaluation study to be useful to specific persons. An evaluation probably will not be useful if the evaluator does not know the interests of his audiences. During an evaluation study, a substantial amount of time may be spent learning about the information needs of the persons for whom the evaluation is being done. The evaluator should have a good sense of whom he is working for and their concerns.

Responsive Evaluation

To be of service and to emphasize evaluation issues that are important for each particular program, I recommend the *responsive evaluation* approach. It is an approach that sacrifices some precision in measurement, hopefully to increase the usefulness of the findings to person in and around the program. Many evaluation plans are more *preordinate,* emphasizing statement of goals, use of objective tests, standards held by program personnel, and research-type reports. Responsive evaluation is less reliant on formal communication, more reliant on natural communication.

Responsive evaluation is an alternative, an old alternative. It is evaluation based on what people do naturally to evaluate things: they observe and react. The approach is not new; but it has been avoided in planning documents and institutional regulations because, I believe, it is subjective, poorly suited to formal contracts, and a little too likely to raise the more embarrassing questions. I think we can overcome the worst aspects of subjectivity, at least. Subjectivity can be reduced by replication and operational definition of ambiguous terms even while we are relying heavily on the insights of personal observation.

An educational evaluation is responsive evaluation if it orients more directly to program activities than to program intents, if it responds to audience requirements for information, and if the different value perspectives of the people at hand are referred to in reporting the success and failure of the program. In these three separate ways, an evaluation plan can be responsive.

To do a responsive evaluation, the evaluator, of course, does many things. He or she makes a plan of observations and negotiations and arranges for various persons to observe the program. With their help, the evaluator prepares for brief narratives, portrayals, product displays, graphs, etc. He or she finds out what is of value to the audience and gathers expressions of worth from various individuals whose points of view differ. Of course, the evaluator checks the quality of his or her records and gets program personnel to react to the accuracy of the portrayals. He or she gets authority figures to react to the importance of various findings and audience members to react to the relevance of the findings. The evaluator does much of this informally, iterating, and keeping a record of action and reaction. He or she chooses media accessible to his or her audiences to increase the likelihood and fidelity of communication. The evaluator might prepare a final written report, or he or she might not — depending on what the evaluator and the clients have agreed on.

Purpose and Criteria

Many of you will agree that the book edited by E.F. Lindquist, *Educational Measurement,* has been the bible for us who have specialized in educational measurement. Published in 1950, it contained no materials on program evaluation. The second edition, edited by Bob Thorndike (1971), has a chapter on program evaluation. Unfortunately, the authors of this chapter, Alex Astin and Bob Panos, chose to emphasize but one of the many purposes of evaluation studies. They said that the principal purpose of evaluation is to produce information that can guide decisions concerning the adoption or modification of an educational program.

   People expect evaluation to accomplish many different purposes:

to document events,

to record student change,

to detect institutional vitality,

to place the blame for trouble,

to aid administrative decision making,

to facilitate corrective action,

to increase our understanding of teaching and learning.

   Each of these purposes is related directly or indirectly to the values of a program and may be a legitimate purpose for a particular evaluation study. It is very important to realize that each purpose needs separate data; all the purposes cannot be served with a single collection of data. Only a few questions can be given prime attention. We should not let Astin and Panos decide what questions to attend to, or Tyler, or Stake. Each evaluator, in each situation, has to decide what to attend to. The evaluator has to decide.

   On what basis will he choose the prime questions? Will he rely on his preconceptions? Or on the formal plans and objectives of the program? Or on actual program activities? Or on the reactions of participants? It is at this choosing that an evaluator himself is tested.

Most evaluators can be faulted for over-reliance on preconceived notions of success. I advise the evaluator to give careful attention to the reasons the evaluation was commissioned, then to pay attention to what is happening in the program, then to choose the value questions and criteria. He should not fail to discover the best and worst of program happenings. He should not let a list of objectives or an early choice of data-gathering instruments draw attention away from the things that most concern the people involved.

Many of my fellow evaluators are committed to the idea that good education results in measurable outcomes: student performance, mastery, ability, attitude. But I believe it is not always best to think of the *instrumental* value of education as a basis for evaluating it. The "payoff" may be diffuse, long-delayed; or it may be ever beyond the scrutiny of evaluators. In art education, for example, it is sometimes the purpose of the program staff or parent to provide artistic experiences — and training — for the *intrinsic* value alone. "We do these things because they are good things to do," says a ballet teacher. Some science professors speak similarly about the experimental value of reconstructing certain classical experiments. The evaluator or his observers should note whether or not those learning experiences were well-arranged. They should find out what appropriately selected people think are the costs and benefits of these experiences in the dance studio or biology laboratory. The evaluator should not presume that only measurable outcomes testify to the worth of the program.

Sometimes it will be important for the evaluator to do his best to measure student outcomes, other times not. I believe that there are few critical data in any study, just as there are few critical components in any learning experience. The learner is capable of using many pathways, many tasks, to gain his measure of skill and aesthetic benefit. The evaluator can take different pathways to reveal program benefit. Tests and other data-gathering should not be seen as essential; neither should they be automatically ruled out. The choice of these instruments in responsive evaluation should be made as a result of observing the program in action and of discovering the purposes important to the various groups having an interest in the program.

Responsive evaluations require planning and structure; but they rely little on formal statements and abstract representations, e.g., flow charts, test scores. Statements of objectives, hypotheses, test batteries, and teaching syllabi are, of course, given primary attention if they are primary components of the instructional program. Then they are treated not as the basis for the evaluation plan but as components of the instructional plan. These components are to be evaluated just as other components are. The proper amount of structure for responsive evaluation depends on the program and persons involved.

Substantive Structure

Instead of objectives or hypotheses as *advanced organizers* for an evaluation study, I prefer issues. I think the word *issues* better reflects a sense of complexity, immediacy, and valuing. After getting acquainted with a program, partly by talking with students, parents, taxpayers, program sponsors, and program staff, the evaluator acknowledges certain issues or problems or potential problems. These issues are a structure for continuing discussions with clients, staff, and audiences, and for the data-gathering plan. The systematic observations to be made, the interviews and tests to be given, if any, should be those that contribute to understanding or resolving the issues identified.

In evaluating TCITY, Craig Gjerde and I became aware of such issue-questions as:

Is the admissions policy satisfactory?

Are some teachers too permissive?

Why do so few students stay for the afternoon?

Is opportunity for training younger teachers well used?

Is this Institute a ''lighthouse'' for regular school curriculum innovation?

The importance of such questions varies during the evaluation period. Issues that are identified early as being important tend to be given too much attention in a preordinate data plan, and issues identified toward the end are likely to be ignored. Responsive-evaluation procedures allow the evaluator to respond to emerging issues as well as to preconceived issues.

The evaluator usually needs more structure than a set of questions to help him decide what data to gather. To help the evaluator conceptualize his ''shopping list,'' I once wrote a paper entitled ''The Countenance of Educational Evaluation'' (Stake, 1967). It contained the matrix, the thirteen information categories, shown in figure 17–1. You may notice that my categories are not very different from those called for in the models of Dan Stufflebeam and Mal Provus.

For different evaluation purposes, there will be different emphases on one side of the matrix or the other: descriptive data and judgmental data. And, similarly, there will be different emphases on antecedent, transaction, and outcome information. The ''Countenance'' article also emphasized the use of multiple, and even contradicting, sources of information.

The article also pointed out the often-ignored question about the match-up between intended instruction and observed instruction and the even more elusive question about the strength of the contingency of observed outcomes upon observed transactions under the particular conditions observed. I think these ''Countenance'' ideas continue to be good ones for planning the content of the evaluation study.

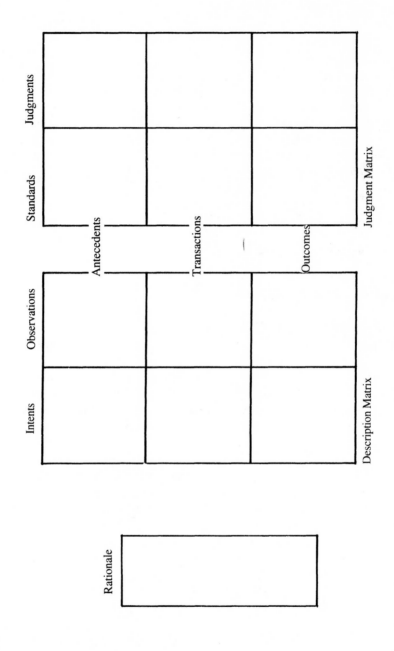

Figure 17–1.   A Layout of Statements and Data to Be Collected by the Evaluator of an Educational Program.

I like to think of all of these data as observations: intents, standards, judgments, and statements of rationale. Maybe it was a mistake to label just the second column *observations*. Thoreau said: "Could a greater miracle take place than for us to look through each other's eyes for an instant?"

Human observers are the best instruments we have for many evaluation issues. Performance data and preference data can be psychometrically scaled when objectively quantified data are called for. The important matter for the evaluator is to get his information in sufficient amount from numerous independent and credible sources so that it effectively represents the perceived status of the program, however complex.

Functional Structure

"Which data" is one thing, but "how to do the evaluation" is another. My responsive-evaluation plan allocates a large expenditure of evaluation resources to observing the program. The plan is not divided into phases because observation and feedback continue to be the important functions from the first week through the last. I have identified 12 recurring events (see figure 17–2), which I show as if on the face of a clock. I know some of you would remind me that a clock moves clockwise, so I hurry to say that this clock moves clockwise and counter-clockwise *and* cross-clockwise. In other words, any event can follow any event. Furthermore, many events occur simultaneously, and the evaluator returns to each event many times before the evaluation ends.

For example, take twelve o'clock. The evaluator will discuss many things on many occasions with the program staff and with people who are representative of his audiences. He will want to check his ideas of program scope, activities, purposes, and issues against theirs. He will want to show them his representations (e.g., sketches, displays, portrayals, photographs, tapes) of value questions, activities, curricular content, and student products. Reactions to these representations will help him learn how to communicate in this setting. He should provide useful information. He should not pander to desires for only favorable (or only unfavorable) information, nor should he suppose that only the concerns of evaluators and external authorities are worthy of discussion. (Of course, these admonitions are appropriate for responsive evaluation and preordinate evaluation alike.)

This behavior of the responsive evaluator is very different from the behavior of the preordinate evaluator. Table 17–1 illustrates my estimate as to how the two evaluators would typically spend their time.

I believe the preordinate evaluator conceptualizes himself as a stimulus, seldom as a response. He does his best to generate standardized stimuli, such as behavioral objective statements, test items, or questionnaire items. The responses that he evokes are what he collects as the substance of his evaluation report.

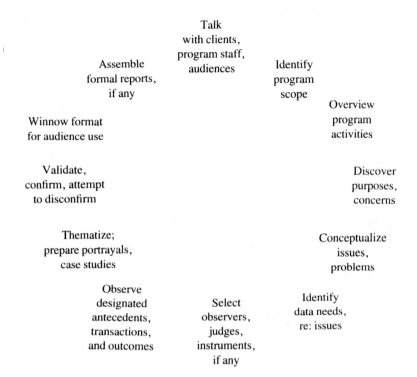

Figure 17–2.   Prominent Events in a Responsive Evaluation.

The responsive evaluator considers the principal stimuli to be those naturally occurring in the program, including responses of students and the subsequent dialogues. At first, his job is to record these, learning both of happenings and values. For additional information, he assumes a more interventionalist role. And, with his clients and audience he assumes a still more active role, stimulating their thought (we hope) and adding to their experience with his reports.

Philosopher David Hawkins (1973) respondeed to the idea of reversing S–R roles in this way:

> . . . I like the observation that one is reversing the S and R of it. In an experiment one puts the system in a prepared state, and then observes the behavior of it. Preparation is what psychologists call "stimulus," . . . In naturalistic investigation one does not prepare the system, but looks for patterns, structures, significant events, as they appear under conditions not controlled or modified by the investigator, who is himself now a system of interest. He is a resonator, a respondent. He must be in such an initial state that (a) his responses contain important information about the complex of stimuli he is responding to, and (b) they must be maximally decodable by his intended audience.

Table 17-1. Comparison of Preordinate and Responsive Evaluators

	Preordinate	Responsive
Identifying issues, goals	10%	10%
Preparing instruments	30%	15%
Observing the program	5%	30%
Administering tests, etc.	10%	—
Gathering judgments	—	15%
Learning client needs, etc.	—	5%
Processing formal data	25%	5%
Preparing informal reports	—	10%
Preparing formal reports	20%	10%

In the next section of this paper, I will talk about maximally decodable reports. Let me conclude these two sections on structure by saying that the evaluator should not rely only on his own powers of observation, judgment, and responding. He should enlist a platoon of students, teachers, community leaders, curriculum specialists, etc. — his choice depending on the issues to be studied and the audiences to be served. The importance of their information and its reliability will increase as the number and variety of observers increase.

Portrayal and Holistic Communication

Maximally decodable reports require a technology of reporting that we educational measurements people have lacked. We have tried to be impersonal, theoretical, generalizable. We have sought the parsimonious explanation. We have not accepted the responsibility for writing in a way that is maximally comprehensible to practicing educators and others concerned about education. According to R.F. Rhyne (1972):

> There is a great and growing need for the kind of powers of communication that helps a person gain, vicariously, a feeling for the natures of fields too extensive and diverse to be directly experienced.
>
> Prose and its archetype, the mathematical equation, do not suffice. They offer more specificity within a sharply limited region of discourse than is safe, since the clearly explicit can be so easily mistaken for truth, and the difference can be large when context is slighted (p. 93–104).

We need this power of communication, this opportunity for vicarious experience, in our attempts to solve educational problems.

One of the principal reasons for backing away from the preordinate approach to evaluation is to improve communication with audiences. The conventional style of research-reporting is a "clearly explicit" way of communicating. In a typical research project, the report is limited by the project design. A small number of variables are identified and relationships among them are sought. Individuals are observed, found to differ, and distributions of scores are displayed. Covariations of various kinds are analyzed and interpreted. From a report of such analytic inquiry, it is very hard, often impossible, for a reader to know what the program was like. If he is supposed to learn what the program was like, the evaluation report should be different from the conventional research report.

As a part of my advocacy of the responsive approach, I have urged my fellow evaluators to respond to what I believe are the natural ways in which people assimilate information and arrive at understanding. *Direct* personal experience is an efficient, comprehensive, and satisfying way of creating understanding, but is a way not usually available to our evaluation report audiences. The best substitute for direct experience probably is *vicarious experience* — increasingly better when the evaluator uses "attending" and "conceptualizing" styles similar to those that members of the audience use. Such styles are not likely to be those of the specialist in measurement or the theoretically minded social scientist. Vicarious experience often will be conceptualized in terms of persons, places, and events.

We need a reporting procedure for facilitating vicarious experience, and it is available. Among the better evangelists, anthropologists, and dramatists are those who have developed the art of storytelling. We need to portray complexity. We need to convey the holistic impression, the mood, even the mystery of the experience. The program staff or people in the community may be uncertain. The audiences should feel that uncertainty. More ambiguity rather than less may be needed in our reports. Oversimplification obfuscates. Ionesco said (Esslin, 1966):

> As our knowledge becomes separated from life, our culture no longer contains ourselves (or only an insignificant part of ourselves) for it forms a *social* context into which we are not integrated.

> So the problem becomes that of bringing our life back into contact with our culture, making it a living culture once again. To achieve this, we shall first have to kill "the respect for what is written down in black and white . . . ." to break up our language so that it can be put together again in order to re-establish contact with "the absolute," or as I should prefer to say, with "multiple reality"; it is imperative to "push human beings again towards seeing themselves as they really are" (p. 298).

Some evaluation reports should reveal the "multiple reality" of an educational experience.

The responsive evaluator will often use portrayals. Some will be short, featuring perhaps a five-minute script, a log, or scrapbook. A longer portrayal may require several media: narratives, maps and graphs, exhibits, taped conversations, photographs, even audience role-playing. Which ingredients best convey the sense of the program to a particular audience? The ingredients are determined by the structure chosen by the evaluator.

> Suppose that a junior-high-school art program is to be evaluated. For portrayal of at least one issue, "how the program affects *every* student," the students might be thought of as being in two groups: those taking at least one fine-arts course and those taking none. (The purpose here is description, not comparison.)

> A random sample of ten students from each group might be selected and twenty small case studies developed. The prose description of what each does in classes of various kinds (including involvement with the arts in school) might be supplemented with such things as (1) excerpts from taped interviews with the youngster, his friends, his teachers, and his parents; (2) art products (or photographs, news clippings, etc., of same) made by him in or out of class; (3) charts of his use of leisure time; and (4) test scores of his attitudes toward the arts. A display (for each student) might be set up in the gymnasium which could be examined reasonably thoroughly in 10–20 minutes.

> Other materials, including the plan, program, and staffing for the school, could be provided. Careful attention would be directed toward finding out how the description of these individual youngsters reveals what the school and other sources of art experience are providing in the way of art education.

It will sometimes be the case that reporting on the quality of education will require a "two-stage" communication. Some audiences will not be able to take part in such a vicarious experience as that arranged in the example above. A surrogate audience may be selected. The evaluator will present his portrayals to them; then he will question them about the apparent activity, accomplishments, issues, strengths, and shortcomings of the program. He will report their reactions, along with a more conventional description of the program, to the true audiences.

> These twenty displays could be examined by people specially invited to review and respond to them. The reviewers might be students, teachers, art curriculum specialists, and patrons of the arts. They might also visit regular school activities, but most attention would be to the displays. These reviewers should be asked to answer such questions as: "Based on these case studies, is the school doing its share of providing good quality art experience for all the young people?" and "Is there too much emphasis on disciplined creative performance and not enough on sharing the arts in ways that suit each student's own tastes?" Their response to these portrayals and questions would be a major part of the evaluation report.

The portrayal will usually feature descriptions of persons. The evaluator will find that case studies of several students may represent the educational program more interestingly and faithfully than a few measurements on all of the students. The promise of gain is two-fold: the readers will comprehend the total program, and some of the important complexity of the program will be preserved. The several students selected usually cannot be considered a satisfactory representation of the many — a sampling error is present. The protests about the sampling error will be loud; but the size of the error may be small, and it will often be a satisfactory price to pay for the improvement in communication.

There will continue to be many research inquiries needing social survey technology and exact specification of objectives. The work of John Tukey, Torsten Husen, Ralph Tyler, Ben Bloom, and James Popham will continue to serve as models for such studies.

Often the best strategy will be to select achievement tests, performance tests, or observation checklists to provide evidence that prespecified goals were or were not achieved. The investigator should remember that such a preordinate approach depends on a capability to discern the accomplishment of those purposes, and those capabilities sometimes are not at our command. The preordinate approach usually is not sensitive to ongoing changes in program purpose, nor to unique ways in which students benefit from contact with teachers and other learners, nor to dissimilar viewpoints as to what is good and bad.

Elliot Eisner (1969) nicely summarized these insensitivities in AERA monograph no. 3. He advocated consideration of *expressive objectives* — toward outcomes that are idiosyncratic for each learner and that are conceptualized and evaluated *after* the instructional experience; after a product, an awareness, or a feeling has become manifest, at a time when the teacher and learner can reflect upon what has occurred. Eisner implied that sometimes it would be preferable to evaluate the quality of the *opportunity* to learn — the *intrinsic* merit of the experience rather than the more elusive *payoff,* to use Scriven's terms.

In my own writing on evaluation, I have been influenced by Eisner and Scriven and others who have been dissatisfied with contemporary testing. We see too little good measurement of complex achievements, development of personal styles and sensitivities. I have argued that few, if any, specific learning steps are truly essential for subsequent success in any life's endeavors; I have argued that students, teachers, and other purpose selected observers exercise the most relevant critical judgments, whether or not their criteria are in any way explicit. I have argued, also, that the alleviation of instructional problems is most likely to be accomplished by the people most directly experiencing the problem, with aid and comfort perhaps (but not with specific solutions or replacement programs) from consultants or external authorities. I use these arguments as assumptions for what I call the *responsive evaluation* approach.

Utility and Legitimacy

The task of evaluating an educational program might be said to be impossible if it were necessary to express verbally its purposes or accomplishments. Fortunately, it is not necessary to be explicit about aim, scope, or probable cause in order to indicate worth. Explication will usually make the evaluation more useful; but it also increases the danger of misstatement of aim, scope, and probable cause.

To layman and professional alike, evaluation means that someone will report on the program's merits and shortcomings. The evaluator reports that a program is coherent, stimulating, parochial, and costly. These descriptive terms are also value-judgment terms. An evaluation has occurred. The validity of these judgments may be strong or weak; their utility may be great or little. But the evaluation was not at all dependent on a careful specification of the program's goals, activities, or accomplishments. In planning and carrying out an evaluation study, the evaluator must decide how far to go beyond the bare bones ingredients: values and standards. Many times, he will want to examine goals; many times, he will want to provide a portrayal from which audiences may form their own value judgments.

The purposes of the audiences are all-important. What would they like to be able to do with the evaluation of the program? Chances are they do not have any plans for using it. They may doubt that the evaluation study will be of use to them. But charts and products and narratives and portrayals do not affect people. With these devices, persons become better aware of the program, develop a feeling for its vital forces, and develop a sense of its disappointments and potential troubles. They may be better prepared to act on issues, such as a change of enrollment or a reallocation of resources. They may be better able to protect the program.

Different styles of evaluation will serve different purposes. A highly subjective evaluation may be useful but not be seen as legitimate. Highly specific language, behavioral tasks, and performance scores are considered by some to be more legitimate. In America, however, there is seldom a greater legitimacy than the endorsement of large numbers of audience-significant people. The evaluator may need to discover what legitimacies his audiences (and their audiences) honor. Responsive evaluation includes such inquiry.

Responsive evaluation will be particularly useful during formative evaluation when the staff needs help in monitoring the program, when no one is sure what problems will arise. It will be particularly useful in summative evaluation, when audiences want an understanding of a program's activities, its strengths and shortcomings, and when the evaluator feels that is his responsibility to provide a vicarious experience.

Preordinate evaluation should be preferred to responsive evaluation when it is important to know if certain goals have been reached, if certain promises have been kept, and when predetermined hypotheses or issues are to be investigated. With greater focus and opportunity for preparation, preordinate measurements made can be expected to be more objective and reliable.

It is wrong to suppose that either a strict preordinate design or responsive design can be fixed upon an educational program to evaluate it. As the program moves in unique and unexpected ways, the evaluation efforts should be adapted to them, drawing from stability and prior experience where possible, stretching to new issues and challenges as needed.

Appendix A

Table 17-2. Nine Approaches to Evaluation

Approach	Purpose	Key Elements	Purview Emphasized	Protagonists (see references)	Cases Examples	Risks	Payoffs
Student Gain By Testing	to measure student performance and progress	goal statements; test score analysis; discrepancy between goal and actuality	Educational Psychologists	Ralph Tyler Ben Bloom Jim Popham Mal Provus	Steele Womer Lindvall-Cox Husen	oversimplify, educational aims; ignore processes	emphasize, ascertain student progress
Institutional Self-Study By Staff	to review and increase staff effectiveness	committee work standards set by staff; discussion; professionalism	Professors, teachers	National Study of School Evaluation, Dressel	Boersma-Plawecki Knoll-Brown Carpenter	alienate some staff; ignore values of outsiders	increase staff awareness, sense of responsibility
Blue-Ribbon Panel	to resolve crises and preserve the institution	prestigious panel; the visit; review of existing program and documents	Leading Citizens	James Conant Clark Kerr David Henry	Flexner Havighurst House et al. Plowden	postpone action; over-rely on intuition	gather best insights judgment
Transaction-Observation	to provide understanding of activities and values	educational issues; classroom observation; case studies; pluralism	Client, Audience	Lou Smith Parlett-Hamilton Rob Rippey Bob Stake	MacDonald Smith-Pohland Parlett Lundgren	over-rely on subjective perceptions; ignore causes	produce broad picture of program; see conflict in values
Management Analysis	to increase rationality in day-to-day decisions	lists of options; estimates; feedback loops; costs; efficiency	Managers, Economists	Leon Lessinger Dan Stufflebeam Mary Alkin	Kraft Doughty-Stakenas Hemphill	over-value efficiency; under-value implicits	feedback for decision making

Approach	Purpose	Method	Style	Proponents	Proponents	Limitations	Contributions
Instructional Research	to generate explanations and tactics of instruction	controlled conditions, multivariate analysis; bases for generalization	Experimentalists	Lee Cronbach Julian Stanley Don Campbell	Anderson, R. Pella Zdep-Joyce Taba	artificial conditions ignore the humanistic	new principles of teaching and materials development
Social Policy Analysis	to aid development of institutional policies	measures of social conditions and administrative implementation	Sociologists	James Coleman David Cohen Carol Weiss Mosteller-Moynihan	Coleman Jencks Levitan Trankell	neglect of educational issues, details	social choices, constraints clarified
Goal-Free Evaluation	to assess effects of program	ignore proponent claims, follow checklist	Consumers	Michael Scriven	House-Hogben	over-value documents & record keeping	data on effect with little co-option
Adversary Evaluation	to resolve a two-option choice	opposing advocates, cross-examination, the jury	Expert: Juristic	Tom Owens Murray Levine Bob Wolfe	Owens Stake-Gjerde Reinhard	personalistic superficial, time-bound	information impact good; claims put to test

Of course these descriptive tags are a great over-simplification. The approaches overlap. Different proponents and different users have different styles. Each protagonist recognizes one approach is not ideal for all purposes. Any one study may include several approaches. The grid is an over-simplification, intended to show some typical, gross differences between contemporary evaluation activities.

Appendix B

TCITY–1971 Evaluation Report: An Advocate's Statement[1]

No visitor who took a long, hard look at TCITY-71 kept his skepticism. A young visitor knows how precious it is to discover, to be heard, to belong. An older visitor knows the rarity of a classroom where teachers and students perceive each other as real people. To the non-visitor, it doesn't seem possible that a summer school program can deliver on all these promises to over 800 kids, but TCITY-71 did.

Every curriculum specialist fears that by relaxing conduct rules and encouraging student independence they may be saying good-bye to the hard work and hard thinking that education requires. TCITY-71 teachers and students made learning so attractive, so purposive, that free-ranging thought returned again and again to curricular themes: awareness of the human condition, obstacles to communication, ecological interactions, etc.

TCITY excels because of its staff. Its students give it movement. Its directors give it nurture. Its teachers give it movement, nurture, and direction. It would be incorrect to say that Mr. Caruson, Mr. Rose, and the teachers think alike as to the prime goals and methods of education, but collectively, they create a dynamic, humanistically-bent, academically-based curriculum.

The quality of teaching this summer was consistently high, from day-to-day, from class to class. Some of the teachers chose to be casual, to offer "opportunities," to share a meaningful experience. Others were more intense, more intent upon sharing information and problem-solving methods. Both kinds were there, doing it well.

The quality of the learning also was high. The students were tuned in. They were busy. They responded to the moves of their teachers. They improvised; they carried ideas and arguments, indignations and admirations, to the volleyball court, to the Commons, to the shade of campus elms and Cannon River oaks. The youngsters took a long step towards maturity.

True, it was a costly step. Thousands of hours, thousands of dollars, and at least a few hundred aggravations. But fit to a scale of public schools budgets — and budgets for parks, interstate highways, and weapons of war — TCITY-71 rates as a *best buy*. Eight hundred kids, give or take a few, took home a new talent, a new line of thinking, a new awareness — a good purchase.

It cannot be denied that other youngsters in Minneapolis and St. Paul deserve an experience like this. They should have it. Some say, "TCITY is bad because it caters to the elite." But a greater wisdom says, "Any effort fixated on giving an equal share of good things to all groups is destined to share nothing of value." For less advantaged youth, a more equitable share of educational opportunities should be guaranteed. But even in times of economic recession, opportunities for the talented should be protected.

TCITY-71 has succeeded. It is even a best buy. It satisfies a social obligation to specially educate some of those who will lead — in the arts, in business, in government, in life. The teachers of TCITY-71 have blended a summer of caring, caprice, openness, and intellectual struggle to give potential leaders a summer of challenge.

TCITY–1971 Evaluation Report: An Adversary's Statement[2]

TCITY is not a *scandalum magnatum*. But it is both less than it pretends to be and more than it wishes to be. There is enough evidence at least to question certain facets of the Institute — if not to return a true bill against it. Costly, enlarging, innovative, exemplary: these Institute attributes are worthy of critical examination.

How costly is this Institute? Dollar costs are sufficient to give each group of six students $1,000 to design and conduct their own summer experience. Over 100 Upward Bound students could be readied for their college careers at Macalester. About 25 expert curriculum specialists could be supported for half a year to design and develop new curricula for the high school.

What is the cost of removing 800 talented leaders from the local youth culture? What is the cost of widening the experience gap between Institute students and their parents? . . . and their teachers in "regular" high school? . . . and their non-Institute friends? Not enough here to charge neo-fascist elitism. Enough to warrant discussion.

The Institute abounds with self-named innovators and innovations, with alternatives to the business-as-usual education of high schoolers. Note that the Institute is not promoted as an exemplary alternative *to* schooling. It seeks to promote the development of alternative forms of education *for* schools. And it is failing to do even that job. What is TCITY doing to demonstrate that TCITY style of life could be lived in schools as we know them? Where in the regular school is the staff so crucial to the life of the Institute? . . . the money? . . . the administrative leadership? Where are the opportunities for the teachers, principals, superintendents to come and live that life that they might come to share in the vision? . . . and where are the parents? TCITY should be getting poor grades on affecting the regular school program.

There are other dimensions of TCITY that puzzle the non-believer:

How long can in-class "rapping" continue and still qualify as educative self-exploration? Are there quality control procedures in effect during the summer program: For example: when one-third to one-half of a class is absent from a scheduled meeting, should not that be seen as an educational crisis by the instructor?

What does TCITY do to help students realize that the Institute standards are necessarily high; that the regular schools norms and expectations do not count;

that a heretofore "best" becomes just a "so-so"? There are unnecessarily disheartened students in TCITY.

Is it unreasonable to expect that more than 2 of 22 teachers or associate teachers would have some clear idea or plan for utilizing TCITY approaches or curricula in their regular classrooms next fall?

Few students — or faculty — understand the selection procedures employed to staff the teaching cadre and to fill the student corps. Why should it be a mystery?

The worst has been saved for last. This report concludes with an assertion: the absence of crucial dimension in the instructional life of TCITY, that of constructive self-criticism, is a near-fatal flaw. The observation and interview notes taken by the adversary evaluator over four days contain but five instances of students engaging in, or faculty helping students to become skillful in, or desirous of, the cultivation of self-criticism. The instances of missed opportunities were excessive in my judgment. Worse: when queried by the writer, faculty and students alike showed little enthusiasm for such fare. Is it too much to expect from Institute participants after but four weeks? Seven may be insufficient. The staff post-mortem, "Gleanings," are a start — but it seems odd to start at the end.

The paucity of occurrence is less damning than the absence of manifest, widespread intent. Certain classes accounted for all the instances observed. They did not appear to be accidental. The intent was there. An Institute for talented high school youth cannot justifiably fail to feature individual and group self-criticism.

Notes

1.   Prepared by R. Stake, not to indicate his opinion of the Institute, but as a summary of the most positive claims that might reasonably be made.

2.   Prepared by T. Denny, not to indicate his opinion of TCITY-1971, but as a summary of the most damaging charges that might reasonably be made.

References

Coleman, James S. et al. *Equality of Educational Opportunity.* Washington, D.C.: U.S. Department of Health, Education and Welfare, Office of Education, 1966.

Cronbach, Lee. "Course Improvement Through Evaluation." *Teachers College Record,* 64 (1963), 672–83.

DuBois, Philip H. and Mayo, D. Douglas (eds.). *Research Strategies for Evaluating Training* (AERA Monograph Series on Curriculum Evaluation). Chicago: Rand McNally & Co., 1970.

Eisner, Elliot W. "Instructional and Expressive Educational Objectives: Their Formulation and Use in Curriculum." In: W. James Popham, Elliot W. Eisner, Howard J. Sullivan, and Louise Tyler, *Instructional Objectives* (AERA Monograph Series on Curriculum Evaluation). Chicago: Rand McNally & Co., 1969.

Esslin, Martin. *The Theater of the Absurd*. London: Eyre & Spotteswoode, 1966.

Flexner, Abraham. *Medical Education in the United States and Canada*. A report to the Carnegie Foundation for the Advancement of Teaching. New York: The Carnegie Foundation, 1910. Reprint. New York: Arno Press, 1970.

Gallagher, James; Nuthall, Graham A., and Rosenshine, Barak. *Classroom Observation* (AERA Monograph Series on Curriculum Evaluation). Chicago: Rand McNally & Co., 1970.

Grobman, Hulda. *Evaluation Activities of Curriculum Projects* (AERA Monograph Series on Curriculum Evaluation). Chicago: Rand McNally & Co., 1968.

Hawkins, David. University of Colorado, Boulder, Colorado, (Personal communications). 1973.

Husen, Torsten (ed.) *International Study of Achievement in Mathematics*. New York: Wiley, 1967.

Levine, Murray. "Scientific Method and the Adversary Model: Some Preliminary Suggestions." *Evaluation Comment,* 4 (1973), 1–3.

Lindquist, Everett, F. (ed.). *Educational Measurement*. Washington: American Council on Education, 1950.

Lindvall, C.M. and Cox, Richard. *Evaluation as a Tool in Curriculum Development* (AERA Monograph Series on Curriculum Evaluation). Chicago: Rand McNally & Co., 1970.

MacDonald, Barry, "Evaluation and the Control of Education," In: D. Tawney (ed.). *Evaluation: The State of the Art*. London: Schools Council, 1975.

Parlett, Malcomb, and Hamilton, David. *Evaluation as Illumination: A New Approach to the Study of Innovatory Programs*. Edinburgh: Centre for Research in the Educational Sciences, University of Edinburgh, Occasional Paper no. 9, 1972.

Provus, Malcolm. *Discrepancy Evaluation*. Berkeley, California: McCutchan, 1971.

Rhyne, R.F. "Communicating Holistic Insights," *Fields Within Fields — Within Fields,* 5 (1972), 93–104.

Rippey, Robert M. (ed.). *Studies in Transactional Evaluation*. Berkeley, California: McCutchan, 1973.

Scriven, Michael S. "The Methodology of Evaluation." In: Ralph Tyler, Robert Gagne, and Michael Scriven (eds.), *Perspectives of Curriculum Evaluation* (AERA Monograph Series on Curriculum Evaluation). Chicago: Rand McNally & Co., 1967.

Scriven, Michael S. "Goal-Free Evaluation." In: Ernest House (ed.). *School Evaluation: The Politics and Process*. Berkeley, California: McCutchan, 1973.

Smith, Louis M., and Pohland, Paul A. "Educational Technology and the Rural Highlands." In: Louis M. Smith, *Four Examples: Economic, Anthropological, Narrative, and Portrayal* (AERA Monograph on Curriculum Evaluation). Chicago: Rand McNally & Co., 1974.

Stake, Robert E. "The Countenance of Educational Evaluation," *Teachers College Record,* 68 (1967), 523–40.

Stake, Robert E. and Gjerde, Craig. *An Evaluation of TCITY: The Twin City Institute for Talented Youth*. Paper no. 1, Evaluation Report Series. Kalamazoo, Michigan: Evaluation Center, Western Michigan University, 1975.

Stufflebeam, Daniel L. et al. *Educational Evaluation and Decision Making*. Itasca, Illinois: Peacock, 1971.

Thorndike, Robert L. (ed.) *Educational Measurement*. Washington, D.C.: American
    Council on Education, 1971.
Tyler, Ralph W. "Eight-Year Study." In: E.R. Smith and Ralph Tyler *Appraising and
    Recording Student Progress*. New York: Harper, 19042.
Tyler, Ralph W. *Basic Principles of Curriculum and Instruction*. Chicago: University of
    Chicago Press, 1949.
Womer, Frank. *What is National Assessment?* Ann Arbor: National Assessment of Educa-
    tional Progress, 1970.

18 EPISTEMOLOGICAL AND METHODOLOGICAL BASES OF NATURALISTIC INQUIRY

Egon G. Guba and Yvonna S. Lincoln

Introduction

It is important, at the outset, to recognize what naturalistic inquiry is and what it is not. Naturalistic inquiry is a *paradigm of inquiry;* that is, a pattern or model for how inquiry may be conducted. While it is frequently asserted that its distinguishing features are: that it is carried out in a natural setting (and hence the term *naturalistic*), that it utilizes a case-study format, and that it relies heavily on qualitative rather than quantitative methods, none of these features define naturalistic inquiry. While all of these assertions are essentially correct, no one of them, nor indeed all of them together, capture the full significance of the term *paradigm*. Paradigms differ from one another on matters much more fundamental than the locale in which the inquiry is conducted, the format of the inquiry report, or the nature of the methods used. Paradigms are axiomatic systems characterized by their differing sets of assumptions about the phenomena into which they are designed to inquire.

There are many different paradigms of inquiry. We are all intimately familiar with most paradigms, which we use on virtually a daily basis. So, for example, our system of jurisprudence is based on an adversarial paradigm; religious faiths on theological paradigms; and peer reviews of research proposals on a judgmental paradigm. Those persons concered with *disciplined* inquiry, however, in the sense that term is defined by Cronbach and Suppes (1969), have used almost exclusively what is commonly called the scientific paradigm, which we will here term the *rationalistic* paradigm.[1] A second paradigm, which is also aimed at disciplined inquiry and which is currently receiving a great deal of attention, we term the *naturalistic;* it is this paradigm that this paper explicates.

One may well ask why anyone would contemplate the use of a competing paradigm when the rationalistic one has gained such widespread legitimacy and achieved such conspicuous successes. How could one doubt the efficacy of the scientific mode for all inquiry? John Stuart Mill urged social science investigators to adopt the scientific methods as long ago as 1843; can there be any question, a century and a half later, that his advice was well-founded?

It seems to us that a variety of evidence may be cited in counter-argument. First, we believe that the judgment that the rationalistic paradigm has enabled conspicuous successes in social and behavioral inquiry is mistaken. Data collected in these arenas has not proved to be aggregatable; where, for example, is the useful residue of the more than 100 years of psychological and educational research? Investigators have, moreover, repeatedly found it impossible to apply the paradigm according to its own basic principles; random sampling, for example, is virtually impossible for both political and ethical reasons. The impact of research on practice is conspicuous by its absence; for example, evaluation data remain unused and the practice of most social institutions, such as schools, hospitals, and prisons, is still based primarily on experience.

Second, we question the utility of the rationalistic paradigm as typically practiced (and as it will be described here) on the ground that it reflects a discredited epistemology of science — positivism. It is apparent that sophisticated scientists can no longer accept positivism; even a casual acquaintance with the field of particle physics provides ample evidence of its inadequacies, as for example, the Heisenberg Uncertainty Principle (Tranel, 1981). Yet practitioners of scientific inquiry, in the hard but especially in the soft sciences, continue to act as if positivism were valid, thereby accepting a position that is essentially analytic, reductionist, empiricist, associationist, reactivist, nomological, and monistic. As we shall see, this posture is inconsistent with the characteristics of many social/behavioral phenomena.

Finally, we suggest that the rationalistic paradigm, like all paradigms, rests upon certain fundamental axioms or assumptions and that the particular axioms of rationalism can be but poorly fulfilled in social/behavioral inquiry. It is our intention to devote a major segment of this paper to a discussion of the rationalistic axioms and their naturalistic counterparts, and to deal with the question of which set of axioms is better fulfilled in the phenomenological field customarily designated as *social/behavioral*.

But, as we shall demonstrate, the motivation for considering naturalistic inquiry as an alternative paradigm is not founded simply on the desire to avoid the shortfalls of rationalism. Naturalistic inquiry has many characteristics to recommend it on other grounds. So, for example, it offers a contextual relevance and richness that is unmatched; it displays a sensitivity to process virtually excluded in paradigms stressing control and experimentation; it is driven by theory grounded in the data — the naturalist does not search for data that fit a theory but develops a theory to explain the data. Finally, naturalistic approaches take full advantage of the not inconsiderable power of the human-as-instrument, providing a more than adequate trade-off for the presumably more objective approach that characterizes rationalistic inquiry.

Even without depending on these claims for the advantages of naturalistic inquiry, however, it seems clear that the examination of an alternative paradigm has utility, since such examination forces out otherwise hidden assumptions and meanings. If it is true that the examined life is ''better'' than the unexamined, it is surely the case that the examined paradigm is better than the unexamined.

This paper has two major purposes:

1. To distinguish the rationalistic and naturalistic paradigms on five basic axioms, and to describe, in addition, six postures on which practitioners of these paradigms have traditionally differed.
2. To suggest some methods for responding to four basic criteria for trustworthiness (analogues to the traditional rationalistic criteria of internal and external validity, reliability, and objectivity) that might be used by naturalists to counter charges of lack of discipline (sloppiness).

The Basic Axioms that Distinguish the Naturalistic from the Rationalistic Inquiry Paradigm

Axioms may be defined as the set of undemonstrated (and undemonstrable) propositions accepted by convention or established by practice as the basic building blocks of some conceptual or theoretical structure or system. Before undertaking an examination of the axioms that underlie the two paradigms of interest to us here, it may be useful to undertake a small digression to clarify the nature of axiomatic systems.

Probably the best known and most widely experienced system of axioms is that undergirding Euclidean geometry. Euclid set himself the task of formalizing everything known about geometry at his time — essentially, that meant systematizing the rules-of-thumb used by land surveyors, who could not provide any proof of their validity other than experience. It was Euclid's powerful insight that these rules could be *proved* by showing them to be logical derivatives from some simple set of *self-evident truths*. Euclid began with four such axioms (Hofstadter, 1979):

1.   A straight line segment can be drawn joining any two points.
2.   Any straight line segment can be extended indefinitely in a straight line.
3.   Given any straight line segment, a circle can be drawn having the segment as radius and one end-point as center.
4.   All right angles are congruent.

With these four axioms, Euclid was able to derive the first 28 of the eventually much larger set of theorems. But the 29th proof he attempted was intractable; Euclid had to assume it instead as a fifth axiom:

5.   If two lines are drawn which intersect a third in such a way that the sum of the inner angles on one side is less than two right angles, then the two lines inevitably must intersect each other on that side if extended far enough.

The modern way to state this axiom is as follows: Given a line and a point not on that line, it is possible to construct only one line through the point parallel to the given line.

As compared to the first four axioms, the fifth seems strained and inelegant; Euclid was sure that eventually he would be able to find a way of proving it in terms of the first four. But his hope was not to be realized within his lifetime, or indeed, ever; two millenia of effort by mathematicians have failed to provide a proof.

Early attempts to prove this axiom/theorem were of what mathematicians would call the direct variety; later, mathematicians fell back on indirect proofs, one variant of which is to assume the direct opposite of what one wishes to show and then to demonstrate that this opposite assumption leads to absurd conclusions (theorems). It was exactly this approach, however, that culminated in so-called non-Euclidean geometries. Not only were the consequences of non-Euclidean assumptions not absurd, they were in fact of great utility. One such geometry is called Lobachevskian; this form takes as its fifth axiom: "Given a line and a point not on that line, it is possible to draw a bundle of lines through the point *all of which* are parallel to the given line." Now this axiom flies in the face of all human experience; yet it yields results of great interest, for example, to astronomers. One of the theorems provable from the Euclidean fifth axiom is that the sum of angles in a triangle is 180°, but the sum of angles in Lobachevskian triangles *approaches* 180° as triangles become "small." Earth-size triangles must all be small, since no such triangle has ever yielded a sum of angles less than 180°. But astronomically sized triangles are very much larger, and astronomers find that Lobachevskian geometry provides a better "fit" to the phenomena that they investigate than does Euclidean.

From this digression, we may deduce several crucial points:

1. Axioms are arbitrary and may be assumed for any reason, even if only for the sake of the game.
2. Axioms are not self-evidently true, nor need they appear so; indeed, some axioms appear very bizarre on first exposure.
3. Different axiom systems have different utilities depending upon the phenomenon to which they are applied. These utilities are *not* determined by the nature of the axiom system itself but by the interaction between these axioms and the characteristics of the area in which they are applied. Thus, Euclidean geometry is fine for terrestrial spaces but Lobachevskian geometry is better for interstellar spaces.
4. A decision about which of several alternative axiom systems to use in a given case is made by testing the fit between each system and the case, a process analogous to testing data for fit to assumptions before deciding on which statistic to use in analyzing them.

Thus, the axioms to be described below should not be judged on the grounds of their self-evident truth, their common sense qualities, or their familiarity to the inquirer, but *in terms of their fit to the phenomena into which one proposes to inquire.* When the rationalistic axioms fit, the rationalistic paradigm should be used; when the naturalistic axioms fit, the naturalistic paradigm should be used.

Five axioms differentiate the rationalistic and naturalistic paradigms; these five axioms are summarized in table 18–1. Immediately following is a formal statement of the five axioms in both their rationalistic and naturalistic versions. We attend to the question of which set provides a better fit to social/behavioral phenomena in a following section.

Axiom 1:   The Nature of Reality

- *Rationalistic version:* There is a single, tangible reality fragmentable into independent variables and processes, any of which can be studied independently of the others; inquiry can converge onto this reality until, finally, it can be predicted and controlled.

- *Naturalistic version:* There are multiple, intangible realities which can be studied only holistically; inquiry into these multiple realities will inevitably diverge (each inquiry raises more questions than it answers) so that prediction and control are unlikely outcomes although some level of understanding (*verstehen*) can be achieved.

Table 18–1. Axiomatic Differences Between the Rationalistic and Naturalistic Paradigms

Axioms About	Rationalistic Paradigm	Naturalistic Paradigm
Reality	Single, tangible, convergent, fragmentable	Multiple, intangible divergent, holistic
Inquirer/respondent relationship	Independent	Inter-related
Nature of truth statements	Context-free generalizations — nomothetic statements — focus on similarities	Context-bound working hypotheses — idiographic statements — focus on differences
Attribution/explanation of action	Real causes; temporally precedent or simultaneous; manipulable; probabilistic.	Attributional shapers; interactive (feed-forward and feed-back): non-manipulable; plausible.
Relation to Values to Inquiry	Value-free	Value-bound

Note: In certain of our previous writing (Guba, 1978, 1981; Guba & Lincoln, 1981) we have focussed on only the first three of these five axioms. However, the latter two now seem to us as equally if not more important.

Axiom 2:   The Inquirer-Objective Relationship

• *Rationalistic version:* The inquirer is able to maintain a discrete distance between himself and the object of inquiry.

• *Naturalistic version:* The inquirer and the object interact to influence one another; this mutual interaction is especially present when the object of inquiry is another human being (respondent).

Axiom 3:   The Nature of Truth Statements

• *Rationalistic version:* The aim of inquiry is to develop a nomothetic body of knowledge; this knowledge is best encapsulated in generalizations which are truth statements of enduring value that are context-free; the stuff of which generalizations are made is similarities among units.

• *Naturalistic version:*   The aim of inquiry is to develop an ideographic body of knowledge; this knowledge is best encapsulated in a series of working hypotheses that describe the individual case; differences are as inherently interesting as (and at times more so than) similarities.

Axiom 4:   Attribution/Explanation of Action

- *Rationalistic version:* Every action can be explained as the result (effect) of a real cause that precedes the effect temporally (or is at least simultaneous with it).

- *Naturalistic version:* An action *may* be explainable in terms of multiple interacting factors, events, and processes that shape it and are part of it; inquirers can, at best, establish plausible inferences about the patterns and webs of such shaping in any given case.

Axiom 5:   The Role of Values in Inquiry

- *Rationalistic version:* Inquiry is value-free and can be guaranteed to be so by virtue of the objective methodology which is employed.

- *Naturalistic version:* Inquiry is value-bound in at least five ways, captured in the corollaries which follow:

  Corollary 1: Inquiries are influenced by *inquirer* values as expressed in the choice of a problem, and in the framing, bounding, and focussing of that problem.

  Corollary 2: Inquiry is influenced by the choice of *paradigm* which guides the investigation into the problem.

  Corollary 3: Inquiry is influenced by the choice of *substantive theory* utilized to guide the collection and analysis of data and in the interpretation of findings.

  Corollary 4: Inquiry is influenced by the values which inhere in the *context*.

  Corollary 5: With respect to Corollaries *1* through *4* above, inquiry is either *value-resonant* (reinforcing or congruent) or *value-dissonant* (conflicting). Problem, paradigm, theory, and context must exhibit congruence (value-resonance) in order to produce meaningful results.

The decision about which paradigm to use depends, we again assert, on an assessment of the area to be studied to determine the degree of fit between the axioms of each paradigm and the area. If we *limit ourselves to consideration solely of the area commonly designated as social/behavioral inquiry,*[2] we make the following observations about fit:

Axiom 1: The nature of reality.   In the hard and life sciences there can be little doubt that there exists a tangible reality, which is the focus of inquiry: actual events, objects, and processes found in nature that can be observed and often measured. The utility of breaking this physical world into variables is well demonstrated by such terms as time, mass, velocity, acceleration, distance, charge, and the like. Such variables can all be studied independently and related to one another in functional expressions.

In the social/behavioral sciences, however, the class of phenomena typically addressed in inquiry *has no reality* in the physical sense. That is not to say that tangible objects, events, and processes do not enter into human behavior. However, it is not these tangibles that we care about but the meaning and interpretation people ascribe to them, for it is these *constructions* that mediate their behavior. These constructions do not have reality but exist only in the minds of people. As Filstead (1979) suggests, "There are multiple realities. . . . Individuals are conceptualized as active agents in constructing and making sense of the realities they encounter." (p. 36) There are as many constructions as there are people to make them.

Nor are these constructions equivalent to perceptions. We are not belaboring here the well-known fable of the blind men and the elephant. If that fable *were* to provide a useful metaphor, it would do so *only if there were no elephant.* We mean to suggest precisely that there is no tangible reality that can be touched as the blind men touched the elephant. The fable deals with their perceptions of the elephant; we deal with constructions that are developed from whole cloth in the mind of the constructor.

Since these constructions reside wholly in the minds of people, they are substantially inaccessible and must be dealt with in holistic fashion; they cannot be divided into parts or variables. Further, since the realities are multiple, it is futile to expect inquiry to converge. One cannot converge on a common or typical reality since each is idiosyncratic. The more people one explores, the more realities one emcounters; inquiry diverges as a result. Every inquiry finally raises more questions than it answers.

Axiom 2: The inquirer-object relationship.   In the hard and life sciences, it is not unreasonable to posit the ability of the inquirer to maintain a discrete distance from the phenomenon under study. Balls rolling down inclined planes, chemicals interacting in a test tube, or cells subdividing under a microscope are unlikely to be influenced by the fact that someone is watching, nor is the watcher likely to be influenced (in any way adverse to the investigatory outcome) by what he observes. In the social/behavioral sciences, however, the *reactivity* of subjects (Campbell & Stanley, 1963; Webb et al., 1966) is well recognized. It is commonly understood that objects of inquiry,[3] when they are human, may react to inquirers of their inquiry methods. Less appreciated is the fact that the inquirer is *also* subject to interaction. Just as the inquirer may shape the respondent's behavior, so may the respondent shape the inquirer's behavior. Nor should it be supposed that the interpolation of a layer of objective instrumentation between the inquirer and the respondent(s) is sufficient to overcome or offset this interaction. Images of what the respondent may be like or how he or she might respond guide the inquirer in devising his or her instruments. Images of what the inquirer wants, or what he or she will do with the responses, guide the respondent in dealing with the instruments. Images of what the respondent meant by a response guide the inquirer in coding, interpreting, and even in accepting the respondent's return, and so on.

Far from deploring inquirer-respondent interactivity, the naturalist exploits it. If interactivity could be eliminated by some magical process, the naturalist would not think the trade-off worthwhile, because it is precisely this interactivity that makes it possible for the inquirer to be a *smart* instrument, honing in on relevant facts and ideas by virtue of his sensitivity, responsiveness, and adaptability. More of this will be said below.

Axiom 3: The nature of truth statements.   The development of generalizations is said by many to be the ultimate aim of inquiry. Why would anyone want to invest time and effort in a study that can yield no more insight than the single occurrence has to offer? Context-free statements of enduring truth value are clearly prized. The question that confronts us is whether they are achieveable.

In the hard and life sciences, that question must be answered with a resounding *Yes*. Statements like $F = ma$ and $e = mc^2$ are derivable in physics, for example, and they hold, whether tested in the eighteenth or twentieth centuries, on earth, Mars, the moon, or anywhere else in the universe. Such statement form the cornerstones of most disciplines, indeed, the phrase *nomothetic science* implies exactly the development of law-like generalizations which provide dependable bases for prediction and control.

There is a real question, however, whether generalizations can be made that will be true forever. Cronbach (1975) utilizes an interesting metaphor to make the counterpoint. Generalizations, he asserts, are like radioactive substances; they decay and have half-lives. He gives numerous examples from the hard as well as the social/behavioral sciences, for instance: the failure of DDT to control pests as genetic transformations make them resistant to the insecticide; the shifting of stars in their courses so as to render star maps obsolete; the suggestion by Ghiselli that the superiority of distributed, over massed, practice may not remain valid from one generation to another; and Bronfenbrenner's conclusion that class differences in parenting observed in the 1950s were just the reverse of those observed in 1930. Thus, it is dubious whether generalizations can be made about human behavior with impunity. Time is an enormously important factor, and who can offer an example of human behavior that is context-free?

Now this argument should not be interpreted to mean that there can *never* be any transfer from one situation to another. What we mean to say is that statements cannot be made about human phenomena that are likely to be true for even a substantial number of years (not to mention forever) or for any substantial number of contexts (not to mention any and all contexts). Conditionals, contingencies, and disjunctions must all be taken into account (Wiles, 1981). Moreover, differences in times or contexts are as important to know about in making the judgment of transferability as are similarities. The naturalist, then, is concerned with developing an adequate ideographic statement — thick description — about the situation he is studying, in order to make judgments about transferability possible, should anyone care to ask that question.

Axiom 4: Attribution/explanation of action.   The search for causality is the mainspring that drives conventional research. Even such authors as Cook and Campbell (1979) who recognize that causality is a slippery concept nevertheless define designs as serving "to probe causal hypotheses" (p. ix), see causal connections as "real," even if "imperfectly perceived" (p. ix), and address their book to those "who have already decided that they want a causal question answered" (p. 2). For them, the question is not whether to entertain a concept of causality but *which* concept to accept.

The meaning to be imputed to the term *causality* has been under discussion for centuries, despite which, as Cook and Campbell note, "the epistemology of causation . . . is at present in a productive state of near chaos" (p. 10). Causality was originally conceived in a common sense way in *if-then* terms, probably because of the tendency of early scientists to view the world as a huge machine. In the early eighteenth century, David Hume noted that causality was never directly observed but merely *imputed* by the observer when two events were physically contiguous and temporally adjacent. He espoused a *regularity* or *constant conjunction* theory of causality that denied the need for the concept of causality at all. Later, an *essentialist* view emerged, based on the idea of necessary and sufficient conditions; essentialists sought functional laws expressing inevitable cause-effect relationships (Weir, 1980). Currently an activity theory of causation placing heavy emphasis on manipulation as the test for inferring cause-effect relationships has wide currency, lending legitimation to the notion that the best test for cause-effect relationships is the experiment (Cook & Campbell, 1979). Cook and Campbell (1979) themselves opt for the *critical-realist* position:

> The perspective is realist because it assumes that causal relationships exist *outside of the human mind,* and it is critical-realist because it assumes that these valid causal relationships cannot be perceived with total accuracy by our imperfect sensory and intellective capacities. (pp. 28–29; emphasis added).

Formulations such as these have meaning (to some degree) within the rationalist paradigm insofar as it is applied to the hard and life sciences. There seems to be little question about the appropriateness of seeking cause-effect relationships when one is talking about gas laws, electric circuits, or the impact that mashes the fender of an automobile. But these ideas are highly suspect when applied to the arena of social/behavioral inquiry. The realities that we are dealing with are constructed and exist *only* in the minds of people; if the realities are constructed, why not the attributions or explanations of causality? And if that is reasonable, emergent attributional and/or semantic theories of causation (if that is now the proper term) are more likely to be meaningful than any of the formulations that have developed in relation to the other inquiry areas. In these views, causality is not merely empirical or contingent but depends heavily on meaning. Questions such as, "Is the treatment applied via a particular instructional program effective in increasing student learning?" imply a cause/effect relation between treatment and student learning, but the nature of that relationship surely depends on what is meant by treatment and student learning and what the criteria of effectiveness are taken to be. In other words, *causality* is a construction less traceable by empirical linkages than by plausible semantic/attributional linkages. The concepts of constructed reality and attributed causality are congenial to and supportive of one another.

Thus, the naturalist argues, there can be no certain way of determining cause-effect; indeed, the very concept of causality seems to have outlived its usefulness. Positivists, such as Hume, believed the concept of causation to be unnecessary; naturalists believe it to be archaic. Instead, the naturalist prefers to think of multiple factors and conditions, all of which *interact,* with feed-back *and* feed-forward, to *shape one another*. Actions can be understood not as having been *caused* but as having *emerged* from the constant interplay of its shapers, all of which are themselves part of the action, indistinguishable from it, shaping and being shaped simultaneously. While rationalists seem to have given up certainty in specifying causal relationships and have fallen back on probabilistic statements, the naturalist is satisfied to tease out *plausible* connections between phenomena.

Axiom 5: The role of values in inquiry. The customary presupposition of rationalists is that inquiry is *value-free,* that is, that the outcomes of the inquiry are guaranteed by the methodology employed by rationalists to be purely empirical. The data, it is often said, "speak for themselves"; that is, they transcend the values of both inquirers and respondents. Naturalists, on the other hand, presuppose that inquiry is inevitably grounded in the value systems that characterize the inquirer, the respondent, the paradigm chosen, the substantive theory selected, and the social and conceptual contexts. Values cannot be set aside, methodologically controlled, or eliminated. It is more reasonable to acknowledge and take account of values, insofar as one can, than to delude oneself about their importance or to hope that methodological hedges will compensate for their intrusion.

Values, naturalists insist, may enter into and influence the course of inquiry in five ways, all of which are *by definition* excluded in the strict rationalist construction:

1. Values influence decisions about what to study, how to study it, and what

interpretations to make of the resulting data. The evidence for such influences is overwhelming (Bahm, 1981; Homans, 1978; Kelman, 1979; Krathwohl, 1980; Scriven, 1971), and most rationalists are willing to concede at least this form of value intrusion.

2. Inquiry is influenced by the paradigm selected to guide the investigation. The rationalist, for instance, who believes that reality is singular and convergent, will impose that construction on the findings, even when hearing respondents assert again and again that *their* constructions of the problem, or of their lives, are at variance with both those of the investigator as well as those of other respondents. Thus, the rationalist proceeds much as does a court of law, constructing and reconstructing into a singular reality that which represents *truth* to him or her.

3. Inquiry is influenced by the choice of substantive theory, which dictates the methods chosen to collect and analyze the data, and ways of interpreting the findings. The substantive theory (like the methodological paradigm) is a construction, having roots in assumptions and values. Freudian constructions of personality are very different from Skinnerian; bureaucratic organization theory from loosely-coupled theory. If seeing is believing, it is also true that believing is seeing.

4. Inquiry is influenced by the multiple value and belief systems which inhere in the context in which the inquiry is carried out. Contextual values include those stemming from individuals and those which inhere in social/behavioral, human, and organizational phenomena. A study of school curricula in a fundamentalist community is very different from a similar study in an upper-middle class suburb.

5. Finally, inquiry may be characterized as being either *value-resonant* (reinforcing or congruent) or *value-dissonant* (conflicting). So, for instance, an inquirer could bound a problem to be studied, choose the paradigm within which he or she will operate, choose a substantive theory to guide the inquiry, and still have to determine whether the inquiry is value-resonant or value-dissonant with the context in which he or she will take the inquiry. When making this decision, problem, paradigm, theory, and context must exhibit internal coherence, value-fit, and congruence (value-resonance)[4] in order for the inquiry to be deemed appropriate and fitting, and in order to produce meaningful findings.

The naturalist admits the role that values play in shaping an inquiry *and* appreciates the possibility of difficulties arising if there is value-dissonance. While he cannot eliminate value effects (any more than can the rationalist), he endeavors to set up whatever safeguards he can, to expose and explicate the values whenever possible, and to test insofar as he can for value-resonance. In this latter regard, we may note that the naturalist's propensity for grounding his inquiry (see below) provides a virtual guarantee of value resonance, since the subjects' constructions and the substantive theory are both extracted from the data rather than laid on them.[5]

Some Characteristic Postures

While the axioms represent basic distinctions in premises between the rationalistic and naturalistic paradigms, certain postures typically assumed by practitioners following these two orientations also provide important insights into the differences between them. These postures are not compelled by the axioms, in the sense that they are necessary, logical derivatives (like the theorems of a geometry); yet they are relatively congenial or reinforcing to the practice of the paradigms and probably would be insisted on by each paradigm's adherents.

Six of the most common postures are described below. It should be noted that, unlike the case of axioms where either-or decisions must be made, postures could often be compromised. Yet compromises are infrequently found. The reason for this apparent intransigence cannot be laid to the obduracy of the proponents, however; rather, it stems from the fact that the collectivity of postures support and reinforce one another in extremely synergistic ways. Each is, in a sense, a raison d'etre for the others, and to compromise on any one of them is to considerably weaken the collective power of all.

Preferred methods.   We have already noted that the rationalistic and naturalistic paradigms are often treated as though the major differentiating characteristic is their relative preference for quantitative or qualitative methods. It is likely that, among the six postures that will be briefly described here, the quantitative-qualitative distinction is the one that can be most easily and sensibly compromised. Cook and Reichardt (1979) have referred to the distinction as "unhelpful," and have called for more widespread utilization of both types of methods, a call with which we can agree. Each approach has advantages: quantitative methods have greater precision and are mathematically manipulable, while qualitative methods are richer and can deal with phenomena not easily translatable into numbers. For the naturalist, the propensity toward the use of qualitative methods is less accounted for by these advantages, however, than by the fact that qualitative methods are normally preferred by a human using himself or herself as a prime data collection instrument. Techniques such as interview, observation, use of non-verbal cues and unobtrusive measures, and documentary and records analysis seem more appropriate in that case.

Source of theory.   Rationalists prefer *a priori* theory; indeed, they are likely to insist that inquiry without *a priori* theory is impossible. Theories always exist, they say, even if only at the implicit level. It is better to make them explicit than to be uncertain about what is guiding one's inquiry. The naturalist suggests that it is not theory but the inquiry problem that guides and bounds an inquiry. *A priori* theory constrains the inquiry and introduces biases (believing is seeing). In all events, theory is more powerful when it *arises from* the data rather than being imposed *on* them. It is better to find a theory to explain the facts than to look for facts that accord with a theory. Again, there is something to be said for each point of view. Surely rationalists would not wish to devise theory that was never shown to have any relation to facts, nor would the naturalist insist that each inquiry had to establish its own theory de novo. Yet the naturalist, using himself as instrument, building on his or her tacit as well as propositional knowledge and unrolling the inquiry design as the study proceeds, would find *a priori* theory uncongenial, preferring to develop the theory as his or her collection of facts grew and his or her insights into their possible meanings matured.

Knowledge types used.   Rationalists confine the types of knowledge admissible in any inquiry to *propositional* knowledge (Polanyi, 1966), that is, knowledge that can be cast into language forms (sentences). In view of their insistence on *a priori* theory and their interest in shaping inquiry preordinately around certain questions and hypotheses derived from it, such a tendency is not surprising. Naturalists, intent upon the use of the human as the prime data collection instrument and wishing to utilize the capabilities of that instrument to the fullest, also admit and build upon *tacit* knowledge: intuitions, apprehensions, "vibes," which, while not expressible at any given moment, nevertheless occur to the inquirer by virtue of his or her training and experience.[6] Of course, the naturalist seeks to recast his tacit knowledge into propositional form as soon as possible, since without so doing he cannot communicate with others — and probably not even with himself — about his findings. Yet to confine the inquiry itself only to those things that can be stated propositionally is unduly limiting from the naturalist's viewpoint, since it eliminates to a large extent the characteristic that is the major warrant for the use of the human-as-instrument.

Instruments.   The rationalist prefers non-human data collection instruments, because they appear to be more cost-efficient, have a patina of objectivity, and produce information that can be systematically aggregated. The naturalist prefers humans-as-instruments because of their greater insightfulness, their flexibility, their responsiveness, the holistic emphasis they can provide, their ability to utilize tacit knowledge, and their ability to process and ascribe meaning to data simultaneously with their acquisition. Just as a "smart" bomb need not be dropped accurately on target to find its way unerringly to it, so the *smart* human instrument need not begin with a precise problem statement, theory, hypothesis, or method in order to find its way unerringly to what is most salient in a situation. As Hofstadter (1979) points out, there is an exact trade-off between perfection and adaptability;

the more perfect an instrument is for some use, the less adaptable to others. The human instrument, while admittedly imperfect, is nevertheless exquisitely adaptable. For the naturalist, with his or her propensity for grounded theory and emerging design, the human instrument is the ideal choice.

Design. The rationalist insists on a preordinate design; indeed, it is sometimes asserted that a good design specifies in dummy form the very tables that will ultimately be found in the report. The naturalist, entering the field without *a priori* theory or hypotheses (mostly), is literally unable to specify a design (except in the broadest process sense) in advance. Instead, he or she anticipates that the design will emerge as the inquiry proceeds, with each day's work being heavily dependent on what has gone before. Given his or her other postures, the naturalist has no choice but to opt for an emergent (rolling, cascading, unfolding) design. Of course there is no reason why the naturalist should not be as specific as he or she can, without constraining his or her options.

Setting. Finally, the rationalist prefers to conduct studies under laboratory (contrived, controlled, manipulable) conditions in order to exclude from the inquiry any influences other than those at which the inquiry is aimed; that is, to exclude all confounding variables. The naturalist, on the other hand, prefers natural settings, arguing that only in such settings can one arrive at reasonable formulations and interpretations. If theory is to be properly grounded, the inquirer must observe the facts as they normally occur, not as they are contrived in an artificial context.

It should now be clear why we asserted earlier that these six postures constitute a synergistic set. Compromises are, of course, possible on each posture, but each supports the others; one cannot argue for the naturalist's preference on any one posture without invoking his preferences on other postures as well. It is difficult to imagine a naturalist at work who could be content with a mix-and match strategy, however desirable that might be from the point of view of achieving a rapprochement.

The Trustworthiness of Naturalistic Inquiry

After some two centuries of experience with rationalistic inquiry, several criteria of importance have been identified for judging the trustworthiness of its findings. It is not unreasonable to ask whether naturalistic inquiry can also meet those criteria; or, in the event that the criteria are deemed inappropriate, meet some new criteria that are more appropriate and of approximately equal power in differentiating good from bad, inadequate, or untrustworthy research. Such criteria have importance for designing, monitoring, and judging an inquiry, whether from the perspective of the inquirer, a monitor (for example, a sponsor, an administrator, or a dissertation committee), or an editor who might be asked to publish the results of such research.

Guba and Lincoln (1981) have summarized the four major traditional criteria into four questions, to which they suggest the naturalist has an equal obligation to attend:

1. *Truth Value:* How can one establish confidence in the truth of the findings of a particular inquiry for the respondents with which and the context in which the inquiry was carried out?
2. *Applicability:* How can one determine the degree to which the findings of a particular inquiry may have applicability in other contexts or with other respondents?
3. *Consistency:* How can one determine whether the findings of an inquiry would be consistently repeated if the inquiry were replicated with the same (or similar) respondents in the same (or a similar) context:?
4. *Neutrality:* How can one establish the degree to which the findings of an inquiry are a function solely of the conditions of the inquiry and not of the biases, motivations, interests, or perspectives of the inquirer?

The terms typically utilized within the rationalistic paradigm in relation to the four questions are, respectively, *internal validity, external validity, reliability,* and *objectivity.* Guba (1981) and Guba and Lincoln (1981) propose four analogous terms within the naturalistic paradigm to supplant these rationalistic terms: *credibility, transferability, dependability,* and *confirmability,* respectively.

The translation of the conventional terms into these four naturalistic terms requires some justification (Guba, 1981; Guba & Lincoln, 1981):

Credibility. Internal validity is best demonstrated through an isomorphism between the data of an inquiry and the phenomena those data represent. While such isomorphism cannot be directly represented in either paradigm, the naturalist does have at least indirect access to the multiple realities he deals with; since they are constructions in the minds of people, he can *ask* those people whether he has represented *their* realities appropriately. Thus, the crucial question for the naturalist becomes, ''Do the data sources find the inquirer's analysis, formulation, and interpretations to be credible (believable)?''

Transferability. In the rationalistic paradigm, generalizability (external validity) is demonstrated by showing that the data have been collected from a sample that is in some way representative of the population to which generalization is sought. The naturalist, while discounting generalizability, nevertheless believes that some degree of transferability is possible if enough ''thick description'' is available about both sending and receiving contexts to make a reasoned judgment possible.

Dependability. In the rationalist paradigm, reliability is a matter of replicability; a study ought to be *repeatable* under the same circumstances in another place and time. If there are discrepancies or deviations between two repetitions of the same study, the difference is charged to unreliability (error). The naturalist cannot be so cavalier, however, because, first, designs are emergent so that changes are built in with conscious intent, and second, emergent design prevents an exact replication of a study in any event (since a second inquirer might choose a different path from the same data). The naturalist defines the concept of dependability to mean *stability* after discounting such conscious and unpredictable (but logical) changes.

Confirmability. As Scriven (1971) has noted, the rationalistic concept of objectivity is based on a quantitative notion of inter-subjective agreement. But clearly, 50 million Frenchmen can be and have been wrong; what is important is not that there be quantitative agreement but qualitative confirmability. The onus of objectivity ought, therefore, to be removed from the inquirer and placed on the data; it is not inquirer certifiability in which we are interested, but in data confirmability.

It is premature to expect that naturalists would have evolved as sophisticated a methodology for dealing with trustworthiness as have rationalists, especially since the latter have had literally centuries to work on refinements. However, Guba (1981) has attempted what he himself characterized as a primitive effort. His formulations will be summarized here by way of illustration of the proposition that methods of dealing with the trustworthiness of naturalistic inquiries are forthcoming and can be expected to be expanded on in the near future (Lincoln & Guba, *forthcoming*).

With respect to *credibility,* Guba suggests the following as means either to safeguard against loss of credibility or to continually test for it:

Prolonged engagement at a site: to overcome distortions introduced by the inquirer's presence, to test for ethnocentrism (Lincoln & Guba, 1981), to test biases and perceptions of both inquirer and respondents, and to provide time to identify salient characteristics of both the context and the problem.

Persistent observation: to gain a high degree of acquaintance with and *verstehen* of pervasive qualities and salient characteristics, to come to appreciate atypical but critical characteristics, and to eliminate those which are irrelevant.

Peers debriefing: to keep the inquirer honest, to provide him or her with the opportunity to test his or her growing insights against those of uninvolved peers, to receive advice about important methodological steps in the emergent design, to leave an audit trail (see below), and to discharge personal feelings, anxieties, and stresses which might otherwise affect the inquiry adversely.

Triangulation: whereby a variety of data sources, different perspectives or theories, different methods, and even different investigators are pitted against one another in order to cross-check data and interpretation (Denzin, 1978).

Referential adequacy materials: that is, documents films, videotapes, audio recordings, pictures, and other raw or slice-of-life materials are collected during the study and archived without analysis; these materials can later be utilized by the inquirer or others, especially an auditor (see below), to test interpretations made from other analyzed data.

Member checks: whereby data and interpretations are continually checked with members of various groups from which data are solicited; done on a continuous basis throughout the study and again at the end when the full report is assembled, using the same members from whom the data were originally collected or other surrogates from the same groups, or both.

   With respect to *transferability,* Guba has suggested that the inquirer engage in, or provide:

Theoretical/purposive sampling: that is, sampling intended to maximize the range of information which is collected and to provide most stringent conditions for theory grounding.

Thick description: by which is meant providing enough information about a context, first, to impart a vicarious experience of it and second, to facilitate judgments about the extent to which working hypotheses from that context might be transferable to a second and similar context.

   With respect to *dependability,* Guba has suggested:

Use of overlap methods: one kind of triangulation process, which, while usually advocated in support of validity, also undergirds claims of reliability to the extent that they produce complementary results.

Stepwise replication: a kind of split-halves approach in which inquirers and data sources are split into two roughly equal halves to be investigated independently, provided, however, that there is frequent exchange between the two teams to allow for the common development and unfolding of an emergent design.

The dependability audit: modelled on the fiscal audit, but limited to that part of the auditor's role which deals with *process.* In a fiscal audit, the first concern of an auditor is whether the accounts were kept in one of the several modes that constitute acceptable professional practice; to reach that judgment the auditor must, of course, be supplied with an "audit trail," which delineates all methodological steps and decision points and which provides access to all data in their several raw and processed stages.

   With respect to *confirmability,* Guba has proffered:

Triangulation: as described above.

Practicing reflexivity: that is, attempting to uncover one's underlying epistemological assumptions, reasons for formulating the study in a particular way, and heretofore implicit assumptions, biases or prejudices about the context or problem. The most appropriate means for this exploration and presentation takes the form of a reflexive journal, kept in the field.

The confirmability audit,   a counterpart to the dependability audit, in which the auditor takes the additional step of verifying that each finding can be traced back through the several analysis steps to the original data and that interpretations of data clusters are reasonable and meaningful, in much the same way that a fiscal auditor would verify at least a sample of entries in a bookkeeping journal to be certain that each represented a *real* transaction and that the *bottom line* accurately represented the current fiscal situation (Lincoln & Guba, 1982).

   The criteria posed, while not theoretically elegant formulations, do have utility at several stages of the inquiry process; they aid reviewers in making *a priori* judgments about the quality of proposed research; they aid the inquirer in monitoring himself or herself and in guiding activities in the field; and, finally, they may be used to render ex post facto judgments on the products of research, including reports, case studies, or proposed publications. The final reports ought at the very least to include — as do rationalistic paradigm reports — statements about what the inquirer actually did to satisfy each of the four sets of criteria, and reports from dependability and confirmability auditors (if used) concerning their verification of his or her processes and conclusions.

   Carrying out even all of these steps (usually not logistically or fiscally possible in an actual inquiry) will not guarantee the trustworthiness of a naturalistic study, but will contribute greatly toward persuading a reader and consumer of the data's meaningfulness.

Summary

We have tried to argue here that we are in the midst of a paradigmatic revolution (Kuhn, 1970), centered about the growing concern that the paradigm which has typically been utilized for scientific (hard and life sciences) inquiry has served poorly when applied to the social and behavioral sciences. It is time for a new paradigm, which takes account of the nature of social experience. We believe that paradigm to be the naturalistic.

   The naturalistic paradigm has emerged, in part, from intense scrutiny of the assumptions and epistemological axioms which undergird rationalistic inquiry. We have tried to make explicit the nature of the epistemological assumptions essential to the two paradigms and have addressed persistent criticism that the latter is soft, non-rigorous, and attentive to relevance over rigor.

While it is true that rationalistic inquirers do not accept the axioms we have imputed to them here without reservation, we have tried to deal with them in their purest form, as they can be traced through the philosophy of science and scientific writers. By doing so, we believe, the reader is able to see the sharpest of contrasts and to understand better why it is maintained that there can be no compromise on axiomatic assumptions (just as one cannot accept a compromise between Euclidean and Lobachevskian geometry), although there may be compromises on various postures that are typically ascribed to the two paradigms.

Thus, we have accounted for five major axiomatic differences: the nature of reality, the nature of the inquirer-object (or respondent) relationship, the nature of truth statements, assumptions about causal relationships, and the role of values within disciplined inquiry. Along those assumptions, we have argued, there can be no compromise. The inquirer must choose one set of assumptions (axioms) or another to undergird his inquiry. The choice is an empirical issue, determined by fit.

Along certain other dimensions, called *postures,* however, compromise may be possible, although we would argue that, like dominoes, one choice may impel the inquirer to make other choices which traditionally have characterized naturalistic inquiry.

Finally, we have argued that, while several centuries of rationalistic inquiry has allowed the development of rather strict and inviolable canons of rigor, the naturalistic school is only beginning to develop an arsenal of weapons against the charge of non-rigor or untrustworthiness. We have demonstrated that it is possible to consider the questions of internal validity, external validity, reliability, and objectivity within the framework of naturalism, but argued for concepts which are more germane — credibility, transferability, dependability and confirmability. We proposed criteria by which external reviewers of naturalistic research might judge the trustworthiness of those studies. While these criteria do not provide unassailable defenses against charges of untrustworthiness, they nevertheless assure the consumer of such research that appropriate steps have been taken to produce data from human sources and contexts that are meaningful, trackable, verifiable, and grounded in the real-life situations from which they were derived.

The naturalistic paradigm seems to us to have much to recommend it. We urge that it be given a fair trial.

Notes

1.   In previous writing (Guba, 1978, 1981; Guba & Lincoln, 1981), we have referred to what we here call the rationalistic paradigm as the *scientistic* or the *scientific* paradigm. The use of even the less pejorative of these latter two terms now seems to us inappropriate on two counts. First, readers have

tended to view the naturalistic paradigm as *less* scientific (or even as nonscientific), and have, therefore, denigrated it as less valid. Second, several critics have accused us of setting up a straw man, on the grounds that vanguard scientific thinkers have moved beyond the nineteenth century logical positivism of which our descriptions are at times reminiscent. It is undoubtedly true that many scientists now think differently, but that change does *not* characterize, in our opinion, the large majority of scientists who engage in inquiries in either the hard or soft sciences. It is to that level of practice that our criticisms are directed, and it is of that moribund culture that are descriptions are apt. However, to avoid the unintended meanings that some readers have drawn from our work, we have shifted to the term *rationalistic* to describe the paradigm that guides so much conventional inquiry.

2.   An appreciation of the constraints which this limitation places on the subsequent discussion is crucial to an understanding of the points we will make. We are not dealing with tangible objects, events, or processes as would the physicist, chemist, or biologist. Nor do we mean to include those aspects of human studies that can be labeled as genetically or developmentally mediated. Study of such matters is undoubtedly better guided by the rationalistic paradigm than by the naturalistic. We *are* dealing, however, with the large majority of studies undertaken by psychologists, sociologists, anthropologists, educational researchers, and evaluators — including evaluations of other social-process fields such as social work, law enforcement, or health services delivery.

3.   We find the use of the term *object* of inquiry, when applied to a human, pejorative; we prefer the term *respondent,* which carries the connotations of interaction and equality.

4.   For two instances of value-resonance problems, see Guba (1982) in the field of reading and Lincoln (1982) in the field of special education.

5.   It is ironic that the naturalist does permit the data to "speak for themselves" in the sense of grounding theory in them, a use never contemplated by the rationalists who are fond of using that phrase as an assertion of their objectivity.

6.   The distinction made here is similar to that between a connoisseur and a critic of art. The connoisseur need only "feel" a painting to appreciate it; the critic must cast his feelings into language in order to convey his critique. Connoisseurship is a private art, but criticism is a public art (Eisner, 1979).

References

1.   Bahm, A.J. "Science is not value-free." *Policy Sciences,* 2 (1981), 391–6.

2.   Campbell, D.T., and Stanley, J.C. "Experimental and quasi-experimental designs for research on teaching." In: N.L. Gage (ed.), *Handbook of Research on Teaching.* Chicago, Illinois: Rand, McNally and Company, 1963.

3.   Cook, T.D. and Campbell, D.T. *Quasi-Experimentation: Design and Analysis Issues for Field Settings.* Chicago, Illinois: Rand, McNally and Company, 1979.

4.   Cook, T.D., and Reichardt, C.I. (eds.) *Qualitative and Quantitative Methods in Evaluation Research.* Beverly Hills, California: Sage Publications, 1979.

5.   Cronbach, L.J. Beyond the two disciplines of scientific psychology. *American Psychologist,* 30 (1975), 116–27.

6.   Cronbach, L.J. and Suppes, P. *Research for Tomorrow's Schools: Disciplined Inquiry in Education.* New York, New York: Macmillan Company, 1969.

7.   Denzin, Norman K. "The logic of naturalistic inquiry." In: Norman K. Denzin, (ed.) *Sociological Methods: A Sourcebook.* New York, New York: McGraw-Hill Publishing Co., 1978.

8.   Eisner, Elliot, *The Educational Imagination.* New York, New York: The Macmillan Company, 1979.

9. Filstead, W.J. "Qualitative methods: a needed perspective in evaluation research."
    In: T.D. Cook and C.I. Reichardt (eds.), *Qualitative and Quantitative Methods in
    Evaluation Research*. Beverly Hills, California: Sage Publications, 1979.
10. Glaser, B.G., and Strauss, A.L. *The Discovery of Grounded Theory*. Chicago,
    Illinois: Aldine Publishing Company, 1967.
11. Guba, Egon G. *Toward a Methodology of Naturalistic Inquiry in Educational Evalua-
    tion*. Monograph Series, no. 8. Los Angeles, California: Center for the Study of
    Evaluation, University of California, 1978.
12. Guba, Egon G. "Criteria for assessing the trustworthiness of naturalistic inquiries."
    Educational Communication and Technology Journal, 29 (1981), 75–92.
13. Guba, Egon G. "The search for truth: naturalistic inquiry as an option." Paper
    presented at the annual meeting of the International Reading Association, Chicago,
    Illinois, April 1982.
14. Guba, Egon G., and Lincoln, Yvonna S. *Effective Evaluation*. San Francisco,
    California: Jossey-Bass Publishers, 1981.
15. Hofstadter, D.R. *Gödel, Escher, Bach: An Eternal Golden Braid*. New York, New
    York: Basic Books, 1979.
16. Homans, G.A. "What kind of a myth is the myth of a value free social science?"
    Social Science Quarterly, 58 (1978), 530–41.
17. Kelman, H.C. *A Time to Speak: On Human Values and Social Research*. San
    Francisco, California: Jossey-Bass Publishers, 1979.
18. Krathwohl, D.R. "The myth of value-free evaluation." *Educational Evaluation and
    Policy Analysis*, 2 (1980), 37–45.
19. Kuhn, T.S. *The Structure of Scientific Revolutions*. International Encyclopedia of
    Unified Science. Vol. 2, no. 2 (2nd ed.). Chicago, Illinois: University of Chicago
    Press, 1970.
20. Lincoln, Yvonna S. "The utility of naturalistic inquiry for special education studies."
    Paper presented at the annual meeting of the Council on Exceptional Children,
    Houston, Texas, April 1982.
21. Lincoln, Yvonna S. and Guba, Egon G. "Do evaluators wear grass skirts? Going
    native and ethnocentrism as problems of utilization in evaluation." Paper presented to
    the Joint Annual Meeting of the Evaluation Network and the Evaluation Research
    Society, Austin, Texas, September 1981.
22. Lincoln, Yvonna S. and Guba, Egon G. "Establishing Dependability and Confirma-
    bility in Naturalistic Inquiry Through An Audit." Paper presented at the American
    Educational Research Association, New York, April 1982.
23. Lincoln, Yvonna S., and Guba, Egon G. *Issues in Naturalistic Inquiry*. In preparation.
24. Mill, J.S. *A System of Logic* (1843). New York, New York: Longmans, Green, and
    Company, 1947.
25. Polanyi, M. *The Tacit Dimension*. New York, New York: Doubleday and Company, 1966.
26. Scriven, M. "Objectivity and subjectivity in educational research." In: L.G. Thomas
    (ed.) *Philosophical Redirection of Educational Research*. 71st Yearbook of the
    National Society for the Study of Education. Part 1. Chicago, Illinois: University of
    Chicago Press, 1971.
27. Tranel, Daniel D. "A lesson from the physicists." *Personnel and Guidance Journal*,
    59 (1981), 425–8.

28.   Webb, E. et al. *Unobtrusive Measures*. Chicago, Illinois: Rand McNally and Company, 1966.
29.   Weir, Eric. "Types of explanation in educational evaluation." *Paper and Report Series,* no. 34. Research on Evaluation Project, Northwest Regional Educational Laboratory, Portland, Oregon: The Laboratory, 1980.
30.   Wiles, D.K. "The logic of $Y = f(X)$ in the study of educational politics." *Educational Evaluation and Policy Analysis,* 3 (1981), 67–74.

19 EDUCATIONAL CONNOISSEURSHIP AND CRITICISM: Their Form and Functions in Educational Evaluation

Elliot W. Eisner

The major thesis of this paper is that the forms used in conventional approaches to educational evaluation have a set of profound consequences on the conduct and character of schooling in the United States. Unless those forms can be expanded so that they attend to qualities of educational life relevant to the arts, it is not likely that the arts will secure a meaningful place in American schools. To understand why we evaluate the way that we do, it is important to examine the sources through which evaluation became a kind of field within American education. If we examine the past, we will find that since the turn of the century, since the early work of Edward L. Thorndike, there has been a strong aspiration among psychologists to create a science of education which would provide educational practitioners — administrators as well as teachers — with the kind of knowledge that would permit prediction through control of the process and consequences of schooling. Laws that would do for educational practitioners what the work of Einstein, Maxwell, and Bohr have done for physicists were the object of the educational scientist's dream. This yearning for prediction through control was, of

Eisner, Elliot W. "Educational Connoisseurship and Criticism: Their Form and Functions in Educational Evaluation." *Journal of Aesthetic Education*, nos. 3–4, 10 (July–October 1976), 135–50. Copyright 1976 University of Illinois Press, Champaign, Illinois. Reprinted by permission of author and publisher.

course, reflected in the desire to make schools more efficient and, presumably, more effective. Educational research was to discover the laws of learning that would replace intuition and artistry with knowledge and prescribed method. The hunt was on for the one best method to teach the various fields of study that constituted the curriculum. This aspiration to discover the laws of learning was allied with the efficiency movement in education that sought to install scientific management procedures in schools through time-and-motion study of teaching practice.[1] It reflected then, as it does today, the need to discover the principles and practices that would give us efficient and effective schools.

This desire was, of course, based upon a particular view of the world and of man's position within it. That view was scientific in character. The task of educational research was to treat educational practice as a nomothetic activity, one guided by the unique characteristics of the particular situation. Describing the philosophic differences between the nomothetic and the ideographic, George Henrik von Wright writes:

> All these thinkers [Droysen, Dilthey, Simmel, Max Weber, Windelband, Rickert, Croce, and Collingwood] reject the methodological monism of positivism and refuse to view the pattern set by the exact natural sciences as the sole and supreme ideal for a rational understanding of reality. Many of them emphasize a contrast between those sciences which, like physics or chemistry or physiology, aim at generalizations about reproducible and predictable phenomena, and those which, like history, want to grasp the individual and unique features of their objects. Windelband coined the label ''nomo-thetic'' for sciences which search for laws, and ''ideographic'' for the descriptive study of individuality.[2]

As for evaluation practices, they were to be objective; that is, they were to describe in quantitative, empirical terms whether or not the goals of the curriculum were achieved.

If I dwell upon these matters of the past, it is because I believe they are crucial for understanding what we do today and why. Arts education might not be possible except in the skimpiest form in institutions that are controlled by unexamined assumptions which create a climate, establish a tone, and foster a set of priorities that are inhospitable to the kind of life that work in the arts might yield. Although scientific and technological approaches to the methods of schooling have made some important contributions, I believe they have had at least four major deleterious consequences. Let me identify these.

First, because scientific assumptions and scientifically oriented inquiry aim at the search for laws or law-like generalizations, such inquiry tends to treat qualities of particular situations as instrumentalities. The uniqueness of the particular is considered ''noise'' in the search for general tendencies and main effects. This, in turn, leads to the oversimplification of the particular through a process of reduction aimed at the characterization of complexity by a single set of scores. Quality becomes converted to quantity and then summed and averaged as a way of standing for the particular quality from which the quantities were initially derived. For the evaluation of educational practice and its consequences, the single numerical test score is used to symbolize a universe of particulars, in spite of the fact that the number symbol itself possesses no inherent quality that expresses the quality of the particular it is intended to represent.

The distinction between symbols that possess in their form the expressive content to which they are related and those symbols which, through associative learning, we relate to certain ideas is an extremely important one. The art symbol exemplifies the former, while the word or number exemplifies the latter. Scientific activity yields propositions so that truth can be determined in relation to its instrumental value, a value dependent upon its predictive or explanatory accuracy. Artistic activity creates symbolic forms, which themselves present directly an idea, image, or feeling which resides within rather than outside of the symbol.

Second, the technological orientation to practice tends to encourage a primary focus on the achievement of some future state and, in the process, tends to undermine the significance of the present. Take, as an example, the concern in recent years with the formulation of behavioral objectives. Objectives are things that are always out of reach. They are goals towards which one works, targets we are urged to keep our eyes upon. Objectives are future-oriented, and when the future becomes increasingly important to us, we sacrifice the present in order to achieve it. In elementary schools, both teachers and students are bedeviled by extrinsic rewards, such as token economies. Children are rewarded for the achievement of objectives that themselves have little intrinsic appeal, and teachers may one day be paid in relation to their ability to produce certain measurable outcomes. When the future becomes all-important, it must be achieved at all costs. At the secondary level, it leads to the pursuit of high scores on scholastic achievement tests and at the university level to the destruction of experiments and the stealing of books in pre-med programs. Not only must objectives be achieved, but one must also be sure that others do not achieve them. The present is sacrificed on the altar of tomorrow.

Third, scientific and technological approaches to schooling lead, as I have already said, to the attempt to *objectify* knowledge. Objectification almost always requires that at least two conditions be met. First, the qualities to which one attends must be empirically manifest, and second, they must be convertible to quantity. In this way, both reliability and precision can be assured; hence, conclusions about a state of affairs can be verified.

That these procedures themselves rest upon certain beliefs which cannot themselves be verified by procedures that the beliefs espouse, does not seem to pose a problem for those who espouse them. But, in addition, these procedures, based as they are on a particular conception of truth, also bring with them some negative injunctions. For example, one must not emotionalize one's language when talking about children, educational practice, or educational goals. Intimation, metaphor, analogy, and poetic insight have little place in such a view. For example, instead of talking about children, we are urged to talk about subjects. Instead of talking about teaching, we must talk about treatments, Instead of talking about aims and aspirations, we must talk about dependent variables, performance objectives, or competencies. And to increase *objectivity,* instead of talking in the first person singular, the third person singular or first person plural is better form. Somehow, if *the author* or *we* conclude something, it is more objective than if *I* do.

This shift in language would not present much of a problem if it only represented a shift in language, but the problem exceeds the matter of language per se. It is a symptom of a larger difficulty encountered in trying to understand human beings. The problem is that in de-emotionalizing expression and proscribing suggestive language, the opportunity to understand empathically and to communicate the quality of human experience diminishes. As long as measurable forms of manifest behavior are our exclusive referent, the quality of experience will be neglected. Inference about experience has little place in radical behaviorism, but radical behaviorism, exemplified in the work of Thorndike, Watson, Hull, and Skinner, has held a central place in American educational psychology. To know what people feel, to know what behavior *means,* we must go beyond behavior.[3]

Fourth, when one seeks laws governing the control of human behavior, it is not surprising that one would also seek the achievement of a common set of goals for that behavior. When one combines this with the need to operationalize such goals quantitatively, the use of standardized tests becomes understandable. The standardized test *is* standard; it is the same for all students. It not only standardizes the tasks students will confront, it standardizes the goals against which they shall be judged. These tests, de facto, become the goals. When this happens, uniformity becomes an aspiration; effectiveness means, in practice, that all students will achieve the same ends. Individualization, regardless of what it might mean, becomes defined in terms of providing for differences in rate; differentiation in pace rather than in goal, content, or mode of expression is the general meaning of individualization. Standardized achievement tests do not now provide the means for assessing the significant personalization of teaching and learning. In a technological orientation to educational practice, the cultivation of productive idiosyncracy — one of the prime consequences of work in the arts — becomes a problem.

The major points that I have been trying to make thus far are two. First, the forms of evaluation that are now employed to assess the effectiveness of school programs have profound consequences upon the character of teaching, the content of curriculum, and the kinds of goals that schools seek to attain. Evaluation procedures, more than a reasoned philosophy of education, influence the educational priorities at work within the schools. Second, these evaluation procedures rest upon largely unexamined assumptions that are basically scientific in their epistemology, technological in their application, and have consequences that are often limited and at times inhospitable to the kinds of goals the arts can achieve.

Recognition of the assumptions, character, and consequences of conventional forms of educational evaluation is insufficient to bring about change in the ways in which we evaluate. Something more must be provided. That something more is an alternative or a complement to what now prevails, and it is the articulation and testing of this alternative that my present work aims at.

I have chosen to start with a set of premises about education that are quite different from those underlying the dominant conventional approaches to educational evaluation and to the study of educational practice. I do not believe that education as a process, or schooling as an institution designed to foster that process, or teaching as an activity that most directly mediates that process, is likely to be controlled by a set of laws that can be transformed into a prescription or recipe for teaching. I do not believe we will ever have a ''Betty Crocker'' theory of education. Teaching is an activity that requires artistry; schooling itself is a cultural artifact; and education is a process whose features may differ from individual to individual, context to context. Therefore, what I believe we need to do with respect to educational evaluation is not to seek recipes to control and measure practice, but rather to enhance whatever artistry the teacher can achieve. Theory plays a role in the cultivation of artistry, but its role is not prescriptive; it is diagnostic. Good theory in education, as in art, helps us to see more; it helps us think about more of the qualities that constitute a set of phenomena. Theory does not replace intelligence and perception and action; it provides some of the windows through which intelligence can look out into the world. Thus, one of the functions that theory might serve in educational evaluation is in the cultivation of *educational connoisseurship*.[4]

Educational connoisseurship, about which I will have more to say momentarily, is but half of a pair of concepts that I believe to be particularly promising for thinking about the conduct of educational evaluation. The other half of this pair is the concept of *educational criticism*. Each of these concepts, educational connoisseurship and educational criticism, have their roots in the arts — and for good reason. Because I believe teaching in classrooms is ideographic in character, that is, because I believe the features of classroom life are not likely to be explained or controlled by behavioral laws, I conceive the major contribution of evaluation to be a heightened awareness of the qualities of that life so that teachers and students can become more intelligent within it. Connoisseurship plays an important role towards this end by refining the levels of apprehension of the qualities that pervade classrooms. To be a connoisseur of wine, bicycles, or graphic arts is to be informed about their qualities; it means being able to discriminate the subtleties among types of wine, bicycles, and graphic arts by drawing upon a gustatory, visual, and kinesthetic memory against which the particulars of the present may be placed for purposes of comparison and contrast. Connoisseurs of anything — and one can have connoisseurship about anything — *appreciate* what they encounter in the proper meaning of that word. Appreciation does not necessarily mean liking something, although one might like what one experiences. Appreciation here means an awareness and an understanding of what one has experienced. Such an awareness provides the basis for judgment.

If connoisseurship is the art of appreciation, criticism is the art of disclosure. Criticism, as Dewey pointed out in *Art as Experience,* has at its end the re-education of perception.[5] What the critic strives for is to articulate or render those ineffable qualities constituting art in a language that makes them vivid. But this gives rise to something of a paradox. How is it that what is ineffable can be articulated? How do words express what words can never express? The task of the critic is to adumbrate, suggest, imply, connote, render, rather than to attempt to translate.[6] In this task, metaphor and analogy, suggestion and implication are major tools. The language of criticism, indeed its success as criticism, is measured by the brightness of its illumination. The task of the critic is to help us to see.

It is thus seen from what I have said that connoisseurship provides criticism with its subject matter. Connoisseurship is private, but criticism is public. Connoisseurs simply need to appreciate what they encounter. Critics, however, must render these qualities vivid by the artful use of critical disclosure. Effective criticism requires the use of connoisseurship, but connoisseurship does not require the use of criticism.

What is also clear, when one thinks about it, is that education as a field of study does not have — as does literature, music, the visual arts, drama, and film — a branch called educational criticism. Yet educational practice and the outcomes of such practice are subject to critical techniques. We do not have, for example, journals of educational criticism or critical theory. We do not have programs in universities that prepare educational critics. We do not have a tradition of thought dealing with the formal, systematic, scholarly study and practice of educational criticism. My work at Stanford is aimed at precisely these goals. With a group of doctoral students I have, over the past two years, been attempting to flesh out the issues, the concepts, the criteria, the techniques, and the prototypes of educational connoisseurship and educational criticism. To do this, we have been visiting schools around Stanford to study classrooms and to create criticism, and we have been creating educational criticism within Stanford University itself by critically describing the classrooms and courses offered within the School of Education. In addition, we have been making videotapes of classrooms and have been using these as a basis for our own education and the testing of our own criticism. Thus far, two doctoral dissertations[7] have been completed in which educational criticism is the major conceptual tool; and two more doctoral students, whose dissertations also employ educational criticism as a dominant mode of inquiry, will receive their degrees in June 1976. In short, we have been working at the task of creating a new way of looking at the phenomena that constitute educational life within classrooms.

In pursuing these aims, we have engaged in a kind of dialectic between the conceptualization of educational connoisseurship and educational criticism as theoretical categories and the actual writing of criticism and its attendant problems, such as what the role of the educational critic is when that person is in a classroom. This dialectic has informed both aspects of our work, the theoretical and the practical. Before I share with you an example of our work, let me say a few words about three major aspects of educational criticism.

What is it that one does when one writes educational criticism of a classroom, or a set of curriculum materials, or a school? There are three things that one does. One describes, one interprets, and one evaluates or appraises what one sees.

The descriptive aspect of educational criticism (and these three distinctions are not intended to suggest that they are independent or sequential) is an effort to characterize or render the pervasive and purely descriptive aspects of the phenomena one attends to. For example, critical description might tell the reader about the number or type of questions raised in a class, the amount of time spent in discussion, or the kind of image or impression the teacher or the room gives to visitors. Descriptive educational criticism is a type of portrayal of the qualities that one encounters without getting into — very deeply, at least — what they signify. Following Clifford Geertz, the descriptive aspect of criticism is fairly thin, although we recognize that all description has some degree of thickness to it. Let me give you an example of what is largely descriptive educational criticism written by one of my students.

Last Thursday morning I visited the auditorium of San Francisco's James Lick Junior High School. I had already stood in this room many times, for many years, in many schools. Recent visits remind me how my body has grown taller and heavier. The scuffed floorboards' squeaks feel less congenial. The looming balcony now appears less exotic. My eyes no longer trace geometric patterns in the familiar tan ceiling.

Although I lean on the rear wall, I feel close up to the stage. Between it and me wait twin sections of permanent wooden seats, each twelve across and maybe twenty-five rows deep. In front of the first row I watch the busy pit area, where several adults, some with flash cameras, mingle purposefully amid a baby grand piano, a drum set, several stools and benches, three conga drums, a folding table holding a tenor saxophone in its open case, and two microphone stands. Dark curtains close the raised stages.

About half the seats, those in the rear, are empty. The front half of the auditorium contains an exquisite kaleidoscope of several hundred junior high kids — standing, sitting, turning, squirming, tugging, slapping, squealing, calling, talking, clapping, laughing, waving. A few stare silent and motionless. Most smile. They make a multicultural mix, of obscure proportions. Here and there an adult, probably a teacher, joins the crowd or stands back to oversee.

Their combined voices swell ceaselessly, like the ocean's face, as though smiling in rhythm with the crowd's surging spirit. Occasionally a single voice calls or whistles to jar this bussing blanket's penetrating caress.

From behind the curtain, a grinning, slim, gray-haired man in a dark blue suit walks down to the audience, talks briefly with someone, picks up the tenor sax, and returns backstage. He leaves the curtains parted about a foot, revealing there people hurrying across the bright stage in last-minute urgency. Indistinct musical sounds from backstage join the audience's hum.

Small groups of kids from nearby schools file in quickly, filling all the remaining seats.

A man carrying a guitar peers out through the curtain, and then walks down to the pit, followed by the tenor sax man. They greet several adults already standing there in the right-hand corner.

A spotlight focuses several different size circles on the curtain. The lights onstage darken. The kids quiet, and their adults come to stand along the walls.

A serious-looking man of average build and thin, straight, gray hair, wearing dark slacks, a dark brown turtleneck shirt, and a beige sportcoat, strides directly to the microphone in the center of the pit. In the next ten minutes he and two other adults greet the audience and progressively, systematically introduce the morning's program and their guest, Mr. John Birks Gillespie. The last speaker — Mr. Smith, the school's music director — is the tenor sax player. His final words succumb to the kids' impatient applause.

Now, from the right corner, Dizzy Gillespie struts playfully across to the microphone — a middle-aged Tom Sawyer in a bulky, white, knit cap that hints broadly toward mischief. A brash musical rebel and innovator thirty-five years ago, now Dizzy is a jovial, stocky, black man, with faint white hairs on his chin. Clutching his spangled trumpet against a black-and-white checked sportcoat which reveals his dazzling red shirt, he thanks Mr. Smith and greets his audience.

Hearing his first words, I expect to see Louis Armstrong's eyes and Bill Cosby's grin. Dizzy savors his voice; it flows gently — slow-paced and melodic. His audience sits rapt. Their posture shifts with his frequent vocal pitch and tempo modulations. I can barely recall the kids' homogenized chatter from a few minutes earlier.

For about ten minutes, he shares comfortable, chuckly stories about his trumpet and his own music education. Everyone seems to be listening, alert and smiling, and commenting with commotion, which Dizzy encourages.

Abruptly, he announces "What we're gonna do now is play for you," and with one foot he taps 1 . . . 2 . . . 1, 2, 3, 4. The drummer and two guitar players, who followed his entrance, now lean into a comfortable number, which Dizzy leads in a moderate tempo. The piece seems unfamiliar to the kids, and they respond to the contrast between its tasty, pattering verse and the soaring chorus. All through the tune, the kids focus their attention on Dizzy, himself. Perhaps sensing this, he plays with their enthusiasm, making games for all to share. For example, turning to face the lead guitar player toward the end of the tune, he dances and sways while the guitar solos a chorus. Simultaneously, many kids are bouncing in their seats.

As the applause following this number dwindles, Dizzy cries out "Como estas usted?" and, responding to the kids' shouted replies, he announces that the next selection will be Latin. As though addressing a favorite toy, he sits behind the conga drums, develops a minute-long monologue about rhythm in jazz, and clowns with his face and voice while adjusting the microphone stand.

He describes a call-and-response routine for the song, demonstrates the kids' part (they fling their right fists while shouting "Oh!") and its cue (he sings a call), and drills them in the routine a few times. The kids conclude each practice with applause, laughter, and chatter; and they seem eager for more. Continuing, Dizzy announces that many people clap their hands on the wrong beats. They should clap on "two and four, as in 'oom-cha, oom-cha, oom-cha.' '' By now the kids are clapping solidly on the off-beats. Dizzy lets them take a few more measures and, with the other three musicians, begins the song.

He arches over the three congas with eyes closed, eyebrows raised, mouth slack open, and head pointing up to the right corner of the balcony. As though keeping six apples submerged in three pails of water, he moves his hands intently, rapidly, and gracefully. The kids find themselves creating part of the music they hear. Many clap, smile, talk, watch, and listen. Few are quiet. No one seems bored. Everyone seems involved.

Leaning toward the mike, Dizzy leads several repetitions of the kids' call-and-response routine. He returns briefly to the congas, before stepping up with his trumpet, which he plays, eyes closed, pointing the horn's bell to the same corner of the balcony. Returning to the mike, he chants a hushed "Swing low, sweet chariot, . . ." Opening his eyes and raising his hands, he replies, ". . . coming for to carry me home." The kids join this response and continue singing these familiar lyrics to their conclusion. Now standing upright, Dizzy sings a series of scat breaks — bursts of explosive syllables cogently declaring an impromptu rhythmic notion. Many kids answer each break by singing back its echo. Finally, he surprises us with an extended, complicated break. The kids respond with applause and laughter, and Dizzy ends the number here, laughing himself.[8]

The interpretive aspect of educational criticism represents an effort to understand the meaning and significance that various forms of action have for those in a social setting. For example, just what do the extrinsic rewards for reading mean to the third graders who keep charts of the number of books that they have read? What do the eager, outstretched, waving arms and hands signify to both teacher and students when student compete for the opportunity to provide the teacher with the right answer? What kinds of messages are being given to students by the allocation of time and its location in the school day to the various subject matters that constitute the curriculum? To answer these questions requires a journey into interpretation, an ability to participate empathically in the life of another, to appreciate the meanings of such cultural symbols as lists of books read, hand-waving, and time allocation. The interpretive aspect of educational criticism requires the judicious and informed use of a variety of social sciences and the practical wisdom born of experience in schools.

The third aspect of criticism is evaluative. It asks, "What is the *educational* import or value of what is going on?" To deal with the educational import of classroom life is, of course, to do more than to describe or to interpret it; it is to make some value judgments about it with respect to its educational significance. It is this aspect of educational criticism that most sharply differentiates the work of the educational critic from the work of an ethnographer, psychologist, or sociologist. Educational critics ultimately appraise what they encounter with a set of educational criteria; they judge the educational value of what they see. To make educational value judgments requires not only the ability to see educational subtleties occurring in the classroom and to be able to interpret their meaning or explain the functions they serve; it is also to have a background sufficiently rich in educational theory, educational philosophy, and educational history to be able to understand the values implied by the ongoing activities and the alternatives that might have otherwise been employed.

This latter aspect of the evaluative character of educational criticism — to be able to consider the alternatives that might have been employed — requires also a sense of the practical realities of classroom life. Each of us undoubtedly holds some pristine vision of educational virtue that we would like to see schools display, yet most of us realize that these images of educational virtue are seldom fully realized. Practical contingencies keep intruding. Lest we come down too hard on situations that do not live up to our highest hopes, it is important to recognize what is and what is not possible in the course of daily educational life.

Thus, the ultimate consequence of educational criticism is evaluative in the sense that something must be made of what has been described and interpreted. The task of the critic is not simply one of being a neutral observer (an impossible position in any case), nor is it one of disinterested interpretation. The critic uses what he or she sees and interprets in order to arrive at some conclusions about the character of educational practice and its improvement.

Although I have said that educational connoisseurship can have as its subject matter anything that can be perceived or experienced and, by implication, that educational criticism can describe what connoisseurship provides, it is time now to be more specific about what can be attended to in educational practice. What are the potential candidates for critical attention? Obviously the particular functions criticism is to serve and the particular audience to which it is directed will influence, if not determine, what is criticized and how it is shared. Yet, in general one can focus upon the qualities of the relationship that exists between teacher and student and the kinds of devices that the teacher employs to stimulate interest, to reward, to explain, and to manage. Teachers seldom have the opportunity to get informed feedback on their teaching. They read how they are doing in the reflections found in the eyes of children. Although this is a relevant source of information, it is neither an exhaustive nor an adequate one. Informed educational criticism may give teachers a view of their teaching that they simply would never otherwise possess.

The character of the discourse within the classroom is another candidate for critical attention. How do the children participate? What is the quality of what they and the teacher have to say? To what extent do they participate both psychologically and verbally in what transpires? Is their enthusiasm feigned or real? Is what they are learning worth their time and effort? And just what are they learning? Is it what is being taught, or are they learning other things that are conveyed by the manner of teaching and the organization and structure of the school day? What about the materials they use, the textbooks, the learning kits, the visuals with which they come in contact? What do these materials teach? How are they laid out? What does their format suggest? What messages are held between the lines of textbooks, which for so many children occupy central roles in their school experience?

What about the relationships among the children themselves? Is it competitive or cooperative? Is the class a collection of individuals or a community? What is the pervasive quality of educational life that children in this particular classroom lead? How is time allocated within the school day? How are the various subjects taught? What values are conveyed by the ways in which time and space decisions have been made?

What is the quality of the work that children create? What is the character of their expression — verbal, written, visual, and musical? Over time, what kind of development is evident? In what ways is the development of intellectual curiosity and autonomy displayed? In what ways are they treated when they are expressed?

These questions represent some of the potential candidates for attention in the effort to create telling educational criticism. To be sure, these very questions reflect a conception of educational value. Only a fool would choose to attend to the trivial.

Finally, I wish to say a few words about the problems of validity, or, put another way, can educational criticism be trusted?

In determining the validity of educational criticism — that is, whether there is any justification for what the critic says is happening, what it means, and what its educational worth is — we discover three possible sources of disagreement between two or more critics. You will recall that I said that educational criticism has three aspects: descriptive, interpretive, and evaluative. Two critics, for example, might agree on what is occurring, agree on what it signifies, but disagree on what its educational value is. Or two critics might agree on what is occurring, disagree on what it signifies, but agree on its educational value. This occurs when two people like what they see, but for different reasons. Still another source of disagreement is when two critics see two different things, but agree upon their significance and agree upon their educational value. I am sure you can play out the rest of the hand, but the point is that the reasons why critics might agree or disagree in their critical disclosures are several. One cannot know them without analyzing the grounds or basis of what they have to say.

Although these conditions make the problems of validating educational criticism complex, there are still some useful criteria to apply. One of these criteria deals with determining the extent of structural corroboration within the criticism itself, and another deals with the criticism's referential adequacy.

Structural corroboration is a process that seeks to validate or support one's conclusions about a set of phenomena by demonstrating how a variety of facts or conditions within the phenomena support the conclusions drawn. It is a process of demonstrating that the story hangs together, that the pieces fit. One of the best examples of structural corroboration can be found in Agatha Christie's *Murder on the Orient Express*. What the detective did to solve the puzzling crime was gradually to piece the puzzle together so that the conclusion that all of the passengers on the train had a hand in the murder was cogent. The evidence was persuasive because each component corroborated the other. In the end, a structure was created whose parts held together.

American jurisprudence is largely based upon a combination of structural corroboration and multiplicative corroboration. Structural corroboration is sought as two lawyers present the facts of the case to prove or disprove the innocence or guilt of their client, and multiplicative corroboration is practiced when twelve members of a jury concur or fail to concur that the evidence is sufficiently coherent and cohesive to remove any reasonable doubt.

But one of the liabilities of structural corroboration, as Geertz (1973) has pointed out, is that nothing can be so persuasive and coherent as a swindler's story. Something more must be added.

It is here that referential adequacy comes into play. Since criticism's aim is the re-education of perception, good educational criticism, like good criticism of anything else, should help readers or listeners see more than they would without the benefit of the criticism. In this sense, the test of criticism is empirical, more empirical than numbers usually signify. The test of criticism is empirical in the sense that one asks of the criticism whether the referents it claims to describe, interpret, and evaluate can be found in the phenomena to which it attends. Is the teacher's enthusiasm really infectious? Do the children really support each other? Is the room really a celebration of the senses? The referential adequacy of educational criticism is determined by looking at the phenomena and finding what the critic has described. To the extent that criticism is effective, it should illuminate qualities of teaching and learning that would otherwise go unseen. By making these aspects of educational life visible, the teacher, supervisor, school administrator, or school board member is in a position to make judgments about them. Thus, educational criticism provides educational policy and the more narrowly defined aspects of educational decision making with a wider, more complex base of knowledge upon which to deliberate.

I would like to conclude by coming back full circle to the issues with which I began. Educational evaluation has had a particular tradition in this country. It is one that conceives of knowledge as scientific and believes that precision is a function of quantification. This tradition has made important contributions to the conduct of education; but as an exclusive mode of inquiry, it possesses limits which, in the long run, exclude more from our understanding than they include. The time is ripe for broadening the base from which inquiry in education can go forward. It is time for a more catholic sense of possibility; we need, in my opinion, to widen our epistemology. In practice, this means recognizing that the forms which humans create, the forms of art as well as the forms of science, afford unique opportunities for conceptualization and expression, and hence for communication. What we can know is shaped by the intellectual structures we are able to use. Many of those structures are framed in forms of knowledge that are nondiscursive. Since educational evaluation has, I assume, as its ultimate objective the improvement of the quality of educational life students lead, I see no reason why we should not exploit the various forms of understanding that different knowledge structures can provide. Educational connoisseurship and educational criticism represent two modes through which we come to understand and express what we come to know; but these modes themselves represent only a small portion of the possibilities in the conduct of educational evaluation. Someday we will make use of criticism not only in a poetic or artistically discursive mode, we will exploit the possibilities of film, video, photography, graphic displays, and the like. But that story will have to wait for another paper and another time. What we need today is a breakthrough in conception, a wedge in the door of possibility. Educational connoisseurship and educational criticism, it seems to me, offer some promising possibilities, not only for broadening the base of educational evaluation, but for those of us in the arts committed to the improvement of the process of education.

Notes

1.   Raymond Callahan, *Education and the Cult of Efficiency* (Chicago: University of Chicago Press, 1962), passim.

2.   George Henrik Von Wright, *Explanation and Understanding* (London: Routledge and Kegan Paul, 1971), p. 5.

3.   Clifford Geertz, *The Interpretation of Culture* (New York: Basic Books, Inc. 1973).

4.   Elliot W. Eisner, "The Perceptive Eye: Toward a Reformation of Educational Evaluation" (Invited address, Division B, Curriculum and Objectives, American Educational Research Association, Washington, D.C., March, 1975).

5.   John Dewey, *Art as Experience* (New York: Minton, Balch and Company, 1934).

6.   Max Kozloff, *Renderings* (New York: Simon and Schuster, 1969).

7.   Elizabeth Vallance, *Aesthetic Criticism and Curriculum Description* (Ph.D. dissertation, Stanford University, 1974); Dwaine Greer, *The Criticism of Teaching* (Ph.D. dissertation, Stanford University, 1973).

8.   This descriptive educational criticism was written by one of my doctoral students, Robbie Schlosser. I am grateful for his permission to use his work in this article.

20 THE EXPLICATION MODEL:
An Anthropological Approach to
Program Evaluation
Kent L. Koppelman

A fundamental problem in evaluation models as they have been developed, discussed, and implemented is the dichotomous perception that has underscored many other controversies in education. Educators, like the Roman god Janus, seem to have two opposing views: some perceive education as an art; others perceive it as a science. The artistic perspective insists upon the complexity of the elements in an educational activity, which are inextricably mingled in a dynamic interaction. This interaction is to be viewed and evaluated holistically and subjectively because it cannot be broken down except in artificial ways and therefore cannot be objectively measured. The scientific perspective, reflected by those who emphasize behavioral objectives, does not deny that complexity, but asserts that to understand something we must begin somewhere. We must identify a basis for understanding, and then proceed logically and systematically to further clarify and comprehend the structure and function of the whole. Renzulli (1972) has described the dichotomy this way:

> Two irresistible forces in education seem hell-bent on a collision course, and I am afraid that our friend the evaluator is going to be caught squarely at the point of impact. The first

Koppelman, Kent L. "The Explication Model: An Anthropological Approach to Program Evaluation." *Educational Evaluation and Policy Analysis,* no. 3, 1 (July-August 1979), 59–64. Copyright 1979, American Educational Research Association, Washington, D.C. Reprinted by permission of author and publisher.

irresistible force is the behavioral objectives movement . . . one cannot deny the value that it has had in helping to build evaluation and accountability models and to advance the science of education beyond the vagueness and lack of specificity (of the past). . . . There is still another irresistible force growing in education today — a renewed concern for the total development of the individual as a human being, dealing with such difficult-to-measure objectives as self-actualization, Consciousness III, and sociability. (p. 301)

Evaluation models reflect this dichotomy. The rational design of the Tyler model is admirable, and yet it is difficult to disregard the criticism of the model based on its failure to deal with important aspects of education such as the unintended outcomes of an educational activity. A more subjective approach to evaluation, an ethnography for example, is impressive for its capacity to incorporate unintended outcomes and other subtle aspects of the educational environment, but this approach also has its weaknesses. Ethnography is primarily criticized for its failure to provide an appropriate measure of what the students are learning. In other words it may not do justice to an assessment of measurable behavior. The problem here should not be misunderstood as the need to determine which perspective is correct, but to accept the validity of both and to create evaluation models that attempt to satisfy the basic demands and overcome the obvious weaknesses of both.

It is at this point that anthropology becomes an appropriate area for consideration. Anthropologists have long faced the issue of artistic versus scientific in their approach to field work. Their struggle with this issue is analogous to the perspective dilemma in education because both groups are trying to understand complex human activity and trying to develop or improve methodologies so that accurate and comprehensive results may be obtained. What makes anthropology especially important here is that some anthropologists are coming closer to a synthesis of the art and science perspectives, incorporating many of the advantages of both approaches to field work (Brim & Spain, 1974). They are combining the breadth and insights of subjective observations, based on the extensive data collection involved in field notes, with the objective concern for a focus and a replicable technique. In the same manner, the *Explication Model* is an attempt to create an evaluation model based upon the development to reconcile art and science in anthropology.

The choice of the term *explication* to identify this model is especially significant because it describes the fundamental purpose of this approach to evaluation. In the first place, the use of explication is an attempt to avoid the pejorative aspects of the term *evaluation*. For those engaged in evaluation, the term is associated with improvement; an evaluation should discover the strengths and weaknesses of a program so that the former can be understood and built upon while the latter can be analyzed and modified. The final result should be an improved program. Although this description technically would be more appropriate for formative evaluation, even summative evaluations are efforts to understand the relationship of goals, procedures, and outcomes. Such efforts should result not only in a judgment about a specific program, but also in learning something about educational processes in general.

The difficulty with the term is that the teachers who are implementing a program question whether it is the program that is being evaluated, or themselves. They know that an evaluation, by any standard dictionary definition, means a judgment of the worth or value of something; so it is very easy for teachers to interpret an evaluation as a judgment of their value or worth as a teacher. Without even considering the issue of job security, most people react to the prospect of someone measuring their worth with chagrin if not hostility. This may result in many teachers being defensive about the evaluation and even lead to a rejection of the evaluator's conclusions. As Wilson (1974) has noted,

> Practitioners in the schools often complain that evaluators and researchers who work with schools do not understand the *realities* of schools and classrooms. As a result, many of the suggestions derived from research are dismissed as being irrelevant to educational realities. (p. 6)

Semantic issues are often illusory and can represent a means for avoiding substantive concerns, but, in the case of evaluation, the semantic problem is a valid issue. An evaluation signifies a process that is defined positively by those who do it, and negatively by those subjected to it; that presents a problem for the process. Given the contradictory perceptions of the term *evaluation,* a different term may be necessary to more accurately depict the function of this kind of process. I am suggesting the word *explication* because it has the primary meaning of clarifying, explaining, and interpreting, and the additional meaning of developing a theory or principle. This term incorporates both of the essential functions of the evaluation process as evaluators like to describe it: to clarify the present status and to develop ideas leading to results that are more consistent with the intended goals of the program.

This is the reason this model is described as an anthropological approach. Anthropologists avoid value judgments because their aim is to understand, and their concerns are phenomenological. This approach uses the teacher as a focus because it will not attempt to judge that teacher but attempts to understand the relationships between the teacher's behavior, the intended outcomes for events, and the students' response. The Explication Model begins with an acceptance of the complexity of what is to be understood. It recognizes that a program is not an inert thing, but an interaction of many elements. The teacher is a vital element in the interaction, and as such represents an appropriate center from which to relate all of the other activities. As Forehand (1974) has written,

> Rather than seek either to decompose or to by-pass curriculum as a variable, one might try to redefine it at the point of its effect, that is, at the point of interaction between the teacher and students. The materials, lesson plans, and other accoutrements of course development are relevant only as they are reflected in the behavior of teachers. (p. 110)

Forehand's statement provides a clear direction, but it also presents some problems. Primarily the problem is one of describing how one attempts to gather data at the point of the curriculum's effect.

One way is to be there while it is happening, taking careful notes based on continuous observation over an extended period of time. That approach, referred to earlier, is called an ethnography. Ethnographies have been criticized for being too subjective, too expensive, too affective in their priorities. To offset these criticisms, I have incorporated into the model several elements that should result in a broader picture of the program than that provided by one person's observations. The basic data-gathering technique is called *systematic observation.* A systematic observation requires that the ethnographer establish certain guidelines for the observations. Anthropologists devised this technique "so that what one anthropologist reports from his observations will differ only minutely from what a fellow anthropologist (or anyone else trained by the same rules) would have observed in the same situation" (Edgerton & Langness, 1974, p. 39). This represents an attempt to combine the benefits of direct observation with objectivity, and it is the heart of this approach.

The first step in the model (see figure 20–1) is to ask the teachers involved in the program to submit a written statement of the goals of the program as they understand them. The teachers would also be encouraged to include their personal goals for their individual classrooms. After receiving a copy of each teacher's statement, the evaluation coordinator would meet with the teachers to discuss the formal goals of the program as outlined by the program developers. At this point, the teachers would be given a copy of their original goal statements and asked to make any final additions or corrections to their earlier statement if they felt such changes were necessary. The teacher statements and their revisions would be given to the coordinator.

The next step would be for each teacher to submit some names of students from each of their classes. The coordinator would explain that these students are to be trained and used (on a voluntary basis) as documenters of the classroom activity.

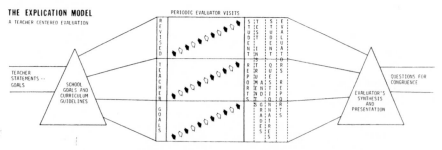

Figure 20–1.   The Explication Model: A Teacher-Centered Evaluation.

This is the reason the guidelines for observation are so important for this model. If the guidelines are clearly defined, then, like the anthropologist in the field, the coordinator can "train local assistants who belong to the culture to perform the task with them" (Edgerton & Langness, 1974, p. 42). Since the evaluation coordinator will be making periodic observational visits, the student observers will be able to ask any questions they may have and clear up any confusion they may be encountering. These students will make a daily record of the activities of each day in class. The categories for such observations will depend upon the goals of the program and the individual teacher. If an affective goal was cooperation, the student would make an entry like this:

Cooperation — spent fifteen minutes in small group work on a project due on Friday.

The time element is very important, since the student observer would be expected to account for what happened in the entire class period each day. The student would also be expected to describe the activity being relegated to a certain category as a further step to ensure the objectivity of the daily record.

The objectivity of the student's daily record is of utmost importance for the model to function. It would be emphasized to both teacher and student that this daily record is to be an objective statement about the types of activities and time allotments made for them, not a judgmental account. That students are capable of performing this task successfully was illustrated in a recent ethnographic evaluation of a desegregated school. One research team (Cassell, 1978) finally allowed some interested students to take field notes, and discovered that the students "had their field note style down pat; the students' notes were written in the same style, and noted similar phenomena as did the fieldworkers" (p. 15). The research team concluded that in their subsequent evaluations they would involve students in field note-taking and do so early in the study. Still, if any teachers expressed concern about having a student keep such a daily record, they would be encouraged to keep a daily record and give that to the coordinator periodically. The evaluation coordinator would compare the teacher's daily record with the student's to see if there were any inconsistencies in the time estimates or in the activities recorded.

The evaluation coordinator would periodically visit the teacher's classes for two consecutive days every three weeks, recording his or her observations and collecting students' reports. The evaluation period could last from nine weeks to a semester, but the longer time period would be recommended for a more effective evaluation. Each coordinator would be responsible for three teachers in the program. At the end of the observation period, the coordinator would gather together the student reports, receive copies of the test instruments and the students' grades, and collect questionnaires provided to all of the students and pertaining to their assessment of what they have learned and their feelings about the program. These questions would be based on the formal statement of program goals and on the teacher goal statements. All of this data would be kept separate, according to the teacher whom it concerns.

The coordinator would review the data collected, which includes teacher goal statements, revised teacher goal statements, program goals, student reports, test instruments, student grades, student questionnaires, and the coordinator's own field notes. The coordinator would write an assessment of each teacher in terms of what goals seemed to have been achieved, and what goals were not, citing the sources used to form those conclusions. These assessments would be for the coordinator's benefit, to clarify perceptions regarding each teacher. With these assessments in mind, the coordinator would write a single report to be submitted to all of the teachers and administrators involved with the program. This report, as illustrated in figure 20–1, should attempt to synthesize the individual assessments, while focussing on the relevant questions concerning the areas where the program did not achieve its goals. These questions should serve as a springboard for a discussion of the problems or inconsistencies that exist. The coordinator would meet with the teachers and administrators to monitor a discussion of these questions. The purpose of the discussion would be eventually to reach some conclusions regarding what changes were needed in the development of the program. The goal for the coordinator would be to help the teachers reach a consensus about the direction in which they want to go. That is the intent of an explication process: to expose the disparities between aims and outcomes in order to stimulate curriculum development and congruence.

The fact that disparities and incongruencies are exposed underscores the important point that the Explication Model does not avoid judgments. It involves teachers in the judgments and provides for formal student input in the data-gathering process on which the judgment will be based. The coordinator is not dictating conclusions to the teachers, but working with them to achieve a mutual goal — an improved program — through mutual effort. One ethnographic evaluator on an initial visit to the school (prior to beginning the evaluation) told the teachers that "any one person in the school does not have the luxury to sit back and see how all the pieces sort of work, fit together; and that, being an observer, I could possibly do this for them" (Cassell, 1978, p. 8). Having done this, the evaluation coordinator in the Explication Model presents the pieces as they seem to fit and works with the teachers to complete the picture. The key to this approach to evaluation is that everyone has an active role to play in it, and that makes the process a meaningful one.

References

Brim, J.A., and Spain, D.H. *Research design in anthropology: Paradigms and pragmatics in the testing of hypotheses*. New York: Holt, Rhinehart, & Winston, 1974.

Cassell, J. *A fieldwork manual for studying desegregated schools.* Washington, D.C.: National Institute of Education, 1978.

Edgerton, R.B., and Langness, L.L. *Methods and styles in the study of culture.* Corte Madera, California: Chandler & Sharp, 1974.

Forehand, G.A. "Problem areas in designing and implementing curriculum evaluation research." In: D. Payne (ed.), *Curriculum evaluation.* Toronto: Heath, 1974.

Renzulli, J.S. "The confessions of a frustrated evaluator." *Measurement and Evaluation in Guidance,* 1972, 5, 298–305.

Wilson, S. *The use of ethnography in educational evaluation.* Chicago: Center for New Schools, Inc., 1974. ERIC Document Reproduction Service no. 126–147.

21 DESIGNING EVALUATIONS OF EDUCATIONAL AND SOCIAL PROGRESS BY LEE J. CRONBACH:
A Synopsis
Anthony J. Shrinkfield

During the past 40 years, Lee J. Cronbach has concerned himself with many aspects of evaluation of social science programs. Much of his thinking in these areas has culminated in a book entitled *Designing Evaluations of Educational and Social Programs* (Cronbach, 1982), a lengthy and erudite work, the preliminary version of which was completed in April 1978. Containing 374 pages, the book includes some new aspects for the design of educational evaluations, while discussing the pros and cons of some of the design concepts already in use.

In his introduction to the issues of planning evaluations, Cronbach states that designing an evaluation investigation is an art because each design has to be decided according to its appropriateness to each new undertaking. He points out that the evaluator must be aware of the choices that are available so that the advantages that accrue from each feature of the design must be balanced against any sacrifices that each choice entails. The design, therefore, becomes a matter of planning for allocation of investigative resources, based upon a selection of questions that are considered to be most apt and guided by practical and political considerations.

All quoted passages in this chapter are from L.J. Cronbach, *Designing Evaluations of Educational and Social Programs,* San Francisco: Jossey-Bass, 1982. Reprinted with permission of the author and publisher.

The strong contrasts between some of the remarks of the adherents of the scientific approach to evaluation and the enthusiasts for the holistic or naturalistic approach suggest a polarization so strong that no reconciliation is possible. However, Cronbach believes that the conflict is exaggerated and that the more an evaluative effort becomes a program of studies (rather than a single study) the more place there is for a mixture of styles. The need for political awareness, open-mindedness, and good communications by the evaluator in both the design and operational stages of an investigation runs through all that Cronbach writes.

Because of the length of Cronbach's book, no attempt will be made to cover all its material in this brief paper. If, however, you find the points raised interesting, you may be assured that they are well worthy of further exploration by reference to the complete text. This paper will select from Cronbach's work those thoughts that fit into the general context which deals with investigative components and resources for an evaluation, such as the place of various styles in evaluation design, identification of research questions, and the importance of evaluator/ decisionmaker communications. In addition, this paper will introduce Cronbach's concept of the elements in an evaluation design — units, treatments, and observations (*uto*).

Introduction to the Issues

Thoughtful Planning for Flexibility

Cronbach is convinced that a premium should be placed upon planning of an evaluation that will withstand certain kinds of challenge because evaluations (in Cronbach's opinion) are intended to serve a political function. The challenges to the information arising from evaluations will often be politically motivated. This is an inescapable statement of any evaluation. To accommodate a wide range of legitimate expectations about the outcome of an evaluation, the planning of the evaluation should be something akin to the planning for a program of investigation. Thus, at its best, the evaluation has the same flexible responsiveness to its own findings as it has to the changing concerns of the political community. As he or she plans (and replans) a fully professional study, the evaluator strives to make it more likely that voters, managers, operating personnel, and/or policymakers will give serious consideration to the findings. Nothing else justifies the effort vested in both the planning and the actual evaluation.

Evaluations are most often undertaken at the request of an administrator. It is possible that the administrator may wish to reduce the evaluator to a technician, setting forth questions to be answered and asking him or her to apply skills of sampling, measurement, and statistical analysis without reflecting on the implications of what he or she does. Cronbach, however, envisages an evaluator asking for, and obtaining, much fuller responsibility so that the evaluation may be more worthwhile. While he or she cannot, and should not, substitute his or her judgment for that of the sponsoring agency, the evaluator should have license to offer views about the agenda for investigation. Administrators, then should ask competent evaluators to think about the design possibilities before any decision to proceed is made.

Cronbach believes that no one individual has the breadth of qualifications to make all the judgments that go into design and interpretation; almost always, responsibility must be shared by a team. This approach has certain advantages as it brings in multiple perspectives and promotes healthy professional debate. Planning, therefore, is likely to occur at two levels — general planning to set priorities and allocate responsibility to teams, and detailed within-team planning that should result in designs based on the experience and interactions of those constituting the team. Thus, evaluation design and studies become thoughtful, evolving processes and not simply mechanically objective, conforming to a set pattern.

It is of greater importance to reflect upon events than to rely upon what Cronbach calls "mindless data-processing." Like Carol Weiss (1972), Cronbach believes that evaluation must be viewed as a way of illuminating complex mechanisms as treatment realizations vary, as the process as well as the outcome is to be studied, and as information from a field test is most likely to be used in decisions about actions other than the one tested.

The Profitable Evaluation

Designs are planned on the basis of some conception of what an excellent evaluation is or does. The best design is that which promises to increase the social benefit from the evaluation — the choice of design alternatives is made on the basis of how evaluations can influence social affairs. Social institutions learn from experience, and so do program clients and political constituencies. Evaluation, in Cronbach's terms, is intended to speed up the learning process by communicating what otherwise might be overlooked or wrongly perceived.

To be profitable, an evaluation must have as its core "scientific activities," for if the observations reported are not true to reality or if the interpretations are poorly reasoned, an evaluation cannot have much value. On the other hand, a study that is technically admirable falls short if what the evaluator learns does not enter the thinking of the relevant political community, such as clients, program staffs, bureaucrats, and interested citizens.

As a result of the scientific approach, evaluators' work may generate insights in others; thus, the evaluator is an educator whose success is to be judged, at least in part, by his success in communication. Cronbach believes that this teaching begins when the evaluator first sits down with members of the policy-shaping community to elucidate their questions. It then continues in every contact the evaluator makes with program participants or with others in his or her audience. The end report is only one of the means of instruction at his or her disposal. The evaluator's work as a teacher lies as much in the matter of raising questions as it does in providing answers. Especially in value-laden matters, the evaluator's responsibility (as an educator) is to help others to ask better questions and determine actions appropriate to their aims.

Cronbach stresses that at all stages of an evaluation, from design to reporting, excellent information is essential. Like Wilensky (1967), Cronbach believes that excellent information is:

1. *clear* because it is understandable to those who must use it
2. *timely* because it reaches them when they need it
3. *reliable* because diverse observers (using the same procedure) see it in the same way
4. *valid* because it is cast in the forms of concepts and measures that capture reality
5. *wide-ranging* because major policy alternatives promising a high probability of attaining organizational goals are posed or new goals are suggested.

If the communications from the evaluation are the product that counts, the following questions should be raised regarding the completed evaluation:

1. Did each section of the audience attend to the message?
2. Did they understand it?
3. Did they find it credible?
4. Were the questions that were significant to them answered as well as possible?
5. Did the answers alter their preconceptions?
6. Was the dialogue leading to the decisions enriched and elevated as a consequence of the evaluation?

If the communications are such that all of these questions can be answered positively, then the evaluation plan and procedures must be judged good. One obvious difficulty in making such a judgment is that which arises from reaching consensus, for in a politically lively situation there is a policy-shaping community and not a lone decisionmaker. All those who play roles in approving the program or in advocating alternatives are part of that community. Moreover, ideally, the evaluator will strive to reach normally silent citizens whose voices should be raised and questions anwered by appropriate communication.

An evaluation should reduce uncertainty regarding alternatives that confront its audience. In addition, it ought to complicate views that are too simple and too certain. Although the evaluator may not be able to persuade all segments of the political community to make the fullest use of his or her feelings, the evaluator nevertheless must plan in that direction.

An evaluation design should lead to a study that will clarify issues for participants and highlight any ways in which they operate under false assumptions or take action without sufficient understanding. Thus, the highly profitable evaluation is one full of suggestions for future realizations of issues and clarifications of meanings.

Cronbach points out that conventional programs of evaluation center attention on a single agency or technique or intervention. While this strategy is useful and necessary, it may all too easily be short-sighted as it may not lead towards an understanding of the basic problem. The implication for evaluation seems to be clear. The more difficult it is to sustain optimistic hopes regarding a particular line of intervention, the more important it is for the evaluation to contribute to basic understanding of the phenomenon. When an evaluation achieves this, it can reasonably aspire to advance societal understanding of the problem area.

Conflicting Approaches to Evaluation

The strong contrasts between some of the remarks of the adherents of the scientific approach to evaluation and the enthusiasts for the holistic or naturalistic approach suggest a polarization so strong that no reconciliation is possible. However, Cronbach believes that the conflict is exaggerated and that the more an evaluative effort becomes a program of studies (rather than a single study) the more place there is for a mixture of styles. An evaluation, in other words, is a place for every kind of investigation and only in this way is it likely that the full truth of a situation may be assessed.

The difficulty for the evaluator, however, is that he or she has to decide on the distribution of investigative effort in a particular project at a particular time and so the trade-offs in design must be the center of concern for the evaluator. A particular study, therefore, may demand more emphasis upon the experimentalist rather than the naturalistic predilections. For his part, Cronbach has used both approaches according to the nature of the study. On the whole, however, his monograph gives more weight to the planning of structured evaluations than to the planning of case studies or the illuminative approach. He feels that as yet there is little cumulative thought about the more naturalistic approaches because there has been no exchange of views comparable to that regarding approximations to experiments. Consequently, issues that divide the various approaches, such as the naturalistic and experimentalist, remain beneath the surface.

Consensus in Design Elements

Cronbach points out that there is general agreement that society should innovate. Social institutions and services are seldom what they could be, and even arrangements that once worked well sometimes fail under changing social conditions. Some form of evaluation for improvement, therefore, is necessary.

There is also agreement that evaluation should be empirical and that events should be examined on sites where the program is being tried. Neither humanistic nor behavioristic/scientific evaluators are likely to argue with this as a general statement of need. The humanist tradition, however, may assert that a program is worthy in its own right. Moreover, any conclusions reached about facts gathered are inferences beyond the data. They are fallible and rest on assumptions, presuppositions, or working hypotheses: thus, conclusions are plausible to a greater or lesser degree. It must always be remembered that statistical estimates are attended by uncertainty.

Nevertheless, unwitting consensus between humanists and behaviorists may be perceived when advocates of experimentation begin to speak of understanding or insight, for it is then that they come much closer to those favoring naturalistic studies. Naturalistic investigators spread resources over the numerous treatment, process, and outcome variables, and comb subsets of data for patterns. They report and interpret many relations that are by no means statistically significant. In other words, they opt for bandwidth at the expense of fidelity, thereby striking a compromise between emphasis upon strong control and parsimony on the one hand and total lack of controls on the other. To sum up, there seems to be some consensus among important writers in the field that circumstances are rare where one may depend wholly upon statistical methods in evaluation and their attendant statistical inferences.

When designing a study, the evaluator must make certain choices. These may include, perhaps, a standard treatment that is unlikely to operate in the absence of the investigator's pressure for reducing variabilities (that is, the traditional experimental method) or a naturalistic approach which will allow for heterogeneous interpretations of the institution under normal operating circumstances. However, Cronbach insists that the evaluator "can choose a plan anywhere in the range from the fully reproducible, fully-controlled artificial study, to the opportunistic, wholly unconstrained, naturalistic study."

Balance in Evaluation Design: Summary

Discussion in the last section indicates that some evaluators in the design and practice of their study may plan to use both the scientific and the humanistic approaches. On the other hand, some may insist upon applying a uniform style to a particular study.

Those who favor formal summative tests also favor objectivity in observation and analysis. By contrast, those who call for case studies are likely to advocate impressionistic interpretation. The first group stresses the fixed character of the hypothesis that is under challenge at the moment; the second, the emergent quality of research questions. When the evaluator cannot adequately specify in the planning stage the most significant variables, the study then proceeds in a context of discovery. The discovery grows out of the collected data, which are interpreted in the light of the investigator's prior experience (direct and vicarious). Strong designs, on the other hand, are appropriate if variables can be clearly defined and hypotheses clearly formulated. The whole point of the strong design in basic science is to provide an objective, reproducible, and indisputable challenge to a prediction from theory.

Cronbach states that there is no necessary conflict between experimental control and use of qualitative information or subjective interpretation, or between open-minded exploration and producing evidence that is objective. This means that even a formal experiment can incorporate interviews of program operators and clients in an open-ended fashion, and ultimately apply "blind coding to obtain machine-compatible data." On the other hand, quantitative, highly-structured data may be used for case study hypothesis construction. Some writers, moreover, make it clear that they would combine strong design with subjective interpretation. Scriven, in particular, wishes the evaluator to report whether the treatment is good or bad and thus bring his or her own values into play. For his or her part, the naturalistic observer may inject objectivity into a study by documenting incidents as they occur and also by use of additional observers focussing on particular aspects of the program being evaluated.

In planning and carrying out an evaluation, a sophisticated evaluator will emphasize some preferences for the methodology to be employed rather than others in his or her endeavor to facilitate resolution of a particular political problem at a particular time, and he or she will "harden his study in some respects and keep it loose in other respects. Seemingly, even the strongest advocate of some one style of evaluative inquiry is prepared to endorse the opposing style as suited to some tasks."

Cronbach summarizes the thinking about the continuum between scientific and humanistic designs in evaluation with the following statement:

> The rhetoric that makes polar opposites of experiments and naturalistic case studies is useful only to bring critical questions to attention.

In actual planning, it almost always makes sense to introduce some degree of control — in data collection, if not in manipulation of treatment, — and to make some naturalistic observation of events within the planned structure. The balance between the styles will vary from one sub-question to the next and may well shift (in either direction!) as the evaluative program proceeds.

Cronbach's Concepts of the Elements in an Evaluation Design: UTO

The conclusions drawn from an evaluation should indicate what is expected if a certain plan of intervention is adopted in a certain type of situation. These conclusions may be predictions about program delivery, the reaction to clients, behavioral change, institutional change, and so on. The designer of an evaluation should strive to ensure (as far as he or she can) that the inferences contained in his or her conclusions are as valid as possible and as persuasive as possible. Ultimately, ''validation consists of a critical scrutiny of the logic of each interpretation and of the research operations behind it.''

Units, Treatments and Observing Operations

Cronbach presents a theory upon which recommendations for design may be based. His abstract conception characterizes the sample, the domain the sample purports strictly to represent, a domain in which the decisionmaking community is interested, and the relations among these three. The three abstract concepts are: units, treatments, and observing operations.

An evaluator attends to:

1. units — either individuals or classes
2. treatments — a unit is exposed to the realization of a particular treatment, e.g. a teacher selects and organizes lessons and proceeds in what may be either a lucid or a confusing style; thus, even with a so-called standard treatment realizations inevitably vary
3. observing operations — the evaluator obtains data before, during, and/or after the treatment; he or she administers a certain form of test or sends a certain visitor to the class to record particular kinds of impressions — these are observing operations.

When discussing a particular study, Cronbach refers to the units actually in the study, the treatment realizations and the observations as *uto* respectively. As each *u* is paired with at least one *t* and *o,* there is formed the *uto,* a symbol that refers to the study as realized — or to any member of the class of studies that might be realized under a particular specification. Thus, *uto* may refer to data on a single unit or to data on the whole sample.

When units are selected, local settings are inevitably included. For instance, if teachers are being studied, they are observed in a social context and not as isolated individuals. A teacher is influenced by supervisors, by tensions that arise from interpersonal relationships, and by union negotiations (to mention some of many likely influences). In addition, there is a larger setting. The intellectual and political climate of a situation impinges on all units. Moreover, outcomes in one situation at one time are not necessarily to be expected some years later, even within that same unit.

UTOS: The Domain of Investigation

Cronbach states that corresponding with *uto* are domains *U, T* and *O*. These combine with *S* in *UTOS,* a concept that will be explained later. By definition, *UTO* specifies the class of unit-treatment-operation combinations which the investigator purports to describe on the basis of *uto*. For instance, a day-care program may meet certain specifications intended for children from a defined class of families with reference made to evidence of particular kinds, such as health ratings by a physician, mother's report on the use of the time the service makes free for her, and acceptance of the service by defined sub-groups in the community. This specification of a class of unit-treatment-operation combination is an example of *UTO*. Cronbach defines *UTO* as the "universe of admissable observations." It follows that any observed *uto* is presumed to fall within the domain that interests the investigator.

If the definition is adequate, independent readers will agree as to which instances of units, realizations, or operations fall within *UTO*. Moreover, the range and distribution of *uto* within *UTO* should (ideally) match the interests of the investigator. As Cronbach points out, the domain may be broad or narrow. For instance, one study may investigate independent study methods based on data accepted from any school that says it has an individualized learning methodology to offer students; another study may define a specific kind of individualized learning methodology and confine attention to instances of one particular kind of activity only. It is important to note that when the definition changes, the question under direct investigation also changes.

Cronbach stresses that the ideal design defines a *UTO,* and then plans for selecting a *uto* to represent it. To the extent that the design is logical and is carried out strictly, one can legitimately infer from the findings in *uto* the findings probable in *UTO*.

The *u, t* and *o* are random elements. The evaluator thinks of the *u* as having been sampled from a population and controls the sampling to the degree that he or she considers practicable. He defines the collection of units that is of interest — the population *U* — and carefully draws a representative sample. The report from observations of a particular occasion *o* is taken to represent what would have been reported on all other occasions; ideally (if costs were not a barrier) one would like to have data from every *o* in *O*. A similar point of view applied to *t* and *T,* as the designated treatment defines a class of realizations about which the investigator is concerned, and the realizations are a sample from the domain. The point is that, typically, *U, T* and *O* in an evaluation are all subject to sampling and to the pitfalls of sampling. It must be clearly borne in mind by an evaluator at the design stage of the study that both behavior and variations in responses may contribute to imperfect generalizations resulting from data gathered, however carefully, by the sampling process.

The concept of an heterogeneous population U from which samples are drawn is not unusual. In $UTOS$ Cronbach extends that concept. He points out that in most social research, t and o are thought of as fixed, while in a program evaluation they are not. Whether he or she realizes it or not, the data interpreter generalizes over treatment realizations just as he or she generalizes over schools or students. Similarly, the observing procedure actually carried out is one of many allowable realizations of a plan. The S in $UTOS$ represents a setting S which should be regarded as fixed. By this convention, each study has one setting only (although units are associated with sites within that setting).

Definitions of the Elements of uto and UTO

The *unit* is the smallest independent entity within which the influence of the treatment effect is fully operative. The unit may be thought of as a system. It is sufficiently complete and autonomous that its experiences and responses are not influenced by the experiences and responses of parallel entities.

Very often, the objects under investigation have a nested structure as, for example, pupils within classes, within schools, within districts, and within states.

> Which level is taken to be the unit depends upon one substantive conception of the mechanism through which the proposed intervention operates and on the level at which the intervention will be installed.

The choice of unit is a subtle, design decision. It must be realized that the assumption of independence is weakened by taking the highest level of the hierarchy as the level of the unit. On the other hand, it may be advantageous to define the sampling plan at several levels.

For the design of the study, the central issue is to judge what are independent *treatment* units. The choice of units for sampling follow from this, together with the strength of inference from u to U.

In any manipulative study, the evaluator specifies a type of action that he will take to influence what happens to the units. The treatment *specified* for the unit is T while the treatment unit actually experienced is t. The actual treatment events t are unlikely to be entirely consistent with the investigator's specifications as there is bound to be variation on what is planned at the design stage of the study. Cronbach points out, for example, that when a set of instructional materials is field tested, a full description of the actual t will include the pace at which the teachers schedule the work, the exercises designed, the rewards made available to students and so on. These actual descriptions of t vary from a generalized statement T to include what is generally spoken of as delivery — those elements of a planned treatment which unit u actually received. The specification of T may, of course, include directives and guidelines and supervisory procedures, qualifications of personnel delivering the treatment, instructional materials, and details for treatment events; or, on the other hand, it may be no more than a global specification, such as "individual progression within classes," with each and every realization that carries this label being admitted.

Observing operations include tests, interviews, classroom visits (in the case of schools), tape recordings of dialogues and procedures for coding the remarks, and use of archival data. There may, in addition, be observation of background characteristics of initial and final status of achievements, of abilities and attitudes, and of various intermediate or processed variables. In the design stage of an evaluation, the ideal is to specify procedures so clearly that another investigator would be able to collect comparable data. Lamentably, this is not normal practice.

In the natural sciences, Cronbach points out that procedures are likely to be so well standardized that the distinction between the class O and the instance o is of little importance. By contrast, behavioral measures cannot be closely standardized. The usual emphasis in operational definition is placed on specifying a rather homogeneous class of procedures. It follows that the specific o falling within the class is likely to agree. Those who are to make use of the evaluation report, however, are often more interested in a broadly defined construct. Rather than choosing a single procedure to be applied to all subjects, the evaluator may best represent the interests of his client by defining a domain of diverse activities associated with the concept under investigation. For instance, rather than saying that reading comprehension is to be measured, it may be preferable to specify a number of different forms of reading comprehension; all these tasks become elements in O.

Cronbach emphasizes that the class O is to be specified with as much care as U and T as a vague label for the variable to be measured is insufficient and possibly misleading.

*UTOS: The Domain of Application

A further refinement of *UTOS,* one which Cronbach considers basic to his argument, is the development of the concept of *UTOS. The asterisk is placed first (thus "star *UTOS*") because an asterisk at the end might suggest *UTO* in $S*$.

Only a small fraction (if any at all) of an audience for a report is centrally interested in the *UTOS* that defined the study. More than likely the hearer is interested in particular aspects of the report. This particular concern of the hearer is referred to by Cronbach as *UTOS, a concept that differs from the original in some respect. For this hearer, the evaluation has value and purpose only as it serves to provide plausible extrapolation from a reported observation to the circumstances of *UTOS, with its individualistic interpretation of observations.

It follows that if an evaluation is to be useful, results should reduce uncertainty about whatever *UTOS enter policy discussions after data (based on observations) are recorded. It also follows that, in the design of a study, the evaluator has to anticipate, as best as possible, the U^*, T^*, and O^* that clients or audiences for the report will wish to know, and some considerations must also be given (as shown below) to the S^*.

The question "Will it work with *our* students?" expresses concern for the specificity of a U^*. Cronbach points out that an outcome difference found in a laboratory situation may not hold up in everyday school situations, or a difference found in a representative national sample may not be found either in the wealthiest or the most isolated school districts. The point is made that U and U^* differ, and that the importance of their differences "has to be weighed when actions affecting U^* are taken."

If the original O was narrow, audiences are likely to show an interest in O^* and receive greater satisfaction by the closer definition afforded by O^*. For instance, a mathematics course may well appear to be successful when O is tailored only to the lessons covered. Some critics may well argue, however, that graduates of the mathematics course are deficient in the area of problem solving. A preferred measure of O^* covering such additional questions about the course, may well be adopted.

As has been mentioned earlier, the audience for the evaluation is really concerned with whether or not to adopt the experimental T of the original study. As the study progresses, discussions about it will suggest variations to improve on the original plan. Each such variation becomes a T^*. Cronbach suggests an interesting example of this phenomenon:

> When the first returns on compensatory education came in, few discussants confined attention to the conclusion about the *UTO* on which data were collected. One reaction contemplated a change in treatment: "It is all very well to report negatively on Head Start (T); but does not that show that compensatory treatment needs to continue for a longer time (T*)?" So follow through was mounted as a *T** (and later evaluated directly).

It is interesting to note that the treatment domain can change when considerations move from *UTOS* to **UTOS* — "even when the operational specification of T remains unaltered." If U changes to U^* or S to S^*, the frequency of realizations changes because the way a treatment is realised depends on the local settings and participants and such factors as organizational and social climates. Thus, S^* may be a significant aspect of **UTOS* when the population of realizations changes.

Those whose task it is to interpret the results of an evaluation have this question on their minds: "How much difference does the change from *UTOS* to such-and-such a **UTOS* make?" It is possible that the change is not of great consequence "either because the phenomenon under study is impervious to social change or because the change is too small to matter." Moreover, if a question is to be directly investigated, it could be cast in the form of a parameter of a *UTOS* that is to be estimated. Cronbach points out that the parameter may be a mean, a regression coefficient, or a proportion of cases in a category. Where questions are not directly investigated they could be cast in the form of a parameter of $*UTO$ in which an estimate is sought. As an example, a person responsible for a program may wish to know what the value is of a particular indicator of a student motivation ($O*$) if a particular ruling regarding multicultural education (a $T*$) is issued to all high school districts of one state ($U*$).

$*UTOS$, the domain of application, is a central and basic aspect of the planning of any evaluation that is to offer specific and needed information for audiences.

Identifying the Research Questions

Cronbach states that:

> Questions for an evaluation come chiefly from uncertainties of members of the decision making community, or from disagreements among members, each of whom is certain about his or her answer. To identify the most pertinent questions is a first step in designing an evaluation; to distribute effort appropriately among them is the second.

The evaluator, Cronbach considers, is not a free agent in choosing questions to investigate because a sponsor may be willing to support certain inquiries and not others. Other constraints pertain. An administrator may be unwilling to conform to an experimental scheme for a number of reasons, or informants may have limited willingness to supply data. On the other hand, communications between the evaluator and the sponsor before the design stage may encourage the latter to accept suggestions for broadening the inquiry.

Two phases of planning are described: the *divergent* phase of listing possible questions and the *convergent* phase of assigning priorities among them.

In practice, the two activities go on simultaneously. It would seem wise for an agency proposing to sponsor an evaluation to go through both the divergent and convergent planning processes before it asks an evaluator to work out an operational plan. Consequent exchanges and negotiations between the evaluator-designate and the sponsor will lead to a revised list of questions. The process of amendment will inevitably continue after field work is launched.

The Divergent Phase

This phase opens the minds of both the evaluator and the sponsor to the widest possible range of questions to be entertained, at least briefly, as prospects for investigation.

Sources of questions. While planning which individuals or groups should be candidates for questions that are important to a study, the evaluator must plan to seek out a wide variety of informants. As a result of this, omissions will result from informed choice and not from the restricted vision of the sponsor or the administrator or whoever has central responsibility.

Cronbach contends that "the evaluator engages to produce something — information — that has value to consumers and for which they are willing to pay." Thus, the decision about which product to deliver is an economic one to which both sides of the supply-demand factors contribute.

The evaluator has certain advantages over the sponsor in envisaging questions to be answered:

1. He brings a fresh set of biases
2. The evaluator may be in a better position than the sponsor to collect and appreciate the questions current in non-political circles (as well as political)
3. From his or her knowledge of past research, the evaluator can recognize the challenges and counter-interpretations to which the study is subject and thus can suggest specific controls needed to bolster the plausibility of its answers
4. The evaluator knows the state of *his* or *her* art and can inform the sponsor (or manager) how adequately a given question can be answered at any given scale of expenditure.

However, in the end, it is the sponsor's estimate of the political and administrative relevance of the many questions which directs the evaluator. The point to be made is that the sponsor should not have to make these decisions unaided.

Treatments and Processes.   In the social services area, it is likely that the place where the evaluation is to occur will not be subject to modification for purposes of the study. In other instances, the services are open to manipulation; treatments may be arranged to provide a direct test of an innovative proposal. In either case, as Suchman (1967) points out, the evaluator requires a list of treatments that might be worth installing for investigation or worth locating where they presently exist.

Both the sponsor and the evaluator should be aware of different pressures from partisan groups, who will suggest some candidates for questions or groups for treatments. Other candidates may be suggested, with profit to the study, by persons further removed from the center of political action. At the stage of listing candidates, friction should not exist. Later, political realities will make some questions far more appropriate and useful than others — but this will be discussed in the convergent stage.

Behind any program proposal are two concepts: one regarding the ways in which existing social conditions and the services already offered combine to produce an unsatisfactory result, and the other regarding the ways in which the alternative service will produce a more satisfactory result. Cronbach, therefore, advocates a sketch for intervention in which the various likely events are laid out in tabular or flow-chart form. This in itself, should bring to the surface questions that will be valuable when the process of intervention and its effects are clarified by the evaluation process. It should be noted, however, that the hypothesized process and the particular questions to be raised (for evaluation) will differ with each program variant. This is true whether the variations were planned or were recognized when realizations took form in various sites.

The intensity of the intervention must be included in the design. Should a larger team be trained to meet this perceived need? The intensity of intervention may also be centered around questions about intermediate stages of the program that is being introduced. If the final outcomes are not what the proponent had hoped for or anticipated, evidence of these intermediate stages and processes will be useful. To monitor and record such evidence, it is likely that a considerable team has to be trained and employed for the study.

Outcomes. The goals stated by the sponsor or by proponents of the intervention are a significant source of questions for the divergent phase. The list ought to include goals of others of whom questions are asked in relation to the evaluation and ought also to include intermediate outcomes.

Cronbach warns that even a well-specified list of goals is necessarily incomplete as a source of questions if it does not give attention to unwanted outcomes. The evaluator must, therefore, direct some attention to side effects as well as goals. It is also important to note that in the educational context, increments of progress are welcome no matter where the student is on the scale. Thus, the global intention that a program is to "achieve its goals" is to be considered circumspectly by the evaluator. At the time when the study is designed, the only reasonable question is: "What outcomes should we attend to?." Whether the level reached is satisfactory must be judged after the evaluation is completed "through a process of political negotiation." Even though the evaluation staff ought to press for clear statements about the outcome variables that the program planners have in mind, in the divergent stage it is important to keep in mind that hard-to-define and assess variables, such as affective outcomes, must not be dropped from sight.

Cronbach contends that the divergent list ought to include outcomes that are expected to become observable only after the evaluation has been completed and reported. He says that often it will be appropriate to bank the data so that a later follow-up can give a clearer picture of long-term consequences. It is to be expected that long-run differences between treatments will not match those on the immediate post-test.

As part of his or her planning, it is important that the evaluator talks to persons who have some images of the program and of what partisans hope (or fear) or of how they expect various effects to develop. Again, it must be emphasized that a wide range of factions within the decision making community should be approached so that the evaluator may learn to perceive the program through the eyes of the various (biased) sectors of the community, including the professionals who would operate the program, if adopted, and the citizens to be served. It is essential to learn the hopes and fears of these sectors.

Moreover, the evaluator has the responsibility to bring into the total picture those values for which there is no effective political voice. He or she achieves this by reaching out for sources that do not readily press their views on him or her. To consult many sources is a divergent step.

The Convergent Phase

The convergent phase stresses the necessity of questions to be raised by a wide diversity of individuals and groups. Some questions should be dropped for practical reasons. Cronbach points out that there are at least three reasons for reducing the range of variables treated systematically in an evaluation. They are:

1. *cost* — there will always be a budget limit
2. *attention span of the evaluator* — as a study becomes more complicated, it becomes increasingly more difficult to administer, the mass of information becomes too great to consider, and, consequently, much of information is lost in the course of data reduction and synthesis
3. *attention span of the decision making community* — very few persons want to know all there is to know about a program and, indeed, few have the time to offer the evaluator all their opinions.

The divergent phase, therefore, identifies what could *possibly* be worth investigating. The convergent phase is dedicated to deciding what incompleteness is most acceptable. The evaluator is likely to invest time and effort in the study of a particular question (or plan to do so) when there is:

1. great prior uncertainty about the answer
2. a prospective large yield of information
3. low cost of the inquiry
4. a high degree of leverage for the choices on which the information would bear (the term *leverage* is discussed next).

When an original list of questions is framed, it is done so in terms of U, T, and O, which are significant to some participants in decision making. In addition, the list may contain questions about artificial conditions that shed indirect light on a practical concern. In the convergent process, however, some of these questions are picked out to become *UTO* of the field study after they are further specified.

Leverage. Cronbach defines leverage as referring to the "weight of a particular uncertainty in the decision making process." In planning an evaluation to have future influence, an evaluator, in conjunction with the sponsor or administrator, may need to judge what leverage information on a particular issues is expected to have. After the study has been completed, judgment about leverage may be made from the response of the community to the evidence presented in the report. A matter that receives appreciable attention from the whole community has great leverage. It may also have leverage if it is significant to an interest bloc or to an uncommitted group whose support or opposition would be crucial. An issue influencing large decisions, such as ''go-no go'' has more leverage than an issue whose resolution would affect minor details of the plan.

Leverage, therefore, has two aspects: the importance of the issue or choice on which the evidence bears, and the weight the evidence brings to bear. The evaluator must consider how much influence each of the conceivable answers to a question is expected to have.

Cronbach points out that it is in examining leverage that the evaluator explicitly considers the values of participants. Nothing on the divergent list of questions deserves consideration if the findings are not value-laden for at least some of the decision making. Things that would be merely nice to know do not qualify for an investment of evaluative resources. Discussing prior uncertainty, Cronbach considers that, with things being equal, attention should be given to the question about which uncertainty is greatest; that is, when two questions seem to be equally open to investigation, greater resources should be invested in the question for which the community's uncertainty is more widespread and intense.

Accordingly, the evaluator is advised to make a priority scale for investigative effort:

1. If a question has high leverage and high uncertainty, it deserves investment to bring down the uncertainty.
2. If leverage is low and uncertainty is high, investment is warranted.
3. If leverage is high and prior uncertainty low, incidental information should be collected.
4. If leverage is low and uncertainty is low, the investigator should do no more than to keep open the channels for incidental information.

Planning for Communication

The Utility of Findings

The usefulness of an evaluation depends on the degree to which members of the decision making community become aware of its findings and consider them plausible. Cronbach also believes that information is invariably lost in moving from the field observations to the report. Some observations are never communicated by the observer to the rest of the team, some are lost in the process of encoding and statistical summary, while some are lost because not everything can be placed in a report. Once a report is written, the information passes through further filters as some information may be squeezed out or altered and, indeed, the sponsor himself may suppress some findings. Moreover, the audience perceives selectively and may tend to over-simplify information, or assimilate new information in the light of old beliefs instead of correcting those beliefs.

Cronbach warns that an audience has limited time only, and many social issues and programs compete for its attention. It is a rare person who gives an evaluative report on a public question a thorough reading. Moreover, few in the audience can grasp the solid technical account of procedures and analysis.

The point to be emphasized is that the reporting task of the evaluator is different from the task the scientist usually faces. The scientist reports to a select audience that shares his or her language and style of thought. The evaluator, however, speaks to numerous and scattered audiences, most of whom receive only secondary and watered-down accounts. The evaluator who finds that his or her report has been misinterpreted finds it difficult, or even impossible, to address his or her reply to those who have misinterpreted his or her statements.

Cronbach addresses two questions:

What might be reported that would facilitate the evaluation user's thinking?

What does this imply for the earlier field operations of the evaluation?

Direct Communication

The evaluator should consider the possibility of increasing direct communication. Such communication would be comparatively informal because of the audience to be reached and because public knowledge should be as timely as possible. He points out that perhaps the most potent report is the informal conversation — in the office of the legislator or around the conference table.

The evaluator, Cronbach considers, has a role much like that of a journalist who investigates matters of public interest, judges what merits public attention, and packages it in a form that attracts attention. Persons within the evaluation team have rich experience and reasonable opportunity to exchange views within the team and with informants. They are, therefore, in a good position to carry out the reporting task of the journalistic function as well as the investigative task. If the team restricts itself to formal reporting, it leaves to outsiders the delivery of its message.

Evaluators are understandably suspicious of constraints on their reporting. This kind of tension can only be resolved when the political system makes clear the role which evaluations play. In Cronbach's view, the public interest will be best served by institutional arrangements that free evaluators to speak directly to all those who will participate in decisions about programs. It is important, therefore, that at least some members of the evaluation team should have skills of informal communication. Cronbach agrees with Stake, who advocates the designing of evaluative reports for a broad community, often employing unconventional forms of communication, such as press releases and speeches and the dramatic reproduction of program events like logs and scrapbooks to bring home the message. The aim is to give the audience a feeling for the program and the experience of participants, rather than an abstract summary alone. It is necessary that the evaluator who foresees that he or she will want to report vividly should begin early to amass material that will add color and realism to his or her otherwise bald and unconvincing narrative.

Cronbach has found it profitable for observers to file narrative accounts of revealing incidents seen in classrooms and of remarks of program participants. These memoranda need not be in a polished form, but they should provide sufficient context and continuity. They should be factual, rather than interpretative. In Cronbach's opinion, "the anecdotes add wonderfully to the interest and belief the report commands."

Reporting, whether of anecdotal information or formal measurement and statistics, must be highly selective. Shorter and longer reports, with small technical content or perhaps a great deal, can reasonably be synthesized to some brief statements by omitting analyses and data sets that seem unlikely to influence decisions. Nevertheless, the complete report may display a few items to illustrate any patterns of differences and a few representative of the no-difference category, thus obviating the proclivity felt by some evaluators to flood the reader with a display of all the differences.

Extrapolating from Findings

Cronbach firmly believes that decision making audiences have both the right and the need to extrapolate as much as they sensibly can from the results of any study. He states:

> It is emphatically not sufficient to conclude an evaluation report with the standard cautionary warning . . . .: "The findings reported apply to the conditions and population we have studied. Further research is required to extend the conclusions to other conditions and populations." The world *must* extend the conclusions to get on with its business, and the evaluator is in a good position to recognize plausible extensions.

The evaluator may, therefore, offer alternative predictions, consistent with different sets of beliefs. These could lead to a promotion of discussion in which conflicting interpretations could be aired.

The suggestion that the evaluator should carry his or her interpretation as far as he or she is able, with appropriate caution, suggests that he or she will be wise to keep comparatively rich descriptive records. Cronbach emphasizes the value of periodically re-appraising the study design so that consequent surprises and puzzles can be given close attention. It is then possible to explain intermediate unintended outcomes, which will have possible consequences for the future of the program, before continuing research operations about that program.

The Promise of Evaluation

Flexibility of Design

A large section of Cronbach's book: *Designing Evaluations of Educational and Social Programs,* deals with an elaboration of controls used to strengthen inferences and to make some conclusions more plausible. In a sense, the listing of available controls in this book is a kind of checklist for the evaluator. He points out that some of the controls that strengthen inference cost very little, either in terms of resources or of relevance. Specifying what *UTO* one intends to study, for example, is nearly cost-free. Arriving at the specification itself brings the evaluator face-to-face with choices that might otherwise be made inadvertently.

Cronbach goes on to say that there may never be a social program where *all* evaluation resources ought to go into a tightly controlled study to support inferences to a narrow *UTO*. Nevertheless, in many instances, tightly controlled sub-studies might be useful within an evaluative effort. In other instances, it would be wise to structure an investigation so that a strong inference may be reached and to make intensive studies of some sites of units within the samples by naturalistic and even impressionistic methods "that enable the investigator to learn about events and processes that were not anticipated." As has been pointed out earlier, it may be possible to combine the statistical comparison of the experimental and control averages with intense studies of individuals or groups of people by naturalistic methods.

Evaluations and Politics: Limitations

Cronbach strikes the word of warning that evaluations will inevitably disappoint if they are expected to *resolve* political conflicts.

> The reasonable aspiration of the evaluator is to produce information that less systematic observation of the program would not have produced, or information that is more plausible, and hence more influential than similar reports from less systematic observations would have been. A narrow-band investigation tries to accomplish this by offering good information on a few of the relevant questions; to the same end, a wide-band investigation produces more comprehensive but somewhat less dependable information. The choice among such options comes down to a judgment about leverage, i.e. about influence of decisions.

In other words, the plan for the evaluation that is too broad and therefore too thin in one context may be quite appropriate in another. The targeted study that focuses narrowly and obtains strong information, limited in scope, may be just right for one context, but may be quite inappropriate for another.

Cronbach looks upon evaluations as short-term inquiries, expected to illuminate decisions that are on the "current political agenda or just over the horizon." The value of an evaluation is not limited to its contribution to these kinds of decisions alone. Society learns from its experience with the program and learns more clearly from the contribution made by the evaluation. The evaluation contributes to the thinking about problems in a particular social milieu and so generates new ideas and feelings out of which arise the possible areas of change and methods of support. The worth of an evaluation, therefore, is not confined to its influence on the fate of the program being studied. Cronbach stresses that insofar as the evaluation illuminates the phenomenon, it may have a lasting influence on the way the problem is understood and on the shape of future programs.

Other Considerations

Cronbach considers that evaluation will have greater promise when designs and studies place emphasis upon the value of accounting for successes and failures rather than simply measuring outcomes. Fresh insights are needed, and, therefore, the investigator must not restrict himself or herself to questions identified in advance, important as these are. It is also important for the evaluator not to delay his or her report until fully satisfied that he or she has all possible answers. On the contrary, the evaluator may need to tell the decision making community what he or she has learned well before the treatment has run its full course. This is one reason why design, planning, observation, and interpretation (to decisionmakers) should go on simultaneously rather than successively.

Along similar lines, Cronbach suggests that the evaluating plan should free some staff time for reflection at each stage of the work. Such reflection should prohibit, for example, too premature a focus upon controversial social issues or recalcitrant social problems. It may offer to decisionmakers wiser counsel than otherwise would be possible.

Cronbach believes that a description favoring a particular style of evaluation or emphasizing certain controls is of limited applicability. By his theory, evaluators should be called on to exercise judgments about substantive and political, as well as methodological, matters. The evaluator should not make judgments unassisted; rather he or she should draw on the sponsor, professional colleagues, or politically interested parties.

Evaluators making use of such advice to locate and properly weight evaluative questions will need a broader training than they have typically received. Political, philosophical, and organizational theory can be as important in planning a potentially influential evaluation as knowledge of statistics and theory of, say, child development.

Like Stufflebeam and Stake earlier, Cronbach asserts that when evaluation is divided among members of a team, the team must work as a single unit if insight is to flourish. While members of the team must be fully conversant with all major aspects of the study, those at the center of the project must assume the greatest responsibility for setting priorities, making sense of observations, and gleaning first-hand experiences from clients and course participants. In this way, the team as a whole will gain the correct perspective and properly interpret computer printouts and other reports. It is necessary, then, for some members of the team to have first-hand field observations and to communicate these to other members of the team.

Finally, Cronbach states that evaluation could be dangerous if society was to curtail programs which the evaluator condemns and to expand those which he or she praises. The evaluator has a valuable and satisfying contribution to make because he or she can discover facts and relations that casual observers would miss. It is Cronbach's belief that evaluators will have greater influence in future years, with the improvement of the art and with society coming to rely on "systematic studies for the enlightenment they offer."

References

Campbell, Donald T. "Factors relevant to the validity of experiments in social settings." *Psychological Bulletin,* 54 (1957), 297–312.

Campbell, Donald T. "The social scientist as methodological servant of the experimenting society." *Policy Studies Journal,* 2 (1973), 72–75.

Campbell, Donald T. "Assessing the impact of planned social change." In: G.M. Lyons (ed.), *Social research and public policies.* Hanover, New Hampshire: Public Affairs Center, Dartmouth College, 1975.

Cronbach, Lee J. "Course improvement through evaluation." *Teachers College Record,* 64 (1963), 672–83.

Cronbach, Lee J. *Designing Evaluations of Educational and Social Programs.* San Francisco: Jossey-Bass, 1982.

Cronbach, Lee J. et al. *Research on classrooms and schools: Formulation of questions, design, and analysis.* Occasional paper. Stanford Evaluation Consortium, Stanford University, California, 1976.

Cronbach, Lee J. and Associates. *Towards Reform of Program Evaluation.* San Francisco: Jossey-Bass, 1980.

House, Ernest R. "Justice in evaluation." In: G.C. Glass (ed.), *Evaluation Studies Review Annual,* vol. 1. Beverly Hills, California: Sage, 1976, 75–99.

MacDonald, Barry. "Evaluation and the control of education." In: D. Tawney (ed.), *Curriculum evaluation today: Trends and implications.* London: Macmillan Education, 1976, 125–36.

Riecken, Henry W., and Robert F. Boruch, (eds.). *Social Experimentation*. New York: Academic Press, 1974.

Rossi, Peter H., and Walter Williams. *Evaluating social programs: Theory, practice and politics*. New York: Seminar Press, 1972. '

Scriven, Michael. "The methodology of evaluation." In: R.W. Stake et al., *Perspectives on curriculum evaluation. AERA Monograph Series on Curriculum Evaluation*, no. 1. Chicago: Rand McNally, 1967, 39–83.

Stake, R.E. "The Countenance of Educational Evaluation." In: *Teachers College Record*, 68 (April 1967), 523–40, 63, 146.

Suchman, Edward A. "Action for what? A critique of evaluative research." In: R. O'Toole (ed.), *The organization, management, and tactics of social research*. Cambridge, Massachusetts: Schenkman, 1970.

Suchman, E.A. *Evaluative Research*. New York: Russell Sage Foundation, 1967.

Weiss, Carol H. (ed.). *Evaluating action programs: Readings in social action and education*. Boston: Allyn and Bacon, 1972.

Wilensky, Harold. *Organizational intelligence: Knowledge and policy in government and industry*. New York: Basic Books, 1967.

THE PROGRESS OF EDUCATIONAL EVALUATION:
Rounding the First Bends in the River
Nick L. Smith

We have been asked to comment on the status of educational evaluation, to address the questions, ''What have been the key developments so far?'' and ''What are the needs for future growth?'' This is a bit like asking someone who has been rafting down a churning river all morning how the trip is going. We haven't been at this evaluation business very long, and we are not terribly sure whether we are adroitly navigating each new turn or merely trying to keep upright through the changing economic currents, the encroaching banks of legislative and judicial control, and the shoals of special interest groups. We have had to gain our balance quickly, having been launched in the swift currents of the Elementary and Secondary Education Act (ESEA) legislation in the mid-sixties. While it does seem useful to consider for a moment where we in evaluation are likely to journey over the next several years, our experience is short and our perspective does not extend much beyond the next bend.

Smith, Nick L. ''The Progress of Educational Evaluation: Rounding the First Bends in the River.'' Proceedings of the 1980 Minnesota Evaluation Conference on Educational Evaluation: Recent Progress, Future Needs. Copyright 1980, University of Minnesota Press, Minneapolis, Minnesota. Reprinted by permission of author and publisher.

Evaluation: Secure or Insecure

Boulding (1980) distinguishes between secure and insecure science and points out that each discipline has "more secure" knowledge or images that are well-supported and not likely to change much over time. Other elements of the discipline are "less secure" and subject to change. Overall, how would we characterize our understanding of educational evaluation? Is our knowledge more or less secure?

Following Boulding's analysis, we would have to say that our knowledge is insecure to the extent that it is based on a small and possibly biased sample of phenomena; it covers only a small area of a complex field; it covers a short span of time; and it is influenced by rare, nonreproducible events. Given these criteria, we have to conclude that our knowledge of evaluation is far from secure.

Our knowledge is based on a small, biased sample in that our attention has been focused almost exclusively on the evaluation of educational *programs* within local district settings. What is even more restrictive is that we have paid relatively little attention to anything but federally funded educational programs. The evaluation of educational personnel, materials and products, and broad systems has definitely not received as much support and interest as program evaluation. Our understanding of evaluation is further biased in that we have tended to focus on public rather than private education, basic and compensatory rather than special or supplemental education, and elementary and secondary versus preschool or higher and continuing education. I am not arguing that these areas necessarily deserve greater attention; I am only pointing out that our collective experience is more limited in these areas.

To date, we have also covered only a small area of a large and complex field. Educational evaluation has been narrowly viewed by many to be concerned only with the use of cognitive knowledge in the improvement of formal decisions made in specific organizational settings. Only recently has that view been broadened to include such issues as the role of political and economic forces in the decision making and the non-decision making uses of evaluation. Still on the horizon are such concerns as the impact of personal influence and historical trends in educational decision making, the relationships between values and fact in education, and alternative means of valuing.

Certainly we would all agree that our span of experience with evaluation is extremely short; and, consequently, our knowledge of evaluation is insecure from this perspective.

Is our understanding of evaluation based on rare events? Was the popular concern with the quality of education that was launched with the Sputnik a rare event? It provided the inspiration, as well as the resources, for the early work in educational evaluation. If it was a rare occasion, was it a fortunate occurrence that beneficently formed the nature of evaluation, or was the evaluation of the 1970s misshaped by a social artifact of the late 1960s? It is obviously too soon to answer these questions from a historical perspective. It will take some time before we can assess whether evaluation as it was practiced in the 1970s charted the main course for the future of evaluation or if it provided only a short trip down a minor tributary.

With so little experience to draw on, it is difficult to state definitively how secure our knowledge about educational evaluation is. I believe, however, that all indicators suggest that our understanding is highly insecure. We can expect major shifts in emphasis, expanding horizons, and radical alternatives to emerge as educational evaluation continues in its current period of expansive growth. Like shooting the rapids, living through such turmoil will result in greater security in the knowledge gained upon reaching the other side.

Evaluation: Past and Present

What have we accomplished in evaluation? Where do we stand today? If we continue the historical perspective suggested by Boulding, then we must also ask whether an enterprise only 15 years old really has a past. For such a short period as this, the first two questions can be answered by a statement of the field's present status.

Before moving on to the topic to which I want to devote most of my attention, the future of evaluation, I would like to share my perception of where we presently are in this field. During the past 15 years there has been a lot of effort put into thinking about evaluation: what it is, what it can be, and what it should do. Much of this intellectual activity can be traced through the articles on the so-called evaluation models: the countenance model, the discrepancy model, the CIPP model, the goal-free model, and so on. These papers helped us to develop alternative views of evaluation, but were less helpful in showing us how to do evaluations.

Doing evaluations has become a big business in the last 15 years. The number of evaluators has grown dramatically as federal, state, and local resources have been increasingly diverted to this new form of management aid. The perception of evaluation as the decision-maker's best friend is reflected in the management orientation given to most evaluations in education. In the local schools, evaluation activities serve administrative rather than instructional needs, are designed to aid formal decision making, are goal or objectives based, and are heavily dependent on measurement and testing procedures (Lyon et al., 1978).

In the last few years, an increasing number of individuals have begun to offer alternatives to this traditional view of educational evaluation by advocating naturalistic (Guba, 1978), responsive (Stake, 1975), or critical (Eisner, 1975) approaches to evaluation. Evaluators have also come to view themselves more formally in recent years. The evidence of this crystallization of a professional identity is readily apparent: we now have evaluation journals, evaluation societies, evaluation standards, and various types of evaluation awards. From a part-time activity for educational researchers in the mid-1960s, we seem to have developed a new professional identity for the 1980s.

Evaluation: The Future

There are three questions one might ask about the future of evaluation: What *will* happen, what *should* happen, and what *can* happen.

Answering the question of what *will* happen requires either a crystal ball or expertise in the techniques of forecasting, depending on your epistemology. Since I have neither a crystal ball nor facility for forecasting, I am left with the expedient strategy of making guesses based on the assumption that yesterday portends tomorrow.

I anticipate that evaluations conducted within local school districts and state departments of education will continue to be heavily management focused, with major emphasis on the use of testing to inform administrative decisions. There also will be an expanding array of alternative approaches to evaluation. While they will capture much attention, these new approaches will be used only in an increasing number of specialized applications and will not replace the current dominant approach.

One of the more exciting changes in evaluation will be that it will continue to become increasingly interdisciplinary. There is already a concerted movement, evident in a few evaluation journals and societies, to combine many social science disciplines (psychology, sociology, economics, political science, history, law, anthropology, and others) with most of the areas of evaluation practice (education, criminal justice, health, social service, industry, the military, private foundations and federal oversight) to form a full-spectrum view of evaluation theory and practice. This increasing catholicity will greatly enrich the thinking on evaluation and will promote the sharing of methods and perspectives across diverse areas of evaluation practice. In fact, this movement is as likely to have a hybridizing influence on the disciplines of social science as it is to enrich the theory and practice of evaluation. If we are exceedingly fortunate, this cross-fertilization will result in more of those rare individuals who can make significant contributions across a number of disciplines, such as Michael Scriven and Donald Campbell. Undoubtedly, this diversification of evaluation will be a mixed blessing to the evaluation practitioner, who will be faced with an expanding array of methodological options and potential social roles.

Of course, many of evaluation's current issues will continue to be of concern; we will continue to deal with:

improving the relevance and utility of evaluation studies;

increasing the role of evaluations in providing equal educational opportunity;

improving the cost-efficiency of evaluation efforts;

expanding the role of consumers and stakeholders in evaluative activities;

integrating evaluation effectively within legislative, judicial; and administrative functions;

making major advances in the ''assessing value'' side of evaluation;

strengthening the evaluator's ability to deal with moral and ethical problems; and

creating a professional identity or identities to guide the future of evaluation.

How would we answer the question of what *should* happen in evaluation? I suppose one could proffer a reasoned argument based on an empirical needs assessment of the profession. I do not believe, however, that professions, or any social organizations, for that matter, follow such a rational model; their directions are dicated by broad social forces and the energetic activity of a small number of influential leaders. The currents of the river and the hard work of the few individuals holding the paddles are what determine whether we negotiate the next turn successfully, capsize, or beach on a shoal. Therefore, I find personal statements of what direction evaluation should take to have more significance than generalized arguments of desirable conditions.

Rather than list a number of activities that I believe would contribute to evaluation theory and practice in the coming years, I will emphasize the one area that I think can make the greatest contribution: the conceptual and empirical study of evaluation practice. We need research on evaluation; we especially need grounded, empirical studies of evaluation practice. We have almost no descriptive information on the practice of evaluation, few field studies of evaluation impact, and scant attention to the empirical study of evaluation method. I have discussed the need for this type of work elsewhere (Smith, 1979, 1980a, 1980b) and will not belabor the point here, except to outline the focus of this research.

Research on evaluation should focus on: understanding the nature of the *contexts* within which evaluation takes place; providing information on the effectiveness of the various evaluation *methods;* improving the *utilization* of evaluation results; and explicating the empirical connections between the evaluation problem, local context, evaluation method, and evaluation utilization. With such background research, it would be possible to begin developing a theory of evaluation practice. This long-term activity of providing an empirical basis for evaluation practice would do the most, I believe, to improve the profession of educational evaluation.

The third question concerning the future of evaluation is what *can* happen. This question calls for a kind of vision infrequently practiced in evaluation, or in science, for that matter. Loren Eiseley (1973) describes Frances Bacon as one of the few individuals with this capacity. In his book on Bacon entitled, *The Man Who Saw Through Time*, Eiseley says,

Bacon was the first great statesman of science. He saw its potentiality in the schools; he saw the necessity of multiplying researchers, establishing the continuity of the scientific tradition, and promoting government supported research for those studies which lay beyond private means and which could not be accomplished ''in the hourglass of one man's life.'' (1973, p. 36)

And Bacon saw this over 400 years ago!

We can attempt to follow Bacon's example of seeing what is possible in the future, noting, however, a comment made by Archbishop Richard Whately, ''Bacon's wisdom is like the seven-league boots which would fit the giant or the dwarf, except only that the dwarf cannot take the same stride in them'' (Eiseley, 1973, p. 47). You must measure for yourself the length of our visionary strides into the future.

To provide a glimpse into the future of what is possible in evaluation, I have prepared five vignettes, which might be called ''scenarios of the possible'' (my thanks to Adrianne Bank for suggesting this term). These scenarios describe possible new methods. I have extrapolated from some of the emerging new approaches in evaluation to generate these fantasies; but in order to give them reality, I wrote these scenarios as if the methods were now fully developed. These are clearly fantasies at present, but they do suggest what could happen in evaluation; and, as Boulding notes, ''. . . fantasy is part of the appropriate methodologies of all fields of human knowledge'' (1980, p. 836).

The Investigative Approach

Jonathan, in the outer office of the State Superintendent of Public Instruction, waited impatiently with the results of his latest investigation. The Superintendent had to be made aware of what Jonathan had found so that he could take action before either the legislature or the newspapers learned what was going on.

Jonathan worked as a special assistant to the Superintendent. He did in-house evaluative studies, usually following up leads of illegal, unethical, or incompetent behavior within the state education system. Jonathan's position had been created by the Superintendent, who was elected during a period of reduced public support and funding for the state educational program on the campaign promise that he would clean up corruption and waste within the educational system. Jonathan's reports were frequently politically sensitive, and his position had to be protected by being attached directly to the State Superintendent.

Jonathan thought back over the latest investigation. As usual, he had attempted to reconstruct a sequence of events through the review of extensive documentation and by interviewing key informants. He had been able to establish a plausible chain of events including effects, causes, and participant intents. Jonathan's methods have improved over the last several years of practice, but they basically grew out of the approaches used by investigative journalists, congressional investigative teams, criminologists, and field researchers in the social sciences.

Jonathan usually provided his services when quick studies were needed; he worked in naturalistic settings under considerable pressure. While he often did short review studies as a means of providing information to the Superintendent when he was drafting new policy, Jonathan worked mostly on uncovering fraud or incompetence. He relied on existing information sources, collecting data primarily through interview, observation, and document review. Most recently he had conducted evaluative investigations of the state materials procurement procedures (there had been charges of kick-backs), of sex discrimination in the hiring of elementary school principals, and of charges that certain professional schools had obtained copies of the state certification tests and were giving their students an unfair advantage in passing the state professional exams.

Jonathan's methods provided one of the few evaluation approaches which allowed for quick field studies. Nevertheless, his investigations frequently established only strong prima facie cases and did not provide incontrovertible evidence. Since the objects of his investigations were often highly controversial, his was a stressful position.

Jonathan reconsidered the details of his current investigation, doublechecking that he had pursued every avenue and had built a report that would stand up to public scrutiny in the newspapers, and, if necessary, in the courts.

The Hearings Approach

Mario slowed his pace as he crossed the street. He did not want to be too early for the meeting of the Citizen's Advisory Committee. It was always difficult to keep the committee's attention on the prepared agenda when he arrived early and became embroiled in a discussion of the latest political issues in the case. Mario worked for a private foundation, although much of the resources for his evaluative work came from state and federal government subsidies and from citizen contributions. It was Mario's job to help minority and special interest groups conduct public evaluations of broad issues concerning the public interest. In this position, he acted as master methodologist, as non-partisan chairman, and occasionally as individual counselor. As he continued down the street, Mario reflected on how much more involvement and influence minority groups now had in education as a result of the types of public evaluations he and others were helping to create.

The committees of specialists and lay public, which Mario organized and worked with, gathered evidence about the multiple arguments surrounding an issue of public concern. They then employed public hearings to scrutinize and, ideally, resolve major points of disagreement. Although there were now several variants of this basic approach, the model derived originally from the hearing procedures used in Congress, legal trials, public environmental impact studies, and national investigative panels. This approach was increasingly being used not only to heighten the participation of various minority groups in education, but also when public values, citizen input, and the analysis of educational problems were seen as more crucial than the collection and analysis of technical data. Relevant data, arguments, and position statements were prepared and presented under various types of hearing formats.

Mario had a diverse methodological background, since it was important for him to be able to summarize multiple types of data (such as research findings, case studies, and anecdotal information) within coherent position statements. His training and special interest in public activism were also important, since he had to conduct public hearings so that useful analyses and closure could be reached. Because of the frequently sensitive topics being evaluated, Mario also had to be politically astute.

Approaching the building where the meeting was to take place, Mario reassessed the progress; it appeared that the hearings scheduled for next month would allow for a sharing of diverse viewpoints on the problem. Unfortunately, as was usual with this approach, some complex issues were being overly simplified, and the process was being subjected to political influence by certain groups. Nevertheless, having presented the State Board of Education with the anticipated roster of witnesses who would be making prepared statements at the hearing, Mario felt confident that this study would have some influence in shaping the state's policy in the area.

The Criticism Approach

Su-Lin sat in the staff lounge of a small elementary school reviewing the lesson plans of several teachers. She was one of the better-known evaluation critics in this region and was currently involved in a study of experiential materials used in values education. As a private consultant, she had done a series of independent evaluations of educational programs. In a number of cases she had been hired by state and local agencies to perform external evaluation critiques of materials and programs.

Following her usual strategy, Su-Lin was reviewing materials prior to doing some classroom observation. Drawing on her extensive experience with similar projects, she would then conceptually analyze the materials under study to assess their quality and to illustrate how their constituent elements contributed to that quality. While most critics specialized in product evaluation, Su-Lin had done some work in program evaluation as well. Her primary focus was on the program's or product's quality and its relation to current public needs and interests. Using techniques of critical analysis, she derived insights about how the product's or program's form and content contributed to its function. She then shared these insights with her clients.

This criticism approach to evaluation had developed through the adaptation of criticism methods used in the fields of poetry, art, music, film, and architecture. The approach also had been significantly influenced by consumer advocate interests in evaluation and had been used in studies of materials in basic skill areas, such as math, reading, and computer use. Su-Lin had just completed a study of classroom climate and student-teacher relationships in several vocational schools.

Su-Lin's training had involved extensive prior experience with the types of materials she routinely evaluated. Her effective written communication skills were also essential in her work, as was her intimate understanding of the techniques of conceptual analysis and of the history of professional criticism in her particular area of expertise.

Su-Lin's work involved the use of seasoned, experienced judgments of quality and was one of the few approaches which allowed one to judge a current product in light of a large number of similar previous efforts. Her best insightful critiques had done much to illuminate those elements of various products which contributed to their quality. Unfortunately, the criteria and experience employed in making these judgments usually could not be made public because they resided within Su-Lin; and so, to some extent, her clients had to validate her professional judgments through their own experience with similar products.

As Su-Lin left the staff lounge and walked down the hall, she was greeted by two passing teachers who immediately recognized her, since she was one of a small number of regionally-known educational critics. The children filed into the classrooms. She quietly took a seat in the rear to begin her observation of this class, which was like hundreds she had seen in the past, but was also in its own way unique.

The Optimization Approach

Having refilled her coffee cup, Katherine returned to her desk to study the latest computer printouts. Her current study concerned an evaluation of the allocation of remedial mathematics materials across the 37 schools in the large school district for which she worked. Katherine's work in evaluation required high technology as well as considerable expertise and material resources. Many other evaluators doing the kind of work she did were employed in large state and governmental agencies and in the largest school districts.

As usual, Katherine was attempting to model the system under study to analytically assess its parameters and to maximize its functioning. Her work involved the evaluation of complex systems where the optimization of operations, resources, and impact were of primary importance. Modeling procedures and computerized mathematical analysis were her standard tools. Focusing primarily on concrete, quantifiable parameters, her work was highly analytic and oriented toward better control of the system.

Although the approach Katherine used in educational evaluation had been employed for many years now, its history was even longer. It had been derived from similar procedures used in operations research, cost-benefit analysis, management control theory, and general system analysis. She had had extensive academic preparation in mathematical modeling, computer analysis, and optimization techniques. Understanding the design of human systems was also a significant element in her training. As was common, most of her studies concerned the optimization of educational subsystems; for example, work in facilities, transportation, student counseling, and some work in instructional design.

Katherine found the figures she had been looking for. She was always pleased when the modeling procedures resulted in an efficient redesign of system elements. Being able to quantify and optimize system operations gave her pleasure; however, she continually had difficulty with the nonquantified factors, such as personal values, student morale, and the nonrational influences in human affairs. Her use of the strong analytic tools was especially effective when system control and optimization had been a primary educational goal. Preparing the data for the next round of simulations, Katherine thought how well this particular study seemed to be going.

The Representation Approach

Billy sat in his study at home preparing notes to teach his university class on evaluation the day after tomorrow. Most of his presentation would concern his recent evaluation of a summer film institute. Using the representational approach to evaluation, which was highly favored by people associated with arts education, he spent much of his time evaluating film workshops, art and museum exhibits, plays, and dance theater. His approach was to capture the experiences of participants in these activities, to analyze those experiences in an appreciative sense, and then to construct a surrogate experience so that nonparticipants could make their own assessments of the quality of the activities' educational and artistic offerings. Thus, his work most often resulted in evaluations that were shared experiences rather than written reports.

Billy had arrived at this approach to evaluation only recently, spurred by his interest in representing a particular educational program or event to an external audience. He had been successful at using a variety of techniques to recreate educational experiences, including photographs, mime, plays, musical compositions, paintings, and stories; and he had used these to share an educational experience with audiences, so that they could make their assessments of its quality and worth. This approach to evaluation had developed from a combination of procedures used in art, music, theater, and case-study work.

Billy's training had required him to increase his understanding of how an experience could be altered through various forms of representation. He had developed a sensitivity to participant reactions and had acquired good observational and interview skills. What he liked most about the approach to evaluation, however, was that it required much creativity in producing a first-hand, high-fidelity surrogate experience that enabled persons in the audience to make their own assessments of the educational program's quality. Most of these evaluations were conducted by experts in some area of the arts, and Billy was pleased to be a part of that group.

Billy continued preparing his class notes, outlining the major points he wished to raise. This approach to evaluation was one of the few models suitable for use in the arts — the criticism approach being another. In contrast to the criticism approach, which provides an external assessment of a program's or event's quality, the representational approach depends heavily upon the fidelity of a surrogate experience and on the audience members to make their own assessments of quality. Of course, these evaluations tend to be non-replicable and are usually of greatest utility to people who are already familiar with events like the one being evaluated. Billy wanted to emphasize to his students that this was a specialized form of evaluation; one which most involved the clients in making their own assessments of quality and which concurrently increased the clients' capacity for doing more of their own evaluations.

Do these scenarios help us envision what can happen in evaluation? I think they do begin to suggest alternatives and options that are only dimly perceived at present. They are not much like the pre-post test/experimental design approach that is currently dominant in educational evaluation; but then some radical alternatives might prove very useful. After all, part of completing a successful rafting trip depends on knowing when to carry the raft around the rapids rather than shooting through them.

We have only just started our evaluation trip. The current is swift, and we have only made the first few turns in the river, so our vision is limited. Perhaps considering visions of what is possible ahead will help us deal with the future of educational evaluation as it unfolds before us.

References

Boulding, Kenneth E. "Science: Our common heritage." *Science,* 207 (4433), 1980, 831–36.
Eiseley, Loren. *The man who saw through time.* New York: Charles Scribner's Sons, 1973.
Eisner, Elliot W., *The perceptive eye: Toward the reformation of educational evaluation.* Stanford Evaluation Consortium, Stanford University, California, December, 1975, (ED 128408; TM 005591).
Guba, Egon G., *Toward a methodology of naturalistic inquiry in educational evaluation.* Los Angeles: Center for the Study of Evaluation, University of California, 1978.
Lyon, Catherine D.; Doscher, Lynn; McGranahan, Pamela; and Williams, Richard.

Evaluation and school districts. Los Angeles: Center for the Study of Evaluation, University of California, 1978.

Smith, Nick L. "Requirements for a discipline of evaluation." *Studies in Educational Evaluation,* 5 (1979), 5–12.

Smith, Nick L. "Studying evaluation assumptions." *Evaluation News,* no. 14, (Winter 1980), 39–40. (*a*)

Smith, Nick L. *Evaluating evaluation methods.* Paper presented at the annual meeting of the American Educational Research Association, Boston, April 1980. (*b*)

Stake, Robert E. (ed.) *Evaluating the arts in education: A responsive approach.* Columbus, Ohio: Charles E. Merrill, 1975.

III THE STANDARDS AND THE NINETY-FIVE THESES

23 THE STANDARDS FOR EVALUATION OF EDUCATIONAL PROGRAMS, PROJECTS, AND MATERIALS:
A Description and Summary
Daniel L. Stufflebeam and George F. Madaus

In 1980, a Joint Committee appointed by 12 organizations[1] concerned with educational evaluation issued one of the most significant documents to date in the field of educational evaluation. It consisted of a set of 30 standards to be used both to guide the conduct of evaluation of educational programs, projects, and materials and also to judge the soundness of such evaluations. The document, entitled *Standards for Evaluations of Educational Programs, Projects, and Materials,* [2] was published in 1981 by the McGraw-Hill Company. The standards were the result of an extensive developmental process, which involved the work of about 200 people and required more than four years to complete. The committee's work did not stop with the publication of the standards, and it presently works to promote sound use and conducts a process of ongoing review and development. This chapter briefly describes the development of the standards and the nature of the standards, and summarizes them for the reader.

Development of the Standards

As the work of the 1974 Joint AERA, APA, NCME Committee revising the Standards for Educational and Psychological Tests drew to a close, there was concern that the use of tests in program evaluation had not been adequately covered in the proposed revision. A committee member was asked to prepare a memorandum identifying areas where test standards might be applicable in program evaluation. After considering the memorandum, the Joint Committee decided not to delay the release of the 1974 *Standards* and made a recommendation in the *Standards* that a companion volume dealing with program evaluation be considered by a succeeding joint committee. After publication of the 1974 *Standards*, APA then asked 20 experts in evaluation to respond to the memorandum; the AERA and NCME boards also took the matter under consideration. The general conclusion was that standards were needed to guide the practice of educational evaluation, and there was strong support for the decision to move ahead with the Project to Develop Standards for Educational Evaluation.

Developing standards is a controversial practice, and in initial deliberations both the pros and cons associated with the development of standards for educational evaluation were inventoried. The perceived benefits to be derived from setting standards included: a common language to facilitate communication and collaboration in evaluation, a set of general principles for dealing with a variety of evaluation problems, a conceptual framework by which to study evaluation, a set of working definitions to guide research and development on the evaluation process, a public description of the state of the art in educational evaluation, a basis for accountability by evaluators, and an aid to developing public credibility for the educational evaluation field.

The committee was also mindful of risks associated with any standard-setting effort, including: promoting a field that possibly is not needed; legitimizing practices that may prove harmful; concentrating attention on matters of relatively little importance, while diverting attention from major issues; encouraging bad practices because they are not explicitly prohibited in the standards; and impeding innovation in evaluation. (An account of the Joint Committee's assessment of these alleged risks as well as their plan to counteract them can be found in the *Standards*.)

It was decided that, on balance, the potential benefits outweighed the risks and that a corpus of standards would benefit the field and promote better evaluations. Since the initial 1974 decision to articulate standards in educational evaluation, a number of events confirm the correctness of that decision. There have been increased efforts by federal agencies and federal programs (e.g., Title I) to provide direction and criteria to improve the practice of evaluation. Professional organizations, such as the Evaluation Research Society, began independent efforts to provide professional standards for their membership. Additionally, there have been strong recommendations to Congress and to federal agencies, both increasingly dependent upon evaluation information, to better define and plan their evaluations through the use of professional standards.[3]

The Joint Committee is unique, and a few words about its membership are in order. Initially, the committee included only representatives of AERA, APA, and

NCME. Because evaluations are commissioned, designed, conducted, reported, and used by diverse groups, the original committee opened its membership to include the perspectives of the consumers of evaluations. Consequently, the groups eventually represented on the committee ranged from the technically-oriented groups that began the process to a variety of practitioner-oriented groups (cf. note 1).

There is perhaps no feature of the Joint Committee as important as its representative nature. Although the committee decided at the outset that it would not seek endorsement from sponsoring organizations, it has had their support throughout. Sponsoring organizations provided time and space at annual conferences for national hearings on the *Standards;* they released information about the project in their newsletters; they provided money for field testing; they provided representatives to the committee; and they lent their names to the standard-setting project.

The broad composition of the Joint Committee ensured: a ready-made constituency for the *Standards;* a comprehensive awareness of problems in the field; and practical standards designed to help all the participants in an educational evaluation. The heterogeneity of the committee was a constant source of strength; it militated against jargon, promoted clarity, and brought multiple perspectives to the task of standard development.

There were, of course, trade-offs associated with the committee's heterogeneity. It led to decisions not to treat complex technical issues in depth and to avoid the controversial area of personnel evaluation. Finally, the committee's composition made it vulnerable to criticism that the task of setting standards should include only evaluators, a position it explicitly rejected. While the expansion of the Joint Committee made the development process sometimes tumultuous and consensus difficult, in the end the committee unanimously adopted the *Standards.* Further, the committee provided a forum for a diverse professional coalition interested in educational evaluation — a coalition with considerable strength. Finally, the committee established not only a product but a process as well, a process that ensures that the *Standards* are a living rather than static document, a document that continuously will be studied and improved.

While the committee could have opted to develop standards internally — no easy task given the size and diversity of the committee — it chose instead the more difficult course of involving a variety of groups in the standard-setting process including: a panel of writers, a national review panel, a field test group, and about 100 participants in national hearings. Further, the Joint Committee continually sought divergent views, allowed room at meetings for debate, and developed procedures to handle controversial standards and minority reports. In general, the committee pursued a strategy of repeated cycles of development and evaluation in arriving at the final product.

This systematic and widespread involvement in the standard-setting effort by many groups and individuals, while adding to the time and cost of the process, greatly enhanced the quality and credibility of the committee's work. Because of this increased participation, it became imperative that the committee clearly define its mission and audiences, and clarify its relationship to each new audience identified during the developmental process. This in turn resulted in the committee's feeling a responsibility toward those practicing evaluation and those affected by evaluations.

Nature of the Standards

Four aspects of the document will be discussed here: its focus and boundaries, its scope, its depth, and its usability.

Focus of the Standards

The focus and boundaries of the book are reflected in its title: *Standards for Evaluations of Educational Programs, Projects, and Materials*. This title is intended to be descriptive and not to promise more than is delivered. By the word *standards,* the Joint Committee meant widely shared principles for assessing the quality of an evaluation, not mechanical rules or levels of performance. The committee was concerned only with evaluations in education. Further, the standards deal only with the evaluation of programs, projects and materials. All other kinds of evaluations are excluded.

Scope of the Standards

The Joint Committee developed 30 standards that are grouped according to four attributes of an evaluation — its utility, its feasibility, its propriety, and its accuracy.

The utility standards reflect the general consensus found in the literature concerning the need for program evaluations that are responsive to the needs of clients. In general, the utility standards require evaluators to acquaint themselves with various audiences that have a stake in the evaluation results, to ascertain their information needs, and to report the relevant information to these audiences clearly, concisely, and on time.

The second set of standards are concerned with feasibility and speak to the realization that evaluation procedures must be cost-effective and workable in real world settings. The feasibility standards require that the evaluation plan be operable for the setting and be as parsimonious with valuable resources as is practical. Overall, the feasibility standards require evaluations to be realistic, prudent, diplomatic, politically viable, and frugal.

The third group of standards deal with propriety and reflect the fact that evaluations can affect many people in different ways. This group of standards are meant to insure that the rights of persons affected by an evaluation are protected. The propriety standards require that evaluations be conducted legally, ethically, and with due regard for the welfare of those involved in the evaluation as well as those affected by the results.

The final group of standards deal with accuracy, that is, with the question of whether an evaluation has produced sound information. These standards require that the information obtained be technically adequate and that conclusions be linked logically to the data. The overall rating of an evaluation against the 11 accuracy standards is an index of the evaluation's overall validity.

Table 23–1 presents a summary of the 30 standards, organized by each of the four attributes.

Table 23–1.   Summary of the Standards for Evaluation of Educational Programs, Projects, and Materials.

A   Utility Standards
The utility standards are intended to ensure that an evaluation will serve the practical information needs of given audiences. These standards are:

A1   Audience Identification
Audiences involved in or affected by the evaluation should be identified, so that their needs can be addressed.

A2   Evaluator Credibility
The persons conducting the evaluation should be both trustworthy and competent to perform the evaluation, so that their findings achieve maximum credibility and acceptance.

A3   Information Scope and Selection
Information collected should be of such scope and selected in such ways as to address pertinent questions about the object of the evaluation and be responsive to the needs and interests of specified audiences.

A4   Valuational Interpretation
The perspectives, procedures, and rationale used to interpret the findings should be carefully described, so that the bases for value judgments are clear.

A5   Report Clarity
The evaluation report should describe the object being evaluated and its context, and the purposes, procedures, and findings of the evaluation, so that the audiences will readily understand what was done, why it was done, what information was obtained, what conclusions were drawn, and what recommendations were made.

Table 23–1.   (continued)

A6   Report Dissemination
Evaluation findings should be disseminated to clients and other right-to-know audiences, so that they can assess and use the findings.

A7   Report Timeliness
Release of reports should be timely, so that audiences can best use the reported information.

A8   Evaluation Impact
Evaluations should be planned and conducted in ways that encourage follow-through by members of the audiences.

B   Feasibility Standards
The feasibility standards are intended to ensure that an evaluation will be realistic, prudent, diplomatic, and frugal; they are:

B1   Practical Procedures
The evaluation procedures should be practical, so that disruption is kept to a minimum and that needed information can be obtained.

B2   Political Viability
The evaluation should be planned and conducted with anticipation of the different positions of various interest groups, so that their cooperation may be obtained and so that possible attempts by any of these groups to curtail evaluation operations or to bias or misapply the results can be averted or counteracted.

B3   Cost Effectiveness
The evaluation should produce information of sufficient value to justify the resources extended.

C   Propriety Standards
The propriety standards are intended to ensure that an evaluation will be conducted legally, ethically, and with due regard for the welfare of those involved in the evaluation, as well as those affected by its results. These standards are:

C1   Formal Obligation
Obligations of the formal parties to an evaluation (what is to be done, how, by whom, when) should be agreed to in writing, so that these parties are obligated to adhere to all conditions of the agreement or formally to renegotiate it.

C2   Conflict of Interest
Conflict of interest, frequently unavoidable, should be dealt with openly and honestly, so that it does not compromise the evaluation processes and results.

C3   Full and Frank Disclosure
Oral and written evaluation reports should be open, direct, and honest in their disclosure of pertinent findings, including the limitations of the evaluation.

Table 23–1.   (continued)

C4   Public's Right to Know
The formal parties to an evaluation should respect and assure the public's right to know, within the limits of other related principles and statutes, such as those dealing with public safety and the right to privacy.

C5   Rights of Human Subjects
Evaluations should be designed and conducted so that the rights and welfare of the human subjects are respected and protected.

C6   Human Interactions
Evaluators should respect human dignity and worth in their interactions with other persons associated with an evaluation.

C7   Balanced Reporting
The evaluation should be complete and fair in its presentation of strengths and weaknesses of the object under investigation, so that strengths can be built upon and problem areas addressed.

C8   Fiscal Responsibility
The evaluator's allocation and expenditure of resources should reflect sound accountability procedures and otherwise be prudent and ethically responsible.

D   Accuracy Standards
The accuracy standards are intended to ensure that an evaluation will reveal and convey technically adequate information about the features of the object being studied that determine its worth or merit. These standards are:

D1   Object Identification
The object of the evaluation (program, project, material) should be sufficiently examined, so that the form(s) of the object being considered in the evaluation can be clearly identified.

D2   Context Analysis
The context in which the program, project, or material exists should be examined in enough detail so that its likely influences on the object can be identified.

D3   Described Purposes and Procedures
The purposes and procedures of the evaluation should be monitored and described in enough detail so that they can be identified and assessed.

D4   Defensible Information Sources
The sources of information should be described in enough detail so that the adequacy of the information can be assessed.

D5   Valid Measurement
The information-gathering instruments and procedures should be chosen or developed and then implemented in ways that will assure that the interpretation arrived at is valid for the given use.

Table 23–1.   (continued)

D6   Reliable Measurement
The information-gathering instruments and procedures should be chosen or developed and then implemented in ways that will assure that the information obtained is sufficiently reliable for the intended use.

D7   Systematic Data Control
The data collected, processed, and reported in an evaluation should be reviewed and corrected, so that the results of the evaluation will not be flawed.

D8   Analysis of Quantitative Information
Quantitative information in an evaluation should be appropriately and systematically analyzed to ensure supportable interpretations.

D9   Analysis of Qualitative Information
Qualitative information in an evaluation should be appropriately and systematically analyzed to ensure supportable interpretations.

D10   Justified Conclusions
The conclusions reached in an evaluation should be explicitly justified, so that the audiences can assess them.

D11   Objective Reporting
The evaluation procedures should provide safeguards to protect the evaluation findings and reports against distortion by the personal feelings and biases of any party to the evaluation.

Depth of the Standards

The depth to which the Joint Committee developed each standard can be best understood by considering the format common to all 30 standards summarized in table 23–1. Each standard starts with a descriptor (i.e., Formal Obligation), followed by a statement of the standard (i.e., "Obligations of the formal parties to an evaluation [what is to be done, how, by whom, when] should be agreed to in writing, so that these parties are obligated to adhere to all conditions of the agreement or formally to renegotiate it"). This in turn is followed by an overview of the standard, which includes its rationale and definitions of key terms. Finally, each standard includes lists of pertinent guidelines, pitfalls, and caveats. The guidelines consist of procedures that will prove useful in meeting the standard; the pitfalls describe common mistakes to be avoided in implementing the standard; and the caveats warn against overzealousness in applying the given standard, which would detract from meeting other standards. Each standard concludes with an illustration of a situation in which the standard is violated, and discusses corrective actions that could be taken to better adhere to the standard.

Usability

From the outset, the committee was concerned that people with widely divergent technical backgrounds could understand and use the *Standards*. To meet this aim, the committee avoided jargon and presented their ideas simply and directly. The committee also developed a functional table of contents shown in table 23–2 which shows the standards most applicable to each of 10 common evaluation tasks. The standards are listed down the side of the matrix, while, across the top, the 10 familiar evaluation tasks are arranged. The X's in the various cells indicate that the committee felt the standard was applicable for the given task. While the Joint Committee believes that all of the standards are applicable in all evaluations, the functional table of contents helps evaluators quickly to identify those standards which are most relevant to given evaluation tasks.

The authority of the *Standards* ultimately derives from their logic and their usefulness rather than from endorsements by authoritative bodies. To promote that usefulness, the committee has attempted to articulate standards which are prescriptive of sound practice rather than descriptive of all practice. The committee has provided a theoretical and functional organization for the standards, and they have developed the items through a rigorous, interactive process involving both evaluators and those groups that are often the consumers of or subjects in an evaluation.

Conclusion

This chapter has provided an overview of the *Standards* — its development and current form.

The *Standards* developed by the Joint Committee certainly will have to be applied, researched, revised, and updated. Plans for all of these activities are presently being developed. All things considered, however, there is reason to speculate that educational evaluation will be stronger because of these *Standards;* both consumers and professionals will benefit from their existence and from their use in evaluating evaluations (meta evaluations); and adherence to the *Standards* will improve the quality of professional practice. We feel that it is to the advantage of evaluation professionals and to the advantage of the emerging profession of evaluation to study the *Standards,* use them, and report on their effectiveness.

Notes

1. American Association of School Administrators, American Educational Research Association, American Federation of Teachers, American Personnel and Guidance Association, American Psychological Association, Association for Supervision and Curriculum Development, Council for American Private Education, Educational Commission of the States, National Association of Elementary School Principals, National Educational Association, National Council on Measurement in Education, and National School Boards Association.

2. *Standards for Evaluations of Educational Programs, Projects, and Materials.* Developed by the Joint Committee on Standards for Educational Evaluation, McGraw-Hill, 1981.

3. Boruch, Robert F. and David S. Cordrary. *An Appraisal of Educational Program Evaluations: Federal, State and Local Agencies.* Evanston, Illinois: Northwestern University, 1980.

Table 23–2 Analysis of the Relative Importance of 30 Standards in Performing 10 Tasks in an Evaluation.

	1. Deciding Whether to do a Study	2. Clarifying and Assessing Purpose	3. Ensure Political Viability	4. Contract	5. Staff the Study	6. Manage the Study	7. Collect Data	8. Analyze Data	9. Report Findings	10. Apply Results
A1 Audience Identification	X	X	X	X		X			X	X
A2 Evaluator Credibility	X		X	X	X	X	X			X
A3 Information Scope and Selection				X			X			
A4 Valuational Interpretation		X	X				X	X	X	X
A5 Report Clarity						X			X	X
A6 Report Dissemination			X	X		X			X	X
A7 Report Timeliness				X					X	
A8 Evaluation Impact	X	X	X						X	X
B1 Practical Procedures			X							
B2 Political Viability	X		X	X	X	X	X	X		X
B3 Cost Effectiveness	X	X	X			X	X			
C1 Formal Obligation	X		X	X		X	X			X
C2 Conflict of Interest	X	X	X	X	X	X				X
C3 Full and Frank Disclosure			X	X					X	
C4 Public's Right to Know			X	X					X	X
C5 Rights of Human Subjects			X	X		X	X			X
C6 Human Interactions			X			X	X			
C7 Balanced Reporting				X			X		X	X
C8 Fiscal Responsibility			X	X		X				
D1 Object Identification	X	X		X			X	X	X	
D2 Context Analysis	X	X					X	X	X	X
D3 Described Purposes and Procedures	X	X		X		X	X		X	X
D4 Defensible Information Sources			X				X		X	X
D5 Valid Measurement							X		X	
D6 Reliable Measurement							X			
D7 Systematic Data Control						X	X			
D8 Quantitative Analysis							X	X		
D9 Qualitative Analysis								X		
D10 Justified Conclusions		X						X	X	X
D11 Objective Reporting			X		X				X	X

24 NINETY-FIVE THESES FOR REFORMING PROGRAM EVALUATION

Lee J. Cronbach and Associates

Editors' note

In their landmark book in the field, entitled Toward Reform of Program Evaluation, *Lee J. Cronbach and seven of his colleagues argue the need for a comprehensive transformation of program evaluation. They provide their readers with an in-depth assessment of evaluation as it stood at the end of the 1970s. They point out a wide range of areas in program evaluation in need of improvement. They lay bare many issues, unwarranted assumptions, and problems associated with specific evaluations commissioned to inform public policy (e.g., the now-famous New Jersey Negative Income Tax study). They go on to propose an alternative way of conceptualizing program evaluation, a conceptualization geared towards facilitating the improvement of programs through efforts to enlighten the various parties to the program. Finally, they offer a wide range of suggestions designed to move the field of program evaluation in the direction they propose. Following the precedent of that earlier reformer, Martin Luther, they codified their arguments and recommendations into 95 theses.*

Excerpted from: Lee J. Cronbach and Associates. *Toward Reform of Program Evaluation*. San Francisco, California: Jossey-Bass, 1980.

405

These theses, along with their authors' introduction to them, appear below. The ideas offered by the multidisciplinary team reach beyond Cronbach's more methodological writings represented elsewhere in this anthology, integrating ideas about method in a broad theory of evaluation as a political process. A careful study of the theses and the supportive material should provoke useful discussion and debate, which can only help to improve the field of program evaluation.

The Ninety-five Theses

This book calls for a reformation in evaluation, a thorough-going transformation. Its priests and its patrons, as well as those who desire its benefits, have sought from evaluation what it cannot, probably should not, give. The proper mission of evaluation is not to eliminate the fallibility of authority or to bolster its credibility. Rather, its mission is to facilitate a democratic, pluralistic process by enlightening all the participants.

Evaluation has vital work to do, yet its institutions and its ruling conceptions are inadequate. Enamored of a vision that "right" decisions can replace political agreements, some who commission evaluations set evaluators on unrealistic quests. Others among them see evaluation chiefly as a means to strengthen the hand of the commissioning authority. Evaluators, eager to serve and even to manipulate those in power, lose sight of what they should be doing. Moreover, evaluators become enthralled by technique. Much that purports to be theory of evaluation is scholastic: evaluations are endlessly categorized, and chapels are dedicated to the glorification of particular styles. Latter-day theologians discuss how best to deify such chimeras as goals and benefits. The technicians debate over numerological derivations from artificial models — "How many angels . . .?" all over again. All too rarely does discussion descend to earthy questions, such as, "Is worthwhile information being collected?"

Budgets for evaluations have jumped to startling levels, but few individuals and organizations are prepared for the intricacies of evaluation research. The federal procurement machinery and timetables for delivery of results are inimical to reflective planning and interpretation. Organizations and individuals undertake tasks that are beyond their capabilities. Evaluation results are challenged and discredited because no adequate critical process precedes their release. Professional ideals can become casualties when everyone scrambles to keep in step with budgetary and legislative calendars. It is none too soon to reflect, to repent (a little), and to entertain bright visions of a wholesome marriage between social research and social action.

Perhaps the best way to bring about a change in thought is to provoke argument. Following Luther's precedent, we set forth our principal points in the form of 95 theses. Being removed from their context and stripped of qualifying phrases, the theses neglect subtleties; reading the theses is no substitute for reading the book. This section is intended to entice into reading the argument with care those who might otherwise ignore it or skim the surface. That should make them eager to join in the needed debate about fundamental issues.

Ninety-five Theses

1. Program evaluation is a process by which society learns about itself.
2. Program evaluations should contribute to enlightened discussion of alternative plans for social action.
3. Evaluation is a handmaiden to gradualism; it is both conservative and committed to change.
4. An evaluation of a particular program is only an episode in the continuing evolution of thought about a problem area.
5. The better and the more widely the workings of social programs are understood, the more rapidly policy will evolve and the more the programs will contribute to a better quality of life.
6. Observations of social programs require a closer analysis than a lay interpreter can make, for unassisted judgment leads all to easily to false interpretations.
7. In debates over controversial programs, liars figure and figures often lie; the evaluator has a responsibility to protect his[1] clients from both types of deception.
8. Ideally, every evaluation will inform the social system and improve its operations, but everyone agrees that evaluation is not rendering the service it should.
9. Commissioners of evaluations complain that the messages from evaluations are not useful, while evaluators complain that the messages are not used.
10. The evaluator has political influence even when he does not aspire to it.
11. A theory of evaluation must be as much a theory of political interaction as it is a theory of how to determine facts.
12. The hope that an evaluation will provide unequivocal answers, convincing enough to extinguish controversy about the merits of a social program, is certain to be disappointed.
13. The evaluators' professional conclusions cannot substitute for the political process.
14. The distinction between evaluation and policy research is disappearing.
15. Accountability emphasizes looking back in order to assign praise or blame; evaluation is better used to understand events and processes for the sake of guiding future architects.
16. Social renovations disappoint even their architects.
17. Time and again, political passion has been a driving spirit behind a call for rational analysis.
18. A demand for accountability is a sign of pathology in the political system.
19. An open society becomes a closed society when only the officials know what is

going on. Insofar as information is a source of power, evaluations carried out to inform a policymaker have a disenfranchising effect.

20.   The ideal of efficiency in government is in tension with the ideal of democratic participation; rationalism is dangerously close to totalitarianism.

21.   The notion of the evaluator as a superman who will make all social choices easy and all programs efficient, turning public management into a technology, is a pipe dream.

22.   A context of command, with a manager in firm control, has been assumed in nearly all previous theories of evaluation.

23.   An image of pluralistic accommodation more truly represents how policy and programs are shaped than does the Platonic image of concentrated power and responsibility.

24.   The evaluator must learn to serve in contexts of accommodation and not dream idly of serving a Platonic guardian.

25.   In a context of accommodation, the evaluator cannot expect a ''go/no-go'' decision to turn on his assessment of outcomes.

26.   What is needed is information that supports negotiation rather than information calculated to point out the correct decision.

27.   Events move forward by piecemeal adaptations.

28.   It can scarcely be said that decisions about typical programs are *made;* rather, they emerge.

29.   The policy-shaping community does not wait for a sure winner; it must act in the face of uncertainty, settling on plausible actions that are politically acceptable.

30.   It is unwise for evaluation to focus on whether a project has attained its goal.

31.   Goals are a necessary part of political rhethoric, but all social programs, even supposedly targeted ones, have broad aims.

32.   Legislators who have sophisticated reasons for keeping goal statements lofty and nebulous unblushingly ask program administrators to state explicit goals.

33.   Unfortunately, whatever the evaluator decides to measure tends to become a primary goal of program operators.

34.   Evaluators are not encouraged to ask the most trenchant questions about entrenched programs.

35.   ''Evaluate this program'' is often a vague charge because a program or a system frequently has no clear boundaries.

36.   Before the evaluator can plan data collection, he must find out a great deal about the project as it exists and as it is conceived.

37.   A good evaluative question invites a differentiated answer instead of leaving the program plan, the delivery of the program, and the response of clients as unexamined elements within a closed black box.

38.   Strictly honest data collection can generate a misleading picture unless questions are framed to expose both the facts useful to partisans of the program and the facts useful to its critics.

39. Before laying out a design, the evaluator should do considerable homework. Pertinent questions should be identified by examining the history of similar programs, the related social theory, and the expectations of program advocates, critics, and prospective clients.

40. Precise assessment of outcomes is sensible only after thorough pilot work has pinned down a highly appropriate form for an innovation under test.

41. When a prototype program is evaluated, the full range of realizations likely to occur in practice should be observed.

42. Flexibility and diversity are preferable to the rigidity written into many evaluation contracts.

43. The evaluator who does not press for productive assignments and the freedom to carry them out takes the King's shilling for selfish reasons.

44. The evaluator's aspiration to benefit the larger community has to be reconciled — sometimes painfully — with commitments to a sponsor and to informants, with the evaluator's political convictions, and with his desire to stay in business.

45. Managers have many reasons for wishing to maintain control over evaluative information; the evaluator can respect all such reasons that fall within the sphere of management.

46. The crucial ethical problem appears to be freedom to communicate during and after the study, subject to legitimate concerns for privacy, national security, and faithfulness to contractual commitments.

47. With some hesitation, we advise the evaluator to release findings piecemeal and informally to the audiences that need them. The impotence that comes with delay may be a greater risk than the possibility that early returns will be misread.

48. Nothing makes a larger difference in the use of evaluations than the personal factor — the interest of officials in learning from the evaluation and the desire of the evaluator to get attention for what he knows.

49. Communication overload is a common fault; many an evaluation is reported with self-defeating thoroughness.

50. Much of the most significant communication of findings is informal, and not all of it is deliberate; some of the most significant effects are indirect, affecting audiences far removed from the program under investigation.

51. An evaluation of a particular project has its greatest implications for projects that will be put in place in the future.

52. A program evaluation that gets attention is likely to affect the prevailing view of social purposes, whether or not it immediately affects the fate of the program studied.

53. Advice on evaluation typically speaks of an investigation as a stand-alone study that will draw its conclusions about a program in complete isolation from other sources of information.

54. It is better for an evaluative inquiry to launch a small fleet of studies than to put all its resources into a single approach.

55. Much that is written on evaluation recommends some one scientifically rigorous plan. Evaluations should, however, take many forms, and less rigorous approaches have value in many circumstances.

56. Results of a program evaluation are so dependent on the setting that replication is only a figure of speech; the evaluator is essentially an historian.

57. An elegant study provides dangerously convincing evidence when it seems to answer a question that it did not in fact squarely address.

58. Merit lies not in form of inquiry but in relevance of information. The context of command or accommodation, the stage of program maturity, and the closeness of the evaluator to the probable users should all affect the style of an evaluation.

59. The evaluator will be wise not to declare allegiance to either a quantitative-scientific-summative methodology or a qualitative-naturalistic-descriptive methodology.

60. External validity — that is, the validity of inferences that go beyond the data — is the crux; increasing internal validity by elegant design often reduces relevance.

61. Adding a control costs something in dollars, in attention, and perhaps in quality of data; a control that fortifies the study in one respect is likely to weaken it in another.

62. A strictly representative sample may provide less information than a sample that overrepresents exceptional cases and deliberately varies realizations.

63. The symmetric, nonsequential designs familiar from laboratory research and survey research are rarely appropriate for evaluations.

64. Multiple indicators of outcomes reinforce one another logically as well as statistically. This is true for measures of adequacy of program implementation as well as for measures of changes in client behavior.

65. In project-by-project evaluation, each study analyzes a spoonful dipped from a sea of uncertainties.

66. In any primary statistical investigation, analyses by independent teams should be made before the report is distributed.

67. Evaluations of a program conducted in parallel by different teams can capitalize on disparate perspectives and technical skills.

68. The evaluator should allocate investigative resources by considering four criteria simultaneously: prior uncertainty about a question, costs of information, anticipated information yield, and leverage of the information on subsequent thinking and action.

69. A particular control is warranted if it can be installed at reasonable costs and if, in the absence of that control, a positive effect could be persuasively explained away.

70. The importance of comparative data depends on the nature of the comparison proposed and on the stage of program maturity.
71. When programs have multiple and perhaps dissimilar outcomes, comparison is invariably judgmental. No technology for comparing benefits will silence partisan discord.
72. Present institutional arrangements for evaluation make it difficult or impossible to carry on the most useful kinds of evaluation.
73. In typical federal contracting, many basic research decisions are made without consulting the evaluators who will do the work.
74. The personal scientific responsibility found in ordinary research grants is lacking in contract evaluation; the "principal investigator" is a firm with interchangeable personnel.
75. Though the information from an evaluation is typically not used at a foreseeable moment to make a foreseen choice, in many evaluations a deadline set at the start of the study dominates the effort.
76. Evaluation contracts are increasing in size, but tying many strands into a single knot is rarely the best way to get useful information.
77. Large-scale evaluations are not necessarily better than smaller ones.
78. Major evaluations should have multiple sponsorship by agencies with different perspectives.
79. Decentralizing much evaluation to the state level would be a healthy development.
80. Society will obtain the assistance that evaluations can give only when there is a strong evaluation profession, clear about its social role and the nature of its work.
81. There is a boom-town excitement in the evaluation community; but, in constant dollars, federal funding for evaluation research has regressed in the last few years.
82. It is inconceivable that evaluators will win their battle for appropriate responsibilities if they remain unacquainted with one another, insensitive to their common interests, and fractionated intellectually.
83. For any suitably broad social problem, a social problem study group should be set up. It would be charged to inform itself by weighing, digesting, and interpreting what is known. It would foster needed investigations and make the policy-shaping community aware of what is and is not known.
84. Honesty and balance in program evaluation will be increased by critical review of the performance of evaluators and sponsors.
85. Oversight by peers is the most promising means of upholding professional standards and of precipitating debate about strategic and tactical issues.
86. The best safeguard against prematurely frozen standards for evaluative practice is multiple, independent sources of criticism.
87. There is need for exchanges more energetic than the typical academic discussion and more responsible than debate among partisans.
88. Reviews of evaluation should be far more frequent than at present, and reviews from diverse perspectives should appear together.

89.   For the prospective evaluator, basic training at the doctoral level in a specific social science is preferably to training restricted to evaluation methods.

90.   Training in evaluation is too often the stepchild of a department chiefly engaged in training academicians or providers of service.

91.   Case-study seminars scrutinizing diverse evaluative studies provide a needed interdisciplinary perspective.

92.   Internships with policy agencies that use evaluation sensitize future evaluators to the realities of evaluation use and nonuse. These realities are hard to convey in a classroom.

93.   The evaluator is an educator; his success is to be judged by what others learn.

94.   Those who shape policy should reach decisions with their eyes open; it is the evaluator's task to illuminate the situation, not to dictate the decision.

95.   Scientific quality is not the principal standard; an evaluation should aim to be comprehensible, correct and complete, and credible to partisans on all sides.

Note

1.   Following Keeney and Raiffa (1976, p. 515), we use the masculine pronoun throughout this work for the evaluator or scientist. Other significant persons (decisionmakers, clients, citizens, and so on) are referred to by the feminine pronoun. Another convention: we frequently speak of *the evaluator* in this work, but the tasks of the evaluator are so multifarious that no one person is versatile enough to perform them all. Hence, the term *evaluator* often refers here to a team or cooperating set of teams. The team members are to be seen not as specialists working on distinct subtasks but as persons who share responsibilities for each judgment.

Index

413

Contributing Authors

Peter W. Airasian, Boston College

Dale Carlson, California State Department of Education

Lee J. Cronbach, Stanford University

Elliot W. Eisner, Stanford University

Robert E. Floden, Institute for Research on Teaching, Michigan State University (1980)

Egon G. Guba, Indiana University

Ernest R. House, University of Illinois at Urbana-Champaign

Kent L. Koppelman, Iowa State University

Yvonna S. Lincoln, University of Kansas

George F. Madaus; Center for the Study of Testing, Evaluation, and Educational Policy; Boston College

W. James Popham, University of California at Los Angeles, and Instructional Objectives Exchange

Martin Rein, Woodshunt Institute of Technology College

Anthony Shinkfield, St. Peter's College, South Australia 5069

Michael S. Scriven, University of Western Australia

Nick L. Smith, Northwest Regional Educational Laboratory

Robert E. Stake, Center for Instructional Research and Curriculum Evaluation, University of Illinois at Urbana-Champaign

Andrés Steinmetz, New Measures, Inc.

Daniel L. Stufflebeam, Western Michigan University

Ralph W. Tyler, Director Emeritus Center for Advanced Study in the Behavioral Sciences

William J. Webster, Dallas Independent School District

Stephen S. Weiner, Stanford Evaluation Consortium, Stanford University

Robert S. Weiss, Harvard Medical School

Robert L. Wolf, Indiana University